EXPORT & IMPORT

Winning in the Global Marketplace

Export & Import

Winning in the Global Marketplace

A practical hands-on guide to success in international business, with 100s of real-world examples + exercises

Leif Holmvall

Export Pro Inc.
Sharon, Ontario, Canada
www.exportpro.com

Library and Archives Canada Cataloguing in Publication

Holmvall, Leif, 1941-
Export & import: winning in the global marketplace: a practical
hands-on guide to success in international business, with exercises + 100s
of real-world examples / Leif Holmvall.

Includes bibliographical references and index.
ISBN 978-0-9681148-1-0

1. Exports. 2. Imports. 3. Export marketing. I. Title. II. Title: Export
and import.

HF1414.4.H635 2010   382   C2010-906203-5

Thanks:

To my wife, Hyacinthe, and my children, Camilla and Christer, for all the input and editing of my book.

To Bill Milne, Knut Arnet, Lennart Bergh, and Richard Gottlieb and all my business associates and former students who have given me input and comments on my books.

Disclaimer and Terms of Use

1. This book will give you ideas for conducting international business. As an author, I am not in the position to provide you with legal advice or comprehensive instructions on how to go about doing international business.

2. Consider the purpose of this book to be similar to when you get a driver's license: it gives you the basis to get started. However, once you have that license, it is up to you to practice and become more confident in your skills. After completing this book you will continue to learn, adapt and adjust the activities to your specific company and the market(s) you have selected.

3. I suggest that you obtain the competent professional advice necessary, whether it relates to planning and implementing a global business venture, legal and government regulatory issues or others, such as foreign rules and regulations. For each country you do business with, you can use this book as a guideline and source of ideas, resources and references and to enhance your understanding of what is necessary to conduct international business. Also, remember that the global market is constantly changing. It is up to you to keep researching, consulting with appropriate specialists and obtaining the most up-to-date information necessary. It would be impossible for me to cover every aspect of international businesses - most likely the result would be a book of thousands of pages and even at that size, some material would be obsolete the day of printing.

4. The information contained in this book is accurate to the best of my knowledge. The opinions expressed are the author's. I make no warranty, express or implied about the resulting accuracy, completeness, or usefulness of any information from other sources, products, or processes disclosed. Reference to any specific commercial product, process or service by trade name, trademark, manufacturer or otherwise, does not necessarily constitute or imply its endorsement or recommendation.

5. The author/publisher makes no guarantees about any of the concepts presented and accepts neither liability nor responsibility to any person or organization with respect to any loss or damage caused indirectly or directly by use of the information in this book.

If you do not accept this disclaimer and terms of use, then you should not use the information contained herein as the only resource for your business venture.

Ordering Information

This book is available at quantity discounts for bulk purchases over 50 books. For information, contact Export Pro Inc.

Individual sales: Contact your local book store or on-line ordering website. For local purchases, also look at www.exportpro.com for links.

For a list of book distributors, contact Export Pro Inc. at:
http://www.exportpro.com
or visit:
http://www.lightningsource.com/globalDistChannels.aspx
for Lightning Source distribution partners.

For updates, upcoming books, a link to my blog and more resources, visit:
http://www.exportpro.com

For information about the Teachers' Handbook, visit my website or contact Export Pro Inc.

Other books written by Leif Holmvall and still in print:

Internationell Ekonomi - En värld i förändring (in Swedish)
Liber ISBN 9789147088225

Export & Import – Att göra internationella affärer (in Swedish)
Liber ISBN 9789147090990

Note: Export Pro Inc. conducts workshops and training on international business worldwide. For more information visit our website at:

www.exportpro.com

and contact us regarding your special requests.

Table of Contents

Introduction

"The world is a book, and those who
do not travel read only one page."
— Saint Augustine

Going global, competing in the global arena, global business, international business, transnational companies - these are common terms in today's media. The world has become global market place. We compete with everyone, for everything, everywhere, at all hours of the day and night. So what does this mean to you?

As a consumer, you accept that products you seek could be manufactured by foreign companies. You buy 'local' products that are not always purely local. Your selection of goods and services has increased tremendously from several decades ago. You enjoy having access to a broader range of new technologies, products and fashions at more competitive prices than ever before.

Markets will continue to change rapidly. As a business person, manager or owner of a company, you cannot just watch what is happening from the sidelines. You have to understand today's international business realities: yes, you have access to global market opportunities, but you also have increased competition from around the world.

During the last 20 years, international business shifts have been influenced by developing markets and demographics, reductions in duty tariffs and volatility in equity and currency markets. One thing is certain - world trade is expanding at a much faster rate then the world economy and will grow to 30% of GDP by 2015, which is up from 15% in 1990.

- **China** is predicted to overtake the United States as to the world's largest economy by 2040

- **India** will pass Italy (2015), France (2020), Germany (2025) and Japan (2032) in GDP

- **Brazil** will pass Italy (2025) France (2030) and Germany (2036)

- **Russia** will pass Italy (2025) France (2032) and Germany (2037)

(Source: Goldman Sachs)

Welcome to the world of international business!

About 30% of world GDP is now from emerging markets and most of the growth is coming from those markets. In fact, the BRIC countries - Brazil, Russia, India and China - will overtake the traditional G6 (France, Germany, Italy, Japan, UK and the US) countries by 2040 and enjoy a GDP that is expected to be 55% higher by 2050.

Some see this rapid growth from countries with lower input and production costs as a threat. On the other hand, forward-thinkers recognize new opportunities to increase their penetration into fast-growing markets that need products, services and technology for improving infrastructure and productivity.

The United Nations expects world population to increase from 6.6 billion to 8.3 billion by 2030. Of those, 60% will live in urban areas. This will create a huge market for water and sanitary systems, transportation and power generation along with significant increases in infrastructure spending that suppliers of those services can benefit from. Furthermore, water consumption will double during each 20 year period. Over 60% of the world will experience water shortages by 2035. Developing markets can also be a source of components, products and services that support company expansion on the domestic market. As emerging markets become more prosperous they will have greater buying power and in fact, their wage costs will increase, making them less of competition.

Adapting to Survive in International Business

Do you want to find out how to do international business in the most practical way? Are you looking for a hands-on, world-tested approach instead of theories?

Whether you are new to international business or an experienced exporter or importer, you can always learn something new! For those who are starting up, this book will guide you step by step. For those already working in the global arena, the book will expose you to new and different ideas, business concepts, opinions and tools to improve your business ventures overseas.

Export & Import - Winning in the Global Marketplace covers key aspects of international business, consumer goods and industrial sales as well as exporting and importing of products and services. Using hundreds of examples based on my over 40 years of global experience, this book will help you determine if international business is right for you, provide answers to most of your questions and also show you how to conduct international business.

Good education always helps, but it does not take a MBA or Ph.D. to be successful in global trade. Experience in sales and marketing is an asset. Success does not require the perfect product or service or price. It is a question of attitude and understanding how to conduct business in each country.

> *"Never stop learning! Knowledge is like a water tank*
> *with a steady leak in the bottom."*
> *— Gerhard Gschwanther*

The best feedback about my books and teaching/workshops comes from my students, executives I have coached and clients. They have given me comments about what they want to know and also what could be improved. They tell me how they want to use information like you will find in this book: as a school text, as a handbook, as a resource to go back to at any time to find the answers they need. They want examples that are memorable and easy to understand, along with plenty of practical examples and the opportunity to practice on their own. I will weave in information so you get a little bit each time without being overwhelmed, sharing experience that will allow you to more easily absorb ideas as you go along.

Once you have read this book and completed the exercises, you will have gained:

- ♦ A clearer understanding of what it takes to succeed
- ♦ Plenty of new ideas based on real examples
- ♦ A more open mindset to 'going global'

Success in international business is based on:

- ♦ 85% - understanding other cultures and how to do business in foreign countries
- ♦ 10% - your company's dedicated staff, forward-looking management and well organized plans.
- ♦ 5% - your product or service

> *"A prudent person profits from personal experience,*
> *a wise one from the experience of others."*
> *— Joseph Collins*

Learn from My Experience

Over the past forty years, I have shared my experience with thousands of individuals around the world, individuals who have attended my workshops and seminars - business executives and owners, politicians, government representatives and university students and those who have read my other textbooks. I am always surprised at how much an open-minded person can pick up during a 24-hour seminar or that after only four days of intense workshops they are able to apply business concepts for expanding into new international markets. It also takes hard work to become successful, but it is not that complicated, as long as you are adaptable and use common sense.

International business is not a one-person show. It requires a dedicated team; you have to involve everybody in your company. If your management group is not committed to international business and supportive of expansion efforts, success will be difficult. Everyone has to believe in it and become active in promotion.

If you're away from the office and the receptionist doesn't understand the importance of a call from your new partner in Malaysia, s/he will not put in the effort to find the appropriate person in your company to take that call. If the design department in Canada isn't aware that quality standards are more stringent in Japan than in Brazil, your chances of success are poor.

You and your staff have to understand that doing business in China is based on building a relationship over weeks and months or even years of meetings in China and not on a one-hour conversation in a bar in Chicago. If the company accounting department doesn't know how to deal with overseas invoices so that you get payment from another country in foreign currency, you will not make the profits you aim for.

The key ingredient is your attitude

There are a few key Success Principles:

1. Willingness to understand other countries' cultures and ways of doing business.
2. Being prepared to understand the market and act accordingly.
3. Readiness to listen to those who have already conducted international business in a variety of markets.
4. Flexibility, attitude and willingness to learn new concepts and adapt.
5. Teamwork
6. Long term commitment

Some of my students asked an executive of a large international corporation we visited, if their education would help to get them a job. He said yes, but he stated that for his company, 90% of getting a job was the right attitude of the applicant, followed by experience and education.

An extra benefit of using this book is, of course, that you will gain experience and the analytical skills to evaluate information and select the right business approach. If you cannot apply the **six success principles**, no product will make you successful on the international market.

It doesn't matter if your title is Export Manager, Senior Manager of Export or Vice President of Marketing; you need to build a strong team. You may be the coach but your production group and Research & Development departments have to be prepared to adapt production to foreign standards as well as dealing with different planning and product approval requirements. Sales and service materials must be available in a foreign language and presented in formats that suit each local market. The shipping department has to select the right packaging and shipping methods to minimize costs and get your shipments to the new markets quickly, undamaged and without pilferage. - As you can see, every department in your company has a role to play. You will get more details in later chapters. Involve all of your staff, because they are an important part of your company's success internationally. Give them a copy of this book. Teach them how to apply the new approaches you will learn. Allow them to practice their new skills.

"The primary asset of any business is its organisation."
— William Feather

If you are a student or a newcomer to international business, you will learn common sense approaches from this book, but you'll have to practice either on your own or with real-life examples your instructor will provide to you.

International business is a challenge and a joy. It will never be boring. Every day you will learn a lot, you will gain understanding of other cultures, you will meet interesting people and despite the fatigue of traveling, you will benefit from exploring new countries, different foods and unique ways of entertaining. New opportunities will be waiting around every corner once you know what to do and how to do it. By 'going global', your company will grow, you'll make more money and you'll get to work in an environment with more excitement and action than you ever imagined. Entry into new markets will bring experiences unlike any regular day in the domestic market. Your first visitor from overseas and their first order will feel very special.

I have seen small companies grow from three employees to 15 in two years, with a corresponding increase in sales. Why? Because they expanded into new markets. I've seen the same percentage increase in larger companies as well.

Your international business can help you gain market share locally – improvements based on demands from the Global market-place can be applied on the domestic market. Your improved marketing skills will make your domestic marketing more professional. Your company's image will also benefit when you can boast of "distribution in over 30 countries."

Family has to get involved in the business

What could the impact of international business be on your family? Family is part of the business, even if individual members are not directly involved. Your spouse or partner has to understand the necessity of your traveling and working odd hours. There will be travel to a foreign country on short notice. Visits by Japanese business people will require your attention 24 hour a day. They may not appreciate that you want to leave a business meeting to go home and say goodnight to your children late at night. My children grew up receiving gifts, clothing and toys from all over the world. They also got used to having foreign visitors join us at home for dinner or for a weekend fishing trip. Not only did the visitors enjoy being included, my family enjoyed meeting people from other countries and cultures. My son is now over 40 years of age. He was born into international business. He has been working globally and has lived overseas in five countries since the age of 19. His introduction to international business as a young child certainly helped.

"It is a thousand times better to have commonsense without education than to have education without commonsense."
— Lewis E. Pierson

You will learn from my practical hands-on experience gained during more than 40 years of conducting international business in more than 100 countries. Some of the examples you will read about are from my early days in charge of international business for two European companies. Perhaps they are not as applicable as they were years ago; however, some examples are fresh and more recent.

My intention is not give you all of the answers but to get you to think outside your domestic mindset. With so many examples, you will learn how to adapt and become more open-minded about different approaches to international business. You will begin to understand that each market, culture and customer group is different and that each requires a different approach. You'll learn from the mistakes of others. After all of my years in international business, I am still learning and you always will too. There is no way someone can become an expert in this field. There are so many markets and the rules are constantly shifting. You have to keep learning and practicing your skills, so that you grow comfortable with the concepts. Some names and cases I use are real: some have been altered to protect the sources.

When you decide to tackle a new market after reading this book, you will know how to investigate that market, the local culture, the way business is done, how you should dress, if bribing is part of the business environment, whether the clients prefer to negotiate with a young or older person and what factors are important to potential foreign partners.

The world is changing at an accelerating rate. You cannot analyze past performance or today's situation - that is history. You have to study the future and develop new products and services for tomorrow's markets.

> *"The only thing constant in life is change."*
> *— Francois de la Rochefoucauld*

There is a big difference between today and 1969 when I started doing international business. Back then, the markets did not change that much. Being away from the office for five weeks in Latin America or in Asia created a communication problem with the home base. There was no internet, fax or mobile phones. Usually, it took a long time to get a phone call through the international operators, often with a terrible connection and at a high cost. However, because you stayed longer in a foreign location, you worked with the local people, learning to do business with them, experiencing their culture and spending time with them on your days off, sometimes picking up enough of their language to have conversations. You built up friendships and relationships because you received invitations to family and business events. In other words, you learned the most important part of international business - the local way.

Between 1970 and 1974, I did a lot of business with a company in Singapore. In 1990, that same company had a request for some specific products. We happened to have a supplier who could meet their needs. The client called because he still remembered me. That was likely the major reason we got the order. This proves the long term value of personal relationships.

Doing business in Russia today is completely different than when I started in 1969. However, the importance of building relationships in Asia has not changed. Japan used to copy others' products but now they are world leaders in technology. Now China, which is a low-cost labour location, has become well known for not complying with copyright and patent laws. In 1973, Chile had an inflation rate of 700% and tried to protect itself with high import duties and restrictions on foreign investment. Today, Chile is an open market and has become an attractive location for foreign investment. Import duties in India have gone from 300% to low double-digit figures, with more openness to foreign investments.

International business is not based on formulas and theories but on common sense and understanding people. We do business with people and not companies.

If you understand the people you do business with and what they want, you will succeed.

My approach

This book does not include terms like "strategic market research". I will tell you in plain language how to find the key pieces of information you need to succeed in foreign markets. Even if English is not your mother tongue, I have presented the material in simple terms, so that you can easily understand the contents. There are no fancy words or scientific formulas.

I am a firm believer that a book should not be full of abstract facts or theories but full of life, entertaining and enjoyable to read, with a mix of examples and the necessary facts. You may not remember all the facts but you will remember the examples and stories. By showing examples, I will highlight what happens in real life by taking you along on the journeys I experienced.

I promise to give you plenty of ideas. I will tell you about successes but also failures. I will teach you international business logic and give you check lists that can be used for many purposes. I will take you step-by-step in an easy to follow, understandable way, with lots of explanations. I will assist you to be a more successful exporter.

However, the final results will be up to you. As I have said before, if you do not have the right attitude or the willingness to adapt and work hard, you will not be successful. Remember, we don't do business with companies, we do business with people. You have to deliver what these people want, presented their way, with the features and benefits they tell you are desirable. If a personal relationship is more important to them than the product, then that is what you have to offer. If technical details are more important than data on return on investment, you have to supply that.

> *"It is not the strongest of species that survive, nor the most intelligent, but the ones most responsive to change."*
> *— Charles Darwin*

I have taught students at many overseas universities. During the first four days of the program of studies, I teach workshops on how to enter new markets. After those four days, I leave them for three weeks. During that time, they are required to work in teams to complete a professional export project for a new or existing product or service, for an actual company, in a real country. When I return for the next part of the course, the student groups have to make a public presentation of their proposal for entering that market. Often, they have not only done their homework and developed the export plan, they have also visited the country, test-sold the product, identified the right distribution channels, signed up their foreign partner and obtained the first order.

Not only are the students surprised at what they can produce in such a short period of time, the companies they are assisting are more so. All this has been accomplished after only four days' of my lectures in class and a lot of question and answer sessions. Don't believe that it's complicated to do international business. As one of my students stated: "You threw us in front of the train to see if we could solve the problem." You have to learn how to "fly" on your own.

I will not be on hand to assist you, but I promise you that after completing this book, you will have gained a very good understanding of how to conduct business successfully in a foreign market. You will also find useful resources such as web sites. (See more in each chapter and at the end of this book).

I have been a teacher, mentor and coach for a long time. My students continue to share with me stories about their performance and their business experiences. They call or email to ask me questions. Some of these people I worked with as far back as 25 years ago. Their success stories are my reward. This book is based on their feedback and you can be confident that the solutions you read about have been tested by real-world business people.

When You Read My Book, I Promise You Will:

- ◆ Understand that it is not that complicated to do exporting and importing

- ◆ Understand that common sense is the key to your success

- ◆ Realize that it is challenging, profitable and rewarding to do international business.

- ◆ Know if you are ready to try international business, if you have not tried it before

- ◆ Pick up helpful ideas and sources (a valuable second opinion) to become even more successful if you are already involved in international business.

- ◆ Get practical answers to the most common questions about how you can carry out international business on your own

- ◆ Understand the pros and cons of different import and export solutions

- ◆ Have check lists for future use. (See summary in each chapter)

I would appreciate hearing your feedback on Export & Import - Winning in the Global Marketplace: what did you like, what can be improved, what else you would like to learn. I would appreciate you sharing your story/case. I might include these in future editions. Send me an e-mail at book@exportpro.com.

Good luck in your reading and much success in your business ventures.

— Leif Holmvall

Other books on international business

I have found it difficult to find easy-to-read books on a variety of international business issues in the 21st century, whether on selecting markets and representatives, understanding cultures, practical business ideas, legal issues, examples, etc. Therefore, in the future I plan to list books I find useful on my website: www. exportpro.com. So, if you have published a book that you think could match the requirements of a good international business text and you want it listed on the website, send a copy of your book to:

Export Pro Inc.
PO Box 1112
Sharon, Ontario
Canada, L0G 1V0

I will only include books that I can recommend because they meet my criteria.

In 2011, I will have completed updating my website - www.exportpro.com. On an ongoing basis, I will update "Links on the Web" as well as the "Questions and Answers" sections. You will always find the most updated information on the website. I will maintain a blog.

In the next twenty four months or so, I will be publishing another book on the topics of searching, selecting and activating foreign representatives. Check my website at www.cxportpro.com so that you know when it will be available.

Note for teachers

A Teacher's Handbook with Power Point presentations, group work and exams will be available by the end of 2011. Visit my web site www.exportpro.com for information about the "handbook" and where you can buy it. It will include a CD/DVD with Power Point Presentation, Course outlines, Group works or activities to practice as well as suggestion for exams, etc.

Reading Instructions

This brief reading instruction will assist you to get the best results from this book. There are thirteen chapters plus a glossary, links and index. Each chapter is self-contained with information and examples. Most include exercises so that you can practice what you have read. In the first chapters you will find general background that will give you a perspective on the global market and its opportunities and challenges. The following chapters are more focused on each topic. There is a special chapter on Importing, but since many exporting activities are also valid for importing, the chapter only contains coverage of topics very specific to importing. You need to understand the different aspects of exporting before reading this chapter.

To make it easier for you to work through some of the more extensive material, I have divided most chapters into two parts. Part One is basic, to give you key information. Part Two provides additional details and examples. The chapter, "Practicalities and Cultures in International Business", is even more extensive so it has been divided into three parts. To get the most benefit from that chapter, read at least the two first parts. You will find some repetitions in the book, mainly because I want to remind you of some of the more important points. Each chapter has a summary that also can be used as a check list.

I have included numerous references to more sources such as websites, with specific websites related to each chapter. For example, the chapter on Market Research includes instructions for doing market research: however you will find more resources related to market research in other chapters. Those websites should also be used in your market research along with sources on currency and payments in the Risk chapter. At the end of the book you will find a full list of websites for each topic.

Conducting global business is a journey through different cultures. I will be your guide to reaching your international business destinations.

The best approach is to read through all of the information in each chapter, from beginning to end, to get a full understanding of the concepts presented. However, if you want to start with an overview you could always read the first part of each chapter, and then go back later on to study the more detailed information.

I don't want you to just accept what I am saying. For that reason, I will sometimes start with a provocative statement or a faulty solution or provoke you. Sometimes I may point you in the wrong direction with a "confusing" answer in order to get you thinking creatively. That way, you will better understand the right answer, which will always be included. For example, basing your export price on the domestic market or your manufacturing costs may seem logical, but you will learn they have nothing to do with your pricing in overseas markets.

There are topics you can easily find more information about on the web. In those cases I will give you the necessary background and then guide you to additional information. The extra resources will also allow you to access the most updated information such as delivery terms and Incoterms and some examples. I will teach you about the alternatives to getting paid and the pros and cons of different payment methods, but if you want to learn more details on letters of credit, your bank can give you a complete book on the topic, you can locate books at the library or you can read more on the web. I will describe the importance to you of trade agreements and provide an overview of Trade Unions like European Union and NAFTA but for detailed information, I will direct you to useful websites for additional information.

The world and the global business environment are continuously changing. You will have to keep your knowledge up-to-date. I will also keep you updated on my web site - www.exportpro.com - . If you have a suggestion for a good resource, send the link and information to book@exportpro.com and I will add it if I decide it is valuable. We will not link to individual company web sites.

Good luck in your success in international business. I look forward to hearing your feedback.

Leif Holmvall, Export Pro Inc.

Teachers

I will prepare a teachers handbook with Power Point, group work, exams, etc. You can obtain more information by visiting www.exportpro.com or by sending an e-mail to book@exportpro.com

Why International Business?
Part One

In This Chapter:

- ♦ More competition
- ♦ Evolution of markets
- ♦ Global population, labour force/ labour markets
- ♦ Emerging opportunities and environmental influences
- ♦ Other international services, health care/medical tourism, legal, education, international consulting, outsourcing
- ♦ Economies today and in the future
- ♦ Large companies and their influence on international business
- ♦ The power and influence of emerging markets
- ♦ Product life cycles, adaptation and profits
- ♦ Why exporting?
- ♦ Differences between Domestic and International Marketing
- ♦ Who can export and adapting your organization

Example - New competition

You operate a local bakery in Brussels, Belgium. You've been in business for the last 20 years, supplying not only people in your neighbourhood who pick up fresh baked goods on their way to and from work, but also you have supplied bread to local schools. This arrangement has provided you with a steady income, which made you feel comfortable about the future. However, without warning, the business landscape suddenly changes.

You've just been notified that a large international bakery located in Holland has taken away some of your best customers. They have new contracts with five schools you used to service. They also have signed agreements with hundreds of companies in office buildings in downtown Brussels, and will supply them with fresh croissants before 9 a.m. every morning. How did this happen?

The European Union requires that public sector purchasing over a certain monetary value, e.g. for municipal and regional governments, has to be put to public or competitive tender.

That international bakery in Holland submitted the lowest bid and, by law, was awarded the contract for the next three years. There is nothing you can do, even though you have always done business with the school board. You did not bid on the contract. The decision-makers had no choice but to open the bid for public tender and select the best quote. Because the Dutch bakery has established early-morning delivery to schools in Brussels, they can now use this to their advantage and also cover the costs of supplying baked goods to offices in the same area.

Welcome to the world of international competition!

As you can see, previously protected domestic markets are being opened to greater outside competition and your rivals are nibbling away at your territory. What can you do? You have no choice but to expand your business elsewhere and seek new opportunities to expand your market domestically or internationally.

The Evolution of Markets

We live in a world of ongoing political, technological and economic developments. The pace is rapid, as is the extent of change in the marketing environment. In order for today's businesses to survive, managers must understand the impacts of progressively more integrated world economies. To succeed, they must have the skills to forecast and implement plans so that their organizations can keep pace with those changes. They have to continuously analyze the markets and how their company will be affected, so that they can adapt.

What was once classified as a "local market" now includes larger geographic areas and a broader base for products and services. In response to market demands and rapid technological development, goods marketed are no longer mainly raw material-based. The main shift has been to knowledge-based services. Life cycle merchandizing from introduction to obsolescence for products is now much shorter. For example, some electronic consumer product companies like Sony and HP change their product lines two to six times a year.

Developing countries are investing in the newest technology in order to improve their economic competitiveness. What they lack in traditional infrastructure assets is being overcome with products and services that do not require costly assembly, transportation or warehousing. The way industrialized countries target customers has also changed in response to numerous variables – political, economic, sociological, technological, environmental and demographic factors. These will be covered in more detail in the following pages.

Twenty-first century markets are essentially borderless. Transactions can be completed with the click of a computer mouse. Customer service can be delivered from any location in the world with telephone and internet access. Products and services are constantly being developed and adapted for a broader range of demographic and geographic markets. Product life cycles tend to be short and competition is aggressive. No longer is it profitable to develop a product only for the domestic market. Furthermore, domestic markets are quickly influenced by events and suppliers from all over the world.

Surviving on the international market scene requires common sense, flexibility, understanding of individual market characteristics and how to adapt business to each of them. Experience in international business issues does help, but even more critical is an in-depth understanding how other markets function.

"In business, the competition will bite you if you keep running. If you stand still they will swallow you."
— Semin Knudsen

Global Labour Forces and Market Influences

Age

The aging of the Baby Boom generation in industrialized countries has created a substantial number of people over the age of 55. In 2035, 25% of the population in Europe will be over 65 years of age.

This large, well educated, financially stable, influential market segment has significantly affected every aspect of North American and European society for the last 50 years. Men and women are retiring earlier from full time employment and living longer. Their interests and activities have changed over time. Many retirees relocate overseas to countries with better climates, lower costs of living and lower taxes, thus creating new market opportunities. On the other hand, a significant population of older people in a society with a low birth rate has far-reaching social and economic implications. These include longer periods for pension payouts, a smaller percentage of the population contributing to the economy and seniors' demands for recreational, housing and health care services such as hospital beds and pharmaceutical products.

In contrast to the greying workforce in the G-8 nations, many developing countries have up to 50 percent of their population in the under - 25 age group. What does this mean in terms of markets? Industrialized nations have a large part of the population not working or retired. Developing countries have more of their population in the labour force, making them very competitive with respect to availability of workers with lower wage and benefit costs for employers. To put it another way, it would be like competing with a company that has only 5 percent in administration costs while you have to operate with overhead of 35 percent.

Labour markets

Half of the global population earns less than two dollars a day; 80% earn less than $3000 a year. About 40 percent are employed in agriculture, 20 percent in industry and 39 percent in services. As seen in the chart below, over 40 percent of the world's labour force resides in India and China. Both countries have a large low cost labour force, which creates a very strong competitive position as well as a large potential consumer base.

Labour Force by Country – 2010

Rank	Country	Labour force – millions	%
	World	3,232	100
1	China	819.5	25.4
2	India	478.3	14.8
3	European Union	225.4	7.0
4	United States	154.9	4.8
5	Indonesia	116.5	3.5
6	Brazil	103.6	3.2
7	Russia	75.6	2.3
8	Bangladesh	73.9	2.3
9	Japan	65.7	2.0
10	Nigeria	48.3	1.5

Source CIA, The World Factbook 2010
Note: China and India have over 40% of the global labour force

Over 200 million people worldwide are living and working outside of their home or native country. A significant percentage of the population is "telecommuting" or not working out of a traditional office.

What this means for a marketer is that more than half of the population in Europe and North America is working from a home or a satellite office at least one or two days a week. Telephone and video-conferencing have also become part of companies' ways of reducing traveling costs for meetings and conferences. The cell phone has made it possible to reach people all over the world and poses a strong threat to conventional land-line communications.

Skype (http://www.skype.com) is a software application that allows users to make voice and video calls over the Internet, to anyone anywhere all over the world who has a computer. Calls can also be made to local telephone numbers at a low cost, using the computer. Computer-to-computer communications are free; low-cost plans are available for calls to mobile and long distance telephones, making it less expensive to keep in touch with contacts and communicate frequently. Many companies now include a Skype "address" on their business card. Your Skype "address" follows you wherever your computer is.

Environmental Influences

Widespread awareness of environmental issues has generated an array of eco-friendly or "green" products and services for environmental controls and safeguards. There is strong interest in recycling and waste reduction. Today, product formulation, product packaging and distribution are, to a larger extent, driven by customer demands for suppliers to comply with the new trend for environmentally friendly products. Conservation efforts, public interest issues and catalysts such as fluctuating prices for petroleum products push consumer demand for specialized products like alternative fuels and hybrid powered or electric motor vehicles.

The price of petroleum will continue to have a long-term impact on trade and the cost of goods. When crude oil prices reached $140 a barrel in 2008, many industries and individuals were directly affected. If experts' predictions are correct that there will be ongoing shortages of oil and a potential price of $200 a barrel in a few years, world trade patterns will be changed dramatically. Freight prices will at least double since today's cost is $70-100 a barrel. The benefits of low labour costs will, to a great extent, be eliminated because of high freight costs from low labour-cost countries such as China and India. The result will likely be increased trade between countries within shorter transportation distances of each other.

New Opportunities for International Business

Improved communication and transportation methods have transformed the market for new products and services. During the last ten years, utility companies, catalogue order-taking, customer support functions for computer hardware and software, help desks, financial transaction data entry and other sales and support activities have been outsourced to locations beyond the borders of Europe and North America to countries such as India and the Philippines. Although there have been service quality and human resources/labour management challenges, off-shoring represents a low-cost way to deliver customer services.

In regions like North America, Europe and Australia new careers are emerging in sectors that did not exist three decades ago: software engineering, computer game development, optical payload design, infrastructure planning, medical imaging, etc. These and other specialized occupations service growing market niches that in turn stimulate demand for innovative products and services. The lesson is this: move jobs and services abroad and the customers will follow. There is no real limit to what can be offered outside of domestic markets.

Health care has become increasingly costly in many traditional industrialized or developed countries. There are shortages of hospital beds and family physicians. The price of some pharmaceutical products has increased beyond what many individuals can afford, especially those who have minimal or no comprehensive health insurance coverage. People are living longer. Many will need more medications, frequent and complex treatment as they age, but as well as constraints on government spending at all levels have led to long waiting lists. For patients who have the ability to pay for wellness care or for treatment, their approach is, why should we have to wait?

Over the years, increasing numbers of graduates from developing countries have studied the same technical and professional curricula for careers in accounting, health care and engineering. However, their comparable education has been obtained at a much lower cost than in developed countries. Relocating some high-paying jobs to lower-cost locations abroad makes economic sense for both employers and their workers. In fact, many developing countries are now competing directly with traditional service providers for customers in the medical field, to the benefit of local economies.

Medical Tourism

Medical tourism is one of the fastest growing global industries, at a rate of about 30 percent a year. The cost of surgery in India or Thailand is often one-tenth of what it would be in the United States or Western Europe. In addition to standard medical procedures, some hospitals also offer all-inclusive options with travel, hotel, a companion package and arrangements for vacation-recovery after

---

Why Medical Travel/Tourism?

- High healthcare costs in industrialized nations. Many uninsured or under-insured individuals cannot afford the costs at home

- Avoid long waiting lists for surgery or treatments at home

- It is relatively easy and affordable to travel overseas

- Overseas institutions often provide more personalized, customer-oriented care

- International accreditation of foreign hospitals provide quantifiable benchmarks for patient care quality (More than 250 hospitals have been accredited by JCI, Joint Commission International, (2008)

- Some insurance companies offer lower rates for coverage if surgical procedure is completed overseas

surgery. In part, costs are lower because of reduced liability/insurance expenses for physicians, more modest salaries and less overhead. Medical practitioners are board-certified and many have left lucrative practices in other countries to return home for a less hectic lifestyle or to care for aging parents and to focus more on medicine than administrative tasks.

Medical tourism are attracting increasing numbers of "medical tourists", individuals with disposable incomes who are not prepared to wait and who are willing to travel the world for services such as hip replacement, cosmetic surgery, dental treatments and "womb for rent". Costs are consistently lower. Because many of the service providers have been trained in and practiced their speciality in North America and Europe, the quality of services can be higher and delivered at luxurious high-rise hospital "resorts".

Countries such as India, Singapore, Hungary, South Africa, Malaysia, Dubai, Israel, Costa Rica, Brazil and Thailand are the top-ranked health tourist treatment destinations. Australia, Argentina, Belgium, Canada, El Salvador, Guatemala, Hungary, Malaysia, Mexico, New Zealand, Panama, South Korea, Taiwan, Turkey and the UK are becoming increasingly competitive.

In 2007, 600,000 foreigners sought treatment in Thailand, 410,000 in Singapore, 450,000 in India, and more than 350,000 in Malaysia.

According to health.com, about six million Americans travelled overseas for faster access to convenient, economical medical treatment in 2009. Popular procedures include comprehensive physical assessments, orthopaedic surgeries such as spinal fusion and knee/hip replacement, cosmetic surgeries such as facelifts and liposuction, gastric bypass, cardiac care, organ transplants and dental procedures.

With millions of health tourists seeking lower-cost but high quality medical care abroad each year, the sector is expected to generate $100 billion worldwide by 2012. The main consumers are residents of the Americas, the Middle East and Europe.

India is forecast to generate over $2.3 billion in health services revenue by 2012. They graduate more than 30,000 medical professionals every year. After 7 years in medical school, a physician can expect to earn about $400 a month. Compare that with the salaries of doctors in Europe and North America and you can understand why there is price differential.

Diagnostic testing is also being outsourced. Secure internet and high-speed broadband transfers are now so reliable that X-ray images, MRI and CT scans can be sent overseas for evaluation by skilled radiologist whose wages are a fraction of wages in Europe and North America. Completed reports are returned to the referring physicians for discussion with their patients.

Comparison of Overseas Surgical Costs*

PROCEDURE	US	SINGAPORE	THAILAND	INDIA
Approximate cost in US Dollars				
Total Hip replacement	24,000	15,000	10,000	6,300
Hip Resurfacing	48,000	14,000	10,000	7,000
Breast Augmentation	10,000	8,000	3,150	2,200
Eyelid surgery	7,000	3,750	1,413	2,200
Face lift	20,000	6,250	4,799	3,100
Liposuction	7,000	5,000	2,133	2,500
Rhinoplasty	7,300	4,375	3,839	1,800
Tummy tuck	8,500	6,250	3,052	3,400
Coronary Angioplasty	41,000	11,250	4,150	3,500
Coronary Artery Bypass Graft	56,000	12,900	13,250	7,000
Pacemaker	65,000	7,500	5,000	3,500

*Source: www.Healthbase.com

Dental treatments such as cleaning, surgeries and tooth implants are also popular. A porcelain metal crown that costs a patient $600-1,000 in the US is priced at around $80-$300 in India. A porcelain metal bridge that costs $1,800 - $3000 in the US could cost $300 - $800 in India.

The examples illustrate one of the results of open competition for medical services on a global market.

Bumrungrad International (http://www.bumrungrad.com) in Bangkok, Thailand, is one of the largest hospitals in Asia, treating over 400,000 foreign patients per year from 150 countries. With more than 700 nurses and 945 physicians covering 55 sub-specialties (200 are US-board certified and many others were trained and certified in Europe, Japan, or Australia) this private, internationally managed facility provides an extensive array of medical programs and services.

Package prices are available for numerous routine procedures and cover surgical fees, doctor's fees, medicine, lab tests, room charges and other costs for treatment, so there are no surprises when the invoice for services is received.

Patients may be picked up at the airport arrivals gate and escorted through immigration to a waiting limousine, which will transport them to sign in to their hotel/hospital. While their paperwork is being processed, they will enjoy a flat-screen television, complementary refreshments and newspapers in the waiting rooms. Being treated like a VIP means staying in a luxury room with a higher standard of care than most hospitals at home, then recovering in a tropical country where you can buy a decent lunch for less than $3 and have a tailor-made suit or dress made for $100 in two days. You can include your family when you travel and spend time having a relaxing vacation – all at a much lower cost than you would pay at home for the medical treatment, and without long waiting times.

Reproductive tourism

All-inclusive fertility treatment packages and surrogacy services are being promoted to infertile would-be parents around the world. Couples from India and overseas sign a legal contract and pay approximately $8-12,000 to "rent a womb", where, for a fee, an Indian woman will carry a child conceived through in vitro fertilization or artificial insemination, to term. The comparative cost in the US, where willing surrogates are hard to find and the process is highly legalized and regulated, is around $70,000.

The prospective foreign parents are the "renters". The embryo of their biological child is implanted into the healthy Indian woman by a physician at a local medical clinic. Of the $12,000 - $20,000 fee, about $7-10,000 will be paid to the surrogate. The rest is paid for physicians, medical care, hospital costs and food. Many of the surrogate mothers live in rural villages and have husbands and children, but limited income. This money represents the equivalent of 10 - 15 years' salary for a rural Indian family and allows them to build a house, start a business and pay for children's educations. A labourer makes about $1 a day.

Surrogacy treatments bring more than $450 million a year to India. India has about 350 fertility clinics. It is believed that more than 500-600 surrogate babies are born each year to couples from Japan, the U.S., Taiwan, Europe, and Australia plus babies to locals using gestational surrogates.

Ethical and legal concerns have begun to complicate the provision of surrogacy services. Although services may be allowed in the country supplying them, they may be illegal in the country of the "buyer". Other questions are, what happens if the donor parent split up or decide they no longer want their biological child? What nationality does the newborn child have? The government of Canada requires a DNA test to prove that the couple are the biological parents. Many countries in Europe ban surrogate babies from overseas. For Germany, a child's citizenship is based on the nationality of the birth mother, which in this case would be the Indian mother. New legislation is on its way in India that would prohibit gay and lesbian couples from hiring surrogates, because Indian laws ban same-sex marriage. There is also a growing possibility that authorities in India will demand a document from the couple's home embassy confirming that the baby will be granted citizenship in that country.

Other services

Lawyers and investment companies outsource research to lower salary countries like India. Why pay a Wall Street Analyst in expensive office space a salary of $180,000 a year plus benefits, when you can hire the same service in Mumbai, India for $20,000? Customer service functions like call centres are also being outsourced, so that when you have problem with your computer you can call a toll-free number to be connected to a technician in India or the Philippines. The market has changed, and so have the customers.

Education

More universities are establishing campuses and joint venture overseas. In the United States, 3.5% of students are from abroad. China has more than 200,000 students in higher education programs abroad, mainly studying engineering, languages and business. In 2006, over three million students were enrolled in higher education overseas.

Population and Market Influence

Projected population - year 2050 (Billion inhabitants)

1. India   1.57
2. China   1.46
3. Pakistan   1.34
4. USA   0.40
5. Nigeria   0.30
6. Indonesia   0.30
7. Brazil   0.27
8. Bangladesh   0.25
9. Ethiopia   0.19

India and China will account for 33% of the world's population of 9.3 billion

Source Economist and www.photius

Global population is predicted to reach more than eight billion by the year 2020 and 10-11 billion by 2050, an increase of 88 million inhabitants a year. This is equal to the population of Germany. With shifts in demographics and residences, a minority of those people will be living in Europe and North America. In 2009, about 37% of the world's population lived in China and India.

What were formerly characterized as lesser-developed countries are now becoming increasingly industrialized. They have emerged as large potential markets. More critically for other marketers, they will be serious competitors.

Movements of companies and privatization

Besides having to think more internationally, municipal, provincial and federal governments have been dealing with increasing numbers of foreign companies entering their traditionally protected markets.

The migration of people is another reason for shifts in settlement patterns. Privatization of industry that started in countries such as the United Kingdom has spread as an impetus to economic growth. The more prosperous status of the Latin American economy, for example, is largely the result of more open and privatized markets. Markets have been strongly influenced by ongoing hostilities in the Middle East, the former Yugoslavia, South East Asia and in Iraq. On the other hand, we have seen positive developments in South Africa, Latin America and the old Eastern Bloc of Europe.

The political instability in countries like Egypt and Libya in 2011 is another indication what can happen when ordinary citizens try to "force democracy" using the internet and social media in combination with demonstrations.

The unexpected economic downturn during 2008-2011 is an example of what can happen when governments, banks and countries spend more money than they have. Ten years ago, who could have predicted that in 2011, some countries, states and cities could face bankruptcy?

Economies and the Future

These types of developments are tough to forecast. Natural disasters such as the earthquake and tsunami in Japan will have a long-term global impact on agriculture, politics, manufacturing, trade and investment patterns. A potential exporter must balance their desire to expand into new markets with ensuring that investments are not wasted in countries with strong potential for political instability. Choosing the right market and decision-making flexibility - being able to change direction at short notice – are essential to success. The only constant is change!

Economic growth in industrialized countries has slowed. If you live in one of those, your market has been deteriorating for decades and neighbouring countries have also experienced limited expansion. You have to look outside your home territory for new, expanding markets.

Geopolitical uncertainties now drive long-term trends in global capital accumulation, currency flows and exchange rates. As well, there are the constant short-term influences of stock markets, high profile business failures, world events and government fiscal policies. In contrast, some developing countries such as Latin America and Asia have shown tremendous trade and industrial growth.

When you work for a company and want to know about its performance, you look at annual sales and the percentage of sales increases year over year. In many ways, a country is similar to a company. Gross Domestic Product (GDP) is like annual sales and an increase in the percentage of a nation's GDP is like a company's percentage of annual increase in sales.

When you are considering a new market, you must look at population as a basis for market size. However, even with a large population, if per capita income is low, total annual sales or GDP would likely be low compared with other countries that have a smaller population but higher GDP. Also, when the percentage of annual GDP growth is high, you have to determine whether it results from changes to a historically lower level of growth. Look at countries that have shown steady growth over a number of years. Determine if consumers there have sufficient income to afford your product or service. Note that trade in goods and services now represent 25% of global GDP, an increase from 10% three decades ago. The chart below shows a forecast of GDP positions.

GDP development in Ten Key Countries (Billions of US$)

Rank in 2050	Country	2000	2010	2020	2030	2040	2050
1	China	1078	2998	7070	14312	26439	44453
*	European Union *	9395	12965	16861	21075	28323	35288
2	United States	9825	13271	16415	20833	27229	35165
3	India	469	929	2104	4935	12367	27803
4	Japan	4176	4601	5221	5810	6039	6673
5	Brazil	762	668	1333	2189	3740	6074
6	Russia	391	847	1741	2980	4467	5870
7	United Kingdom	1437	1876	2285	2649	3201	3782
8	Germany	1875	2212	2524	2697	3147	3603
9	France	1311	1622	1930	2267	2668	3148
10	Italy	1078	1337	1553	1671	1788	2061

Value in billion dollars EU Trading block. Source www.geografic.org (Goldman Sachs)

In fact, since the figures in the table above were presented in late 2009, the economic climate has changed. By August 2010, China passed Japan to become the second largest economy. The forecast is that by 2030, China will pass the US as the largest world economy.

Even if a nation has experienced steady development it can involve uncertainty and potential risk. Some countries in the newly restructured Eastern Block have shown a relatively fast change in focus by adapting to a market-driven and investment style of business. So if you want to survive on an international market, you have to find new markets and also be aware of the threat of someone stealing part of your domestic market.

Some large corporations have as much in sales as the GDP of many countries. As a comparison, Wal-Mart, an American company with more than 1 million employees, had annual sales of $379 billion in 2009, which is the same as or more than the GDP (sales) of countries like Austria ($379 billion), Norway ($373 billion), Venezuela ($358 billion) and Greece ($342 billion). This means that large corporations can have a major influence on the economies of many countries.

Ten largest corporations in 2009

Rank	Company	Revenue ($millions)
1	Wal-Mart	378,799
2	Exxon Mobil	372,624
3	Royal Dutch Shell	355,782
4	BP (British Petroleum)	291,438
5	Toyota Motor Company	230,201
6	Chevron	210.783
7	ING Group	201,516
8	Total (France)	187,280
9	General Motors	182,347
10	Conoco Philips	178,558

Source - http://money.cnn.com

Some countries have experienced more rapid economic development than others. Corporations that are not that large today will have a much greater influence in the future, because of their location in emerging markets.

Different industry sectors and markets have a large impact on countries' economies and also on the profitability of individual companies. For example, between 2006 and 2007, Tata Steel in India increased sales by 358 percent. Freeport McMoRan Copper and Gold Inc., which have operations in Asia and Spain, increased sales by 209 percent. Today's emerging markets are becoming increasingly strong competitors with traditional industrialized European and North American countries.

While the financial downturn in 2008 had a negative effect on some national economies, others continued to enjoy uninterrupted GDP growth.

Examples of annual sales increases/ GDP growth - 2009

Rank	Country	GDP –% Real growth rate
1	Macau	13.20
4	China	8.70
12	India	6.50
20	Vietnam	5.30
35	Iraq	4.30
113	Brazil	-0.20
220	World average	-0.80
180	European Union	-4.00
213	Latvia	-17.00

Source, World Fact book - https://www.cia.gov/

As you know, 2009 was a year of economic upheaval, so the figures above do not represent normal GDP growth. The usual figure for China would be 10-12% and for the European Union, 2-4%. I suggest that you visit several websites to research country performance when it is time to make your selection of a new market.

Almost 100% of the growth and around 30% of global GDP comes from emerging markets. Because so many factors influence markets and market development, individual country growth and large corporations, from now until 2050 shifts in ranking will continue. As someone in international business, you will have to follow these developments and be prepared to change your priorities, research new market opportunities and adapt how you do business.

What Does International Business Include and What Can You Do?

International business is a two-way process that, among other things, includes:

- Export
- Import
- Joint Ventures
- Licensing
- Strategic partnerships

Benefits of Exporting

Increase your market size = increased sales

If your domestic market is 30 million customers and the world market is 8 billion potential customers, the global market is about 270 times the size of your domestic market. It is simply not possible that you could ever cover a market of that magnitude. Given the population of Canada, the European market offers a population of about 10 times the size of my domestic market. By entering that market, I will spread my risks and, at the same time, gain exposure to a much larger potential market.

More markets and clients = Increased company stability and more constant sales

Indirect exporting

You may already be exporting without knowing it. Say you supply hoses and couplings to a company manufacturing hydraulic systems and selling them on the international market, in 30 countries. So in fact, your products are being sold internationally. When those overseas customers want spare parts and you are set up to supply them, you have created an opportunity to start your international exposure.

> ### Example - Indirect exporting
>
> *A European company supplied computerized control systems to a manufacturer of robotics in Europe. The manufacturer exported the systems to North America. After a number of years, over 300 systems were exported for use in the American automotive industry. As the control system could also be used for other automated systems, the European company decided to set up its own operation in North America. They already had 300 systems installed that needed service and as well, the existing satisfied users could serve as references, and become a good base for expanding the business.*

Spread the risks = less dependence on one market, minimize fluctuations (currency, orders, etc.)

When investing in the stock market, you don't just buy equities from one company; you diversify and spread the risks. Experts say you should never have more than 5% on your investments in one stock. When doing international business, you should use the same philosophy. Perhaps you cannot limit your exposure to 5%, but try to keep it to a maximum of 15%.

If you are fully dependent on your domestic market and that market drops by thirty percent, you'll lose 30% of your business. Let's say that your domestic market is limited to only 10%, then you would lose only 3% (30% of 10%). By taking your business to several markets, you can spread your risks and level out the ups and downs in your sales.

Economic trending varies from country to country, not only because each is in a different development cycle but also because of how industry is structured and what sectors bring the most money into the country. For example, Saudi Arabia relies on the price of oil and global consumption of petroleum products for their wealth. Naturally, when economies are actively expanding, there will normally be higher demands for some products and also higher prices.

Chile, which accounts for 35% of global copper output, is sensitive to fluctuations in consumption of minerals. When the economy is "going at full speed", consumption rises and so do prices. When the economy slows down, consumption and prices also fall. During the economic meltdown of 2008, copper prices fell 45% and Chile's exports declined by 29%. Even a country like China that has a huge domestic market is very dependent on exports. If the economy slows in Europe and North America and customers cut back on their consumption, the Chinese economy will feel the impact.

Increase your product or service range

Have you considered representing and/or manufacturing foreign products for your domestic market or for your trading area?

Example: two-way trades

For many companies, especially in North America, international business means exporting. However, there is always an opportunity for trade in both directions – into and out of your home country.

Let's say you're a German company that manufactures woodworking machinery. You have a limited range of products and you would like to export to Australia. You're looking for a company in Australia that sells woodworking machinery, which is not a market competitor, and which preferably also manufactures a complimentary range of woodworking machinery.

You approach company management and offer to sell or perhaps even manufacture your products under license in Australia and New Zealand. You want to expand your product range so you can become more competitive on your domestic market. You offer to sell the Australian company's products on your domestic market, as well as representing them in Europe from your home base. Your approach succeeds. Now you have a partner who will sell your products in Australia, and you also have access to complimentary woodworking equipment for your domestic market, as well as for export within Europe.

Why invent everything by yourself, when you could find a partner who already has suitable products? Why not spread the risks and benefit from the experience of others by partnering to expand your business and international sales activities?

Increased market and sales

As you've seen in the woodworking example above, by expanding into new markets, you will increase sales. By importing products, you can increase your product range and become more competitive on the domestic market too. If it is possible, you can also arrange to export the products you are representing on the domestic market.

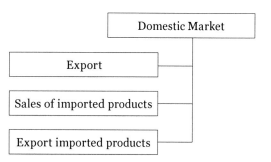

Increase the range of products and services = use other company's technologies rather than developing on your own

Expanding abroad can make it easier for you to source components for domestic production. With suppliers all over the world, you can search for opportunities to further reduce manufacturing costs and increase your competitiveness.

Two-way communications

International business is increasingly about two-way communications for sourcing and distributing products. Advancements in travel options and developments in telecommunications have greatly facilitated market growth. Creative use of inexpensive and accessible fax and video-conferencing, Internet-based communications such as e-mail, online and Net Meetings, Skype and text messaging and the simple telephone have greatly reduced communication barriers, despite the distances involved. Innovations such as on-line advertising and other promotional activities between merchants and consumers have transformed marketing and purchasing patterns. Competition is global and competitors are much more aggressive.

Modern merchandising includes not only tangible goods or hardware, but also systems, software or other kinds of advanced technology. What this means in the market is that now a smaller proportion of the value of non-traditional products is based on the cost of manufacturing than in the past when goods made up the main category of items traded. Value today is based on benefits and knowledge or "soft" products which include education and consulting services. The result is a better return on investment for the client. And price is based on what the customer is willing to pay.

One example is the mobile phone/smart phone. The hardware is actually only a minor part of the product and what you pay. The capabilities of the software is much more important.

Markets Today and Tomorrow

The number of companies and countries involved in international business continues to increase. Competition in industries such as manufacturing of high technology products is intense. Because of this, and rapid product development, the life span of new products has been reduced considerably. Purchasers know that two months after they've bought the latest model computer, another model will come onto the market, faster, with more features and a bigger monitor, and at a lower price.

Distances have shrunk, in part because of better communications and faster methods of transporting goods from one location to another. New opportunities have opened up for companies wanting to establish themselves in the global market. At the same time, companies wanting to compete domestically are under increasing pressure. Company personnel with better business knowledge, the right attitude, a willingness to step outside their "comfort zone" and the ability to make fast decisions will be most likely to succeed in new markets.

"Business is a combination of war and sports."
— Andre Maurots

When products have shorter life cycles, larger markets and more rapid new product introductions are required. A product which in the past had a 20-25 year life cycle (i.e., from introduction to obsolescence), may now have a life of only two to three years. Some of the major electronic goods manufacturers "refresh" or change their entire product line six times a year. They have to maintain a significant market share to remain profitable. These global companies also have to be aware of the characteristics of different markets so that they can phase-in product introduction. This is a common method for extending product life cycles, in a variety of markets.

Product life cycles; from design to phase out

The cycles:

- ◆ Design, planning and introduction phase
- ◆ Growth/expansion phase when sales take off
- ◆ Maturity, when sales begin to level off
- ◆ Stagnation, when the product loses its attractiveness and sales begin to stall
- ◆ Phase out or obsolescence, when the product no longer matches the needs of the market

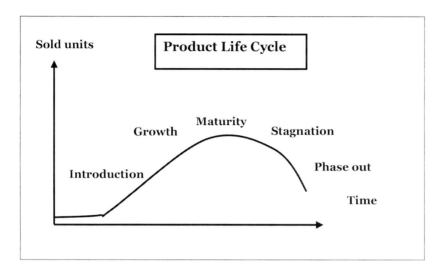

Individual markets develop in different stages. What is considered a high tech product in one country may be too advanced for another market. For example, in a country where labour is cheap and a shovel is the only tool used for digging trenches, it would be impossible to sell a computerized excavator. Not only would it not pay off, but there would be no one available to service the unit.

Example - Obsolete product in established market but modern in new market

In highly industrialized countries, a modern sawmill is a fully computerized system. The system requires few people to operate. A computer scans each log and calculates the optimum cuts based on lumber prices that day.

When those sawmill systems were introduced in Europe and North America around 1970, they were seen as a way to better utilize expensive raw materials as well as cutting labour costs by reducing the work force.

This created a surplus of old sawmills to be sold or recycled somewhere and also limited the market for outdated machines. However, a huge potential market was located in Africa. Now the old sawmills could be exported to a new market and users who were happy to buy more advanced equipment than they had before. An obsolete product in a more developed market represented modern technology in a lesser developed country. In addition to new sales of complete older sawmills in new export markets, the sale of spare parts increased in markets that had not previously needed them.

So what does this mean for you as an exporter? It means that when the life cycle of products developed for higher-technology markets is over, you can now begin to market them to less-developed markets that have matured enough to use your old product. You can extend your product life cycles, increase your markets and sales, and open up demand for spare parts.

Increased sales and product adaptation = Extending product cycle

With an expanding market, you can sell current and older products. By adapting an earlier generation of products for lesser developed markets, you can create a longer life cycle and higher volume of sales.

Older products sold on lesser developed markets = New market life for established products

Product Life Cycles

Selling older products in less-developed markets = New Market Life

Industrialized Countries

Product introduction	Mature market	Aging Market	Obsolete product
Slow sales	Good sales	Reduced sales	No sales

Developing Countries

Product introduction	Mature market	Aging Market	Obsolete product
Slow sales	Good sales	Reduced sales	No sales

Lesser Developed Countries

Product introduction	Mature market	Aging Market	Obsolete product
Slow sales	Good sales	Reduced sales	No sales

Example - Old product finds a new market

Sometimes, you can find opportunities in under-developed markets in more industrialized countries. In 1980, when Canadian consumers were concerned about energy shortages, the demand for old-fashioned cast iron fireplaces exploded. Being a Swede, I knew that companies in Sweden used to manufacture cast-iron fireplaces. In Sweden, they were considered old-fashioned technology. More modern units had been developed using sheet metal construction and fans for better efficiency. All the tools and equipment for manufacturing cast-iron fireplaces had been scrapped long before. However, a company called Jötul in Norway was still manufacturing the old-fashioned fireplaces, and they were able to take advantage of the "new" market for an old product. Jötul still exports large numbers of fireplaces to Canada.

Write off R&D on larger volumes =
Less cost per item and more profit

When a company develops a new product, a lot of time and money is spent on development costs, tooling, etc. A car manufacturer spends hundreds of millions of dollars for every new car model and associated tooling. (Toyota spends $1 million an hour on research). So if they only sell one car, all that cost has to be carried by that one car. By manufacturing hundreds of thousands of cars or sometimes even millions of cars, development costs can be spread over larger volumes and the R&D and tooling costs reduced per unit.

The same is applicable for you, whether you develop software or machinery. Your product development and tooling costs can be dispersed over the expected volume of sales. So if your R&D costs are $300,000 and you sell one thousand units, your R&D cost per unit is $300, (300,000 / 1000). However, if you sell 10,000 units, your R&D cost is only $30 per unit. As you can see, by expanding into larger markets you can increase your sales volume and reduce the R&D costs per unit, which means you make more money. If you can extend your product life cycle, you can increase your sales volume even further and write off R&D quickly.

If you purchased a product like Microsoft Office software and examined the contents of the brightly coloured box, you would find that you received a DVD and a short installation manual. The cost to manufacture this product was most likely less than $5. So why were you charged $200 or even $700? Because you were willing to pay that price, you were convinced you needed the software and its benefits were worth it for you. Do you think the difference between the $200 you paid and the $5 production cost was profit for Microsoft?

You have to remember, though, that Microsoft has spent a huge amount of money developing and marketing their products. The dealer you purchased the software from was making money, too. So when Microsoft calculated the manufacturing cost -- the total cost -- they had to take into consideration the R&D costs and spread them over a large volume of sales. Of course, the more products Microsoft can sell, the more their profits will increase. When the company has written off the costs for R&D, i.e., reached the volume the product cost was based on, the marginal cost will be $5, giving Microsoft an enormous profit.

When we calculate manufacturing costs as well as profits, we tend to forget about this fact. Furthermore, because we complete the wrong calculation, we don't realize that we could make more money. Have you ever had someone ask for a quote on a large number of units at a reduced price, and you couldn't take the order because the price was too low based on your estimated manufacturing cost? Let's look at one example.

Different Ways to Calculate Profit

	Cost of product	**Marginal costs if increasing volume**
R&D	X	
Administration	X	
Material	X	X
Tooling	X	(X)
Labour	X	X

In the first example, the cost of the product is reached using your normal method of calculation, (second column) i.e., research and development, administration, material, tooling and labour. However, if you still have capacity in your factory, the extra cost to manufacture this large order (third column if you have to invest in new tooling) will only be for the material and labour and, in some cases, extra tooling costs.

Below are some figures that allow you to calculate profit on increased sales volume.

Normal calculation

Development cost/R&D for product	$1,000,000
For 50,000 units = $1,000,000/50,000 or	$20 per unit
For 500,000 units = $1,000,000/500,000 or	$2 per unit
Tooling costs are $50,000 for up to 250,000 units	
For 50,000 units = $50,000 : 50,000	$1 per unit
For 500,000 units $100,000 ($50,000 x 2)/500,000 =	$0.20 per unit
Material	$20 per unit
Labour	$12 per unit
Administration	$3 per unit

This is the normal way to calculate your manufacturing cost. Let's look at that order you want to quote. Could you make the product at a lower price and take the order?

Different Ways to Calculate Profits

From the chart above, you can see that your R&D cost is $1 million and that you manufacture 50,000 units with a cost per unit of $20. For 500,000 units, the cost would be two dollars. However, if you have already written off the R&D costs, your marginal R&D cost is zero. You could follow the same calculation for tooling and find that the marginal cost is only $.20 or it could even be zero. In this case, the material cost is the same although it most likely would be lower because of higher production volumes. In this case, it is $20 and administration costs would be zero, with manufacturing costs reduced from $56 to $32.20, for a saving of $22.80.

Activity	Cost for 5,000 units	Cost 500,000 units	Marginal cost
R&D	$20 .00	$2.00	$0.00
Tooling	$1.00	$0.20	$0.20
Material	$20.00	$20.00	$20.0
Labour	$12.00	$12.00	$12.00
Administration	$3.00	$1.50	$0.00
TOTAL	$56.00	$35.70	$32.20

Your potential order of 2,000 units will produce the following results.

Order for an additional 2,000 units - selling price $63

Normal calculation

2000 x ($63 or selling price - $56 or manufacturing cost) =
$14,000 profit ($7 per unit)

Marginal calculation

2000 x ($63 or selling price - $32.20 or manufacturing cost) =
$61,600 profit ($30.80 per unit)

As you can see from this example, you not only achieve better results with a higher sales volume, you can now afford to take low-priced orders and still make some good money. This is applicable to marginal orders and also to when you increase sales to new markets. As mentioned before, you can also increase sales by extending product life cycles through selling older products and services for which you have already paid off development and tooling costs, to less developed markets.

Exporting will make it possible for you to utilize excess production capacity at a much lower cost because of economies of scale. Growth in sales can result in your factory moving from one to two or even three shifts for production. If you can utilize labour-saving technology such as robotics, you could lower the cost of your machinery and building overhead.

Challenge the competition in their own markets = Monitor their development strategies

If you only do business in a domestic market, you may not realize what's happening in other markets. You expect to have plenty of competitors there, but you won't be aware of what they are doing. Suddenly one day, you discover that a foreign competitor has entered your market and is launching new products that you had no clue about. You're concerned that the competitive products are more advanced than yours. You're not prepared.

If you were working in the international marketplace, you could more easily follow trends (product development, what the customer wants) as well as the activities of your competition. You can then better prepare for competitors entering the local market and gather ideas for new products and innovative ways to compete.

Take advantage of currency fluctuations = Increase sales and profit in markets with strong currencies

When you conduct business on the domestic market, you only deal with one currency, except for imported goods. For companies that export, the foreign currency has to be taken into consideration. When you are doing business in foreign markets, you will experience currency fluctuations, some of them in your favour and some of them not. You may invoice in other currencies. (See more about currencies in the Risk chapter later in this book). If your domestic currency becomes weaker in comparison to an overseas currency, you will receive more profit if you invoice in the foreign currency.

Example - change in exchange rates

You are a Swedish company wanting to export to the US. The exchange rate has been seven Swedish krona for each US dollar. This year, however, the dollar is strong and the exchange rate has increased to 8.50, an increase of 21%.

If you were selling in Swedish kronor, your price for the US distributor/customer would be 21% less than before. However, you set your prices in $US, which now gives you 21% more in profits. You launch your new product into the US market. You can keep your original $US price, but introduce a special discount of 15-20% for the first year, in order to assist your American distributor. In this case, you use the strength of the US dollar to enter the market without giving away any of your profits.

Allow flexibility in export pricing = Balance profits and use marginal calculations

When you export, your pricing will have to be different for each market. As will be described in the Pricing chapter, price is based on the market you export to but your profit is based on factors like how long a distribution channel you have, costs for customs duty and freight. By selling to a number of different markets and by using the formulas used for calculating marginal costs, you should be able to sell at a variety of price levels and still make a profit on all of them.

Focus on action/results = Increased activity that energizes staff

When you do business only in your domestic market, there is a tendency to take the market for granted because it is familiar, however, when you enter into a foreign market that is an unknown territory. If you don't want to fail, you must thoroughly research the market. That means you have to find out how the market "looks", where the customers are and their preferences. You also have to investigate the competition and pricing levels and activate your local representatives, in order to compete and win in the market.

Receiving a steady stream of overseas orders and being financially successful creates a very positive atmosphere in an office. Once you know more about the market, you can continuously adapt your business strategy. Going international can also position your company to undertake the same types of activities on the domestic market, such as additional research, product adaptation, etc., which can make you even more competitive domestically. Why? Your organisation becomes more open-minded and action-oriented. Because a broader market provides more stability for a company and greater opportunities for expansion, there could be more promotional opportunities for staff as new positions are created.

Increased range of products

Working in international markets will likely require improvements or adjustments to existing products, to adapt them to a variety of local markets. As mentioned earlier, you have the opportunity to add to your range of products by importing from other markets. Because you are servicing new clients in more markets, you will be exposed to ideas for improving existing products as well as suggestions for new products. These strengthen your ability to compete. As an added benefit, your company will increase its image by working overseas and you will be able to say, "We sell worldwide".

In this chapter, you have read basic information about the importance of doing international business. If you prefer, you can move on to the next chapter. However, if you want more in-depth knowledge on the subject, I suggest you continue to read the second part of this chapter, which follows the Summary. You will find more highlights and coverage of the importance of international business as well as some pros and cons. There are also some exercises that will allow you to practice what you have learned.

Summary

Expanding into new markets is a must for many companies wanting to grow. Why? The domestic market may be too small to allow for profitable development of new products. A company may need a longer life cycle for each product and larger volumes to cover the costs of R&D. Distances between countries are no longer barriers to trade because of better communications, understanding of different cultures and improved transportation. Today, almost any products/services could be manufactured anywhere in the world. The trend has moved from the manufacturing of products and services to development and production of products and services that have been adapted to the requirements of each individual market.

For those companies wanting to expand and thrive, entering the international marketplace is a necessity. The key reasons are:

- Larger markets and opportunities to increase sales volumes

- New markets mean new opportunities (sales, service, uses)

- New types of customers, requiring other types of products, i.e. expanding market

- New types of services, clients needing more than just a product and requesting a complete solution

- The opportunity to develop new products, broaden the product range and increase profits

- Balances market fluctuations

- Extends the life cycle of mature products with sales in less-developed markets

Remember that:

- International business is not only Export. It also includes importing, joint ventures, licensing and strategic partnerships

- International business is about spreading the risks and levelling the financial ups and downs

- Larger sales volumes result in lower R&D and tooling costs per unit. Along with lower administrative costs the result is improved profitability

- International markets = Increased competitiveness. Becoming familiar with competitors in foreign markets make it easier to compete and gain ideas for new products

- You must take into consideration the difference between domestic and international marketing

- Anyone can export. It's important that you make the decision to export, keeping in mind that you are investing for the future. Money won't just roll in, though. There has to be a long-term goal for the investments.

- Successful exporting is based on teamwork. Get all of your staff involved in international business activities from day one.

- Each market will have its own local adaptation demands. You have to adapt your products, your sales materials, marketing strategy, communications, etc.

Why International Business?
Part Two

Why Exporting?

Exporting should be a well planned business venture, but many times, it is an activity decided on by accident and without any real strategy. The reasons can be many:

- You are offered a free trip abroad

- Exporting is popular. Your local government promotes exporting as being good for them and the balance of trade

- A company has too much inventory. Business is slow domestically and the company needs new markets to expand

- News media report that China is an "interesting" market

- The company president attended a seminar presentation describing a foreign country as a potential market.

You know as well as I do that the reasons listed above are not the right ones; however, they are not uncommon. Of course, you shouldn't start exporting because you can buy inexpensive tickets overseas or because you think you'll get to travel to a pleasant country. I have seen foreign companies decide to set up subsidiaries in a particular city, not because the location was right for the market, but because someone liked the area.

Your local government may be promoting the benefits of exporting but that doesn't mean it will be right for you or your company. You should have better reasons, such as increasing sales and long-term profitability. If you happen to have too many products in stock, it won't necessarily help you to export, because perhaps the products are not suitable for export markets. However, if you had planned in advance to expand into more markets and spread your risks, you would not have experienced that inventory problem. You would already be selling to established markets.

That your business is not successful in the domestic market is not a barrier to exporting. If your risks are spread across many markets, then a drop locally will have a limited influence on your company.

China may be an exciting potential market, but you shouldn't decide on a market based on the opinions of other people. You have to pick an investment that is right for you and your company, choose the appropriate timing and determine if your products fit the new market. China is more suitable for those of you who have been exporting before and have the experience and resources. For a beginner, however, the Asian market may not be the right place to start. It's a huge market that takes time to enter. If you are a westerner, the way of doing business there is completely different. It will take a long time to build up the necessary relationships, a step that is very important when doing business there.

Example - Not having the right information

Many years ago, when I still lived in Sweden, my company President attended a seminar promoting the Philippine market. He came back to the office "sold" on the market potential. Of course, the seminar speaker had delivered all the positive aspects of the expected development in the Philippines and spoke highly about growing demands for technology. He had neglected to say that the technology they needed was at a much lower level than our company could supply. The most important thing he didn't mention was that the country did not have any money.

Real reasons for exporting

Many companies want to export because they have grown out of their domestic market. That way, exporting becomes a means of surviving and expanding the business. For most companies, exporting has resulted in better cash flow and creating stability through fluctuating economies. Continuous production can be maintained. Skilled personnel will not be tempted to leave.

No doubt you're beginning to understand that exporting requires more knowledge and resources than will be enough for your domestic market. That places additional demands on you, your managers and staff, requires updated product documentation and more extensive financial controls. With good planning and the right strategy, it is possible for almost any company to prosper. Success at exporting is not only for large corporations. Many small and medium-sized businesses have become profitable in the global marketplace. How?

They keep active with industry organizations and stay current with what's going on in their sector, they are determined to succeed and they have the patience to plans then implement and monitor their plans. They listen to what the market/consumer want and are adaptable to changes that occur. They adapt themselves and their business to foreign markets and make sure they understand the foreign country business practices, cultures and customers.

Exporting is a continuous learning process; feedback is important. Despite the potential offered by expanding world markets, there are many companies who are hesitant to take the first step to going global. Doing business abroad seems to be complicated and too risky, so they decide that it is better to stay home. The biggest hurdles to exporting are, however, not external but internal, i.e., your attitude towards change and your expectations of success.

The most common objections to expanding into new markets are:

- We have never exported
- We're not ready for the market right now
- Our product/service doesn't fit the market
- We aren't allowed to sell our product on that market
- We know nothing about all of the duties, business rules and legislation
- We don't even have the capacity to sell to neighbouring markets
- Who knows if there are benefits to exporting to new and unknown markets?
- We won't make enough money in export markets. Why start with international business when it costs more and perhaps returns smaller margins?
- We don't know how to work with foreign measurements
- We don't need any more business. We have enough problems with the business we do today
- We don't have an adequate amount of information or resources to enter another market
- It will take at least two years before we see any results and that's too long a time to wait for a return on investment
- We don't have enough personnel to cover a much larger territory. Our staff members don't speak the language and besides, they have no clue how to do business in other markets
- Overseas customers live and work in other time zones. We aren't awake or in the office when they are

If these are some of the excuses or attitudes in your company, then it is time to change to a more positive outlook!

You don't need to know every detail about exporting. There are many experts who will be more than willing to help you – freight forwarders, professional trade and industry associations, domestic and foreign government agencies, Chambers of Commerce worldwide, networking, etc. On the following pages, I've provided you with lots of resources for where to look for more information.

> *"Experience is the hardest kind of teacher. It gives*
> *you the test first and the lesson afterwards."*
> *— Anonymous*

The market - yesterday

In the past, the market was small, with the majority of trade taking place locally. Deals were finalized with a hand shake. Products were high quality, had a long life and did not become obsolete. Exporting was not that common and for many reasons, was very time-consuming. Often, trading companies (see Distribution chapter) who specialized in export made the deals. A domestic company would sell their product to the trading company, who then took care of the rest. Back then, changes to products were limited. A company could sell the same product to many countries and after five years, still ship the same product.

Wars that affected many countries destroyed manufacturing capacity and the challenge was not competition but who could deliver products to a continuously expanding market. Shipments took place by boat and communication was by mail, all of which took considerable time. The lead time from first contact to shipment was long but the business relationship that had been built also lasted a long time. This has changed today, with almost instant communications, numerous transportation methods and markets that are more competitive but also easier to reach.

Differences Between Domestic and International Marketing

People who work in other markets have to learn and adapt

- ◆ New marketing environments will require you to change your standard marketing techniques
- ◆ As an exporter, you will be influenced by duties, local rules (written and unwritten) and laws
- ◆ Unfamiliar languages and ways of communicating and transferring information will be challenge at first

♦ Responding appropriately to different cultures and religions may require adaptation by individuals and companies to understand new norms and values and old traditions and ways of living

♦ There will be a variety of currencies and methods of payment as well as unfamiliar business ethics and practices regarding terms of payment

♦ Knowledge levels and availability of information will vary from country to country

♦ Longer transportation routes, different requirements for transport and other forms of packaging must be used

♦ A range of shipping environments and climates will affect your products

♦ The way products are sold will change. You will need to tailor a variety of competitive strategies to the new markets

♦ Differences in technical development, consumer demands, educational levels, sales locations require a flexible approach

Competition

It is not only your company wanting to export; there are a many countries who want to take advantage of global market opportunities. The new generation of products to be developed will have larger markets to grow into.

Adapting Your Organization and Staff for International Business

Expanding into a new market will create knowledge and skill demands on your staff. Train your staff about international business and you will increase opportunities to succeed. However, in many cases you will also need to recruit new staff with special international business competencies. As you start your global business, you may have to contract for external assistance from companies or individuals knowledgeable about foreign languages, legal aspects of trade or specific market experience. Overseas freight or shipping will be somewhat more complicated, with requirements for added documentation, insurance and improved packaging. You'll find more coverage of these topics in later chapters.

You may have to restructure internally or change your business organization, with the result that some of your staff members grow concerned about their ability to cope with new business tasks or about someone else taking over their job. My experience is that after the first hurdles have been overcome, your staff will become more positive about the changes and begin to see the benefits. It is critical that you keep staff involved and continuously informed, through meetings, with emails, newsletters and other forms of communications. Don't forget customer service and support. You will have to ensure your service staff is trained and comfortable with their new responsibilities. Service, user-friendly products and/or detailed instructions will have to be provided in a number of languages.

Companies entering the global market will often experience staff that are against exporting. Usually, they are afraid of the challenges and possible failure. They may worry their jobs could be put at risk. In order to minimize their concerns you can:

♦ Educate staff at an early stage, creating an understanding of your international business plan and sharing knowledge about how to work in international business. Giving them a copy of this book would be a good start!

♦ Inform them early about potential changes and ask for their views, so they feeling more involved and have the chance to become more positive. Let them know that you will provide professional training and opportunities to develop their skills within the company.

♦ As exporting requires teamwork, you have to motivate staff to understand their role and work as part of a team. A seminar or conference over a weekend can create opportunities for learning, information-sharing and discussions about the future.

Who Can Export?

If you are successful in your domestic market and have enough resources, you already have the foundation for success in international markets. On the other hand you don't have to be successful locally. There are companies that conduct the majority of their business internationally. For example, our company, Export Pro Inc., is based in Canada but 98% of our clients are overseas.

It doesn't matter if you are a small, medium or large company. All companies can export. A large company certainly has more resources but internal communications can be more difficult, there are more people to be informed and involved and decision-making may take a long time. A small company has shorter communications channels and faster decision-making processes. It's not difficult for each individual in the company to learn about and understand what's needed in each of the respective markets. In fact, it's often easier for small companies to export, although sometimes, external assistance will be required with more complex issues.

So what's needed to be successful? You have to have a plan, as well as patience, the right attitude and a willingness to learn and adapt to each new market. Good teamwork and a stable organization are important and, of course, company management must be fully committed to entering new markets. Your profitability is really proportional to the energy and commitment you put in new market ventures.

When Is the Right Time To Enter New Markets?

I would say that any time is the right time, but here are some thoughts. Remember that it takes time and preparation to enter a new market, so plan ahead and don't rush into exporting. When markets are down, companies tend to limit traveling and sales programs, but they really should increase their activities in anticipation of the market improving. When economic conditions are slow, you will have more time to study potential new markets. Companies overseas will have more time to listen to your presentations and likely will be more open-minded about adding new products and services to increase their sales.

When the market is booming, companies tend to be too busy to think about expansion or new products. They may not have the capacity to supply more goods or the resources to spend to increase visits to distributors, with the result that their sales teams in the field receive less support. In times like these, I have found it is easier to attract dissatisfied distributors from the competition. They have become unhappy with the lack of support and are willing to switch to someone offering more support. The lesson to be learned is this: a good time to enter new markets is when the economy is slower and there are opportunities to sign up a competitor's best distributors when business is booming.

Exporting – Expense Or Investment?

You have probably calculated return on investment (ROI) before purchasing machinery, expanding a fleet of delivery vehicles, constructing a new factory or developing a new product line. However, because many companies see marketing and export not as an investment but as a cost, they fail to invest in new markets because they can't see an immediate return. If you expect to make instant profits on your export activities, I suggest you have not done your homework and you are cheating yourself. If you happen to achieve immediate profitability, it is probably more because of good luck.

When you buy new machinery, you probably write the cost off over a period of five years. The practical write-off time could be even longer, especially when exporting and manufacturing lead to increases in production volumes over time. Research and development are considered long-term investments. Marketing and sales promotion activities are written off immediately, although marketing is an investment for the future and should be treated that way when you analyze your results. It is important that company management understand that marketing delivers a long-term return on investment and treat the investment accordingly. Export activities will result in increased sales, increased profitability, lower per unit production and marketing costs, reduced research and development costs per unit and increased company stability.

Establishing an international business takes time

The process of establishing your company in a new overseas market could take between three and five years, or twice as long as you might have thought. It will most likely cost you twice as much as your original estimates. Hopefully, you will start to get orders from the market in the first year, but you will also be spending money on traveling, new sales material, market research, etc., which will offset any profits. Therefore, your net result could be a negative. We'll discuss this later on. If you try to do things faster than you have capacity to, you increase the risk of failure. There's even a risk that, if you make some bad business decisions in the new market, you could harm your ability to continue to do business in that market.

When you become more familiar with this method of doing international business, you can complete your planning for more than one market at a time and speed up the process.

Timing/Activities

You can find more detail about each of these sequential steps in the Market Research chapter.

- Initial study of a new market - 6 to 12 months
- Laying out the details for your first visit and visiting the new market - 3 months
- Additional market information (what you didn't know before the trip) - 3 months
- Search for local representative - 4 to 12 months
- Selection process and negotiations with potential representatives - 2 to 6 months
- Test sales and delivery, evaluation - 3 to 6 months (can require another 3 to 6 months to adapt the products to local market)
- Test sales after adaptation - 3 to 6 months
- Education/training of sales and service staff, start-up and sales activities - 3 to 6 months
- Achieving desired sales volumes - another 6 to 12 months

Note: Every market is different. These timelines are a guide to help you get started thinking about the time you need to set aside.

It's important that you appoint someone to be in charge of exporting. As you will find as you read through this book, there are many steps and responsibilities. The knowledge requirements are high. It is even more important to assign responsibility for each market to a specific individual, so that they can become a specialist and act as a resource to others in your company. It is equally as important to designate a staff person to be in charge of coordinating the multitude of tasks involved in exporting, such as designing and printing new sales material, completion of export documentation, changes to packaging, invoicing in different currencies, etc. This is not a sales position but a project management function.

I've told you about a lot of activities that go into international business. So perhaps you're saying to yourself, "If it is that difficult, then I don't think I should work on the international market."

As you will see when you have finished reading "Export & Import - Winning in the Global Marketplace", it is not that difficult. You just need to apply the principles I'm going to teach you and use common sense. You bought this book because you wanted practical advice about import and export; you wanted to learn about global business or how to expand your activities in the international market.

Your first export order is always something special. Traveling overseas, establishing working relationships with contacts in new markets and learning how to succeed in new business cultures are good compensation for the hard preparation work you did before obtaining that first order.

Do remember: successful exporting is not a "one man show". It demands teamwork. Employees, including research and development and the marketing department should make trips overseas to visit to market. This exposure to local conditions creates a better understanding and allows them to learn firsthand what is required so that they can better carry out any adaptations necessary.

Exercise

Answer the questions below. You don't have to go into detail.

1. What are your products/services? To what markets could you sell them?

2. What "old" products/services can you sell to less-developed markets? Which markets?

3. Go back to the marginal cost calculation. Make one for each product/ service listed in questions #1 and #2 and calculate/analyze how you can increase your profit by increasing sales.

4. Going into the global marketplace will create some challenges. List and then analyze the strengths and weaknesses of your company.

5. What would you need to improve or change before you start, such as staff training, hiring people with new/different skills, changing accounting systems, finding external expertise, etc?

6. Set your first goals, e.g., 15% of sales from export markets within two years and/or representing two foreign companies on your domestic market.

7. Select up to four priority foreign markets for the next five years.

8. How do you need to change your product range before you expand into foreign markets?

9. How are you going to adapt your sales and promotion material to suit the foreign markets you have selected?

10. How can you cope with demands for increased production volumes? Do you need foreign components for your products?

Take some time to answer those questions before going on to the next chapter.

Practicalities and Culture in International Business – Part One

In This Chapter:

- ♦ How to succeed on a global market
- ♦ Taking a company going international
- ♦ Optica going international
- ♦ Five keys to international business
- ♦ Culture and its influence on international business
- ♦ Women in international business
- ♦ Travel
- ♦ Gift giving
- ♦ Tipping & gratuities
- ♦ Common errors
- ♦ Language and body language
- ♦ Entertaining
- ♦ Titles and hierarchy
- ♦ Bribing
- ♦ Who can export?
- ♦ Your organisation and what is needed from you

Sometimes things don't work out as expected

In 1975, I was traveling to the former Yugoslavia to negotiate a large contract for a complete sawmill. For the trip, I brought two technical engineers to support me at the negotiations. Those engineers believed that traveling and doing business internationally would be relaxing and without hurdles. We flew from Stockholm to Sarajevo. When we arrived at the hotel, the desk clerk stated there was no hotel booking for us, despite the fact we had a written confirmation. My associates suggested we should go to another hotel. I asked them to sit down in the lobby and said I would fix the problem. How did I do this? By dropping two dollars on the desk for the desk clerk, so she could "find" our reservation.

One of the Yugoslavian ministers visited us at the hotel. He expected to be entertained. He was a very demanding person and had told us in advance that he wanted some "consulting fees" in order for us to get the order. We negotiated for two days, without my technicians knowing that I had already received the order. Every night we had to entertain the Minister and at one point, I left my engineers alone with him. They did not appreciate that.

After three days, it was time for us to return home. We left for the airport only to find out that it was too foggy for the aircraft to take off, so we went back to the hotel. Of course, the hotel was fully booked, but after I dropped five dollars at the reception desk, we had our three rooms back again. The same procedure happened the next day. On the third day, the airport was still fogged in. We gave up and went to the railway station to buy tickets for train to Austria. We booked three tickets and I paid for mine. My friends only had credit cards. Those were not accepted, so I had to bail them out with my cash.

Before the train departed, I bought a couple of bottles of wine and a big package of sandwiches. On the train, we had arranged for seats that could be folded down so we could sleep. In the same area, there were two Yugoslavians travelling to Germany to work. They did not understand English or German.

After about eight hours, the train stopped in the Austrian Alps. It was snowing heavily and we could see a steep ravine on the left side of the train. Snow began building up on the right side of the train cars, eventually covering the windows. We were stuck! After another 10 hours in the Alps, our food supply started to run out. There was no water for the toilets and sinks, so you can imagine what that was like. We played dominos with the friendly Yugoslavians, who shared some of their dried meat and local beer with us.

During the time we were trapped on the train, the anxious wives of the engineers were calling my wife and asking where we were. She was used to my travel experiences so her answer was that we were "probably stuck somewhere where they don't have a phone."

After two more days, we finally arrived in Vienna, Austria and were able to get a flight home. Before this trip, the technicians used to complain that I had more vacation days than they did every year. But the irony was that as a result of being stuck on the train, they were compensated with three extra days because they had been away from home on a weekend. I, of course, was not compensated for working Saturday and Sunday because that was part of my job. That's life, right?

On Monday morning, I picked up some new tickets to go to the Czech Republic but my friends, the engineers, were at home sleeping because they were exhausted.

Welcome to the glamorous world of business traveling.

How to Succeed on the Global Market

Are you ready to enter the global market? Do you know what you need to do?

To succeed in the global marketplace you have to think like an exporter and an importer. When entering a new market, you'll have to be informed about that market and understand how to do business there.

Importer: what would you expect from a foreign supplier before you agreed to represent them? You want someone who understands your business and can guarantee deliveries at the right time, with good service.

Exporter: what about other cultures, attitudes, consumer preferences and even religions? You will quickly realize that things are very different than they are at home.

"The organization can never be something the people are not."
— Pritchett, 1993

If you want to do well internationally, you have to be open-minded and ready to adapt to the many diverse characteristics of the new market. For example, you will find that the titles used are different, depending on the country (doctor, professor, president, etc.), product safety and packing requirements can be strict or lax, there are a variety of business practices, personal relationships may have more or less importance, use of business cards and the rules for appointment times vary from country to country. Some of the customs and foods you encounter will be unfamiliar, which means you have to be well prepared so you won't get unpleasantly surprised.

To start with, let's have a look on what can happen when a company starts an international business. I'll be using a fictitious company, *Optica*, and executives with names like Mr. Press (the president), Ms. Money (manager of finance), etc.

Optica, a Canadian Company Going International

The Optica Company manufactures optical thickness measuring instruments. The products are mainly used in the paper and steel processing industry regulates the thickness of paper and steel sheets during product manufacturing. The founder and former owner, Mr. John Madison, recently sold his shares in Optica to a private equity company.

Up until now, Optica has only sold its products in the domestic market. The new owner has seen the potential of expanding the company by exporting and broadening applications for existing products.

Optica – key personnel

The company has employed Tom Press as the new President. He is a 35-year old engineer with an MBA in economics and marketing. Mr. Press worked for a short time as a stockbroker then held several management positions in his father's international company. His work experience broadened his business outlook and gave him a good base in marketing and production. After that, he worked with a large asset management firm, helping them to activate and restructure recently purchased companies around the world.

John Manuf is the production manager. He began his 20-year career with Optica working on the assembly line. He took night school courses at community college and gradually worked his way up into management. He is 45 years of age, has a very old-fashioned way of thinking. He is uncomfortable with change.

Ronald Mark is a 30 year old sales and marketing manager who started with the company seven years ago after selling excavators for five years. He was promoted three years ago, is a good salesman and has a strong sales network. He is not very effective as a manager.

Ian Devo is in charge of research and development. He has a PhD in applied mathematics but is also an avid competitive athlete. He is forty-five years old and a brilliant inventor who continuously comes up with new ideas for products and process improvements.

Donna Money, Manager of Finance, has a background in the retail sales industry and banking. She is a good comptroller who tries very hard to find ways to speed up customer payments and reduce costs. At 60 years of age, she has been with Optica for 25 years.

Helen Staff, the Manager of Personnel, has come a long way from being a mail room clerk to her current position. She is 50 years old and despite being very traditional, she is very popular with the employees.

Marilyn Admin, the Office Manager, is a 33-year old MBA graduate with a creative approach to business. She is always willing to try something new.

The fictitious company named Optica will be used to demonstrate what can happen when a company starts exporting. We will not go into many details now but you'll get more information as we develop the example.

Optica - time for exporting

Tom Press has just returned from a meeting with the new owners. He recently participated in an export seminar and networked with many successful international business people. Tom is convinced that Optica must begin exporting. He has asked some of his key players to attend a meeting so that he can brief them and gather their comments.

Mr. Press: As you know, one reason our new owners purchased this company was because we have the potential to market Optica products around the world. By exporting, we can broaden our client base and increase sales, write off research and development costs on longer production runs and thereby reduce per unit development costs. One other advantage is that we'll be able to get a better understanding of what the competition is doing.

Mr. Devo: That sounds great, but have you thought of the fact that our products have been developed for the domestic market? If we start exporting, we'll have to redesign them for new markets that have different standards, voltages and electric frequencies. What about and the skill levels of the people who'll be operating the machinery? Today, we only have four models. Expansion could result in us having 20 models and they'll be different enough that we'll have to make a lot of changes. Maybe now we can buy that new CAD/CAM system we've wanted. That will certainly make those adaptations much easier.

Mr. Press: You're right about those adjustments, but our domestic market won't be big enough if we want to really expand the model lines. The ones we have today took two years to develop but most likely they'll only last for only another two to three years before we have to introduce updated designs. Optica will have to invest a lot of money in product development, no matter what.

Because our four models only have a life cycle of 4-5 years, we'd still have to innovate and develop new models. Now, we'll be able to extend product life cycles by selling to less-developed markets where our existing designs will be more than adequate. Another benefit of more sales is that we can spread our R& D costs over bigger production volumes. That will also free up the funds we'll need to adapt to new market. Some of you will have to travel and see firsthand what the markets looks like and to source new components.

Mr. Mark: What about sales and marketing? Do you expect existing staff to take care of the new markets too? I only speak English, so if you want me to take an active role in this, I'll need to learn others. Besides, I have no experience with exporting and neither does any of my staff. The only country outside North America I've been to is Mexico for vacation.

Mr. Press: I understand your concern, Ron. We definitely need more knowledge. Our first step is to get a better understanding about what it means to do international business. For that reason, I've hired a specialist consultant with more than 40 years experience in more than 100 countries. In two weeks, the consultant will begin educating us on the various aspects of exporting. We've booked a meeting room at the local conference centre for the weekend.

Ms. Admin: A weekend? Why?

Mr. Press: The company is covering the costs of getting together on a weekend so that as many Optica staff as possible can be included. Exporting is not something just management takes on – teamwork is essential. It's equally important that Sam on the order desk and Donna in the packing department and staff who will be answering phone calls from all over the world in other languages, know how the process is supposed to work. Interacting with new clients from overseas means we need to understand their cultures and business rules. I agree that international business is new and there will be changes, but the challenges will also be rewarding.

Mr. Manuf: What kinds of changes are you talking about?

Mr. Press: We already have great customer service, but we need to make sure all of our team is comfortable with international business methods, John. Everyone will be involved getting Optica up to speed. Our Information Technology department will have to upgrade our hardware and software systems so we can work with different languages. We're going to have a variety of new pricing schedules, payment terms and methods, so the Accounting department will have to be prepared. Human Resources will get involved with recruitment and training of specialist staff. The people in Shipping will be working with different documents and freight demands. Our Customer Service and support staff will now be providing service to clients and distributors all over the world. We'll need to do some retraining or recruitment to ensure we can offer services in a variety of languages.

By doing international business the company can invest in better sales and marketing material and furthermore afford better market research. Sales material has to be adapted to each market to fit their type of clients and the way of local marketing. Because sales will be based on higher volumes the costs for the printed matter can be reduced. We can probably use only one original for photos and graphics and then adapt the content with different languages. Spare part lists can be produced in several languages. Being in more than one market means we can benefit from domino effect and expand to more markets simultaneously. By being in more markets more of our customer groups can use the same product, we can also increase sales in our domestic market.

Ms. Money: Hold on now. How are you going to finance this venture? It all sounds very adventurous and expensive! I know from when I was with another company, that it took 2-5 years to get established in a new market. We spent a lot of money translating brochures into other languages. I'm not sure if it was worth it. The new payment terms were complicated and it took us a long time to learn to do them properly.

Mr. Press: There will be a learning curve. We know that costs will increase when we start exporting, but we're looking at this as an important long-term investment. Optica's owners will arrange for financing. Government agencies offer export financing supports and training programs we can tap into.

We expect that after a number of years in new markets, company profitability will improve and Optica will become better protected against downturns in the economy. Let me give you some examples.

By selling more equipment, we'll benefit from economies of scale in our production. Set up charges will be lower when we have continuous production instead of in batches and we'll be able to lower our per-unit manufacturing costs. Reduced production costs would put us in a better competitive position domestically.

Once we are in international markets we will be able to source lower priced components and use alternative suppliers. The company will be able to invoice in different currencies, making it possible to utilize the strength or weakness of different currencies. We will also open up the opportunity to get financing from other markets.

The risk of not getting paid could also increase because it's tougher to control. On a short-term basis Optica will probably make less money because of the initial costs of entering each market. I agree that invoicing could be more complicated. Our bookkeeping system has to be adapted for more than one currency. We will have to learn to analyze our sales results based on different exchange rates. All of this will become easier over time.

Mr. Manu: It sounds to me like management will expect higher production volumes of more models. I figure we have 20% extra capacity on the day shift, but we'll have to put on a second or third shift to keep up with production demands. We'll have to increase product inventory so we can meet delivery targets during the start-up period. Will I be allowed to build a new factory to handle the extra work?

Mr. Press: I think we should leave discussion of those complex issues for another time. If Mr. Devo's department develops more advanced products, we could subcontract some equipment production, but this would mean Optica would be more dependent on outside technology and production. Most likely our business will shift more to final assembly and quality control than complete manufacturing. At some point, we'll look into robotics and more automation, which will reduce production costs even more.

Mr. Devo: Increased sales means we can turn over our inventory more frequently and keep storage costs down. And if we sell more equipment, we'll have to produce and ship more spare parts to meet demand. I can talk to some of my colleagues in the industry about their experiences with exporting.

Mr. Mark: You realize there'll be some technical risks and pressures on production. What if we can't keep up? I've heard buyers in some markets don't have good advance planning. Last minute rush orders could put pressure on the production lines. What do we know about sourcing components overseas? And what about our sub-suppliers? They have to be prepared to cope with our increased sales, too.

Ms. Money: I expect we'll have to open new bank accounts. Entering new markets creates more payment risks, too. We'll need better follow-up and reporting so we can track payables and receivables and profits and losses for currency exchanges. Currency fluctuations and billing in foreign currencies could affect our bottom line. Expenses will likely go up for servicing overseas accounts. It's easy for a customer only 20 km away to call us and get service the same day. But for customers on another continent, whose first language isn't English and who isn't near a major city that could be a real problem. Our reputation could suffer if we can't deliver.

Ms. Staff: Your plans sound pretty exciting, but from what I see, we're going to have to reorganize and retrain our staff and recruit new people with the right experience. I'm sure some long-term staff will be worried about how their work will change. And what if they don't want to do different jobs? Will they get laid off?

Mr. Press: Those are all good points you've raised. Our team will have to deal with them one by one over the next few weeks. Going global will require us to complete more paperwork than we do now, for export documentation and for reporting statistical information to governments and to our Board of Directors. After we look at the skills staff have now and what they can learn through training, we probably will have to bring in new staff with different skills. That's where your experience will help a lot.

The international business consultant has some ideas about restructuring our organization with a minimum of disruption. He can also assist with recruiting and selecting qualified staff, like an experienced export manager. It will be his or her job to organize the new Export Department and use as many people as possible from inside the company. We'll have to get used to working with other languages and travelling more often to overseas locations for trade shows, marketing, training distributors and delivering customer service.

Ms. Admin: Luckily, we already have staff from a variety of cultures. But I can see we'll need to recruit others with specific language skills and recent experience working in different countries. My staff can make an inventory of special staff skills, languages spoken, business contacts and training requirements. We are fortunate to have people with Polish, Brazilian, South-East Asian, Russian and Italian background. I'll have the inventory ready before the seminar.

I guess our travel agency can tell us about visas and vaccinations, or we could contact consulates or embassies to find out what they recommend. I'll talk to some of our freight forwarders to get their opinions on the best software for producing shipping and customs documentation. Maybe we can even get them to do the paper work will we all get up to speed on exporting.

Mr. Press: You're on the right track, Marilyn. It's important that we approach this as a positive opportunity otherwise it will be more difficult to get this to work. I'd suggest we all look for tools and techniques to make our life easier.

Ms. Admin: Our word processing software has spell-checkers and dictionaries in different languages. There are also translation programs we can buy. Our travel insurance only covers Canada and the US, so we have to look for international coverage. It can be expensive to get sick overseas. We also have to register our existing trademarks in other countries and make sure we apply for future patents in our key markets.

Mr Press: It's obvious that although becoming international will open up future markets for Optica, there are many steps to be taken before we can say we're successful. I'm encouraged by your questions and ideas and I look forward to your support for this new project.

At the seminar:

Welcome, everyone. This is an exciting time for you at Optica. My name is Martin Exportwise and I'm the facilitator for a series of sessions about exporting. I'll be sharing my experiences doing business in 100 countries and we'll talk about the opportunities and challenges of exporting to international markets. Besides growing your company, you'll be rewarded with more interesting jobs, better knowledge about cultures and world events and new skills. It's not that difficult to export but it does take a combination of common sense, flexibility and know-how.

For these sessions to be productive for all of you there's going to have to be a high level of participation. I'm not going to do all the talking and I encourage you to ask lots of questions. There is no such thing as stupid questions, so don't be shy.

Today, we're going to talk about teamwork and some of the basics of exporting.

Many companies start exporting by accident or as a last resort because they want to sell overstocked or out-dated products. Some start exporting because they're looking for exotic trips abroad or new product lines. Usually, this is a mistake.

After a company has identified that they have the right products and staff, the next step is to take the time to get prepared, which is what we're doing now.

> ### *Example - New application for same product*
> *A company that manufactured submersible pneumatic membrane pumps used for construction projects received an order from an Italian company wanting to pump grape juice from one place to another within several of their wineries. This was an unheard of application for construction equipment but the company jumped at the opportunity. The wineries became satisfied customers. The pneumatic pump manufacturer discovered a unique application for their products. They were able to sell to every market where there was a winery.*

This example gives you some idea of what I mean when I say that you need to be open-minded. Applying your in-depth knowledge of Optica's business will help us all discover potential opportunities.

Five Keys to Being Successful in International Business

- ◆ **Communication**

- ◆ **Commitment**

- ◆ **Thorough preparations**

- ◆ **Well-tested products**

- ◆ **The importance of relationships**

Look at the examples below and identify which ones you think might be similar to your situation.

☞ Communication

You are the foreigner

We tend to bring our domestic mindset for doing business and attempt to apply it to a foreign market. Remember that you are the foreigner and it is **you** who has to adapt.

Say you operate a firm in Spain. A company from Indonesia calls and wants your company to distribute their outdoor furniture products. They tell you: "This is the way we sell outdoor furniture in Indonesia; here is the pricelist and the sales materials we use. You should sell our products the same way."

What would your reaction be? You probably wouldn't appreciate their approach. In the same way, a distributor in your new export market won't appreciate being told they have to sell in the same way as you do in your domestic market. The **local market** determines your activities, prices and ways of doing business, no matter where the market is.

Get to know your new market

The best way to learn about a country is to spend time there. By doing that, you will get a 'feel' for the customs, become familiar with the culture and get your mind ready to do business.

Many years ago when I was conducting a workshop in Sweden to recruit, select and activate representatives, one of the clients was unhappy with the help he got from a consultant he hired to select a distributor for the Spanish market. I asked him how many times he had visited the Spanish market to collect information before setting up a profile for the distributor he wanted. He said he had never been to Spain. My answer to him was this: "So how would the consultant be able to find the right distributor for you without knowing what you were looking for?"

Example - Different skill level

In 1972 we were planning a sales campaign in Morocco. The customers were local construction companies. Together with the president, I was putting together an advertisement for a local industry magazine. The sales manager, who had a lot of experience there, came in and looked at our advertisement. He began to laugh. We wanted to know what was wrong with the text. His reply was that 90% of the potential clients could not read. Of course, we had to change our approach so we could reach the non-reading audience.

Get to know and understand different customs

Values, customs and rules vary considerably, depending on what country you are in. Differences range from how you should greet a client to how to entertain them. For instance, it may be considered impolite to use the word "no", although that is what you mean. It can be practical etiquette like titles such as President, mister, doctor or professor, when you can use the first or last names of people you meet or whether you shake hands or not.

Before you make your first visit, learn about the local culture. Do your research using this book, go online or visit the library. There are plenty of good books on business culture; some of them even describe each country. Invest in one of those. Network and ask for advice from business people who are knowledgeable about local customs. You will be treated better and will gain credibility if the foreign company sees that you have taken the time to gain insight into their unique ways of doing business.

> ### Example - Long time relationship
>
> *I was responsible for marketing construction equipment for a large Swedish company. On a business trip to the Philippines, our company invited a customer to their office. The customer was developing a quarry on an island. I was an expert on that topic and spent three hours with him, describing suitable equipment for his business. After the meeting, the customer thanked me very much and left.*
>
> *My question to the other staff was "what happened?" They told me that the client had purchased the equipment. My reaction was that we hadn't discussed whether this was the right equipment for him. We didn't even talk about price.*
>
> *The staff told me, "We've done business with this company for 50 years. What you suggested was right. We will bill the customer an amount that he will accept."*
>
> *I learned an important lesson. It was a large order but I didn't even understand that I'd closed the deal and received an order.*

When you understand how to do business locally in a new market, you will be successful

The Asian way of conducting business is completely different from the North American way. An Asian business person first wants to get to know you and build up a relationship. You have to be "eye to eye" with your Asian partners to understand their message. Then they will be prepared to get to know and have confidence in your company. They will also want to analyze and test your product for a long time. The North American way is to quickly present an offer, focus on the potential profits and close the deal.

As you can see, these are two completely different approaches to doing business. For an exporter, the demand is for two completely different approaches.

To establish effective business relations, you have to establish mutual trust. The day you understand how to do business the "local way", you will truly understand what adjustments have to be made by you and your company. The day you are able to apply that understanding in different foreign markets, you will be on the road to success.

If you and your foreign partners (e.g., distributors, dealers, representatives, etc.) are not compatible, the odds are 100:1 that they will not be happy with your products and services either. If the relationship is not a good one, it will be difficult to do business and may even create new problems. Be positive and remember that your representative has to believe that you are sincere and interested.

You can sell anything if you understand the customer

Example - Responsibilities in different cultures

One of my team members in Sweden had to implement a sales promotion activity in our subsidiary in Greece. He was very enthusiastic and looked forward to the campaign. He would be supported by staff at the subsidiary. He met with the advertising manager and they reviewed a list of activities. Some of the tasks would be delegated to other staff. After a couple of days, he contacted her to find out what work had been completed. She called her associates; they had done nothing. My colleague soon realized that assigning responsibility in Greece did not work the same way as it did at home. He had to be more forceful when delegating tasks, set deadlines and continuously follow up. Later in the week, when he arrived for the official opening, he found out that the program could not start on schedule because the room was not set up and the catering company still had not arrived. However, in the end everything worked out because the VIPs, including the Minister who was the guest of honour, were also late. No one from the subsidiary was worried, because being late was a local custom.

Keep the channels of communication open

It's not enough to visit a country once and then think that you understand their culture and way of doing business. Conditions are constantly changing - you must keep updated. Make sure to maintain ongoing communications with your market contacts. Be ready to answer their questions. Share ideas and proposals for new activities and products. Ask about how things are going, what assistance or changes they need. Listen and understand, give your support and be prepared to adapt. Make sure you benefit from this unique situation.

"Good listeners generally make more sales than good talkers." — *B.C. Holwick*

Learn the language and the underlying meaning of what is said

Having English as your mother tongue may hinder learning other languages. Being able to make yourself understood in several languages enhances your qualifications and helps your transition into new countries. You will be able to greet people you meet, order food in the local language and ask for directions. Knowing other languages also shows your foreign representative that you have a genuine interest in understanding their market. Encourage your staff to learn more languages. An answer like, "This fax will have to wait until the export manager is back because I don't understand what it says", is not acceptable.

Staff in your export department must have strong oral and written English language skills too. If possible, you should hire individuals with proficiency in other languages. Your company should be prepared to assist staff to develop the necessary foreign language skills they will need to work with representatives from overseas markets.

Most failures result from clashes of culture or values, lack of communication or misunderstandings. Just because someone doesn't 'look you in the eye' does not mean they are not trustworthy. Their actions could be the result of cultural or social training. Many times you think you have understood, but you later find out there was some type of miscommunication. You have to learn to go beyond the words so that you know what the person you are speaking with really means. Check for tone of voice, body language and other visual clues.

Example - Speaking the language

On a visit to Belarus some years ago to teach international business to entrepreneurs and university professors, I was assigned a translator. However, before arriving, I spent some time learning enough Russian words to be able to make a short presentation about myself in their language. I introduced myself and finished by saying that I didn't understand the Russian language and the only thing I knew was "DADNA." Everyone laughed and applauded because Dadna in Russian means 'bottoms up'. I connected with the audience by learning some words of their language and being confident enough to use them.

Example - Different meaning of same word

A British businessman visited a customer in the United States. During the meeting, the American distributor indicated that 'the short-term outlook was bad, but the long-term was pretty good'. The businessman returned home and recommended that his company reduce production for North America. Six weeks later, the British company received a large order. They had to advise the customer that they could not fill the order because they had information the Americans would not have much need for deliveries. What went wrong? Both the businessman and the customer were speaking the same language, English. Someone made a potentially costly mistake.

For the American customer, short-term meant three to four weeks. For the British businessman, short-term meant three to five years. They thought they understood each other. So, who was at fault? Before cutting production, the British company should have clarified what the American customer meant about their market outlook.

When I was in charge of marketing complete saw mills, our Nordic customers could plan their investments two to three years in advance and accept delivery times of six to nine months.

The North American market was completely different. When the price of lumber reached a certain level, the customer's board of directors decided to put a new sawmill into production within six months. A couple of days after the board meeting, the company requested quotes. It took them less than one month to decide on the purchase. After placing the order they expected the sawmill to be in full production in another two to three months, so that they could capitalize on higher lumber prices. To make sales forecasts in such an environment can be very difficult.

⌑ Commitment

Show that you are prepared to commit yourself

Establishing a partnership in a new market requires a long-term commitment.

It's easy to say that you will provide support to a distributor. But arriving on a Sunday afternoon and announcing that you have to leave on Tuesday for another meeting is not a sign of commitment. You must be prepared to stay for meetings as long as necessary to ensure you new partners are satisfied. Bring sales training materials, offer to train their staff in your factory, provide staff to work closely with them on their time schedule, add extra inventory to your warehouse and inform them that you are ready to deliver when sales increase.

In countries where people pay attention to hierarchy and titles, it will be expected that your company will send someone from senior management, at least for the initial meetings. When your president or CEO cannot attend follow-up meetings, arrange for a telephone conference or produce a DVD in which he or she speaks directly management and staff at the new company. If you send a junior manager or someone without high company status, your company may be seen as not having a strong commitment to the new partnership.

You have to demonstrate that you are making a long term investment and intend to be an energetic partner. Make sure you are well prepared for your first visit. Bring promotional material that is specific to their needs and in their language. Invest in repeat visits and make joint customer calls. These steps, along with helping to create advertisements and exhibitions, will help establish a solid base for a productive working relationship.

The real work begins when everybody agrees

We are often too quickly relieved when we have signed up a representative, believing that this has 'locked up' their activities with respect to that market. The reality is that once you have agreed to work together, the actual work starts. Why? Up to this point, you have only convinced the foreign company to sell your products. Now you need to help the company secure the initial sales orders that will get your

marketing program off the ground. Your job is to motivate your foreign representative. This is what differentiates a successful exporter from one who fails.

> ### *Example - Support after first order*
>
> *The President of a Swedish firm and I were in the United States negotiating with a distributor in California wanting to sell our mobility walkers. They placed their first order on Friday afternoon. The President said, "Okay now we are in the American market." Thinking our job was finished, he was ready to go sightseeing.*
>
> *I pointed out to him that he was just getting started.*
>
> *After the Swedish executive and I finished the meeting, we started planning for the next steps. First, he had to get to know the American executives better and establish a relationship. The best way would be for him to invite the distributor to dinner at a restaurant. It is very common for North American managers to bring their spouse along on business trips, so they would expect him to do the same when he made a return visit.*
>
> *Second, we had to make sure that first shipment could be sold quickly to get the distributor ready for another order. We discussed how we could activate the foreign company's sales representatives. If the products were not selling, we would not get established in the market.*
>
> *On Saturday and Sunday, we spent more time analyzing how we could provide sales support and increase inventory, so that we could respond quickly to the new distributor. After coming back to Canada on Sunday night, we faxed a description of all the activities and support we would offer.*

Educate the distributor and your own personnel

One of your first priorities should be to educate your foreign distributor. After all, you
selected them because they were well qualified. But that's not enough. You still have to
transfer important knowledge about your
product and about sales techniques and
providing customer service policies as well
as about competing products. Explain how
you normally market your products and
how they were successfully introduced to
other markets. Work with them to develop
a proposal for what tasks have to be done
based on local market demands.

Your export success is also much dependent on the skills and knowledge of your
domestic staff. Educate them about the
culture and way of doing business in the

new export market. Don't forget to prepare them for the general rules of exporting and the potential challenges they will likely encounter.

Activate

If you want active representatives, you must select the appropriate partners based on knowledge and experience. It's your job to motivate them to work hard on your behalf. Make sure you have a plan for how to activate them once they have agreed to take on your product line. For example, convince them of the benefits of working with you ("make them hungry"), show them how they will benefit from the relationship, how you will support them and get them "up to speed" and earning money.

If you have a representative who does not perform satisfactorily, you have either chosen the wrong one or you have not activated them properly.

Here is your price list and product material. Order!

Of course this won't work! You have to work together to get the representative or distributor to place the first order. You have to work harder to make sure they sell what they have ordered.

You'll be mistaken if you think that by giving your representative product information and price lists the orders will just roll in. It's a very common, and wrong, assumption on the part of an exporter that it's a foreign representative's job to do everything. Rather, success in the market is a joint responsibility. The first sale is just the beginning. The joint venture is not proven until your distributor has sold out and placed another order.

Show that you can correct mistakes quickly

If you don't do anything, you won't make mistakes. But if you are active, some day, something will go wrong. Don't take the "ostrich approach" and try to ignore problems, assuming that your representative will not find out. With immediate action, you can take care of your slip-ups before your representative ever sees them. So if you expect deliveries to be delayed, inform the customer at an early stage and try to minimize the difficulties caused. If you experience technical problems, be proactive and give your representative an explanation of what is being done. As you are building up a long-term relationship, it is critical that you work towards a common goal.

Example – Turning a mistake into something positive

I had just signed up a distributor selling Bobcat utility machine tracks in Toronto, Ontario, Canada. They had previously sold tracks from a competing company. I had convinced the Canadian distributor about the market possibilities and uniqueness of Swedish manufactured tracks. The manufacturer received the first order for a variety of tracks in different dimensions. After the tracks arrived in Toronto, the distributor called me. He was not very happy. One set of tracks did not fit the machinery.

By visiting the customer, I found out that the Swedish company had delivered the wrong tracks. I promised to get back to the distributor in one hour. The time was 3 in the afternoon local time or 9 at night in Sweden. I called the Marketing Manager in Sweden at home and explained what had happened. (I always supply my home phone number and cell phone number and expect the suppliers to do the same). He promised that the next morning he would air freight a replacement set of tracks with the correct dimensions. There would be no cost for the customer.

I was able to call the distributor back within the hour and assured him that the replacement tracks would be delivered within 48 hours. In the meantime, I contacted the Canadian representative of the Swedish company's freight forwarder and asked them to monitor the shipment from departure to arrival to ensure there were no delays. I also contacted the customs broker. Normally it takes two days for a shipment to clear customs, but I had to have it done in two hours. It turned out that 24 hours after the distributor contacted me, he received the right tracks. He was a satisfied customer, and he told me that he had never had such good service before. A mistake was turned into something positive.

You will find more details about shipping and clearing customs in the Shipping chapter.

Prove your interest in the new market

Of course you are interested in your new market. Otherwise, you would not have done the work to get there, right?

We tend to put in a lot of effort into market start-up, conducting research and making sales contacts. Sometimes after that start-up, though, the pace of activity slows down. Successful exporters need to be prepared to follow up – not just today but in the future. You have to maintain an ongoing interest in what is happening in that foreign market.

For example, there will be changes in industry and customer demands. Currency fluctuations will influence your export results. Keep up with what is happening locally. Show that you have an interest in issues that affect your new distributor and ask about the specifics of their market. When you visit or call them up or email them, be informed enough to be able to discuss current affairs, the weather, the global financial situation and even local sports teams. Ask about their families or other non-business topics. A phone call is easy and inexpensive, so call regularly.

(If your phone rate is high, look into using Skype for your long distance phone calls – a low cost solution: www.skype.com.) That will not only show your ongoing interest in the market and in your representative but it will also keep you updated about developments. Invite them to visit your factory to see your facilities and meet staff. Another benefit is that they will better understand your business culture, production and quality control processes as well as the culture in your country.

☙ Thorough Preparations

Before selecting a market, you have to get to know the market. Make several visits to gather key information and verify that your strategy is the right one. If you are not sure, take more time. Visit a cross-section of end users, because they will be your future customers. When you ask, they will tell you who your competition is. They can confirm whether your product is suitable and if your pricing is appropriate. They can also make suggestions about potential distributors.

Example - Studying the market

Steel producers were important customers of one of the foreign companies I worked with. They wanted to expand their sales to the US. In order to get them ready to enter the market, I contacted 200 individuals within the steel industry in Indiana. That project took me one year. Was it worth it? Yes!

Because I was so thorough, I was able to collect useful information about the potential market, product applications, the competition and pricing levels. I also created an interest for the Swedish company's products. Furthermore, I received suggestions from potential clients for five suitable distributors. I did some more research and selected one of those distributors. I could give the distributor excellent market information as well as 200 potential clients, so although my research took a long time, our new distributor was in the enviable position of being able to start selling immediately. Because I had convinced a large number of customers about the product's superiority, I was able to attract a "hungry" distributor who was skilled and ready to go.

Prepare your personnel

As I mentioned before, exporting has to be a team effort. Make sure you have enough personnel with the right skills and knowledge. Keep your staff in the production, order and shipping departments, finance and research and development informed about developments. Inform them about any organizational changes that will be made and clarify job responsibilities.

Let them know the time frame you have set up, provide them with information about the new export market and what you want to achieve. Then tell them what you expect from them. Share suggestions for contacts with your representatives in the new export market and tell them which staff they should keep in touch with at your company.

Your reception staff should not be surprised when someone calls from Mexico with questions or orders, because they will already know it is one of your new distributors.

There will, of course, be increased workloads because you will be serving new clients and markets. These clients will have questions and requests for assistance that only your staff can deal with. You can't just add extra work for your staff and expect them to do the job well without the proper training, customer service information and even extra resources. Staff will be called on to make decisions or resolve problems that may be more complicated than they are used to.

If you want a professional organization with a professional image, you must have professional people. Prepare your staff well in advance and you will all benefit.

> *"Things that are bad for business are bad for*
> *the people who work for the business."*
> *— Thomas E. Dewey*

Adapt your products and materials

Each market has specific demands for types of products, product adaptation, sales and technical/promotional material. The language, technical terms and manufacturing specifications you use have to suit your export market. For example, you might have to change the height of a mobility walker if the people who will be using the device are of a short stature. Depending on a country's voltage, you may have to adapt your electric motors. Some colours are unpopular in parts of the world.

Sales and support materials have to suitable include diagrams and illustrations suitable. Users in North European markets want technical information while North Americans want text that is more promotional in nature. Paper measurements/dimensions and the pre-punched holes for ring binders vary in different countries. If your customers use inches or imperial units they should not have to convert from metric measurements.

Take time to evaluate prospective distributors

Your choice of foreign representative is critical. Take the time to locate potential distributors and evaluate them thoroughly. Once you've interviewed several prospects and made your selection, you'll begin building a long-term relationship. Ask some end users for their opinion about your product/service and where and how they want to buy. That will give you a good indication who to contact as a potential distributor.

When you're looking for a life partner, you take the time before making the decision to live together for the rest of your life. The same process also applies to selecting a foreign partner, whether it is a distributor, joint venture partner or other arrangement. You have to find the right partner who "fits" with your goals for the market and one where the chemistry works well between the two of you. The personal relationship is very important.

Don't settle for someone who is just good enough. Find the best, because they can make the difference between satisfactory results and excellent results. If you select the wrong partner, it can hurt your sales and your company image.

Prepare your professional material in advance

Who are you and what is your company about? Your printed materials are tools for selling yourself and your company as potential partners. You only get one chance to make a good first impression. Before you leave home for your business trip, ensure that what has been prepared is high quality and adapted to that specific local market. This can mean the difference between signing up a new partner or returning home empty handed.

Example - The result of good preparation

I was living in Canada and representing a Swedish company that manufactured industrial equipment. That firm employed 120 people. I wanted to sell their product to a large American company headquartered in Chicago. That company had more than 1700 people.

How did we convince this large firm that had been selling American products for the last 40 years to change to a small unknown Swedish company?

We printed up high graphic sales materials, using the American company's colours and logo. Our presentation on the Swedish company's products was very professional. We included graphs that compared the Swedish company and the competition. We also prepared printed matter that had been specifically adapted to some of their large clients so that they could use the brochures and technical sheets right away. They were so impressed, that not only did we get our first order but they also used the material we had prepared, as their own sales material.

Bring promotional materials you can leave behind

Very often, an exporter will bring along a well-prepared binder. The binder includes a presentation on the company, information about products, advertising and reference material. The material is often of such interest that the local distributor wants to keep it. However, the exporter says: "This is my personal binder, but I can prepare one for you, and send it in two weeks." That is not a good way to start.

Make sure you have prepared multiple binders with the same content and quality as your own. You will leave these with your client.

If you can get your representative eager to sell your product (hungry) by using your binder as an appetizer, then you have the right material. Provide enough sets of binders for their staff too. Since they are hungry, you have to serve what they want immediately.

⌐ Well-tested Products

Test your products on your home market

Never export a product that has not been thoroughly tested and retested. If you are a manufacturer in Sidney, Australia and something goes wrong with a product you have shipped to a client 100 kilometres away, you can send out a technician or schedule a service call. But if your client is in Latin America, that is too far away for you to make immediate repairs.

Test your product in the new market and make adjustments

Although your product can pass tests in the domestic market, it is wise to test it in the export market where circumstances can sometimes be difficult to predict. You would be surprised what things you haven't considered.

The mobility walker manufactured for a tall Swede would be too large for a small person from the Philippines. Door sizes in Japan are narrower than in North America, so make sure your product can fit through their doorways. Clients in Europe and North America are not very particular about the appearance of some products. Japanese customers demand high quality finishes on products. They will not accept just painting over a welded joint; it must be a smooth surface.

Example - Adapting the products

A company in Finland that manufactured excavators decided to introduce the product to California, in the western US. They knew the machinery would be subjected to tougher treatment so they made the machinery more heavy duty. They even let an operator in Finland abuse the machine so that they could find and correct failures when they occurred.

After many improvements and adaptations they invited an operator from California to Finland to test one of the redesigned machines. After two hours, the excavator broke down. They couldn't understand why that happened, since the equipment had been tested and retested. Why did the excavator malfunction when the American operator used it?

When the Finish machine operator saw that the machine couldn't handle the material loaded, he took a smaller load. However, the American operator increased the rpm of the machine in an effort to get more power but the machine couldn't handle it. The Finn took one approach and the American took a different approach to the job to be done. In the end, the Finnish manufacturer had to make more adaptations so that the excavators to be exported could withstand the "mistreatment" of US operators.

Testing a product on the foreign market, with the people who are going to use it will allow you to determine if the quality is adequate and if the product is right for that market, then to make appropriate product improvements.

Example - Different performance than at home

A company I worked with wanted to sell diesel generators in Peru. The generators would be used at 3000 meter above sea level. At this altitude, the air is very thin and machine capacity is reduced by 50%, a fact that must be taken into consideration during manufacturing.

Example - Problem with different electricity

A Danish company supplied Canada with fume extraction equipment for welding, including fans. In Denmark, electric motors operate at 50 Hz while in Canada they run at 60 Hz. Why was this important to know? The difference in electrical frequency created a 20% increase in speed in Canada. This was a load that the Danish-made motors could not handle. A new fan wheel had to be designed to adapt to the higher speed of the Canadian electrical standards.

⌐ The Importance of Relationships

Being successful in business requires good working relationships and a mutual trust that are developed over a long time. As in a marriage, there will be positive and negative experiences, however, it is important to work through your differences together and resolve them when they occur. The same applies to business. It's not the product or service that makes for success; it is the relationships between the people in the companies.

You may have to adapt your way of doing things. Don't just spend time with the president of a company. Spend a lot of time with the staff, service people, subdealers and customers (if appropriate) and get to know them. It's your willingness to work on building up the relationship and your willingness to learn that sets the stage for information sharing and building a strong export business.

"There are more goods
bought by the heart
than the head."
— George Henning

Example - The importance of relationship.

I represented a European company selling mobility equipment people in Canada. Our sales were very good and we had a 55% share of the market. I was paid a commission on sales. The European company got the idea I was earning too much money and wanted to terminate our agent/representative agreement. We came to an understanding that they could free me from my contract, pay me a certain amount of money and release me from any future obligations or non-competition requirements.

I picked up a new product line from a competitor in Europe. After one year of working with them, we had grown to a 50% market share; my former company's market share plunged to 5%. So what happened?

My distributors did business with me and my relationship with them was more important than the product, so when I changed product line, they did the same. The lesson here is this: remember the critical importance of relationships.

You have to be flexible in your approach to the new market

Entering the global marketplace makes it possible for you to expand your business, make more money and create a more stable company.

Don't forget that you are the foreigner in the new export market, and you will have to adjust or risk you will failure. There are many examples from the past and in the recent business press about major companies that tried without success to force their domestic products and practices onto a foreign market.

If you have a great product but a bad relationship with your representative in the foreign market, your business will not work. However, even if you have a less desirable product but enjoy a good working relationship you will have a better chance to get the product accepted.

This is the end of Part One. As this chapter has three parts, I suggest you also read Part Two. If not, at least read the summary of Part Two.

Practicalities and Culture in International Business – Part Two

Culture

This chapter includes some examples of culture differences and business approaches in different countries. I have limited the number of examples because of space and also because some examples might offend some people from other cultures. I suggest that you interview someone familiar with doing business in the country you select so that you can learn directly how business operates there. There are some very good books on the subject, some of which provide details on doing business in specific countries.

Culture is a big part of doing business, but it is dangerous to generalize because cultural differences can vary not only between countries but also within countries. Americans see Europe as a single market and tend to treat it as one country. As you know, however, Europe is made up of many sovereign nations. Each has their own distinct history, culture and business practices. Belgium has a number of cultures as well as several official languages. There are significant differences between business practices in southern and northern regions of some countries and in eastern and western Germany. You have to take these facts into consideration when planning your business. This also applies to your choice of distribution method.

Similarly, the state of New York and the state of Alabama in the United States have very different cultures and distinctive accents. The state of California has 38 million inhabitants. Because of its size, it could almost be treated like a separate country. The same kind of diversity applies to the province of Ontario, Canada that conducts business mainly in English and could be described as somewhat British while the province of Québec, which has French as the official language is more French-European in its outlook and practices. Although they are located in

North America, Canadians dislike being called Americans or to treated as part of the United States, so setting up your head office or main distributor in America to serve Canada will likely be problematic.

China has over one billion inhabitants, dozens of provinces and different regions in the country with a variety of dialects. One of the largest software companies in the world had to spend many years adapting and developing their business in China before they got it right. In his book, *Business the Richard Branson Way: 10 Secrets of the World's Greatest Brand Builder,* Sir Richard Branson said that when launching Virgin Atlantic airline flights to Japan, he knew that they would want slippers, not socks in First Class, that Japanese beer should be served and saucers provided for Japanese teacups. He had done his research and knows his market

So how are cultures different? Here is a very old joke.

Heaven:

- The police are British
- The cooks are French
- The engineers are German
- The administrators are Swiss
- The lovers are Italian

Hell:

- The police are German
- The cooks are British
- The engineers are French
- The administrators are Italian
- The lovers are Swiss

By now, you are beginning to understand that we all belong to unique and interesting cultures.

Women in International Business

The presence of women in international business is more common. However, it is important for women to understand that personal expectations and cultural differences may complicate business in some foreign countries. In others, women are accepted but are not always treated equally to men. Sometimes, they will not be treated any differently.

There are two major issues for women in international business

1. How to adapt to different cultures/countries, including gaining acceptance
2. Personal safety

The female business executive's title should be included on her business card, e.g., Manager of Sales, Export Director, Import & Export Coordinator, etc. It may be challenging for some women from more liberal countries to accept the social, cultural and business limitations in foreign environments. However being flexible and adapting to local practices will often mean the difference between success and failure.

It may be natural for a woman to automatically shake hands when meeting someone she is conducting business with. However, in some parts of the world, touching another person, especially a man, could be considered rude or provocative. Do your research to learn how to dress appropriately, according to the climate and culture. Other influences on women in business include the local religion, perceptions about the social and business status of the woman and the number of women publicly involved in the academic and business world. In some countries, something as simple as a woman wearing a stylish outfit and sitting alone in a hotel lobby, could create the wrong impression.

Personal safety risks for women

♦   Perceptions of your profession and credentials. Dress conservatively. When sitting in a public space such as a restaurant, carry a book or magazine and read it while you wait. If a male approaches you, make sure that you send a clear message that you are not interested. North American politeness can, unfortunately, be mistaken as flirting. If he won't leave you alone, ask a staff person to assist you.

♦   If a stranger asks what kind of job you have, say that you are involved in law enforcement. This normally discourages your questioner.

♦   Always be aware of your surroundings and what is happening around you. If you have concerns, talk to hotel personnel. Many hotels have accommodations and restaurants for women only. Use them.

♦   Of course, never open a door to a stranger, no matter what stories they tell you. People will try to trick you by claiming to be ill or in danger or saying that they have found something belonging to you. Always call down to the front desk and ask for assistance or advice. You can buy a device that hangs on the inside handle of your hotel room door, so that if someone with a pass key tries to enter, a loud alarm will warn you and frighten off the intruder. Always pack a small door stop or wedge that can be pushed under the door to stop it from being opened; some come with an alarm.

♦   There are many terrible stories of women (and some men) who have been drugged in public places then robbed, assaulted or killed. Never allow anyone to bring you a drink, even someone you are acquainted with through a business connection. Ask for a can of soda or an unopened bottle of beer. Pour it yourself. Never leave your food or drink unattended. If you have to leave to go to the bathroom, either take your drink with you or order a new one when you return.

- Carry a high-pitched personal alarm in your pocket, so if you are attacked you can trigger the alarm and the people around will notice something is wrong. You can't rely on chemical substances like pepper spray or mace because they are prohibited in many countries. You could be in trouble for just carrying them.

- If you need to use a rental car or a taxi or hire a driver or tour guide, ask the hotel desk clerk or concierge to arrange one for you. Always make sure someone knows where you are going and what time you expect to return.

- Don't bring valuables with you. Don't even wear costume jewellery or fakes that look like they are valuable. Why make yourself a target for robbery or worse?

Do lots of research before your trip

- Contact your local embassy for up-to-date information about the country you plan to visit. Contact the foreign representative in your country. Talk to business people who have spent time in the areas you will be visiting. Professional groups such as the Canadian Swedish Business Association in Stockholm, the Organization of Women in International Trade (OWIT) in Washington, D.C., or the 300 World Trade Centres in 100 countries can be useful resources.

- Talk to women who have lived and worked in the country you are going to. Those interviews will give you insights into how to dress, where it is safe to travel, how women are accepted in business, etc. There are also numerous websites where you can find a lot of information from women who are world travelers.

Some local information

- In some cultures, smiling or making eye contact with a man can signal that you want their company. Wear dark glasses if appropriate and be careful with your facial expressions. In some countries, it is considered impolite for a woman to shake hands with a man.

- You may look very different from the locals, so everyone will know that you are a foreigner. A tall, blonde Norwegian will stand out in a group of Indonesians. People may stare at you.In Latin America and southern Europe, you may be whistled at. It is not meant to be offensive, but to show appreciation.Don't go out after dark by yourself, or with other women. It will likely be dangerous. Never do anything in a foreign country that you would not do in a large city at home.

♦ In some male-dominated or more traditional countries, a woman's place is at home or in low-level positions and few may have executive jobs. As a woman in business, travelling on your own, you may not be quickly accepted. Be cautious about your conversation. In Saudi Arabia, for example, you should not discuss women's place in society unless your Saudi contact raises the topic. Don't expect to be able to import opinions or behaviours that are acceptable in your home country.

♦ Look at pictures of how local women dress. Wear neutral, rather than bright colours. In some countries, trousers or short sleeves are not worn by 'proper' women. You may be expected to wear a long dress that covers your ankles and sometimes a scarf to cover your hair.

♦ It is possible to meet men for business meetings but for dinner you may be seated with other women in a separate room. It's not about you, but local customs.

♦ If you are married, wear your wedding ring. If you are unmarried, don't wear a ring to fake it.

♦ In most parts of Europe and North America women are treated as equals in business. However, how courtesy is shown can vary a lot. In India, foreign business women are well accepted. In that culture, though, it is important for a female manager to demonstrate to subordinates that you are the person in charge.

♦ In Japan, dress and manners are restrained and formal, but unlike in Europe and North America, a man will not pull out a chair for you or step aside when entering a room. Older people are held in high esteem, more so than a business title.

♦ In China and the Philippines, it is becoming more common for women to occupy important business positions.

♦ If a couple is traveling together, in some countries it is not uncommon for them to be seated apart from one another at meals. The woman will be placed with the male host and the male with the host's wife. It is not considered proper in some countries for a woman to travel solo. Two women traveling together would be more appropriate.

♦ If you are given a gift in Latin America, the male will have to give it to you through his wife or secretary, so it is not construed as a romantic overture.

Example - How to translate a cultural message

Many years ago, I had some male visitors coming to Sweden from Latin America. The only place to eat was at the local hotel where the guests were staying. The dining room also hosted dancing six nights a week. My guests were surprised when several of the Swedish women approached and invited them to dance. They got the wrong message and thought the women were asking for something else. They didn't know that in Sweden, going out dancing is a social event. It is socially acceptable and not uncommon for a Swedish female to invite a man for a dance; however, the invitation is only for dancing.

Summary – Women in international business

Although women in business are more common than in the past, they are not always accepted as equals in some countries. They may be treated differently from men. Before you leave home, learn which countries are more "female friendly" and mentally prepare yourself for travel to those that will be more challenging. Understand the local rules and culture so that you know how to adapt.

More sources

http://www.journeywoman.com/

> a travel magazine for women, the website is a good source of information, on what to wear in different countries and travel tips

http://canada.servas.org/english.htm

> a non-profit service with information about cultures

http://www.womenwelcomewomen.org.uk/

> an international friendship and travel network for women

http://www.voyage.gc.ca/publications/pdf/her_own_way-en.pdf

> Her Own Way: A Woman's Guide to Safe and Successful Travel, Foreign Affairs and International Trade Canada

http://www.weforum.org/pdf/Global_Competitiveness_Reports/Reports/gender_gap.pdf

> This report from the World Economic Forum reports on the global gender gap. Sweden and Norway are at the top of the list with respect to women's empowerment. China ranks 33, India ranks 53 and Turkey and Egypt are at 57 and 58 of the fifty-eight countries listed.

http://www.we-inc.org/resources/

> resource for articles on women and international business

Your First Trip Abroad

You've done your initial research and decided which market you want to enter. Now it's time for your first visit. The first visit will allow you to determine if your decision was correct as well as giving you a sense of the local culture and the way business is conducted.

But before you take this important trip, you have to plan and organize thoroughly.

♦ Make a checklist of what you want to achieve for your business. Plan/ schedule who you should meet with and outline your objectives for each meeting.

♦ List the questions you want answered about your foreign partner, their networks, rules and regulations.

♦ Find out what the weather will be like and how you should dress, so that you can pack appropriately and not bring more than you need.

♦ When you are travelling overseas, you will have to make time to recover from jet-lag and time differences. Give yourself plenty of time to adapt to the climate too.

♦ When you arrive, pay attention to your surroundings and how people behave. Walk around and absorb the differences from your home country.

♦ Be prepared to spend from three days up to a week for your trip, especially if the market is important. Check country calendars to make sure you won't be visiting during holidays, religious holidays or other special events. For example, don't visit Rio de Janeiro during Carnival if you want to get much work done with your business partners. Your potential partner may have a religion different from the country you are visiting. Take that in consideration when planning your trip.

Travel

Wear comfortable clothing and footwear. Air travel is not the time for glamour or uncomfortable high fashion. Pack as lightly as possible – you don't need to carry your entire wardrobe with you on a business trip.

Disease protection. Find out if there are any vaccines, anti-malaria drugs or other health and safety preparations that have to be made in advance, before you enter the country. Websites like the Centers for Disease Control and Prevention list global destinations and travel health information. http://www.cdc.gov/.Depending on your destination, you may be required have certificates of vaccination for yellow fever, typhoid, rabies, cholera or show that you have been treated with anti-malarial drugs, if traveling to a high-risk area. Some jurisdictions demand that you have been tested for HIV or AIDS.

Seat selection. Unless you want to climb over your seat-mates every time you have to use the toilet or whenever you want to stretch your legs, book an aisle seat. You'll have greater freedom of movement as well as a bit more space. Every airline has schematics of the seat configuration of their aircraft – before you confirm your seating arrangements, check out the plan and choose carefully. Sitting by the toilet or the galley area is not desirable! Check http://www.seatguru.com/ for seating diagrams.

Avoid dehydration. One reason that people experience fatigue and jetlag after long flights is lack of water. Aircraft cabins usually have less than 20% humidity and the air is recycled. At home, you likely live in an environment with 40-50% humidity. If you wear contact lenses, you will soon feel how dry the air is. Wear your eyeglasses, so you won't have to worry about eye drops or cleaning solutions.

Drinking alcohol and coffee to compensate for your thirst will dehydrate you. Be prepared to consume a lot of water, and for safety, drink bottled water. I always carry an empty unbreakable half-litre bottle with a tight-fitting lid and get it refilled continuously during my flight. Eat a healthy meal on board.

Luggage. You'd be surprised at how much carry-on some people bring on board, despite airline regulations! Things like suitcases, backpacks, heavy clothing, shopping bags, briefcases, children's toys. Try to board the aircraft early so that you will have room to stow your luggage in an overhead compartment. Sitting for eight hours with a bag between your feet is very uncomfortable.

Label all of you luggage, inside and outside. Make copies of your important papers and your travel itinerary.

Take a photo of your bags before you check in for your flight. You never know when your luggage will be delayed/lost. If that happens, report the missing luggage immediately. Ask for an Amenity Kit, which normally contains underwear, toiletries and a pair of socks. In European Union countries, for example, if your luggage is misplaced when you arrive from overseas, the airline will automatically provide you with a kit and a voucher so that you can buy some replacement clothing. You will later be reimbursed. Many credit card companies have insurance that permits you to buy clothing if your luggage is lost for as little as four hours.

When there is a significant time difference between your home location and your foreign destination, e.g. 12 hours between Toronto and Bangkok, try to start becoming adjusted a week ahead. Gradually change your sleep patterns and eating habits. On the aircraft, set your watch to the new time zone. Once you reach your destination, immediately start working according to local time. Don't go to bed because you'll be tired in the middle of the day and you will have trouble adjusting. Eat regular meals and be careful of alcohol intake.

Don't try to squeeze in too many activities during your first trip. Don't believe everything you hear about the country you will visit. Research, ask questions and find out for yourself.

What to Bring on Your Business Trip

♦ **An open mind and willingness to adapt**

♦ **Company presentation.** Who are you? What is your company about? You are probably not well known. Your objective is to convince your potential clients that your company has the image, skills, capabilities and resources to be a desirable foreign partner. Because you have done your research, you have learned how to present your company and impress your clients in the most appropriate way to gain their interest in doing business. You have to prove that you can offer them what they want. Remember – you only have one chance to make a good first impression!

♦ **Plenty of business cards.** Professional business cards reflect your position in the company. They carry more meaning when they include text in the language of the country you are visiting. In some countries you will hand out a lot of business cards. If you run out, you may, perhaps, not be able to continue with your meetings.

♦ **Stationery.** Bring some company letterhead. It could be useful if you need to write a thank-you letter, make up a price list, etc.

♦ **Promotional and product material.** You are visiting to introduce your company and to sell your products and services. It is essential that you bring professional promotional materials that have been adapted to the country you are visiting. A CD and DVD can be effective and they are easy to carry.

♦ **Price lists.** As you will learn in a later chapter about Pricing, you have to do your homework and bring pricelists that are appropriate and adapted to the new market.

♦ **References.** Perhaps your company is not well known to the foreign company. It is advisable for you to present them with reference lists of existing customers and distributors.

♦ **Freight costs.** Your potential representative needs to know your total pricing structure so they can calculate what the landed cost for your products will be, i.e., costs to their warehouse or how much it would cost to ship your goods to their designation.

♦ **Money.** Most likely you will be using credit cards. However, in some countries and establishments, credit cards are not accepted. Know what the local conditions are. Make sure that before you leave home, you have a quantity of cash in the local currency.

♦ **Carry small bills in the local currency,** so that you can tip taxi drivers, porters and waiters. Bring enough cash for the first few days because if you require more, you can change it on site. Normally, you will obtain a better exchange rate than at home. Be aware that when you use your credit card, some countries may offer to charge your purchase in your local currency, which may be at a more favourable rate than your credit card company would charge. Card issuers normally add a service fee of 1.5 - 3% to convert to your currency. In this example, you live in Italy. When you buy something for $100 US in Panama, the credit card issuer in Italy converts that amount to 80.67 Euros, plus the service fee of 2% for a total of 82.28 Euros. In Thailand, you can get billed in the Thai Bath currency, but if you are using a Canadian Visa card, for example, they can charge you in Canadian dollars. Hotels and many stores offer that choice and before accepting the charge, you can see the charge in each currency and decide which one you want to use. Before you leave home, advice your card issuer of your destinations so any charges you make could be processed without questions.

♦ **Samples.** The best way to showcase your products is, of course, to bring samples that your customers can examine and operate. If you sell excavators, that may perhaps not be possible. In that case, bring along scale models or samples of the materials that go into the product.

♦ **Gifts.** As described later on in this chapter, it is essential for you to bring gifts to your contacts in some countries. Pay careful attention to gift selection and wrapping.

♦ **Valid passport.** For international travel, you have to carry a valid passport. Make sure that the expiry date is beyond the period of your travel. Some countries require that your passport cannot expire within six months of your arrival. Ensure that your travel documentation complies with the rules of countries you will be passing through or staying in.

Example - Need for two passports

A European businessman who travels extensively in Europe, Asia and the Middle East has to use two passports to avoid having entry/exit stamps in the document from certain countries that are involved in diplomatic or military disputes. After concluding a business trip in Israel, he arrived at the airport with is boarding pass and his luggage. He was stopped at the security check-in. Officials spent almost one hour searching through his entire luggage. He almost missed his flight. Why? He had a stamp in his passport from a trip he had taken to Malaysia. Israelis are not allowed to travel to Malaysia and vice-versa. He had the wrong stamp in the wrong passport and had to answer a lot of questions about his travels.

If your country allows you to have two valid passports or more at the same time, this will make it easier for you to use one while the other is being processed for any visas you may require for future travel to countries that require them. However, it is not enough to use two passports when traveling - you have to keep track on which countries are in conflict with each other and make sure that you present the proper documentation when traveling.

You will have similar issues if you have a stamp in your passport from Israel and travel to the Middle East. It can create a problem in many Muslim countries. I suggest in those countries that you carry a "clean" passport without stamps from Israel.

Another issue is that some countries which are under Islamic law don't allow unmarried couples to share a private room or a car. This is applicable to common law and gay couples.

- ◆ **Visas.** Visas are sometimes necessary and they have to be arranged for in advance. It could take days or weeks and there will be various security requirements. Note, there's a difference between a **tourist visa** and a **business visa** and you may need to show a written invitation from your clients to obtain a business visa. Traveling for business on a tourist visa could be considered misrepresentation, especially when you are carrying promotional materials and samples. You could be charged criminally or imprisoned. You may be deported and perhaps barred from re-entering the country in future. Visit http://www.oneworld.com/ow/airports-and-destinations/visa-and-health-information. The web site gives you good information as to visa and medical information.

- ◆ **Materials to leave with your clients.** You're visiting a foreign country to convince potential clients or representatives about your products and services. It is crucial that you use professional promotional material and carry enough to leave behind once they have expressed an interest.

- ◆ **Photos.** If your visit is a long one, you may need to apply for or renew your visa. It will be handy to bring a spare set of professional photos.

- **Driver's license.** In some countries it's impossible to get to your destination or to travel to companies located out of town without renting a car. It could be too expensive to hire a driver or a taxi for days at a time. Check to see if you have to apply for an international driver's license before you leave home. Bring your driver's license, just in case. Vehicle collisions are the most frequent cause of injury among foreign travellers. Wear your seat belt, be careful of overcrowded mini-buses or boats, follow local rules of the road and never drink and drive.

- **Medications**. Carry your prescription medications in your hand luggage, in their original containers, with the physician's and pharmacy's names clearly visible. Bring enough to last well beyond the days of your trip. Some medications are considered to be dangerous or illegal in some areas. Because you've done your research in advance, you'll know if you are required to carry documentation from your health care provider explaining why you need to bring the substance into the country. Even non prescription drugs with codeine can be forbidden. Even for vitamins or health supplements you should you bring your original container.

- **Digestive upsets**. Diseases from food and water are the leading cause of illness for travelers. When traveling, you will be confronted with bacteria that could cause an upset stomach or other intestinal problems. There are plenty of over-the-counter remedies for vomiting or diarrhea – always carry some with you. Food preparation, refrigeration and hygiene standards vary around the world. Use common sense and caution: drink bottled fluids that you can open yourself; wash your hands thoroughly; make sure that the food you eat is fully cooked; don't eat food purchased from street vendors; avoid unpasteurized dairy products.

- **Scheduling.** Make sure that you allow plenty of time for your trip. The worst that could happen is that you have to leave before your business is concluded because you have a flight that you can't change. Be prepared to extend your stay if your business colleagues want you to spend more time with them. You may have experience with quick meetings and quickly closing orders, but doing business in another country won't always be the same. It normally takes longer than you are used to. If you do have some unscheduled time at the end of your business meeting, take a sightseeing tour and purchase gifts for people at home. Don't forget the staff that have helped you plan your successful trip!

- **Camera and tape recorder**. Perhaps you will remember everything when you are back in your office, but exporting is about teamwork. You'll want to share your experiences and show your staff where you have been, who you met and what the new country looks like. Install a high capacity memory card and take plenty of photos. There will be many questions, and the tape recorder will allow you to dictate answers, record new information and have everything handy when you come home. If you use a digital recorder, you can connect it directly to your computer and transcribe it using speech recognition software.

♦ **Bring your telephone**. Check which mobile wireless phone system is used and if your phone will work there. If you have a cellular phone with GSM system (Global System for Mobile) capability, you can purchase a local SIM (Subscriber Identification Module) card that will permit you to make local calls at a low price. Remember to inform your office of the new phone number. When visiting Thailand in November 2009 and 2010. I purchased a local SIM card with 250 minutes of talk-time for $10. Even better, the card supplier gave a 50% discount for most of the calls, so in total, I was able to use about 400 minutes for $10. If you have an extra GSM phone, bring both with you and use one for local calls.

Example - Things will look different

Picture yourself walking around in Athens, Greece. You've been eating a lot of salads and great food cooked in olive oil. Now, you urgently need to go to the bathroom. You search around and find a public toilet, but inside the room you don't see a white fixture like you have at home. What you notice is a handle on the wall above a porcelain hole in the floor that has two indentations or foot prints on either side. Welcome to another experience for an international traveler!

Gift Giving

Gift giving is part of relationship-building in many countries. The protocols associated with exchanging gifts vary. In North America, Europe and Australia, it is not that common. In some countries it's seen more as a social gesture, in others it is a must and in some, a gift could be considered a bribe. Be sure you find out what is appropriate gift-giving behaviour. Sometimes you have to wait until after you have established a working relationship. In the Pacific Rim, which makes up a large part of Asia, the Middle East and Latin America, Japan, Indonesia and the Philippines, there is a long gift-giving tradition so be well-prepared. You may be faced with several apparent refusals before the person accepts your gift. Don't give up, or you will cause offense.

In China, giving and receiving gifts is part of a ritual. Be cautious that you don't give too expensive a gift and keep in mind that there will be a hierarchy you have to respect. If you give to different people, the value must mirror the rank of each individual. It may be appropriate to give one gift for the whole organisation. You should ask the recipient to accept your gift as an honour for your company. Use both hands to hand over the gift, which should be wrapped neatly in red, pink or yellow paper. Never use white paper, which is the colour of death and is used for funerals. Wrapped gifts are not opened in front of the giver.

If you are invited to a home in India, bring a small gift as a token of appreciation. However, be careful when selecting flowers. Ask for advice. Green, red and yellow are acceptable colours for wrapping, but black or white are not. If you receive a gift, don't open it in front of the giver.

Always bring gifts to your first business meeting in Japan, preferably something made in your country. They need not to be expensive. The gift-giving ceremony is more important than the gift itself. Always make a presentation to your key contacts and make sure you use both hands. It's important that the gift is wrapped; most likely, the recipient will not open it right away. Do not use black or white paper.

It is not mandatory to give gifts in Saudi Arabia, but it can be helpful when you visit someone's home or office. Before you leave home, ask for advice about what to give and the appropriate value. Saudis will normally open the package while you are there. Your hosts will be very offended if you offer the wrong type of gift. Avoid alcohol and perfumes containing alcohol, pork and pork products such as pigskin, knives or anything with images of unclothed women. It is inappropriate for a man to give a Saudi woman a gift.

Although gifts are not expected, in most European and North American countries it is a polite gesture, especially if you are invited to someone's home. It is common

Example – Gift giving

You've completed a visit to Lima, Peru, where you finalized arrangements for a local representative to become your distributor. You are due to fly home on Saturday. The president of the distributor's company invites you to dinner on Friday night and tells you he will also be inviting some of his key staff members and their spouses.

You enjoy a long, friendly dinner, you are served a local drink called Pisco sour which is sweet and very powerful. You are being careful about how much you eat and drink. After the meal, your host makes a speech in which he expresses his appreciation for the agreement. He talks about looking forward to a long relationship. He then presents you with a gift, a work of art. It is 1 meter in size square and hand-carved, in leather. You are surprised and grateful and stand up to make your thank-you speech. Of course, you also have to present a gift. An ordinary pen set or company key ring wouldn't be enough. Are you prepared? Luckily for you, your quick-thinking secretary at home anticipated just this situation. Included with your business samples and brochures, she had wrapped and packed several pieces of good quality crystal, together with several ladies' bracelets and a selection of children's toys. Aren't you happy about her thoughtfulness? Next time, be sure you plan on bringing gifts.

in Sweden and Germany to bring a bouquet of flowers for the hostess. Remove the outer wrapping before you present them. In some countries it is very popular for guests to bring gifts for their host's children.

Sometimes you may receive an unexpected gift. For example, after a pleasant dinner, a male visitor may be provided with a female companion for the night. He is expected to accept this, out of courtesy. If you know this is a practice in the country you will be visiting, figure out beforehand how you will deal with this "gift". If you refuse her outright, the host may be upset. The young woman may "lose face" or consider that she's not beautiful enough. Another question is how can you return the favour?

Tipping & Gratuities

Tipping is handled in many ways, depending on where you travel. Keep in mind the wage levels of each country you visit.

In the United States, a hotel porter expects between $2 and $5 to carry your luggage to your room. In 1973, I was travelling in Chile. I handed a porter $2US as a tip. I didn't understand at first why he was so grateful. I found out later that $2 was equivalent to one month's salary. So remember that in countries like Mexico and the Caribbean, which have low wage rates, workers generally rely on tips. In Japan, tipping is not that common.

In China, tipping is not required most of the time because foreigners are usually charged much more than locals. In India, your waiter expects a tip even if they refuse it at first. In Europe, many establishments automatically include gratuities in prices found on menus. In those situations, you can simply round up the amount of the bill when you pay. In Thailand you have to look at the bill. Sometimes tax and/or a service charge are added to your bill, sometimes not.

Before your trip, check what the applicable taxes and tipping policies are. If you are in doubt, ask someone locally. If you plan to tip the housekeeper who cleans your hotel room, do it on the first day. You will then likely get better service for the duration of your stay.

Common Errors Made by a New Exporter

As an exporter, you will enjoy success but you will also make mistakes. Below are some of the common mistakes exporters make.

- ◆ The parent company does not service their export markets when things become busy at home, but then they lose those overseas clients. Pay attention to your partners and clients.

- No commitment from company management. So when the exporter needs support, there is none.

- The company tries to increase sales by taking orders from all over the world. However, because they do not have the international knowledge and resources, they have difficulty rejecting low priority or unsuitable markets. Concentrate and do a good job on a limited number of priority markets instead of a poor job in many.

- The company does not spend enough time researching and selecting the right foreign representative. An appropriately qualified rep is essential to success.

- The company treats foreign representatives as "them," and members of their own organization as "we." A foreign representative is as much a part of the home organization as your own sales people and is as part of your team.

- Unwillingness to modify or adapt products for a foreign market because they work so well at home.

- Not taking advice from professional exporters or consultants. This leads to making the same mistakes as others have and wasting time and money fixing problems that could have been avoided.

- Underestimating initial investment costs and realizing too late that the company cannot afford to export. One step often forgotten in calculations is that payment may not be received until 90 days after invoicing your overseas client. So if products are sent to Australia from Poland and shipping takes six or seven weeks, the importer will not pay until 30 days after they receive the goods, which is close to three months later. Normally, payments are received after 30 days on the domestic market.

- The company fails to produce good quality sales material and instructions adapted to the local business culture and language.

- There are insufficient personnel and financial resources dedicated to technical support and services. They are not taking into consideration the long distances from foreign customers, languages, requirements for instructions and assistance, time zones, etc.

One thing is certain - when you are involved in international business, you will never be able to know everything. The best thing you can do is to get advice so that you don't make the same mistakes that many people have made before.

There is an old expression: You don't have to re-invent the wheel. This means that there are people and organizations with extensive experience in international business and special knowledge about the global marketplace. They are also

Example – Culture and quality

A Swedish company moved their machine manufacturing to Spain. The local labour force did not have the same work ethic as their Swedish counterparts. Quality control was also poor, so the company's customers were not happy. I pointed this out to the Swedish production manager. He told me that he was trying to get the Spanish production workers to take responsibility for the quality of their work, instead of waiting for a supervisor's instructions. What he was trying to do was to make them act more like a Swedish worker who tends to be very independent and responsible for their own quality control. I told him that he would have to accept the Spanish way of thinking and adapt his strategy accordingly because he could never change them to working in the Swedish way.

familiar with a variety of industries. Ask around and you will find knowledgeable individuals who will be more than happy to assist you by sharing their experience and knowledge.

I have worked in international business for more than 40 years. I'm still learning and taking advice from people who are knowledgeable about specialized topics or specific market issues. Remember there is constant change in the market. What was applicable five years ago is likely not valid today.

Most of the time, people fail because they do something wrong and don't know how to fix it. Unfortunately for many of my former clients, they messed up badly and came to me afterwards, asking for help. I would analyze the problem then advise what they should have done, what they should do now and what not to do in future. They've all said, if only we had asked you for help before, then we would not have made those costly mistakes.

> *"It is not the company with the best product and services that succeeds. It is the company that best understands their customers."*
> *— L. Holmvall, Export Pro Inc.*

Summary

I hope exporting and international business are the right activities for you. It takes strong commitment and the willingness to put in real efforts. Combine this with experience and I am sure you will become a very successful exporter if you are not already. Exporting skills are not something you learn overnight but will stay with you forever.

Exporting is also a mental activity

Exporting is very much a question of common sense and goal setting. A recipe for being successful on the export market should include the following ingredients.

♦ Corporate focus on exporting and the patience to wait for results. Activities will be long term.

♦ Export achievements are directly proportional to your commitment, energy, planning and investments. An investment of time and money delivers corresponding profitability.

♦ Setting priorities and selecting the right markets are necessary, but being able to say no to less important markets is also important.

♦ Develop a "gut feel" or intuition for changes on the market, because the market changes rapidly. Forget tradition! Be a bold marketer and look ahead. Understand market circumstances and how they influence long term results.

♦ Team work is the foundation for success. Use the skills of your staff members and don't forget to keep them updated. Information will help overcome internal resistance. Provide export education for team members at an early stage in the export process.

♦ Do your homework. The more informed and prepared you are the better chance you have to succeed. There are many excellent tools you can use to obtain accurate market information quickly and easily.

♦ Remember the five keys to successful exporting: communication, commitment, thorough preparation, well-tested products and relationships.

♦ Don't be afraid to take advice or ask for help. This is an excellent way to increase your opportunities for reaching your goal faster. It is also a low-cost way to avoid making mistakes. Why not use an experienced mentor to guide you through the hurdles?

♦ Adaptation of products and presentation material to suit local requirements increase opportunities for success.

♦ Pay attention to developments in world markets, politics, economies, culture and local ways of doing business will become a regular part of your day-to-day activities. Recognize that **you** have to adapt to a variety of cultures, local business practices, not the opposite.

♦ Select the right partner in a foreign market. Make sure they are well trained and motivate them. It is **your** job.

This is the end of Part Two of this chapter. If you decide not to read Part Three at this time, I suggest you at least read through the Exercise and Additional Information.

Practicalities and Culture
in International Business – Part Three

Adapting to Diverse Cultures

You've learned that before you enter foreign markets you have to understand the local culture. There are 195 countries with over 3,000 cultures in the world. A product that can be marketed in Singapore perhaps won't sell in Argentina. There are many things involved in the way to do business in each country, like marketing, scheduling business meetings, where it is proper to conduct business, etc.

Successful companies use their knowledge about foreign cultures to their advantage; the less successful ones don't really care. Failure to understand cultures can in the long term be very expensive. Each country has its own style.

The way in which people show politeness or good manners can vary greatly. The Japanese say yes even if they don't mean it, because it is not polite to say no. So, when the Japanese nod or move their head in a way that you think means yes, it may mean anything from, "I don't understand you" to "perhaps not". Instead of saying no outright, they may say that "It may be difficult to fulfill but we will try." The same kind of politeness is applicable in Korea. A "no" in France does not have to mean a definite no. On the other hand, you have to get the French to say "yes" a couple of times before you can be sure that is what they mean.

In Sweden, like in North America, it is very common to use a person's first name after you have been introduced. In other countries, it can take a long time before that is allowed; sometimes you have to ask permission. In Germany for instance, it could be disastrous for you to talk to customers using their first name. To go from *Herrn* Doctor Braun to Heinrich may take a long time, and it may never happen.

> *Example – Adapting to another culture*
>
> *We are sometimes exposed to culture shocks when we travel abroad. I had just finished my first business trip to Algeria. It had been completely new experience – the clothing, the smells, the noise, the way of driving – everything was unlike at home in Sweden or any experience in Europe.*
>
> *I was in a cab on my way to the airport in Algiers, trying to catch a flight to go to Casablanca in Morocco. About a kilometre distance from the airport, the cab could go no further because the road was blocked. On the road were tens of thousands of pilgrims sitting, standing, sleeping and chatting. Everyone was making a lot of noise. They were on their way to make a pilgrimage to Mecca. Some were dressed in white – they had made a previous pilgrimage. Others, who were making their first trip, were dressed in beige. There wasn't much time until my flight left, so I had to hurry I had to get out of the cab and pull my luggage behind me in brutal heat, through the crowds. I was dressed in a business suit, which didn't help.*
>
> *Once I got into the airport, I was the only European and I was surprised by the masses of people milling around. When I got to the check-in counter, no one was there – they were all chatting with the pilgrims. To make this even more interesting, everyone was speaking French, a language I barely knew. I actually had to step over the weigh scale, go behind the counter and pull a ticket agent by the arm to help me.*
>
> *Even for me, an experienced business traveler, this was an uncomfortable experience. After that incident, I realized that I would never allow one of my inexperienced staff to travel to such an unusual country with such a completely different culture without a lot of advance preparation and experience in countries with less of a culture difference. In other words, they had to practice in markets that were easier to understand. This does not mean the market has to be close geographically, but culturally similar.*

When you meet someone from North America they'll repeat your first name several times to better memorize it. They will say, Nice to meet you, Robert, tell me about your family, Robert; do you live in the city or in the country, Robert; what kind of hobbies do you like, Robert? After this, they will remember your name as well as all the names of all your family members. The next time you meet, they would say, nice to see you again Robert, how are your wife Anne and your children Karen and Karl.

Would you remember your customer's name and his wife's name? This is important! I suggest you write down the names on the back of their business card and include their hobbies, etc. so that you can talk about them next time. During a phone call, of course, it's much easier because you can just look at the contact information in your computer and find all the details. Be aware, though, that in some countries, it is considered impolite to write on a person's business card, especially in front of the other person. Once again, this shows the value of your advance research.

Gestures, Expressions and Body Language

It is not only spoken language that sends a message but also hand gestures, facial expressions and body language.

♦ When Northern Europeans and North Americans speak they don't usually express themselves using a lot of gestures while in southern European countries like France, Spain and Italy and also in Latin American countries, people use their whole body to express their message.

♦ You'll notice that in Asia, people always seem to be pleasant and smiling. This does not always mean that they are happy. For a Westerner, it could be difficult to translate what they are really feeling if you only consider their expression.

♦ When you hold up your index finger to order a beer in Germany, you will get two beers, as the thumb is number one and the index finger is number two. If you form your index finger and thumb into a circle, for many people that means "okay" or "perfect", but for a Japanese person that gesture means money and for a French person that means zero. In Brazil and Russia, it could be taken as an insult.

♦ A Greek man who shakes his head from left to right doesn't mean no, but yes.

♦ In Muslim nations, Korea and Thailand and parts of Africa, it is a serious insult if you cross your leg over your knee and show the bottom of your shoes because the soles of the feet are considered to be unclean.

♦ Chinese people generally do not look you in the eyes during a negotiation because direct eye contact is considered to be intrusive.

Religion

Religion influences behaviour in many ways - what you are permitted to eat and perhaps when and where meals can be eaten, what you can drink and if smoking is allowed. It also affects what is acceptable clothing and how business is conducted. Religion is a very personal matter and you should avoid any discussions involving faith and beliefs. You also have to be careful about jokes or humour, as something funny in your culture could be offensive to someone else. It is considered disrespectful to visit holy places like churches or mosques and not wear modest clothing. Shorts, uncovered heads or bare arms are usually not allowed. In some holy or religious places you will also have to remove your shoes.

In some countries, religious beliefs guide people's everyday lives and business. So, when you are conducting business in Saudi Arabia and other parts of the Middle East, being aware of and respecting the influence of Islam is critical. The belief system says that nothing happens that is not the will of God. If a deal is completed successfully, it was the will of God; if the deal fails, it was meant to. For non-Islamic people, that can be a difficult concept to understand. The expression *Masha'Allah!* is used when someone hears good news. It is an expression of respect and a reminder that all accomplishments are achieved by the will of God.

Insha'Allah, means if God wills. For example, someone might say to you, "The meeting will take place tomorrow at 11 o'clock, *Insha'Allah (*God willing). Not acknowledging the existence of a Supreme Being or not having religious beliefs is not accepted.

Example – Religion and business

During a business trip to Saudi Arabia, a high-ranking executive mentioned in casual conversation that he was atheist. At a later meeting, he was seated at the end of the boardroom table, far away from the key executives of the company he wanted to establish a partnership with. Why? His attitude about religion was objectionable to his hosts and the result was that he had to return home without being able to complete negotiations.

Punctuality and scheduling

In Nordic countries you are expected to be on time for appointments and meals; you can even arrive early! In North America, it is not considered an insult if you arrive a little bit late for social events but in southern Europe, for instance, it's almost expected that you will be late. In fact, if you arrive on schedule, your hosts may still be getting ready and won't appreciate your promptness! So remember, when inviting someone or when you are being invited, you have to know what acceptable or polite behaviour for the respective country is. In the Middle East, people work on a different schedule than in North America, for example. Arabs work on Sundays but not on Fridays. In Israel, they do not work on Saturday because that is the Sabbath. In some areas of Spain and other Mediterranean countries it's not uncommon for everyone to take a break between 1 and 4 p.m. for the midday meal and a siesta. It's too warm to work during those hours.

In South Africa, punctuality can be very elastic. In Saudi Arabia, time is flexible and meetings can start late and last for many hours. It will be difficult to schedule a series of meetings on the same day. In fact, many Saudis do not even make appointments with a specific start time. Remember that appointments are scheduled between prayer times.

In China, meetings tend to be very long. Sometimes you'll get the feeling there is no clear objective. Punctuality is very important. The first meetings are always about relationship-building. It can take many meetings before you really talk business. In India, meetings can begin and end late, with frequent interruptions. As in China, a meeting normally starts with plenty of social conversation. Make sure you are on time, even though your hosts may not be. It is not uncommon for an appointment to be rescheduled at the last minute, so make sure you have set aside sufficient time to get your business discussions completed. In Japan, it is the opposite and meetings run on time. Always be punctual. Korean and Japanese guests tend to be early.

Punctuality tends not to be important to Brazilians. Their work day can start around 10 o'clock but will also end later in the day. Social events also end at a very late hour. It is good for you to arrive on time, even if you happen to be the first person there and have to wait.

Example – Appointments not on time

Many years ago I had a meeting in the Philippines with an executive for the department of transport. My appointment was for a meeting at 9 a.m. on Monday morning, but I had to wait until Tuesday at 2 p.m. when it finally took place.

Holidays

Closing your company for vacation is very common in many countries. Furthermore, the length of the vacation period varies. Some countries have a one-week vacation while other countries have as much as five to six weeks. The summer months differ around the world, so there can be a lot of variation in scheduling.

If your company closes for holidays, it's not normally a problem. However, you have to make sure that your office is staffed during the shutdown to respond to your customers overseas with everything from customer service to supplying machinery and spare parts. Ensure there is adequate stock in your inventory, so you can continue to supply your distributors. Inform your clients about the company's vacation plans so that they can place advance orders and receive supplies without interruption.

Entertaining - Food, Drinks and Dining

In many countries socializing involves sharing meals; some are very casual and some are more formal. In North America, when a business contact says they will pick you up at 8.a.m in the morning, that usually means the day will start with breakfast at a restaurant or at the company. At the end of the day, the two of you will finish your business with a drink at a bar or perhaps with a meal. It is not uncommon that spouses may be invited. You may also be invited to someone's home for a BBQ and to meet their family.

In Northern European countries such as Sweden and Norway, family life and business life are separate. The business person's spouse seldom participates in work-related meals and it is unusual for a foreign guest to be invited home. In Denmark, eating and drinking are part of doing business, although mid-day meals are normally light. In Finland, every company has two saunas, one for staff and one for entertainment. It is common after work, for visiting clients and company representatives to meet in the sauna. After heating up in the sauna then cooling down with a shower and beer or vodka, they return to the sauna. This happens a

few times. During the last session, a snack of sauna sausage is often cooked on the sauna rocks. The Finns say, "We don't do business with people we have not seen naked". Of course, a visit to the sauna isn't mandatory, but you have to understand that it is a common part of doing business in Finland.

Finland is situated close to Russia and there, a pleasant meal will help cement the working relationship. Socializing used to include a considerable amount of drinking, but that has changed.

"A dinner lubricates business." — *Baron Stowell*

In Italy, not only is a business dinner common but you may also be invited to attend a soccer game or the opera. Don't offend the host by refusing. Dinners are normally attended by small groups of people. Wine is considered food, so don't drink too much because you are supposed to enjoy it in moderation. A glass is normally filled to less than half full. Their philosophy is that you can always pour more later on. There is no competition to drink as much as anyone else. You very seldom see a drunken Italian.

You know that when doing business in Asia, hospitality and relationship-building are very important. Expect to spend long hours with your hosts and share many lengthy meals. If you are invited to a banquet, you will be expected to try different types of dishes, some of which will include unfamiliar meat, seafood and vegetables. It is acceptable to ask what you are eating before you taste it, especially if you have food sensitivities. Many times, meals are served with large amounts of liquor such as local beers and clear (strong) alcohol. Remember that you will be expected to return the hospitality. Arrive on time or even better, 15 to 30 minutes early. Unlike in North America, business is not discussed during the meal. Toasting is very popular and the host always offers the first toast. Do not eat everything on your plate, because that means you are still hungry. Meals normally end with a serving of fruit.

In South Africa, most entertaining is done at local restaurants. It would be unusual for you to be invited to someone's home. Business can be discussed, but usually not during the meal.

In Brazil, you may spend two hours at lunch and up to five hours at dinner. Parties can continue until the early morning hours. Remember it is all part of relationship building. Mostly, social issues are not discussed until the meal has ended, then business topics can be raised in conversation.

In India, lunches and dinners are considered part of doing business. If you are entertaining, remember that Hindus and Sikhs don't eat beef and Muslims don't eat pork or drink alcohol. Many people from India, Pakistan and Bangladesh are vegetarian. Indian food is frequently eaten with the fingers – always use your right hand because the left hand is considered to be unclean. Leave a small amount of food on your plate to show that you are satisfied. If invited to a dinner, dress modestly and take your shoes off when entering someone's home. You can arrive a couple of minutes late at a restaurant but Indian people expect foreigners to be punctual at a private home, even if they are not themselves.

Buddhism does not condone killing even insects, so be cautious about what foods you serve. Orthodox Jews do not eat pork, shellfish and certain parts of the cow. Milk products and meat should not be served on the same plate. The dietary rules are quite strict. I have been in situations where they bring their own food, eating utensils and containers.

In Japan, it is customary to remove your shoes when entering a restaurant. The Japanese host will enjoy choosing your food and explaining its origin and preparation. When you invite a Japanese person to your country, take them to a restaurant that reflects your country's culinary arts and customs. Entertainment consists of going from bar to restaurant and maybe to a special hostess bar that includes karaoke, sumo wrestling, etc. Be aware that it is not normally recommended for women to participate in those activities.

Coffee is a common drink in many places and tea in others. It sometimes is consumed after a meal and occasionally, during the meal. In some countries, you may be served wine, beer or strong alcohol. Your host could be offended if you don't accept a drink. That is their culture. In Japan, you will be offered sake, in Mexico, tequila and the local beer Corona; in Peru, it will be the Pisco sour cocktail, in France and Italy, the beverage of choice is wine and in the Middle East and Arabic countries the choice of drink will be guided by religion.

Example – What to drink and when

My export manager and I were invited to the Czech Embassy in Stockholm at nine o'clock in the morning. We were asked if we wanted something to drink. As it was early morning, we asked for coffee. Ten minutes later, a man arrived and asked if we wanted beer. Of course we said yes, as the host most likely wanted that.

When you invite someone for dinner from another culture, you have to be careful what you offer. At home, you know if someone has a food allergy and you adapt your menu to that. When you are dealing with people from other countries, you have to be sensitive to cultural or religious food restrictions. Some Muslims won't eat meat if the animal has not been slaughtered according to halal rules. (The word "halal" is Arabic for permissible. It describes meat that has been slaughtered and prepared according to Islamic law. There are even special rules for cosmetics – they must use plant extracts and minerals rather than pork and alcohol ingredients that are banned.)

What you eat in one country may be seen as very odd in another one. Ingredients such as snakes, monkey brains or ants are delicacies in some cultures, but disgusting to others. Do you eat salad with the meal, after the main dish (France) or before (North America)? If you eat spicy food in a country like India, Malaysia, Indonesia or Peru, you can't stop the fire with water. You'll have to finish the meal with a banana to neutralize the spices. Do you hold your knife in your right-hand and your fork in the left when you eat? North Americans do it that way, but when they finish using the knife, they put it down and switch the fork to their right hand. Chopsticks are used to eat most kinds of Japanese foods, but you should not stab food with them, stick them into a bowl of rice or point them at another person. That is considered rude.

At a dinner or lunch, where you seat your guests is important in Europe and Asia but not so important in America. Where you place the guest of honour must be done according to what is applicable in a particular country. Even at a company boardroom those same rules apply. Look at how seating arrangements at meetings of high-ranking politicians are arranged, if you want to know how important this is.

Meal times vary, depending on where in the world you are. Some people have a large breakfast; eat a big lunch and then a light dinner after six. Some have a light lunch and sit down to dinner after 8 p.m. Keep in mind that your foreign guests could still be mentally in another time zone. They may not be hungry at your regular meal times.

When traveling, think about what you're eating and when. Perhaps your digestive system is not accustomed to the bacteria in food or water in the country you're visiting and you could become ill. Get the appropriate vaccinations and be careful with what you eat and drink.

Even if you think you recognize the food, it will not always contain the same ingredients. A can of prepared tomato soup that you buy in Holland will be formulated differently than in Indonesia. The product looks the same but the Indonesian soup will be spicier. In India, a hamburger is vegetarian. In Italy and France, you can order alcohol at major fast food hamburger chains. The local cultures come first!

Titles and Names

In some countries, decisions are made by front-line staff. Middle management and titles will not be very important. In other countries, titles and education credentials are of great importance. Executives are the key decision-makers. In England for instance, business people include their organizational title and their education on business cards. Remember that your foreign partner will expect to negotiate with someone who is their equal, i.e., on the same level. That can create a problem if you are not prepared to meet the expectations.

Example – Importance of titles

You are planning to negotiate with the president of an overseas company with a long chain of command. In your company, you are the Product Manager with full responsibility for closing the deal. You are 30 year old and you look young. The president is 60 years old. The reaction is that your company is not really interested in doing business with his company, because they have sent someone who appears to be a junior employee. So what are you going to do? In this case, the solution is to change your title from Product Manager to Vice President, International Sales. Now, the foreign president will be impressed because a young person with a high-level position must be something really special.

Example – Age and status

When I was 36 years old, I looked like 30. I was Swedish Trade Commissioner to Canada and had diplomatic status, with diplomatic license plates on my car. Many people visiting my office expected an older person. I was even stopped by the police now and then, because they wanted to know who owned the car I was driving. They were surprised that such a young person was a "real" diplomat. Because of my diplomatic status, I was treated like someone special whenever I attended events. For me as a Swede, this did not make sense because I thought of myself as just an ordinary business man with a different job to do for my country.

After my appointment as Trade Commissioner was over, I started my own business. I asked the Swedish Ambassador to Canada to officially open my new office. My clients were very impressed and couldn't understand how I could convince the ambassador to attend. For him and for me, it was very natural.

In North America, titles are quite important, so you will find many presidents and vice presidents in a company. When you deal with people in a country like Germany or Brazil, they will often have Dr. in their title, e.g. Herrn Dr. Schmidt.

In some countries, a title is not that important, but age or seniority could be, so the older you appear, the more experience you are expected to have. In this situation an older representative would be the lead person in negotiations. This respect for age is very common in many countries in Asia.

> ### *Example – Older is wiser*
>
> *Several representatives of a Dutch company visited a factory in China to complete a manufacturing deal. The son was President and his father was the Sales Manager. The Chinese factory managers directed all of their questions to the father. Although he was not the President of the company, he was the oldest of the Dutch representatives, so he was seen as the leader and the more experienced.*

Make sure that the title on your business card mirrors your position in the organization and can be easily understood by your customer in the country where you want to do business. In Sweden for instance, the president has the title VD (Verkställande Direktör). Translated into English, that means managing director. However, in English VD is an abbreviation for **v**enereal **d**isease, which is not a very appropriate title. Maybe your job title is Manager of Ground Support or Remedy Engineer, but ask yourself, what does that mean to someone not familiar with your industry? Provide a brief explanation or change the title to something more specific, like, Aircraft & Ramp Equipment Service Manager or Director, Civil and Environmental Engineering Projects.

In China, wives do not normally have their husbands' surnames but keep their maiden or birth name. In Iceland, a woman's last name is a combination of her father's first name and the word for daughter, like Sigurdsdotter, which mean the daughter of Sigurd.

In many Asian and Latin American companies, having a professional business card is a prerequisite to doing business. You will hand out a lot of them. Make sure to bring enough. If you run out, it could be difficult for you to conduct business. When you have business cards printed, it is preferable to have any important information translated into the local language.

Learn the proper way to hand over your business card. In Japan, hold the card between the thumbs and index finger of both hands as you bow from the waist and hold out the card. The higher the status or position of the person you are meeting, the deeper you should bow.

For some people, it's an honour to meet people with a high rank. Using a powerful or important-sounding title or holding diplomatic rank can make a difference in many countries. The title and the rank can be more important than the person's knowledge or abilities!

Example – Who you know is important

I was working as a Marketing Manager for a European company. We were representing a German company. I was 28 years old. The company owner and CEO of the German company was 65 years old. Every time the German owner visited our company in Sweden, he asked to meet with the CEO. The CEO told him I was the one in charge, but that didn't seem to make a difference.

Whenever I visited the company in Germany, I was picked up at the airport by a Mercedes 600 and driver and driven to a hotel. The next morning, I was picked up and driven to the office. The owners never took me out for lunch or dinner.

One day, when I arrived at the airport in Germany, the owners were waiting for me with their personal car and driver. They treated me like a special guest. When we arrived at the hotel, they offered to take me to dinner. I was surprised and couldn't understand the change in behaviour. However, the next morning I got an explanation.

When I reached the office, there was a large picture on the wall of me with the Swedish king. He was using their machine. I had sent the photo as information but this is what changed the way they treated me. In their minds, if I had been able to not only meet the Swedish king but get him to try their equipment, I had to be a very special person. After that, the German President never asked to meet with the CEO of our company and I was always treated to lunch and dinner, whenever I visited his company in Germany.

If you're not sure who to deal with, always start at the top

When doing business overseas it is important to understand who is the boss, who makes the decisions is and how decisions are made. You have to ensure that you follow their procedures but even more important, that you negotiate with the right person.

Example – Negotiating with the right person

I was helping a foreign company located in Canada. The person in charge and who did most of the work was an engineer. I was only involved when he requested me to be. He was negotiating a large order with a mining company in Canada and I asked him if he wanted help. He said no, the technical staff has recommended our equipment and he was sure he would get the order. I asked if he had made a product presentation to the mine manager. He stated that he didn't need to.

He didn't get the order. Why? Because the competition visited the mine manager and convinced him to buy their products. The technical staff had very little influence on the purchasing decision. After that, the engineer always contacted the mine manager. In fact, he would bring me along for the negotiations and after that, we received most of the orders.

Business Relationships and Greetings

How to establish relationships and conduct business will be different in each country you visit. In Asia, people want to know all about you. They also take care of you 24 hours a day when you visit. You are a guest in their country and insisting that you can take care of yourself is not accepted. When they visit you at home, they will expect you to return the favour.

In Southern Europe, you won't spend that much time together after business hours because the family comes first. In Germany and England, it is common to go to a *Bierstube* or pub after business hours. In North America, you will likely meet for breakfast and for something to drink and to eat after work, in a relaxing environment. Spend the time to learn what's appropriate. If you are uncertain about the rules, contact someone with experience working in that country or from their embassy in your home country. There are also many books and web sites that describe the customs of various countries.

Before making their decision, northern Europeans and Germans like to receive information, with plenty of technical details over a long period of time. Americans tend to be fast decision-makers. If they like you, your product and the money they expect to make by doing business with you. In China or Japan, however, you have to be prepared for extensive information-exchange and negotiations to take plenty of time. That could require several visits before they're even willing to talk business.

When a foreign representative visits you and brings their spouse along, you will have to make sure that both of them are well taken care of. If the client's visit extends over a weekend, don't leave them to entertain themselves while you take off for the cottage with your family. If you invite them along, you will improve your relationship and strengthen your chances to do business. Take them out for a round of golf, a walk in the forest or a boat trip. Ask if they would be interested in local attractions like the theatre, a sporting event, museum or a concert. If the spouse enjoys the trip, they will speak positively of the experience but if they are bored or ignored, that could have a negative impact on any business deal. If your business guests are happy with you and the trip, they will, hopefully, invite you and your spouse to visit them.

It is not uncommon for buyers from countries such as Egypt to send someone to inspect the goods they have ordered, before you are allowed to ship. Even though they will pay for their own travel and accommodations, it is smart business for you to treat them well, as you would any business guest.

When you travel as extensively as I have, you will get tired of hotel rooms and hotel food. So when I have foreign business visitors, I usually invite them to our home for lunch or dinner. They very much appreciate a nice meal in a relaxing atmosphere and meeting the family. For them, it provides some insight into the country and culture they are visiting.

Example – Meal with family

When my children were young, I invited a sales manager from the Philippines to my townhouse in Sweden. The visitor missed his own children and he really enjoyed sharing a family meal with us. During my next visit to Manila, I was invited to his home to have dinner with his wife and children. It was an interesting experience because while we ate, the rest of the family (grandma, uncles and cousins) sat along the wall, listening to and watching the tall Swedish guest.

In China, *guanxi* or the personal connection between two people in a relationship is critical to success and will take some time. Business meetings are normally attended by groups of people. It could take hours, days or weeks before you see any progress. Long-term commitment to the business relationship and the age of those involved are also significant. An older person will be shown the most respect. The internal organizational structure is always hierarchical. Directives are issued by senior managers and passed down through the organisation. Many senior managers have a close relationship with the ruling Communist party, which is the behind-the-scenes power in business networks.

In Saudi Arabia, meetings and business relationships are very much influenced by religion. You are supposed to compliment your host, his business organization, the country of Saudi Arabia and the Muslim world. It is important that you use strong eye contact. Direct eye contact is expected in Brazil but not as common in Europe. In Asia, it is not the proper thing to do.

In Saudi Arabia, it would not be uncommon for you to be in a room with many meetings going on at the same time. Participants will drop by to talk with you then leave to talk to other people. Family is important and business is normally family-oriented. Age is honoured. Your hosts may discuss family as well as religion, your personal wealth, etc. Don't expect to conduct business there like you would in Europe and North America; you have to learn the Saudi way.

In India, business organizations and society are very hierarchical, so you have to make sure to negotiate with the top level manager. The work environment is very social and hospitality is closely associated with doing business. Always use formal titles such as Mr., Mrs. or Miss or the appropriate professional title such as Professor or Doctor. Never use someone's first name unless you are asked to do so.

Russia has changed dramatically in the last decade. Before, business was very much based on long term relationships but now business is more short-term. Meetings are more of an information-gathering process than for concluding deals, because in many cases decisions are made at a very much higher level than that of the person you will be dealing with. A company is normally driven by one strong central figure. The boss is always the boss. Make sure that you follow up what is agreed upon verbally, with a written contract. Also remember that the business environment in Russia is not like North America or Europe – there are many social, political and economic complexities and depending on your industry, frequent demands for bribes. This corruption, as well as many special rules and inconsistent interpretations of regulatory requirements make it a challenge to get goods into the country.

Japan is very hierarchical, although most information is channelled downwards in an organisation for approval. Many decisions within a company start as suggestions that move up the hierarchy ladder from front-line workers or subordinates through middle management, to the top. In this way, management decisions are normally more strongly anchored or agreed with in the organisation. That process also means that new business ventures, production methods or products have to be reviewed and agreed on, which takes time.

Because of their history of formality, respect for authority/seniority, consensus building and common standards for orderly behaviour, people living in Japanese society are very familiar with how business and society are supposed to function. For an outsider, it can be difficult to understand. Sometimes you may not be sure what you are agreeing to during a business discussion. There is often a big difference between what is said and what is meant. Rather than saying no, a Japanese negotiator may give you an ambiguous response, because they are trying to be polite. It is not that the Japanese are untrustworthy. In fact, the opposite is true, but there a risk that your communications to them and from them may be misunderstood. Always be polite. Ask several times to clarify that everyone is clear on what has been discussed and agreed and that there really has been an agreement reached. Most meetings in Japan are attended by groups of people.

> ### *Example – Treating foreign visitors*
>
> *A Swedish company in a small northern town was hosting visitors coming from Japan. I was asked how they should take care of their guests. I suggested that the company representatives should pick up the visitors at the airport, pay for their food and hotel costs and take them on a golfing and a fishing tour. Why? Because hospitality is very important!*
>
> *The Swedish company thought it would be expensive, but they followed my advice. The Japanese guests appreciated the hospitality. When the Swedes visited Japan, the Japanese company paid for everything. As you probably know, the cost of living is much higher in Tokyo than in a small town of Sweden, so everything worked out.*

Trust, respect and dignity are the keywords in international business. In Brazil meetings normally start informally, with plenty of small talk. Lengthy dinners and lunches are common, because they use their social opportunities to get to know you. Be aware, though, that Latin-Americans can be temperamental, so don't be surprised by demonstrations of emotion in social and business conversation. Shaking hands is very common. Women often greet each other with a kiss on the cheek.

In Latin America and Europe, greetings may include body contact. Shaking hands is a common way to greet business associates. In North America and Europe, handshakes are normally firm but in countries such as China, handshakes are very soft or gentle. In Italy, Spain, France and Spain you can exchange a kiss on both cheeks when greeting good friends. In the Middle East, you must never have physical contact with someone of the opposite sex. Americans shake hands and sometimes give a hug, sometimes with the opposite sex, but be careful that you understand whether this is allowed or if it will be considered too familiar and frowned upon.

In many Asian countries, people bow when they greet one another. In Thailand, the customary greeting is the *Wai*, where a person presses their palms together near the chest and bows to show respect. They say Hello, "Sawasdee krub" if it is a male greeting you and "Sawasdee kaa" if a female is greeting you. Never try the European approach of kissing someone on the cheek.

Travel expenses

If you are inviting someone to visit your country, who is expected to pay for travel costs? You should investigate this beforehand. Normally, the business person travelling would pay for their trip and hotel costs. As host, you're supposed to cover the cost for meals and hospitality. However, some countries do not have access to Western currencies and may not have funds to pay with. In those cases, you should be prepared to pay the bill. Some countries don't allow a citizen to travel abroad without a formal written invitation. Find out if they need a visa for travel to your country and who is responsible for arranging one. You may have to assist them.

What to wear

You have to dress appropriately in the country you are visiting. You also have to adapt to the type of company and industry you are working with. A two-piece business suit would be suitable in some circumstances and more casual clothing in others. In the state of Texas in the United States or in the Philippines, the weather can be hot and humid. It doesn't always make sense to wear a suit. Sometimes, trousers in a light fabric and a good quality shirt would be appropriate for men and women. Blue jeans are seldom appropriate business attire, unless you are in rough conditions where you also have to wear a hard hat and work boots. Never wear ripped or distressed clothing or garments that don't fit you properly. Don't wear t-shirts or hats with slogans, slang, cartoons or pictures – you never know what may offend someone. Remember, you are representing your company.

If you visit a mine in northern Canada or in Chile, you will have to dress more casually, especially if you're going to visit the mine, but always dress neatly and in clean clothing. If you will be visiting a company head office or meeting with executives from a large corporation, of course you will wear more formal clothing. My advice to you is this: before travelling or attending a meeting, find out what the appropriate dress code is.

Some companies have what is called "casual Fridays" or "dress-down days". That may be fine for staff, but not for someone who is there to conduct business. If you are not sure, it is always better to be well dressed than casual. You can always re-move your tie or jacket, but if you don't have the proper attire, you will not make a good impression. If you can't find someone to ask, take a drive by the office you will be visiting and see what people are wearing. Dress like an important customer.

For women, it is even more critical to understand the importance of the right clothing. In some areas, women in business are still a rarity, so being seen as pro-fessional may require greater attention to the choice and style of garments. In very few businesses is provocative clothing acceptable. Selection of what is proper will be influenced by a country's religion and perceptions of women's place in society. That is a fact of life women have to be prepared for.

Colours

You probably have not given much thought to the importance of colours, but they have different meanings, depending on where you are. Colour can be a powerful tool for conveying a message, either good or bad.

In some countries, green is used to represent something that is good for the en-vironment. Green means 'go'. It is the national colour of Ireland and the flag of Libya, while in Malaysia it represents the jungle and sickness. In Asia, it means youthful and in South America it means death. When you give a red rose to a

Example – Making mistakes

I often ask my customers if they remember the worst mistakes they have made. One company in Norway said they had visitors from Japan and wanted to give them an appropriate gift. The gift they selected was a knife with Viking motifs. The package was nicely wrapped with white paper.

When the Japanese people opened the package and saw what was inside, they got up quickly and left the room. So what happened? In Japan, if you give someone a knife it means suicide. White signifies death. So of course, the message the Norwegians sent was totally inappropriate.

woman in North America it is a symbol of love. In Turkey and some countries of Africa, red means death while in Iran, it means happiness. In some cultures, the colour white signifies purity and is often used for weddings while in other countries it has a completely different meaning.

The colour blue in the US means masculine but it is also stands for authority and loyalty. The color yellow is often used for weddings in places like India and it stands for strength in Saudi Arabia, but it means sorrow in Egypt. It signifies feminine in the Ivory Coast and Ghana, but means death in Mexico. A yellow tag on a product can identify that it is defective.

So as you can see, you have to consider the importance of colours, not just in selecting gifts but in your choices for machinery, packaging, labels, etc.

Communications

There are 5000 languages in the world. The English language contains more than a million words, when you count slang, medical and scientific terms and foreign words used in daily speech. New words are being created every day. Twenty years ago, no one had heard of the *Internet*, or products called *smart phones*.

In Europe, there are 239 languages, although the major languages are English, French, Spanish and German. In addition to the recognized languages there are regional or local dialects and sometimes combinations of several languages. There is no way that you would ever be able to learn about all of these, but you have to get to know the foreign market so that you can produce your sales material in a language used locally.

Business communications

Remember when you communicate to:

- ◆ Use plain language that everybody understands. This means no slang or jargon and few complicated words in product instructions. Remember that some of your customers may not have strong reading skills, so keep your information simple.

- ◆ Use an approach tailored to each country. In North America, you would talk about profits and return on investment. In Germany and Sweden, you would use technical terms. In Japan, you would use communication that builds up the relationship.

One of the reasons companies fail in a foreign market is their inability to share information, so that people understand. Many times, we assume that we understand each other but the words we use may mean completely different things. A direct translation from our own language to another language can lead to problems when the other person's way of thinking is not taken into consideration. There are numerous examples of company and product names that mean something harmless in one language and something ridiculous or offensive in another. You can search on the Internet and find many examples.

In some countries you will have to take a "soft" selling approach where you don't boast about how good your product is. In other markets, if you want to convince a customer to buy your product, you will have to use a hard sell and really promote the benefits.

> ### Example - Presenting your company adapted to the client
>
> *If you're a small company in Holland, you might say that "we're a small company in Holland manufacturing wooden sticks for ice cream novelty products".*
>
> *But you could also say," we are the largest manufacturer of wooden sticks for ice cream in the world and we have been in business for 40 years, selling into 50 markets". This is the same company, but the approach will vary, depending on the client.*

When you prepare sales material for a foreign country, you will translate it from your language. However, you also have to understand what kind of message the foreign consumer has to receive in order to want to buy your product. So, if you are marketing to consumers in Germany, the client wants sales material that includes a lot of technical information about the product. On the other hand, your American client's company wants promotional text that tells them about product benefits and opportunities for them to make money. Where literacy is basic, sales and service material will have to include mainly pictures and diagrams.

Don't ask your brother-in-law, the high school teacher, to translate your sales material. In business, you must find a competent translator who not only knows the language, but who can also edit and rewrite the text and illustrations you have provided so that they conform to what is appropriate in the target country way of thinking.

Remember, when communicating with foreign clients in English, that it is not likely their mother tongue. Don't use specialized terms or sentence structure that is overly complicated. Use basic English so that your information is clear. Double-check with someone to make sure that the message is understood the way you want it to be. When a North American talks about the "bottom line", they mean net profit. In some countries, it could mean the last offer or the best price. For someone who doesn't understand English terminology, they might not know what you mean and look at the last line in your letter.

If you use the word "turnover" in business conversation in England, it means how much has been sold. In the United States, it means how many times you have turned over the stock or inventory in your warehouse. In the US, the term for how much has been sold is "annual sales". You "rent" a car in North America and you "hire" a car in England. In English, the word "pain" means something that hurts but in French, the same word means "bread".

Example – Adapting your language to skill level of client

Many years ago when the phone lines were the not that dependable, I got a call from a client in Mexico who was having technical problems. I spent twenty minutes explaining the cause of the problem and how he could solve it. I asked him if he understood, and he said no. I had used too many technical details in my explanation so I had to start all over again, using plain language.

So what could happen if a translation is wrong? I have listed some real life examples below.

- ◆ **At the ticket office of an airline in Spain.** We take your bags and send them in all directions.

- ◆ **A sign at a doctor's office in Malaysia.** Specialist in women and other diseases.

- ◆ **Zurich hotel.** Because of the impropriety of entertaining guest of the opposite sex in the bedroom, it is suggested that the lobby to be used for this purpose.

Communicating Methods

Communicating through personal visits or by phone allows you to "read" expressions, emotions and tone of voice. Using emails, text messages, letters, the Internet or fax does not open up the same opportunities. It is always better to make a personal visit to the country, at least at the beginning of your business relationship. No electronic technique can substitute for the benefits of social contact as a means of finding out subtle information about a customer, based on their facial expressions or what they say.

Make sure that your name, your company name or product does not have another meaning in the customer's language. Here are some examples for product names that had an unintentional meaning.

Chevrolet *Nova* = In Spanish, no va means you don't go

Ford *Caliente* = Vagabond

GM *Fiero* = Ugly old person

Double-check your company name and product names before entering a market. Don't just look in the dictionary, ask local people because there could be slang meanings or negative interpretations. As you will see in Legal chapter, you have to ensure that the name you want to use has not been taken or registered by someone else.

Here are some ideas for increasing your business by providing information in other languages.

You are an American visiting Greece and looking for a pleasant place to have lunch. You see a menu posted outside the restaurant but everything is listed in the Greek language. You have no idea what meals they offer and what the prices are. If they had displayed a menu translated into English, you would be more interested. There is, however a menu in the Danish language. If you were a Dane, you would appreciate seeing a menu in your mother tongue. Who do you think will attract more customers?

Understanding how your customer thinks

When doing business overseas you need to understand how people think, what's important to them and how you can meet their needs.

> **Example – Presenting the right benefits based on client**
>
> *When we were selling complete sawmills world-wide, customer requirements varied. In Sweden, which had high prices and a shortage of raw material, the priority was to have thin cuts that maximized production from the raw material. When marketing the same equipment in Canada, the selling point was speed and capacity.*

Here is another example of how critical it is to understand the local way of thinking.

> **Example – Understand what the customer wants**
>
> *We were requested to send a quotation for a complete saw mill to a potential buyer in one of the Eastern European countries. I asked my Canadian company to offer prices on two production lines. They said that the buyer would only need one line and that if we offered them two, our price would be too expensive. I explained why I needed a price for two production lines. Our quote even so was about 45% higher than our competitor's price. We got the order.*
>
> *How did that happen when our price was more expensive? We had to think like a customer. The customer in this case was represented by a manager who was making the decision. He was going to become the production manager and general manager of the future mill. His pay would be influenced by how much lumber he could produce compared to the official production capacity of the saw mill. We told him that he only needed one line, but we would quote for two and state the capacity of one line. This would allow him to produce twice as much, thus guaranteeing him a sizeable bonus. His interest was to make money for himself. The company paid for the saw mill, not the manager. But he was responsible for making the final recommendation. We provided him with what was important to him at the same time as we supplied the company with the information they needed. We got the order because we understood who the decision maker was and what his priority was.*

Remember that sometimes there will be restrictions on your ability to sell. NIH is a common term in the US, meaning Not Invented Here. You will find that it may not be popular or patriotic to use a foreign product. So if there is some anti-Chinese sentiment, don't label the product as having been made in China, if you do not have to. In some countries, you will find the opposite situation, where customers believe that an imported product is better than a domestic one.

Bribing

Bribing is influencing someone to do something by giving them a gift, money or some other type of inducement.

You know that you have to adapt your activities to each market. Expect to be faced with decisions and situations that you have never encountered at home. Bribing may be one of those. You may feel strongly that that neither your company nor your country supports bribing. However, the question is when does a simple favour become bribing?

If you have children in your family, you have probably bribed them. Have you ever said, "stop screaming and I'll give you some candy" or "if you behave, you'll get a treat"? So what was this? You bribed the child in order to change their behaviour and get what you wanted from them – to stop screaming or to behave properly. Remember the definition – an inducement or gift in exchange for something. You have to realize that in some countries, people cannot survive on the salaries and wages they are paid. They have to supplement that with other income. This is usually allowed or quietly approved by their superior.

Example - Bribing

It was reported that in 2007, Mexican families spent 8% of their income on bribing or $2.58 billion, an increase of more than 42% from 2006. The survey, conducted by the non-profit group Transparency International, showed that 197 million bribes were paid nationwide in 2007 compared to 115 million in 2005. Like a truck driver stated, "paying off the police is part of my cost of doing business".

Bribing and corruption are everywhere. Someone offers a benefit and someone accepts it; sometimes there are several intermediaries. While bribing happens in business, it more commonly occurs with government representatives, public officials, police, customs officers and people in positions of power or control.

The most common bribes are:

 ♦ to high-ranking politicians or political parties

 ♦ to junior officials or bureaucrats

 ♦ using personal or familial relationships to win public contracts

Bribes can be given to obtain a business contract or a building permit, to speed up processing of documentation or approvals, to eliminate paying fees, taxes, or customs duties and even to prevent being arrested or sentenced to a prison term. However, these are just a few examples because the range of possible bribes is very wide.

So let's see if you have been bribed or have bribed anyone. It is sometimes difficult to understand when a bribe is a bribe or when it is something else. Unfortunately, even if bribing is illegal in many countries, it is still part of doing business.

> *Example – Is this bribing*
>
> *When the young man takes his girlfriend to a nice restaurant, he wants to impress her and get a good table. He gives a maître d' some money, and gets the requested table. Bribing?*
>
> *You are attending a show in Las Vegas. The ticket cost $50 and the usher seats you far away from the stage. Next time you go to a show, you include $20 when you hand the usher your tickets. Now you sit so close to the stage that you can almost touch the people dancing. What did you call the cash you gave to the usher, a consulting fee or a bribe?*
>
> *It is election time in your country. A candidate campaigns on the promise that, "If you vote for me. I will ..." The politician buys your vote and bribes you with your own money! In some countries they promise benefits for poor people if they vote for them. They have bribed the poor by taking money from the rich.*

Do you still feel you have not been involved in bribing? Just continue reading, I am sure you will change your mind.

> *A purchasing manager for an important client has her 50th birthday. You really don't get along with her but despite that, you buy her a nice gift. Why?*

As you can see, it's not that easy to tell when you're crossing the line from a favour to a bribe. You have to understand how it works in a particular country and to adapt your business practices.

Example – Getting a seat on a fully booked flight

I was traveling in the Philippines and had a stopover on the island of Cebu on my way back to Manila. Our flight was delayed, and I was not going to make my meeting in Manila. I went to the airline ticket counter and asked if there was an earlier flight. There was one, but it was fully booked and 40 people were on the waiting list. I handed over my ticket folder with a five dollar bill inside. I asked the airline representative to contact me if there were any changes. After five minutes, there was an announcement, asking Mr. Holmvall to please come to the counter. I got my seat on the earlier flight. My five dollars was gone from the ticket folder. Do you still think a confirmed ticket would have guaranteed a seat on that flight?

When I asked our sales representative in Manila how much he paid in bribes, he said 50%." I get an amount from my manager to pay for favours. I pay the customer 50% and I keep the other 50% for myself."

Example – Speeding up customs procedure

Many years ago, a company I was working for, transferred a production manager to Brazil for four years. He was relocating with his wife and two small children and had to ship over their household furniture, clothing, toys, baby formula and diapers. The ship containing their goods left three weeks before the family did. The production manager had always said that he would never pay a bribe. A few days after arriving in São Paulo, he called and was very unhappy. He had just been told that clearing his container through customs would take three to four weeks. His wife and children were upset because they had no furniture, clothing or baby food. He said I had to do something, fast!

He called again three days later. This time, he was very happy because he had received the container so quickly. I asked him, "So, you don't believe in bribing? He said no, I don't. I said, "How do you think we could get this shipment cleared in two days?" He replied, "Well, I didn't pay it". I told him, "But you accepted that we did it, didn't you? Your contract states that the company has to pay your moving costs, including extraordinary expenses. Do you agree that getting your container through customs quickly was a justifiable expense for your family? He had to agree that now he could understand and accept that bribing was a fact of life.

How do you know what to do you in countries where bribing is part of day-to-day business? First of all, you have to understand how business works. If you have a local representative there, they are the ones who will know the written and unwritten rules as well as how to take care of them.

Here is another example. You show up at the front desk of a hotel in Mexico City. You have a confirmation number for a room reservation but the desk clerk can't find your name or your registration in their records. What do you do? It's your decision how badly you want the room. Are you ready to find another taxi and drive around in a strange town trying to find another room or should you just take out some cash and ask the clerk to look again for your name?

Usually, there is limited risk in offering money to staff in a hotel or restaurant for better service. In business, however, I suggest you refrain from doing it yourself, because offering a bribe may be a criminal offence in that country. If you think you will have to pay a bribe, be very careful and get expert advice in advance. Paying bribes can be very complicated and risky. On the other hand, if you want the business, you will have to find a way to play by the local rules without breaking the law.

Some examples from the media

"Company A group chairman Mr. X is expected to step down after a second round of questioning by an independent counsel investigating allegations of bribery at the consumer electronics giant, according to reports."

"Nine Arrested For Attempted Bribery Of Building Inspectors." Nine people were arrested Tuesday on charges of bribing New York City Department of Building inspectors.

Company Z Fires 20 Staff for Violation of Rules in China. Faced with allegations that it paid bribes to operate in China, the company has fired 20 Chinese employees.

So who are the least corrupt, according to Transparency International?

Corruption in the World
(perceived level of public-sector corruption out of 200 sovereign nations)

The ten least corrupt countries 2009 (points)			The ten worst corrupt countries 2009 (points)		
Rank	Country	Points	Rank	Country	Points
1	New Zealand	9.4	168	Haiti	1.8
2	Denmark	9.3	168	Iran	1.8
3	Singapore	9.2	168	Turkmen-istan	1.8
3	Sweden	9.2	174	Uzbekistan	1.7
5	Switzerland	9.0	175	Chad	1.6
6	Finland	8.9	176	Iraq	1.5
6	Netherlands	8.9	176	Sudan	1.5
8	Australia	8.7	178	Myanmar	1.4

So how do you know when someone wants a bribe? Remember the situation at the hotel check-in desk? Most likely, you would have realized what you had to do to get a hotel room for the night.

If you've done your advance research, you will have collected information about serious poverty, political unrest, ongoing hostilities with other countries, natural disasters or social and economic instability in the country. All of these factors can contribute to creating an environment where you will find corruption in the public and private sectors or a high tolerance for corrupt practices in government and business.

If you look at the lists developed by Transparency International, it won't be hard for you to guess what the expectations will be in a specific country. For example, Zimbabwe is listed as 146th out of 180, which means that corruption is perceived to be widespread. In some countries, you will be given a list of items that they want, for instance: three Mercedes, a big-screen television and home theatre system and a case of scotch whiskey. Check with other people who are doing business in the country, but be very careful and use common sense. If you are unsure about what to do, don't do it.

Example – Bribing or not?

Many years ago, I was involved in negotiations to supply heavy equipment for a large forestry harvesting project in Liberia. Many government ministers were involved. One of them repeatedly pointed out that the products available from our German competitor were much better. You can guess why this topic was brought up. However, in our case, we knew that the project was being financed by the World Bank. The deadline for signing the contract for equipment was the next day. My colleague and I excused ourselves from the negotiations and left the room. We had a brief discussion and when we returned, we stated that our companies were no longer interested in submitting a proposal to the Liberian government. Immediately, the attitude changed. Why? The client had no choice but to work with us. They had no one else to supply the equipment they needed before the contract deadline.

Example – Bribing or Salary?

I mentioned earlier that sometimes, a bribery payment forms part of a salary. We had sold several large wood processing machines for a project in Poland. Ten percent of the total payment had been withheld until the technical documentation was approved by the woman in charge. We tried a number of times to get her to sign off on the approval, but she refused.

Her boss suggested to me that we should invite her to visit our factory. We paid for her travel, her accommodations and all meals. At mid-day on the first day of her visit, we passed by a clothing store on the way to lunch at a restaurant near our offices. She said she wanted to look around. She tried on a coat and some dresses that she really liked. Of course, she didn't have any Western currency. We paid for the items she had selected.

When we returned to the office after lunch, she signed the papers right away. Was paying for her clothing a bribe? Yes, in our eyes it was a bribe. The reality was that her boss couldn't pay the salary she was worth, so we had to help out the boss, so that we could get the approval we needed to complete the last part of the contract.

If you read fiction or even the newspaper, you will have seen stories about large military contracts involving an agent or middleman who received large amounts of cash for services provided. You usually don't find out how much of that money stays in the agent's pocket and how much is paid out to other people. You can only guess.

Say you're dealing with a company in sub-Saharan Africa and you quote a price of $250,000 for an order of farm tools and equipment. The purchasing agent tells you that you will get the order, but only if you increase the quoted price to $300,000 and deposit $50,000 in a bank account in northern England. You are certain this as a bribe. However, in this case, it may not be. The buyer does not have access to money in western currency in his country. Every time they place an order, they have to put aside money for future travel or future purchases.

Reverse bribery - intimidation tactics

One of your competitors, a large international company, does not want you to enter a market they want to control. They will do anything to stop you. They contact a major trade magazine and tell them that if any positive articles are published about your product, they will not advertise any more. They are intimidating the publisher by threatening to withhold their business. Or they could say to a store owner or distributor that if they sell your competing product, they will no longer deliver to them.

As you have read, it is sometimes difficult to know when a gift or simple favour constitutes a bribe. Giving gifts is very common in many countries. Sometimes, it is the excessive value of a gift which takes it into the realm of a bribe. Two bottles of good quality wine would be a nice gift when you visit someone's home in the United Kingdom but two cases of expensive wine may be considered an unspoken request for favours. You have to know the local customs so that you can figure out what's appropriate. As a foreigner in another country, when it comes to bribing, you have to exercise caution. As mentioned before, if bribing is necessary, your local contact might be the person to ask or to take care of it.

Demands on an Exporter
and How It Influences the Company

Skill and experience

We have partly covered this topic in the chapter, *Why international business*. Here are some additional thoughts.

International business will certainly require more skill from your employees. This may mean additional in-house training and education or hiring staff with special business knowledge and skills.

"It is not going to be business as usual. There will be
changes and they have already started."
— Leif Holmvall, Export Pro Inc.

Company organization

Communications – early and often – are essential to keeping your employees informed and on side with what is going to happen. Issuing memos from senior management will not work. You have to be personally involved in the messages that go out about how the company is changing and how your staff will be included. If you present change in the right way and at the right times, opportunities for training, travel and new ways of doing business can be viewed as rewards for improved performance rather than something forced upon them.

Experience shows that staffing and organizational changes will, in the long run, be seen as positive. Quite often, you will encounter resistance to the new idea of exporting. Usually, you will find that individuals are afraid that they won't be able to cope, that they will lose their familiar position in the company or even lose their job. It is your job to reassure them, keep them informed and provide the training and education they need to succeed. If it happens that you have to let some staff go, be honest with them and generous in assisting them to find a new job.

"We live in a world with accelerating changes. If you
want to see tomorrow, you and your organisation have
to adapt to it in order to survive. You have to shake up
your organisation so you do not live in the past
or today but to survive the future."
— Leif Holmvall, Export Pro Inc.

Increased demands for service and support

The international marketplace will require that you deliver better service and/or a variety of easy to service products. Detailed service instructions will have to be produced in different languages. The further away from the foreign market you are, the more reliable your products will have to be, otherwise, your costs will increase and your reputation for quality will suffer

In the short term, you will have to invest in additional product development and production capacity as well as product marketing activities such as market surveys, travel, hospitality, printed matter, telephone and fax, websites and all the other add-ons necessary to introduce your product or service to new markets.

"After you've done a thing the same way for two years, look it over carefully. After five years, look at it with suspicion. And after ten years, throw it away and start all over."
— Alfred Edward Perlman, New York Times, 3 July 1958

Increased travel

Keeping your passports and travel documentation up to date will become routine over time. You cannot conduct international business sitting at home at your computer.

When I was starting out as a salesman, I was given a tie clip with the letters: YC-DBSOYA. Those letters don't make sense to you, do they? What they mean is this: **Y**ou **C**an't **D**o **B**usiness **S**itting **O**n **Y**our **A**ss. Crude, but very true! Get to know a friendly travel agent who regularly works with business travellers. If they deliver good service, use them all the time. They will value your business and work hard for you. You'll realize the value of this arrangement when you are stranded overseas and need a capable travel specialist close to home, to make alternate arrangements for you. Not every location you visit will have email access or the Internet, so you will have to rely on someone you can reach by telephone.

Personal contacts and relationship-building are critical parts of establishing yourself internationally. You also have to see, smell and hear what the new market is like, otherwise, you will be making business decisions without all the information you need. Through good planning and foresight, you can reduce travel costs, even for trips to be taken on short notice. There are regular charter flights to many destinations. They offer direct travel to your destination at a low fare, often with a hotel stay included.

Additional paperwork

International invoices are more specific than what you may be used to. Contracts, international transport documentation, information about country of origin, export and import papers, tax and customs forms are some of the paperwork that will be required. The exporting country will also ask for data for reports on export statistics. The additional paper handling will normally not cause any major problems. Your freight forwarder will be more than happy to help you with documentation as well as provide guidance on what you need to consider in preparing for international business.

Increased costs

Exporting "costs" money. It will take time before you get a return on your investments in going international. There will be longer period of time between invoicing and when you receive payment, either because you have to agree to extended credit terms or your financial transactions are more complex and time-consuming to process. You will read about potential solutions later in the book, in the chapter on Risk.

Company size doesn't limit potential to export

It does not matter if you are small or large, if you have 10 employees or 1,000. All companies can export, whether or not they have extensive resources and specialized personnel. The distances internal communications have to travel in these large companies can be very long and sometimes become difficult. For that reason, it may be harder to ensure that everyone in the company understands what has to happen before exporting can succeed.

A smaller company will likely have shorter lines of communication and a more efficient decision-making process. It is easier to share information that helps staff understand what is required of them. In other words, the smaller company often has better potential for export, but they are frequently more dependent on external experts for help with freight, customs duties, legal questions and culture.

What do you have to do to be successful? First of all, you must have an open mind and be willing to learn how to do business in new ways, in foreign markets. Take the time to learn about, understand and respect the differences you will encounter. You have to be prepared to commit yourself and your company to the challenge of international business. It will not always be easy to learn, mistakes will be made and things will go wrong. Next, you have to maintain a positive attitude towards change, meeting new people and having new experiences with different cultures. Learn to have patience, because your international business will develop over time. Export activities are a long term investment. Remember that your staff and business associates will be watching how you behave – they will take their cues from you, whether they are positive or negative. Communications and relationships are equally important at home and overseas.

In the end, profitability will be proportional to the energy, planning and the commitment you put into your export activities. Working in a global market cannot be a marginal or part-time activity. By working internationally, with the dedication of everyone involved, your company will grow stronger. Don't forget that while change and growth can be seen as intimidating, achieving success is stimulating.

We live in a time of accelerating change. Those who believe they can survive by staying only in a domestic market will one day wake up to a major surprise, because they will have been left behind by those with the courage and foresight to plan for the future. Those who decide to market products and services internationally will be much better positioned. As an exporter, you have a challenging, but very fascinating career ahead.

Exercise and Additional Information

It is time for you to practice what you have learned.

Select four countries you would like to do business with. Contact several business or trade organisations and obtain more information. If you are serious about working with those countries, go to the library and borrow videos or books on the topic. Buy some books on specific countries and cultures. Search Google for "business culture" and "Doing business in" plus the name of the country. You can use key words like "shake hands" for specific topics and do the same search on websites like Amazon, Barnes and Noble or Chapters Indigo.

Contact the embassy for each country or your Trade Commissioner in that country to ask them for material. Banks and chartered accountants normally have handbooks on "How to do business in ......". Ask them for a copy.

Contact your lawyer, if you have one or search on the websites of lawyers specializing in international business. They may have a partner in the country you are interested in and perhaps there is a handbook on doing business there. These publications are normally aimed more towards legal issues like starting a business, taxes, etc.

Contact associations in your country like the Chinese-American Chamber of Commerce. If you intend on doing business in the country, consider joining a professional association.

Based on the information you obtained:

1. Which markets can you consider for an international business project?

2. What do you have to do to adapt to those markets?
    a. Products/services
    b. Sales and marketing
    c. Your own organisation

3.   Make a list and prioritize the countries you could enter, based on an assessment of your company's resources.

4. Make a first draft of a business plan for entering the new overseas market. You can revise it as you read through the book and learn more.

Resources

Language, culture, doing business

http://audiovideo.economist.com - Go to "Doing business in...."There are videos on doing business in different countries

http://www.businessculture.com - Information on doing business in different countries

http://www.worldbusinessculture.com - Information on doing business in different countries

Japanese culture www.culturebank.com-jpntoc.html

www.languageculture.com

www.iorworld.com - Deals mainly with culture

Search Google "culture in business" and you can add the country you are looking for. Also search on "gift giving", "foreign cultures", "food and other cultures", "eating traditions"

http://www.cyborlink.com/besite/international_gift_giving.htm - Gift giving

http://www.4hb.com/0113intergift.html - Gift giving

Search Google for "gift giving in business"

http://en.wikipedia.org/wiki/ - "Bribery"

http://www.allbusiness.com/human-resources/employee-development-employee-ethics/686469-1.html bribery

www.tranparency.org – "Bribing", "corruption"

Later on in this book, I will provide you with more detailed guidance about how to select your market and find the right information.

"It is not business as usual. There is no off-season anymore. There will be changes and they have already started. Are you ready? You are not safe at home unless you can compete abroad."

Finding the Right Information, Selecting Markets and Partners

This chapter will show you how to:

- ♦ **Find the information you need**
- ♦ **Select the right market**
- ♦ **Find your customers**
- ♦ **Locate the right foreign partners**
- ♦ **Complete advanced market research**

The objective of market research is to collect relevant written and statistical information that can be analyzed and then used when you make business decisions.

The most common difficulty that companies expanding globally encounter is a lack of information about markets and ongoing changes. If you are a company executive driving a car with a wind screen you can't see through and your director of finance is looking in the rear-view mirror, what will happen? You're going to crash. The same thing happens in business – when you don't have a clear view of what is ahead of you and your management team doesn't anticipate what's coming, your company will fail.

In this chapter, I will show you how to obtain the information you need, step-by-step. Some you should collect yourself, some you can get free of cost from others, and for some, you will require assistance.

> *"You don't skate to where the puck is.*
> *You skate to where the puck is going to be."*
> *— Wayne Gretzky,*
> *famous Canadian hockey player and coach*

Get your mind into Market Research (using a Mental Approach)

Selling on the international market scene requires a lot of information. Those who are best informed have the best likelihood of succeeding. Even so, many companies still fail. How come? It is not only the facts that count. There is usually one significant ingredient missing.

When we begin, we collect a lot of information about the market including prices, competition and distributor margins. We find the right distributor. Despite this, things don't work out as planned. We blame the distributor for not performing. When we ask why they aren't meeting sales targets, they say that the prices and products are not right, even though we know this is not so. We don't understand why our plans failed. We've done all our homework, haven't we?

What is wrong?

We did not develop a "feel" for the market. Many companies rely on information and facts that other people have collected and they base their strategies on that information. They assume a lot but don't "get to know" the market.

How do we solve this?

We need to develop an understanding of how the market works. We need to "touch", "feel", "taste" and "hear". We have to get our mind to understand it is not like at home. The temperature is different, people dress differently and act differently and things look different. By reading a report you can not get that feeling, you have to go and visit to get the real feel for it. So, if we plan to enter a market, before even collecting too much information, pay a trip to the country and get "the feeling" of the market. Start 6-12 months before the planned start-up and pay a number of visits to the end-users. This will give you a better feeling for the market and the way they do business there. It will furthermore indicate if your product fits the market, what you need to adapt. You will also get information about competition, prices as well as suitable distributors. If you can coordinate your trip with an exhibition you can also walk around and "inhale" the feeling of how products are sold and exposed. Bring a camera so you can show your staff how the new market looks like, when you come home.

With all this as a base you can add the "facts" to decide on how to enter the market. In this case you have already made your intellectual and mind adjustment and will not fail in your efforts due to lack of understanding of the market. It firstly when the company can see the advantages it can decide where and how to enter the international market.

What is the difference between Market Information and Business Intelligence? Market information is data you collect from the market – consumer surveys, sales figures, etc. Business Intelligence is the collection <u>and</u> analysis of market information, so that a company can make informed business decisions and convert those decisions into action. You collect and organize the data; you analyze and understand what it means to you. You create a strategy based on that.

Two shoe salesmen visiting a remote African village look at the information they have collected in two different ways:

Nobody wears shoes here. There is no market.

Nobody wears shoes here. There is a great potential for sales and no competition.

Why Does Introduction of a New Product on a New Market Fail?

♦ Inadequate planning and preparation. The company had no plan and no commitment from management.

♦ There is no marketing strategy. The company goes after every potential seller or they go into business with anyone who wants to sell their product, despite the importance of the market. They accept any distributors who contact them without doing background research into their suitability.

♦ They use insufficient, outdated or unreliable information when they plan.

♦ They do not consider their overseas partner as part of their organization.

♦ They are not willing to adapt.

♦ They fail to do the necessary mental preparation.

"640 K should be enough for everybody."
— Bill Gates, 1982

Why Do Some Companies Succeed?

Successful companies:

♦   Research and develop an in-depth understanding of the market

♦   Visit the market, learn how to do business there through hands-on involvement and confirm that their product/service is right for the market

♦   Take the time to complete advance preparations and make an organizational commitment

♦   Select qualified, competent partners and invest in activating them

♦   Adapt prices and sales materials to the local market.

♦   Communicate with, educate and train their own staff

Market Information and How To Find It

Is market analysis complicated? Successful market analysis is really a question of common sense.

There is a tendency to collect a lot of information, but only a limited amount is relevant and necessary. Eighty-five percent of success in international business is based on understanding other cultures and the way business is conducted in the marketplace, whether it is local or foreign. Remember to include this as part in your research.

Practical Market Research

♦   Conduct your own searches

♦   Use internal resources and expertise

♦   Use external resources

♦   Search the web for information

♦   Use books, trade magazines and continuous media collection. Many periodical magazines produce their own research that is available free or at low cost.

♦   Buy "off-the-shelf" information or custom-made reports.

"If you don't take the time to roll up your sleeves,
you will be caught with your pants down."
— Leif Holmvall, Export Pro Inc.

What you need to do?

♦   What goals do I have?

♦   Identify the business objectives you want to achieve. Research shows that people who write down their goals are, on average, 10 times more successful than those who don't. What do you want achieve by expanding the market. Set up your main goals as well as sub goals, like increasing total sales with 20% per year, spreading risks over at least five markets and/or allowing increased higher R&D costs.

♦   Which are the foreign markets where you can meet those goals? Are distributors and consumers permitted to buy your product/service? Does your country allow you to export your product/service to those markets?

♦   What is the timeframe for your exporting? Are you considering a long term or short term approach?

If you don't have the answers to these basic questions, you won't be able to survey the market properly.

"If you don't know where you are going
any road will take you there."
— Lewis Carroll, Alice in Wonderland

Checklist:

♦   List the kinds of information you need before entering the new market.

♦   Review the list you made and identify which of the items are the most important to your business plans. Now, you can narrow the scope of your search. Research the higher priority questions that you must have answers to. **Limit your search to essential information. Focus, otherwise you will drown in information you won't know how to use.**

♦   When asking for information, use "open" questions such as "Can you tell me what rules there are about importing clothing?" or "What do I need to know to be successful in this market?" This type of questioning will encourage more descriptive answers. Be careful not to use the journalistic approach which is more closed and assertive, because you may not get the answers you need.

♦   Make it personal and use direct contacts by telephone or visits. E-mail and letters do not work – how often do you answer inquiries from people you don't know?

- ♦ To encourage others to assist you, use an approach like this one: "I know you are one of the leading companies in this field. I'd appreciate if you could help me with your advice. "

- ♦ Is there a market for your product/service? Is your product up to date or too advanced for the market? If the latter, sell "old" products, equipment or services to take advantage of the R&D you have already written off for those products.

- ♦ Is the market growing? If the market is for 5000 units a year and you can only supply 500 units, the market size is more than enough..

- ♦ Who are the key clients?

- ♦ What are your resources, e.g., what can your company handle?

- ♦ Contact end users as well as distributors. How is business conducted? If you can't sell your product, it will be tough for the distributor to do business.

"Marketing is very similar to military strategy. If you have limited resources, don't spread yourself too thin by trying to cover too many countries."

Different Ways to Obtain Information

1. Visit the market

    a. One hour with a customer is worth more than 100 spent at your desk.

    b. The feeling you get is important, so confirm that what you expected is correct.

2. Interview people to obtain answers to your questions

    a. Investigate how business is conducted in the foreign country.

    b. Find out about special rules for standards, labelling, language, etc.

    c. Is your product/service right for the market? What is the appropriate price level? Who is your competition? Are they local or overseas?

3. Study reports and industry and trade literature as well as magazines and newspapers.

    a. There are numerous print and online reports available on specific products and geographical areas, either for free or to purchase. (See later in this chapter.)

b. Many trade magazines include descriptions of the specific industry they write about. They usually also include lists of distributors and suppliers in that field. This could be useful when you want to learn more about an industry or when you want to select a local partner. Look also at the advertising - how are products sold and promoted?

c. The business section of local newspapers very often describes specific industries and long term forecasts.

4. Employ someone who already has the information you need

a. For a company entering an export market it is normally less expensive to hire someone with international business experience. Even better, you may be able to recruit someone with experience and who can speak the language of the specific country you are interested in. You can either hire someone on a temporary or contract basis to get you started or for special projects or you could hire someone with the skills and experience you need, on a permanent basis.

b. Use qualified external consultants. This could help accelerate your entrance into the new market.

c. To research a foreign market, you could contract with someone already living there who has useful local contacts and knowledge of your specific industry. However, you still have to visit the country to gain an understanding of local business.

5. Analyze the competition

a. Examine the competition. What can you offer that they cannot? Don't select the home market of your strongest competitor as your first overseas market. They will be operating from a position of strength and will do anything to keep you out.

6. Utilize trade statistics

a. There are official production statistics available for products and for each market. If you sell pulp and paper processing equipment, you can obtain data on manufacturing volumes for the industry as well as development forecasts for the market. You can also find price levels, by type of machinery.

b. You can obtain statistics on imports of processing machinery that tell you which areas/countries the imports are coming from. (See later in this chapter - on Databases)

7. Collect information from industry associations

    a. If you are selling food products, for example, contact your domestic association and ask them for referrals to associations and companies in the country you want to export to.

    b. Contact associations for food products or food suppliers in the overseas country.

    c. You can also contact associations representing food service dealers, food distributors or grocery stores in the country you plan to export to.

8. Visit your local public library to research what information is available about a specific market, industry or country.

9. Buy reports on a specific product and market from companies with a presence on the Internet.

    a. There are companies that sell prepared reports. If you search for "energy drinks + reports + France", you will get results on specific products as well as market research available.

    b. Here are some examples of online market research companies

    www.marketresearch.com

    www.researchandmarkets.com/reports/256811

    www.reportlinker.com

    www.euromonitor.com

    www.frost.com/prod/servlet/frost-home.pag

    www.datamonitor.com

    http://research.thomsonib.com

    www.marketresearchworld.net

10. Obtain information from the trade press

    a. Contact the publisher of a specialist publication that focuses on particular industries or a business sector and ask to interview them and receive reports and articles on your industry and for your specific interest. They are normally interesting in you as you are a potential advertiser.

    b. Many publications or product brands produce buyers' guides that include information about the market, manufacturers, distributors, suppliers, etc.

11. Attend industry trade shows and conferences

   a. At first, you will only **visit** trade shows and conferences. You are not yet ready to exhibit until you have completed your market assessments. If you exhibit too soon, you will alert your competition to your existence and create a market demand you can't yet meet.

   b. You will be able to observe the variety of products available and how companies are promoting products/services similar to yours. Act like a potential buyer and interview your competition. Check pricing so you can compare theirs with yours. (You will find more information below about how to interview).

   c. When you attend a conference, there will be speakers making presentations on markets, products, new technologies, suppliers, etc. You can network or mingle during coffee breaks, luncheons, dinners and cocktail parties and use those opportunities to ask questions of attendees and speakers.

12. Credit checks

   a. Obtain credit history reports on the financial status of your potential partners. In addition to important credit information, you will get more detailed background on the company and their clients. More information is provided in the second part of this chapter.

   b. Use commercial databases (See Part Two of this chapter.)

"Analyzing today's business situation is like reading a history book. To be successful, you have to study the future."

Selecting Your New Market

How do you decide on a market? When you have several choices, which market should you select? How would you know if the product suits the market? Some markets are not too complex to enter, don't have too many restrictions and are not too culturally different.

Here are some questions for you to consider:

 ♦ Which markets could help you meet your business goals?

 ♦ How would you find the right markets?

 ♦ Do you want to expand into five new markets within 10 years or one market over a period of two years?

 ♦ Do you want to find a new market with excellent growth opportunities?

K. HORNE

♦ Are you considering a long-term or short term approach to get the results you want?

♦ Are you willing to invest a little more to develop markets that may take longer to enter but that have much better growth potential?

♦ Are you willing to work in rapidly-expanding markets that take more time and preparation to enter?

Analyze your company before starting

Be honest about your resources – financial, production current and future, staff, time, knowledge and skills.

Will you have or be able to develop the right products/services and adapt them?

How much can you realistically accomplish? Remember also that you have to design new sales material. It normally takes twice as much money and time as you expected. Eliminate those markets that take too long time or are too complicated. Can we take on the extra workload? You will need more resources not only in marketing but also in production, research and development, and service.

Are you only targeting a niche market such as wealthy retired people, women who speak French, young vegetarians or Buddhists? Target group information is easily found in government statistical and census reports. You can also purchase research reports from commercial companies. Concentrate on countries or geographical areas that have sufficient numbers of people in your selected target market. The same applies to industries that may only be situated in certain areas, like mining exploration and ore processing, pulp and paper manufacturing or wine producers. If you export baby diapers, you would start with statistics on the number of children born every year and compare that data with your own country. Be aware, though, that diaper use can vary between countries, based on what kinds of products are used (none vs. cloth vs. disposable) or for how long (6 months, 1 year, two years). You can't just make a simple comparison using the number of births and expect to extrapolate the figures and arrive at an accurate projection. Check what the customs or practices are in that country.

Develop a detailed market profile for each country or distribution area. This will allow you to sort "the wheat from the chaff" and decide on the best possible choice.

The elimination approach

Start by assessing all of the markets that could be of interest.

Eliminate those that:

  o Do not have market demand, sufficient population or growth potential.

  o Would take too much time to develop or cost too much to enter.

  o You don't have the resources for or the market is too complex .

When you have made your short list, identify the pros and cons for each of the possible selections.

An example – Mining equipment

You are a German manufacturer of mining equipment. Many countries could use mining equipment, so that does not help narrow your choice. However, your equipment is intended for use in coal mines. With this information, you can eliminate many markets. Furthermore, since your equipment only works in underground mines, you can now eliminate countries that only have open pit or surface mining operations.

Let's say your final list includes Australia, China, England, India, Indonesia, Kazakhstan, Russia, Ukraine and South Africa.

You remove Kazakhstan, Russia and Ukraine from the list because of potential political risks and the complexity of doing business in those countries.

Your mining equipment is technologically advanced. Based on your early research, you decide that at this time, Indonesia does not have the required skilled operators or trained service staff. In addition, they are not prepared to pay a premium price for your equipment.

You divide the remaining countries on your list into two groups.

  1. Australia, England and South Africa. Those markets are political stable, there is a well established industry and they are familiar with high tech equipment. Those are the key markets to enter now.

  2. China, the largest coal mining market in the world, is too large for you to handle at this time. It will take considerable planning and resources to

enter this market. Your technology is too advanced for Chinese operator skills and knowledge at this time. You would need a joint venture partner there and you would be required to manufacture the equipment in China. It is definitely a market to consider for the future. India is similar to China, although not as large and more open to adopting new technologies. Will it also be a future market? Only more research will answer that question for you.

As you can see, we have now reduced the entire world as a potential market to three high priority markets and two long-term markets that will require more intensive development activities. Now you understand how to select market options for yourself, analyze the pros and cons of a key market and identify where you want to start, based in reliable, relevant information. Complete a chart like the one below to see the pros and cons for each market.

Coal Mining Equipment in Great Britain

Pros	Cons
Market geographically close and culturally similar	Tough local competition from established companies
Currency stable against the Euro	A mature market that will not expand but which has the potential to shrink
Low freight costs	Growing environmental regulations
Easy access for after-sales service	

Complete the same analysis for Australia and South Africa.

Do you think this looks easy? Yes it is, although perhaps not as easy as illustrated in the example. Even with more complex issues to be decided, a common sense approach will help you select the right markets.

If you are a mining equipment manufacturer and you belong to a mining association in your country, the association can help you to find detailed information about the mining industry around the world. They also have associates in many countries. Search Google for "Coal mining underground". From there, you can research general information about the industry.

Summary:

Make the first analysis of a broad range of markets and prioritize as above. Then analyze each individual market and its opportunities, pros and cons. Are the markets you want to enter expanding and can you handle them? If your domestic market today is France, perhaps it would be easier to expand within the European

Union, using the customs free market with shorter distances. Many countries would use the same currency as yours, EURO. However, it is a stagnating market. At some time in the future you will have to look at the expanding Asian or Latin American market.

How could market changes influence you? - Although China, India and Brazil are developing markets, in order to compete they need to improve infrastructure such as trains, airports, highways, phone system, and environmental controls. China must train 2200 airline pilots per year or 40,000 pilots by the year 2025, a potential market for a company making flight simulators.

> *"Knowledge is one of the few assets that multiplies when shared."*

Obtaining country information

The internet is a very effective tool. You can find a wealth of information, with a properly worded search. At the end of this book, I have listed many helpful websites. We will also keep our website, www.exportpro.com, updated with lists of useful resources.

For now, try looking at www.cia.gov/library/publications/the-world-factbook, which provides detailed information for each country and industry.

You can also find country briefings at http://www.economist.com/countries.

For statistics on the European Union, go to the website for the database, Eurostat at http://epp.eurostat.ec.europa.eu/portal/page/portal/eurostat/home. The website called the Gateway to the European Union, http://europa.eu, contains information about the EU, work, business and education, policies, media and official documents, presented in a variety of languages.

If you are looking for specific information about an industry in a country, visit that country's website or search for topics such as "mining association England". You will find results for over 290,000 web sites like http://www.abmec.org.uk and http://www.mauk.org.uk.

Official Statistics and General Information

Every country maintains a website which has useful information and resources about industry, trade, etc. Two web sites for Canada are http://www.dfait-maeci.gc.ca or http://canada.gc.ca/home.html. If you can't find the information you need, contact the country's appropriate government representative.

Contact your local bank branch. Almost certainly, they will have produced a handbook containing information for the most important trading countries. Airline representatives and travel agents can help link you with clients who do business in a specific country.

If you use any of the major accounting or legal firms they will have partners overseas. They likely have handbooks for clients, describing how to do business in various countries or sectors. I did a search on Google for "doing business in China" and found a large number of handbooks, including some produced by the World Bank and various consulting companies. Look at the website http://www.doing-business.org for a variety of information.

If you are member of international service organizations such as Rotary, Lions Club, etc. they will probably have a chapter or club in the market you are interested in. Attend the weekly or bi-weekly events to network and use that networking to seek out information and business contacts. In some countries, churches and religious organizations are good networking sources.

Many countries assign **trade commissioners** to posts in foreign countries. They are professional business consultants. Contact them. Some are knowledgeable but unfortunately, they are not always helpful. Some trade commissioners' charge for their services. They are normally more professional as they have to compete with private consultants. It is worth it to pay their fee, make sure you check their references.

The United States has a fee-based service called Gold Key Service, operated by the US Department of Commerce for American companies. I recommend it. The US has foreign embassies in most countries around the world. They provide market research, arrange appointments with pre-screened potential clients and advise on customs matters and regulations. You can find basic information at: www.export.gov/salesandmarketing/eg_main_018195.asp.

For example, the website with information about Saudi Arabia at

http://www.buyusa.gov/saudiarabia/en/31.html contains background in trade missions, doing business there, promoting products, finding business partners, events of interest, links and more details about other business-related services supplied.

> ## *"The future that we study and plan for begins today."*
> ## *— Chester O. Fischer*

Most foreign countries will have **Trade Commissioners, Consulates and Embassies** in your country. Contact them or even better, arrange a meeting.

There are many trade organizations and **Chambers of Commerce** that support culture and trade between countries, e.g., the Spanish Chamber of Commerce in Hong Kong and the Japanese Chamber of Commerce in Melbourne, Australia. When I searched for organizations in South Africa, I found 17 foreign chambers of commerce. I'm sure there are more. They normally have members who are nationals from a specific country. Contact them because they can give you access to useful contacts and advice.

If you're planning a long term business venture in the country, join a professional organization because then you will be part of is an established network. The website for the Japanese External Trade Organization (JETRO), http://www.jetro.go.jp has information about Japan as well as comparisons between Japan and specific countries, industry market reports, information on standards and regulations and trade and investment statistics. JETRO has offices on every continent. Read their reports and statistics online but even better, find a local office and pay them a visit.

Most large companies conduct business overseas and many maintain subsidiary offices overseas. Contact them, because they can help you with country-specific information. Also, speak with your freight forwarder and ask if they can give you a list of companies that do business in the country you are interested in.

Look in the phone directory under the country name. When I looked in the Toronto telephone book I found 16 companies under "Spanish", 42 with the word "Japan or Japanese" in their names and 12 under "Australia". Even if not all of them can help, some of them will be useful resources.

Regulations, taxes, and duties

The easiest way to find out about import regulations, taxes and duties and whether you need a permit to export to a foreign market is to contact your freight forwarder. They know the relevant rules. If they don't maintain offices overseas, they likely have a partner who can give you the details.

Finding a Foreign Representative

Unfortunately, many companies stumble upon foreign partners by accident. They accept whoever contacts them without completing a proper evaluation.

When you start looking for a life partner or spouse, you don't marry the first one you meet in a bar. You probably wouldn't spend your life with someone who has just contacted you by phone or email. You take your time, get to know them and find out about their background, then you can begin the decision-making process.

Your foreign associate should be a lifetime business partner. You have to ensure that you select them just as carefully. You'll want a partner who shares your approach to business and who can give you credibility. Of course, you can try to set up your overseas business the same way as at home, but that won't work. You have to identify the end user of your product/service in the foreign country. What is important for them and where they do they want to buy?

Example - Children's clothing New York

You want to sell children's clothing in New York. How do you select a distributor? You would bring samples of the type of clothing you want to sell, to New York. You could visit a place like Central Park, where mothers and nannies with small children congregate. Show their clothing samples. Ask them if they like the products, any special features they are looking for, what they are willing to pay and where they would like to buy the clothing. They will give you the name of the stores they go to and prefer to use. Now, you have an indication which stores could be potential dealers.

Visit those stores. Tell them that you have showed your products and interviewed a number of families who showed a great interest. One of the stores they suggested is the one you are visiting. Hopefully, the manager or owner will want more information. Ask how they would prefer to buy, such as directly from you or via an agent or distributor. If they want to purchase from distributors or work with an agent, which ones?

You now have a list of suitable partners who could import your product. Contact them. Tell them you have investigated the market and prices and that some clients have suggested them as one of the store locations or distributors to buy from. Make sure they understand they are "one of" a number of potential partners, so they know they have competition.

It requires some preparatory work, but you will find out if your products are of interest to the market, what consumers are prepared to pay and suitable distribution channels

You're thinking maybe it's easy for clothing products, but you want to sell software to computer game developers. The same procedure would work. Do your research, make a list then contact several game designers. Talk about your product features. Ask if you could demonstrate your program and give them a hands-on experience. How would they like to buy it?

It's all about applying common sense principles to your decision making. You start with the end-user (consumer, buyer, etc.) and work backwards to the starting point, which is yourself. Sometimes you will have to use a variety of distribution channels, depending on what you discover about the end user. For more detail about this process, review the examples in the Distribution chapter.

Example – Automotive service products

You are selling lubrication equipment to service facilities specializing in automobiles, e.g. dealers for different car manufacturers. The service stations use similar equipment: hydraulic lifts, wheel balancers, brake and air conditioning repair equipment, service tools, etc.

Start by finding out what dealers or distributors those service centres use. You could contact the manufacturer of wheel balancers, ask what distributor they use and if they would recommend them. That way, you have the name of an established distributor plus a referral. Distributors are usually looking for items that expand their product range and give them another opportunity to visit their customers. Don't forget the basic question! Ask the service centre manager which companies they would prefer to buy from.

If you select the right partner, you will have a good foundation for building your successful international business. If you select the wrong distributor, it could lead to poor sales and a negative image for your company and your product. Take the time to plan and research.

It's not the product/service that determines success:

- ♦ You have to convince the customer to buy the product by:
  - ○ Giving them what they want to buy
  - ○ Supplying it through a distribution channel the customer prefers

- ♦ Your local representative must be:
  - ○ Convinced about the benefits of selling your product/service
  - ○ Able to identify existing and new market opportunities
  - ○ Organized and able to make money
  - ○ Able to recognize that you will be a good partner

- ♦ You have to adapt your product, your market approach and sales techniques

- ♦ It is up to you to determine, in advance, and convince the client:
  - ○ That there is a market
  - ○ Who the customers are and what their decision-making process is
  - ○ That you can supply the promotional "tools" to encourage customers and decision-makers to buy
  - ○ That you can supply materials that persuade them to actively represent your product/service

- o How you can provide their sales people, service representatives, etc. with the tools and incentives needed to
- o That you can supply the product/services on time, at the right quality and price
- o You can build on your track record

You have to have a "hungry" distributor, someone who is eager to sell your products/service. You also have to activate them and provide them with consistent support and up-to-date information. After sales service is just as important as the initial selling!

Checklist: Foreign Partner

- ♦ Personally contact the business and check all personal references you received
- ♦ Contact existing suppliers to find out about their working relationships, how they handle difficulties or conflict
- ♦ Contact existing clients and ask about the quality and timeliness of service, follow-up
- ♦ Check the structure of ownership, so that you have a better idea what will happen if the company is sold
- ♦ Examine the turnover rate of staff, key reasons why they are leaving and where they are going. How long have the employees remained with the company you are considering partnering with?
- ♦ Get a financial credit history report through a credit bureau
- ♦ Request that the company provide you with a reference letter from their banks, which includes their approved credit level and describes how it has been used.
- ♦ Visit the company's headquarters and branch offices
- ♦ Meet with sales staff and service staff and get a "feel" for how the company operates. Are they positive?
- ♦ Assess the technological level of the products they are selling today. Are they consistent with your products or do they have to be a changed?
- ♦ Is the company selling systems (products and services or even turn key projects) or individual products?
- ♦ Who is delivering their customer and warranty service and how after sales service is delivered?
- ♦ Is it a large or small organization? Does their organization correspond to yours in size or is it a Goliath and David situation?

- ◆ What are their overhead cost levels today, such as for administration, management, etc. - This will influence if they can make enough money selling your products/services.

- ◆ Who are the company's end users/customers? – Do they fit your products/ services?

- ◆ Are management and staff open to new ideas or are they conservative and set in their ways?

- ◆ Are the products/services sold through personal selling using own sales force, dealers or with a catalogue?

- ◆ Who is your contact person? Who is the decision-maker? Are they one and the same?

- ◆ What is their geographical coverage?

- ◆ What kind of customer groups do they deal with today?

- ◆ Ask your potential distributors to prepare a draft marketing plan. How do they plan to introduce the product if they got your business? What sales levels are they expecting and what back-up or support would they need?

"Your survival depends not so much on what happens to you, but how you handle what happens. That is up to you."

Prices and Discounts

If you don't know what you can sell a product for in a particular area, what the distribution margins are and the discounts customarily given, you won't know if you can compete or make money.

There are a number of ways to find out about prices. As mentioned before, when you are interviewing clients, ask what they are willing to pay and the level of discounts they normally receive. For products that are sold in retail stores, it is easy to visit and find out how products are priced. I usually call or have someone else call the competitors about their pricing. If you say that you are a consultant working for a client, you may be surprised at how hungry the salesmen are and the amount of information they can provide.

With respect to distributor discounts, you can ask the distributors themselves as well as the appropriate trade associations.

Using interviews for data collection

The best way to gather direct information is to interview people. However, it is important for you to be selective about what questions you ask, who you ask and the way you conduct interviews. There is a right way and a wrong way.

Develop a list of possible questions that are relevant to your product and market. Print out the questions to help you keep the interview on track. Bring along a pen and paper to write down what you hear. Alternatively, if you are conducting a telephone interview or even when face-to-face, ask if it is ok for you to use a voice recorder so that you don't need to slow down the interview. People almost always will give you permission.

You should start by explaining why you are asking the questions and what you hope to find out. This is called framing or "opening the door" to the interview. Next, ask open questions using phrases like, "tell me about" and do not guide their answers in any way. What is the market for this product? How is distribution done? What is important to clients?

Let the person being interviewed give you their answers. Don't ask for clarification yet. Remember that your body language may give the person clues about the kind of answers you want, so remain neutral in your expression and choice of words.

Once they have answered a question, you can probe or ask for more details so that you collect as much information as possible about the reasons and emotions behind the answers. Then, to confirm that you understood, you can ask closed or "yes or no" questions.

Example - Conducting interviews

One of my staff members had problems getting answers from company staff when calling them on the telephone. Normally, people would hang up on her. On the other hand, I had not encountered any trouble. What was the difference?

She would start the conversation by saying, "My name is Anna and I am calling from Holmvall International Trading Inc. We have a new product."

The person she was talking with thought Anna was another salesperson making a cold call. I used a different approach. I would say, "My name is Leif, from Holmvall International Trading Inc. I know you are the market leader in the construction machinery industry and I would like your advice. I don't want to sell anything. I need your help to understand your industry and products. Can I have five minutes of your time?"

This approach was usually successful. If I wasn't able to talk to them right away, it was because the person was too busy. They'd usually ask me to call back or they referred me to someone else. In that case, I would call the person and tell them who had suggested I contact them. I would then tell them the reason for my call, using a similar script as with the first contact.

Living in Canada and needing to research the Canadian market, there were many times when I would call the competition and ask to speak with a salesperson. I would tell them I needed information to assist my clients in making their decision on future purchases. I asked the salesperson to describe their products, which he or she was happy to do. Was there a market for those products and could they share sales figures with me. What about the competition? Could they send leaflets and a price list? Sales people love to brag and they don't usually check to determine if you really are a potential client. This is one advantage of using someone locally to assist you in collecting market information.

Before you begin your first interview, practice on someone such as a customer or end user or one of your staff who does not have a role in the decision-making process. That way, there is less of a problem if you make a mistake. This pre-testing also provides an opportunity for you to refine your questions or identify additional questions to ask during the actual interviews.

Some typical questions to ask when interviewing an end user:

- What is important for you to know about the product? What features are important?
- Who decides on the purchase
- Where they would prefer to buy the product
- What the normal distribution patterns are in the country
- The price levels and discounts usually applied
- Who the competition is and where they are located
- Are there any special rules or regulations for the product, approvals, etc?
- Can the company provide you with any suggestions on how to proceed in the market?

"I have traveled the length and breadth of this country and talked with the best people, and I can assure you that data processing is a fad that won't last out the year."
— The editor in charge of business books
for Prentice Hall, 1957

Additional topics

Ask your government trade representative and freight forwarder if there are other restrictions.

- Are you allowed to export your product to the country you have selected?
- Is the country allowed to import your product, such as military and equipment or used machinery?

Once you've collected the information, you can complete a variety of market analyses.

Example - Up to date market information

A tire manufacturer in Finland subscribed to weather forecasts for different regions in the country. When there was a high probability for a heavy snowfall the next day, they placed an advertisement in local media for winter tires. When a vehicle owner picked up their newspaper in the middle of a snowstorm, the first thing they saw was an advertisement for winter tires.

Example - Weather forecast for production

Ice-cream, soda pop and beer producers also use weather forecasts when planning their production. When hot weather is predicted, they know that beverage consumption rises and they increase production accordingly.

Telephones for market information

Rural farmers in India rely on SMS messages to their cell phones to help them to know which market is offering the best prices for their produce.

> *"You miss 100% of the shots you never take."*
> *— Wayne Gretsky, Hockey Star*

Does market research sounds easy? It is, when you take a common sense approach. However sometimes your research indicates there is no market. What do you do then? If there is no market or you can't make a profit, you saved a lot of money buy not entering the market. You will sometimes find the product is too advanced. In that case you will have to wait few years.

If you can't generate enough profits, perhaps you can change your sales plan for your product/service. As you will learn in the Distribution and Pricing chapters, by changing your distribution solution you can change something not profitable to something very profitable. You will find different solutions in every chapter that can make a low interest market to a priority market or a market without profitability to a very profitable solution. Therefore after reading all chapters in the book, go back and revaluate the information you obtained in this chapter and the solution at that time. – If it still does not work, don't enter the market.

> *"No person is so dim-witted that they can't give another person advice, and nobody is so brilliant that they don't make mistakes when they only rely on their own knowledge. The person who chooses only to learn from himself has a fool as a teacher."*
> *— Leif Holmvall, Export Pro Inc.*

Summary

- ◆ Because you have been successful in one country does not guarantee that you will be successful on the next one

- ◆ Most failures are based on:

  - ◆ Inadequate preparations
  - ◆ Too little information about the market
  - ◆ Selecting the wrong market
  - ◆ Limited understanding of how to do business there.

- ◆ It is not the company with the best product or service that succeeds; it is the company that best understands their customers

- ◆ Seek out appropriate market information

- ◆ Don't forget that a small market today can become a large market in the future

- ◆ Take into consideration a country's political stability and technological level

- ◆ To what questions do you need answer to be able to make a decision?

- ◆ Limit your search to those

- ◆ Analyze your information and convert what you learn into action

- ◆ Visit the country where you want to do business

- ◆ Ask other people for advice

  - ◆ Those who conduct business there
  - ◆ Those who understand the culture

When you analyze a market, don't just look at potential sales volumes but. It is not enough to have good sales; you have to make money too. So when selecting a market also analyze profitability in the short and long term. A low sales and high profit is better than a high sales and a low profit.

- ◆ Today will be the past, tomorrow

- ◆ The old-fashioned way looks safe, but following past practice is risky.

- ◆ In today's changing market you have to take some risks, but remember, with the correct information and analysis, you minimize risks.

  - ◆ You increase your success in meeting your business targets
  - ◆ You obtain a better return on your investments

- ◆ Markets are constantly changing and change occurs at a rapid pace

  - ◆ Your decision process has to be quick but it has to be well informed.

- ◆ You have to continuously learn about new techniques, future market forecasts, market trends, etc.
- ◆ You have to be prepared to shift the focus of your business.
- ◆ You have to be flexible and keep up to date in order to prepare for change

◆ Analyze the information you collect to stimulate your business ventures and identify new activities

- ◆ If you do nothing, of course, you won't make any mistakes
- ◆ You will not achieve desirable results for your company by waiting to make decisions
- ◆ Market testing and mistakes should be considered useful opportunities to learn and adapt your product, processes or overseas business

"Using old-fashioned methods of doing business is like using a hand pump to bail out water from a sinking ship. You only delay the inevitable." — Leif Holmvall, Export Pro Inc."

This is the end of Part One. You will find more in-depth information, including on databases, when you read Part Two of this chapter.

Finding the Right Information, Selecting Markets and Partners

"There is only one thing for sure in life. Change."
— Leif Holmvall, Export Pro Inc.

To complete research on some products and services, you will require more detailed information and perhaps even professional help. It can be difficult and sometimes impractical to do all of the research on your own.

If you are selling consumer products, you may want to test them in the new market. One strategy would be to offer free samples of your cookies outside the store that might sell them. You can ask taste testers for their comments on your product. However, if you have chosen an overseas market where a different language is spoken, you won't be able to do the work yourself. In this case, you could hire an appropriate local researcher or company to complete the survey. Remember, depending on the product, you won't always need to hire a professional surveyor.

If you can find consultants in the foreign country who are also familiar with your market and who speak both languages, hire them. Not only can they assist you with the research but they can also explain the differences between the two markets and recommend how you should proceed. They can provide on-site support when you visit, assist with negotiations, arrange for local meetings and complete post-meeting follow up.

"Today's problems are often the result
of yesterday's solutions."

Modern Market Research - On-Line Databases

Information + analysis + strategy = success

Databases are collections of information that is organized in a specific way. They can be simple, such as a spreadsheet, telephone directory or a club membership list or more complex relational databases. Users of databases conduct searches or queries for information then manipulate the results and use their findings to help make informed decisions. Unlike Google, which does not sort the results of a search, databases return very specific results, e.g., you can specify what you are looking for.

We are living in an information age. Those who are best informed about markets, market potential, distribution and price levels and use their knowledge have the best chance for success. You have to keep yourself updated about general world events but more specifically changes in the economy, currencies, political situation and labour market, issues in every market you are interested in. Furthermore, you have to keep up to date with the activities of your competitors.

You might be aware that there is information available, but how can you rapidly access that information?

On-line databases

There are more than 5000 commercial databases. About 4000 of those are accessible via your telephone line, a data line or via dial-up, cable or wireless connection to the internet. Each of them provides unique information.

So what is a database? Some examples include: The Economist (credit checks and country data), Dun and Bradstreet (credit reports), International Risk and Payment Review (IRPR), SCAN (international contracts), Reuters (international news), Frost and Sullivan Data Monitor. The New York Times maintains a database of every article published for the last 20 years. There are databases where you can search for global patents, trademark registrations, etc. There are specialized databases for the medical sector, for oil and gas producers and many other industries.

How do you quickly access this information? You can buy a subscription and make a search. The key to getting the most out of a database is to narrow your scope and limit the amount of information you search for.

News articles are produced regularly – sometimes hourly - in newspapers and the trade press, in print and posted on web sites. If you wanted to read all the newspapers published today from around the world, it would take you 365 years. With access to databases, you can search through every newspaper, magazine, patent and trademark for the past 20 years, for a specific piece of information. Then you can sort the results all in a couple of minutes.

Market surveys results are published on an on-going basis. New patents and trademarks are registered daily. Export and import statistics are recorded by most countries, using standardized codes such as HS (Harmonized Commodity and Description System). Financial and company information (about the industry, company operations, physical location, number of employees, assets and liabilities, sales volumes, share capital, owners' backgrounds, number of accounts, territory covered, etc.) is usually available through a database. Irrespective of which part of the world you want information from, you can find it.

Do you want to find import and export statistics for your new export country or for your competitor's country? Are you looking for suitable distributors or complete company data and credit checks, market development, an analysis of which patents your competitor has registered in the last year or newspaper articles about a specific industry? Perhaps you are looking for new suppliers, a company to buy, a patent to license or local trade associations. On-line databases can deliver this and much more.

> *"There is no reason anyone would want*
> *a computer in their home."*
> *— Ken Olson, President, Chairman, and founder*
> *of Digital Equipment Corp., 1977*

Fast Information at Your Fingertips Using Search Words

In the old days, we examined the past and extrapolated what we found to forecast trends. We would hold up a finger to test which way the wind was blowing and we'd make wild guesses about what would happen. Now, we live in the information age, with access to a huge body of knowledge which makes it easy to stay updated on current activities and on predictions for the future.

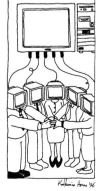

By using modern technology and databases, you can rapidly find relevant data using computers. The problem is not whether there is enough information, but how to find it. We used to get market information by reading newspapers, using library resources and visiting companies. Today, you have the option of going online to read through the contents of library shelves or searching hundreds of locations within a couple of minutes. By connecting to commercial databases, you multiply the information options available.

Today's business decision-makers in departments such as marketing, legal Research & Development and export are like aircraft pilots – they have at their disposal an extensive range of tools that make it possible for them to quickly track how political, financial and trade markets are changing. You can use the same resources to keep yourself updated with what you need to know for your own business decision-making.

One of the major companies maintaining a broad range of databases is Dialog (www.dialog.com). They have packaged hundreds of databases for their clients in such a way that the same search formula can be used. This will allow you to search each database individually and to search all of them at the same time. If you don't know specifically where to search, the multiple search function will deliver results from each database.

I have used those databases for over 20 years. I have given you some examples of searches I completed to show what you can do.

A European company makes birch wooden pins. One customer group is companies that make wooden coat hangers. How can you find them?

I used one of the European databases. There are 55 companies in Europe manufacturing wooden coat hangers.

◇ *19 in Germany*	◇ *4 in France*
◇ *17 in Italy*	◇ *2 in Denmark*
◇ *5 in Sweden*	◇ *2 in Spain*
◇ *4 in Belgium*	◇ *1 in Holland*

Time to search and production of a printout of company, profile, contact name and address less than 2 minutes

Tasks to be done:

♦ Identify distributors in Germany who sell computer software for the transportation and logistics sector. Your client wants this profile in preparation for marketing their software.

Result: 67 companies found. Search time - 4 minutes

♦ Find a newly launched product with the name Power Drain Plug for a distributor.

Result: I found an article in the *Santa Barbara Morning News*, dated August 1992. Search time was 10 minutes and the results included contact information and background on the company.

♦ What's happening in the seniors market in the US and Japan? My client was selling wheelchairs and walkers.

Result: 100+ articles and sources. Search time was approximately 10 minutes. I spent another 15 minutes identifying the most relevant studies and articles

♦ Locate companies in Great Britain specializing in printing cards with a built-in magnetic strip. (For use to produce bus and subway tickets). The company I worked for wanted to find a manufacturer.

Result: 5 companies. Time to search was 7 minutes

♦ Search for component suppliers in Europe. My client was a manufacturer of specialized exercise bicycles and wanted a list of suppliers to meet their increasing need for components.

Result: 74 producers of components in Europe, 39 of whom were in Germany; 14 of those employed more than 100 people. 581 bike manufacturers in Europe, 158 in Italy, 75 in Germany and 158 in England

Search time for full report - 4 minutes.

♦ A European company was seeking distributors who were distributors of compressed air equipment or hydraulic equipment in the US. There is a Standard Industrial Code or SIC that categorizes industries by sector. The general code for Wholesale Industrial Machinery is 5084. For the specific codes I searched for, (see below) I got a list of 2534 companies.

♦ The PC or product codes for pneumatic tools and equipment are 5084 0907, for compressors, except air conditioning, 5084 0903 and for hydraulic systems equipment and supplies, 5084 9905. You can find those codes in D&B handbooks, on the web or online from database suppliers.

♦ This is the search:

♦ S(= select) PC = (5084 0907 or 5084 0903 or 5084 9905), i.e. a search for any of those distributor categories. (It searched for any company that indicate they match any of those product codes.)

658 PC = 5084 0907 (pneumatic tools and equipment)
805 PC = 5084 0903 (compressors, except air conditioning)
1414 PC = 5084 9905 (hydraulic systems equipment and supplies)

(658 companies of the first, 805 of the second and 1414 of the third)

S2 2534 PC = (5084 0907 or 5084 0903 or 5084 9905) for a total of 2534 companies. (The result was 2534 companies. If you add the figures above it will be 2877. Some companies had multi-product codes, therefore the net was 2534 companies)

o   After limiting the number of states in the US to ones we where interested in and narrowing the results to companies with between 15 and 75 employed, I ended up with 120 companies

o   They were sorted by state (Alabama, Arkansas, etc) and a short report printed on each. The short report is inexpensive and lists the company name, number of people employed, industry sold to and contact person.

I selected several companies for the final list and printed out a complete credit report for the past 3 years, (at a much higher cost) with comparisons to other companies in the industry as well as details about share capital, annual sales, customer base, geographical coverage, number of clients, number of employees, size of offices and factories and the backgrounds of owners and executives.

Total time online was about 15 minutes. It took a bit longer to prepare the final report. The cost was several hundred dollars. The final cost will depend on how many reports you ask for and how much detail you want.

♦   I searched on *Export Pro* and *Export Master* worldwide when I registered those trademarks for my company. Not only did the search include registered trademarks but also any place where that combination of words showed up. I could prove to the authorities where I registered the trademarks that there was no conflict that would prevent my registration.

Search time was less than a minute.

♦   I completed a client inventory for one of my distributors, specifying potential clients in California, listing all companies that they could potentially sell to, sorted by telephone number so that their salesmen could easily divide up the clients. Many clients were not even known to the sales people at that time. I also delivered a listing of all noise control consultants in their area. This client base would help them to increase sales, because their products reduced noise levels by 60%.

♦ I researched data on imports of different species of lumber to Japan. The report included the total volume and value of imports as well as details on imports broken down by country, species of wood including the number of cubic meters and the price per cubic meter by country, all for the past three years. Time to search and print the report took about 2 minutes.

"I do not believe you can do today's job with yesterday's methods and be in business tomorrow."
— Nelson Jackson

Example - Not up to date on your competition

A Swedish company requested an information consultant to help them search for information. The consultant wanted to perform an analysis of the competition. However the company thought they already knew everything about their competition. In spite of this, the consultant searched for more data. It turned out that one of the competitors was on their way into the Swedish market. This resulted in a crisis meeting to decide how to respond to, or alternatively, stop the competition. Had the consultant not performed the search, the company would shortly have been at a severe competitive disadvantage.

There are other resources you can use.

♦ Credit checks on countries can be found on websites for The Economist Intelligence Unit (http://www.eiu.com/PublicDefault.aspx) and Dun & Bradstreet's International Risk and Payment Review (IRPR) which delivers analyses of marketing, political, commercial and economic risk covering over 130 countries.

♦ Tenders Electronic Daily (TED) is the online version of the 'Supplement to the Official Journal of the European Union', and lists European procurement opportunities or invitations to tender.
(http://ds.datastarweb.com/ds/products/datastar/sheets/teda.htm)

It is published in the 23 official EU languages and registration and usage are free. You can search this database directly from the European Union website (http://ted.europa.eu) but it is much slower and does not allow you to set up permanent searches.

♦ Summary of Proposed Projects (SOPP) contains information on development projects funded by the United Nations and describes projects by region, country and sector. SOPP is used by companies and consultants to bid on international contracts and track who was awarded contracts
(http://ds.datastarweb.com/ds/products/datastar/sheets/sopp.htm)

♦ Scan-a-Bid (SCAN) is the online version of the UN publication, "Development Business" a twice monthly procurement newspaper published by United Nations. It is used by companies and consultants interested in bidding on projects in Africa, Asia, Latin America, and Central and Eastern Europe that are funded by the World Bank, the Inter-American Development Bank, the Asian Development Bank and other institutions (http://ds.datastarweb.com/ds/products/datastar/sheets/scan.htm)

♦ Market research companies offer prepared reports that can be purchased in full or in part from companies like Frost & Sullivan, Datamonitor, and Euromonitor.

If you don't want to search manually on a regular basis, you can set up a permanent search alert, which means that every time there is a hit on the keywords you selected, the database will send the result to you. For example, if you want to know about requests for tenders for railroads in specific countries, you can set an alert using those words. Even better, use the database code for each type of contract and you will receive a report when a new tender is registered on the database. If you want an update every time your competitor applies for a patent, you can do the same thing. Google alerts allow you to set up and manage email alerts or notifications for specific search terms that appear in news stories, web sites, etc. but the databases allows you to be much more specific and obtain the exact results you want.

Options for data retrieval using commercial online databases are endless. It is definitely a very useful tool if you want current information at a relatively low cost.

You can learn to access all the wealth of database information on your own, but you should know that there is a steep learning curve to becoming effective at conducting searches. Quick, concise, correct searching is a skill that can be difficult to learn. It may not be cost-effective for you to try to learn on your own, especially if you will only need a limited number of searches completed. A better option would be for you to hire a professional called a data retrieval specialist, information broker or online researcher. For a fee, they will search, retrieve information and prepare reports for you. The database supplier can most likely give you some names. Many large libraries also have trained librarians who can do the searches for you. There are also professional groups such as the Association of Independent Information Professionals (AIIP).

"While theoretically and technically television
may be feasible, commercially and
financially it is an impossibility."
— Lee DeForest, inventor

Dialog

From the website, http://www.dialog.com/about, I found the following description: "Dialog online-based information services help organizations across the globe to seek competitive advantages in such fields as business, science, engineering, finance and law. The Dialog portfolio of products and services, including Dialog® and DataStar®, offers organizations the ability to precisely retrieve data from more than 1.4 billion unique records of key information, accessible via the Internet or through delivery to enterprise intranets."

The company has 900 databases to search from including news feeds, scientific data, government regulations, intellectual property data and business intelligence. Here are some websites you can visit to locate more information.

http://support.dialog.com

http://www.dialog.com/about/corporate_capabilities.pdf

http://www.dialog.com/sources

http://support.dialog.com/howdoi/business

http://support.dialog.com/howdoi/business/54810.shtml

The two last ones shows examples of search and reports

http://support.dialog.com/ontap/ a place where you can practice searches

http://library.dialog.com/bluesheets/ data sheets on different databases

At http://support.dialog.com/techdocs/c0018002mi_dlg_dbselguide.pdf you will find a handbook on different databases, as well as in-depth information about what databases are available.

Kompass

Kompass is a global Business to Business database that lists 2.7 million companies, 23 million products and services and over a million trade names in 60 countries. It offers services in 16 languages and is stronger in some countries than others. Type http://kompass.com in the url line. It will probably take you to the Kompass site for your country. The beauty of this program is that you can purchase a CD or DVD containing the search information you wanted, so that you can load it onto your desktop or laptop.

Many databases specialize in certain industries. The ones mentioned in this book can give you broad access and are a good introduction to the power and usefulness of database searches. You can also visit http://spireproject.com/database.htm which contains an overview of additional databases and some useful articles on searches.

This chapter has given you the basics of market and customer analysis. Each chapter that follows will build on this and provide more information on how to find specific information on topics like currency, payments and freight.

Exercise

1. Make a list of the information you think you will need before you can decide on which market to select.

2. List the key topics to be researched before you are ready to enter a new market.

3. Use the elimination method to select a market for your product/service.

4. List five suitable sources for information about the market you selected.

5. Complete a web search using key words and a search engine such as Google. Do the same search but this time, use some of the websites suggested in this chapter or at the end of this book.

6. List resources in your company or business network with the knowledge, language skills or specific information about the country or industry you are considering.

7. Which clients can you visit in the country to get answers to your questions?

8. Which associations are there in your town, province or state or country, with representatives you could interview or who could supply you with a list of contacts to answer your questions?

9. Look up trade statistics for the specific country. You could search for either general statistics or specific data on production, imports by type of product and country of origin.

10. Contact your freight forwarder to ask about:

    a. Customs duties, special taxes or other conditions

    b. Export restrictions from your country or import restrictions in the country you are interested in

    c. Specific contacts they can refer you to

11. Investigate if there are suitable trade shows or conventions you can attend.

12. Visit the websites of databases to learn more about how you can use them.

13. Contact information brokers or librarians to find out more about how they can assist you.

"I think there is a world market for maybe five computers."
— Thomas John Watson, Sr., Chairman of the Board,
International Business Machines (IBM), 1943

Selecting the Right Distribution and Sales Channels – Part One

In This Chapter:

- ◆ **Distribution options**
- ◆ **Indirect exporting**
- ◆ **Direct Exporting**
- ◆ **Own organization overseas**
- ◆ **Contract manufacturing**
- ◆ **Licensing**
- ◆ **Franchising**
- ◆ **Holding companies and tax planning**
- ◆ **E-commerce**
- ◆ **Pros and Cons of different solutions**

There are many components to international business. One is choosing the correct distribution and distributor channel, how your product or service will reach the final end-user. Each distribution alternative has its pros and cons. The key is to adapt to the way of doing business in the foreign market. The purpose of this chapter is to highlight some of the key considerations for selecting distribution options for export markets.

"With over 50 foreign cars already on sale here,
the Japanese auto industry isn't likely to
carve out a big slice of the U.S. market."
—Business Week, August 2, 1968

How to Select Distribution Channels

Selection of distribution options has to be based on what the exporter wants to achieve and the resources they have available. Add to this what is permitted and suitable on the foreign market. Note that we are not talking just about the physical distribution itself but also about your communications channels. Sometimes those will vary, depending on the markets and distribution alternatives. (See later in this chapter.)

Pull versus push

Pull: End user > Distribution channels > You the exporter. In this way you work from the market to find the most suitable distribution method.

Push: Exporter > Distribution channels > End user. You decide on the distribution you want.

I recommend the Pull version. Your end-users decide you how they prefer to buy and from where. With the Push method, you decide how you want to sell. Perhaps your solution will not be what the market wants. You will miss out the feedback from the market.

♦ You are a 35-year-old woman looking for designer jeans, and you're willing to pay a premium to look good. You know which stores sell the jeans you're looking for.

♦ You are a 65-year-old gentleman looking for some durable jeans but you're not willing to spend a fortune. I'm sure you know where to go.

♦ Grandma wants to buy some pretty jeans for her five-year-old granddaughter. Price is not important. She has to find out where to buy them.

If you do not know where the stores are that carry the product you want at the price you are willing to pay, either you could look around, do an online search or ask some friends until you find the right place. It all makes sense, doesn't it?

Of course, this is the approach to use when you look for companies to sell your products overseas.

1. You have to define the target group, you have to talk to them and ask where they would like to buy the product and at which price.

2. When you have found a store for your product, you have to ask the store owner if they want to buy directly from you or if they can suggest a suitable distributor or agent you can contact.

By doing this type of quick survey, you can easily find out what your clients like, how much they are willing to pay and where they want to buy your product. Furthermore, you will have learned where the store wants to buy your product. Easy, isn't it? This is how you find your distributors, dealers, etc. Perhaps you're saying to yourself that this is easy to do with consumer products, but how about industrial goods?

Let's say you want to sell mining equipment to Australia. You travel to the country. You visit a number of mines. You make presentations about your products to find out if they suit the market, what the competition is, what prices you could charge and where customers would like to buy your equipment. The process works for any type of product or service, including yours.

Example - Finding the right distribution

One group of my students had a project to introduce trendy jeans into a country in the European Union. They spent four days there research the target group and stores serving the market. They learned there were only four stores that would be suitable. They visited all four of them; everyone was interested Store representatives suggested the same agent to work with. When my students returned home after that trip, not only had they found out about the target group, the size of the market, price levels, and suitable stores but they had also convinced the stores to sell the products and signed up an agent to represent the company.

Don't believe that it is difficult to do international business. If you use common sense and do your fact-finding in advance, it will be easier than just jumping in with limited information.

Example - Wrong way to select partner

A Swedish company asked me for advice on their licensing contract with a Canadian manufacturer. They had worked backwards and first contacted the largest manufacturer of a specific kind of mining equipment in Canada. Of course, the manufacturer was interested in signing a contract.

I asked the Swedish company if they had been in touch with any mining companies. They said yes. My second question was: So did you ask if they were interested in buying from that company? They had not asked.

I picked up the phone and called four of the largest mining companies. They all said they would not buy from the suggested company, as it was in the wrong location. They wanted a local manufacturer with a facility close to their mines. The Swedish company didn't sign the contract with the large manufacturer. I had to help them find a new partner.

What can you learn from this? Always start with the end-user, confirm that they like your product and find out who they want to buy from and where they want to buy it.

Remember Pull versus Push in the beginning of this chapter. Now you understand why I prefer Pull.

Many companies select the same methods of distribution in foreign markets that they use in domestic markets. Don't make that mistake! Say you're selling wheelchairs. At home, you use local dealers who sell equipment for disabled persons. In the new country you will to do business in, the government assists people who need mobility aids. They have stores that supply wheelchairs free or at subsidized prices. That will be your distribution channel.

In another example, you sell your company's paper towels through 'big box' stores or warehouse outlets in Europe and North America. Now your plan is to enter India and China. Most retail outlets there are family-run (mom-and-pop) or small shops. In India, more than 10 million small stores account for 95% of sales across most categories. Only 4% of India's retail is from 'big box' stores. China has some 23 million retail outlets of which about 78% are small, family-run stores. Do you still want to sell through large outlets if they only count for 4% of the market?

"Focus on your customer's needs! It takes less effort to keep an old customer satisfied than to get a new customer interested."
— Anon

You cannot presume that international business works the same way as domestic business. You, the exporter, will have to tailor the distribution solution to the requirements of a specific market and end-user. It is where and from whom your end-user wants to buy that will determine how you set up your distribution.

How Do Customers Want To Buy?

Different Distribution Same Product

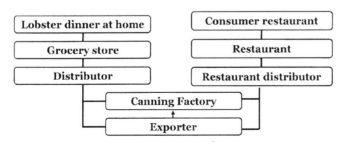

You have some customers who want to buy either whole lobsters or canned lobsters to eat at home. But you also have other customers visiting restaurants wanting a fresh lobster dinner or ordering surf and turf (steak and a lobster tail) or a lobster salad. For you to reach all of those customers, you would need a distribution system that sells to a canning factory, grocery stores and restaurants, which are different distribution channels for the same product.

Understand the importance of starting your planning with the end-user

Before you enter a new market and select a distribution method, you have to decide what you want to achieve and consider the resources you have. If you don't, you cannot develop the right strategy.

You have to analyze your company's Strengths and Weaknesses, but even more, assess how far you want to go. Are you willing to modify your websites and catalogues and adapt your products for different markets? What resources do you have or how much can you afford to put into each market? Can you develop a completely new product range for the markets including new measurements and packaging. (You will find more examples later in the book). These are some key questions you have to consider.

- What do you want to achieve? *A specified sales volume?*

    Start in a new market as a way of entering neighbouring markets. For example, you enter Belgium, which is in the European Union, to establish a base for further expansion into other EU markets.

- What staff resources do you have? *Two in the marketing department or 100?*

    Your resources set the stage for what you can accomplish in a foreign market. A small number of staff limits how many markets you can handle, the speed with which you can enter new markets and the control you could have on foreign distribution.

- Which financial resources do you have? *Limited resources or a big bank account?*

    You need funds for travelling, new sales material, adapting products or services. More capital allows for extending payment times for new markets and for purchasing an operation overseas.

- What kind of control or guidance do I want? Full control (own company in the foreign market) or allowing foreign companies to manage of your local sales?

- How do you want to divide the workload between head office and the local market?

    Keeping most of the workload at home will put pressure on local company resources. Moving people to the new market will reduce the burden. Placing the responsibility on people/organisations on the foreign market reduces some of the burden of the head office.

- What dangers are there in the export market? Could the country experience political instability or financial problems? Are you willing to take those risks?

- What local rules will guide your choices? A foreign country could demand a certain percentage of local ownership.

- What is your long-term goal? *I want to have 40% of my business in export markets.*

    Make the decision before you select the markets and distribution methods. Launching a product in Asia can take time, if you are not already located there. Are you willing to wait for profitable results or do you want to enter a market close to you, with a similar culture?

We've talked about international business in a country and countries, but you should also consider regions. If you enter Germany, your goal may be to expand to other European Union countries. If you enter China, you could also include Hong Kong.

I'm sure you can think of other issues.

Distribution Options

- **Building up your own organization in a foreign location**

- **Partnering with local companies**

- **Utilizing another company's network and contacts**

- **Allowing other companies to manufacture and sell your products**

The final choice will be determined by factors such as local laws and rules regarding foreign ownership and corporate structures as well as your resources and goals.

The examples outlined below will be explained later at greater length. They are included here to pinpoint that the selection of distribution can vary depending on circumstances in each market and your capacity to adapt.

Market Priority 1	Market Priority 2	Market Priority 3	Market Priority 4
Japan Local distributor	*Denmark* Local distributor	*Mexico* Joint-venture	*Ecuador* Trading house
Germany Subsidiary	*France* Local distributor	*Thailand* Joint-venture	*Costa Rica* Representative
Italy Joint-venture	*United Kingdom* Local distributor	*Malaysia* Licensing	*Philippines* Export agent
	Australia Combination representative and dealers		

Note: local distribution could involve a combination of solutions. You can split up distribution based on geographic areas, by type of customer or the size of the client groups.

Perhaps you want to sell directly to a few key clients in a specific market. For a general manufacturing industry you could set up geographic distribution centres. But if you want to sell to the automotive industry you have to set up an arrangement with a specific distributor for this purpose (i.e., approved by the car manufacturers). Car manufacturers source products from all over the world, which could mean that the company you deal with might be in a different country than where the products are to be supplied.

As another example, say you want to sell components to NASA. Missiles and rockets are highly specialized and extremely complex equipment. You can't just knock on the Space Agency's door. You would have to find someone who is approved by them, as an agent for your type of products.

The selection of distribution channels is based on consideration of:

♦ The local market

♦ What the exporting company wants to achieve

♦ What resources the exporting company has for each specific market

♦ What the exporting company is allowed to do in the foreign market

The more resources you commit, the more opportunity you will have to control the market. However, you will likely have limited control over political influences.

There are three primary alternatives to consider when you make a decision about the form your exporting will take:

Three major forms of exporting:

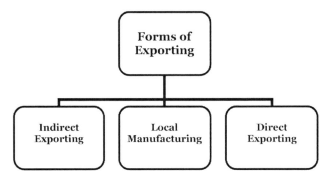

Indirect Exporting,
Such As International Firms and OEM

The exporting company is not directly involved in export activities and uses other services. To facilitate Indirect Exporting, the exporting company can use:

International Firm

These include large engineering or construction companies conducting international business in many markets.

Let's say that a large Australian construction company is awarded a contract to build a hydroelectric power station in Tanzania. They buy excavators from a manufacturer in Australia and ship the machinery to Tanzania. When they have finished the construction job, they sell the machines locally. The Australian manufacturer of the excavators may not have exported before, but because the construction company purchased their products, used them and sold them locally they can be considered to be an exporter. Furthermore, they now have a base for future sales and a market for spare parts.

OEM (Original Equipment Manufacturer)

This is a company that builds machinery to be exported, maybe using your products as components of their final product or as an integral part of a complete system.

In this example, you are a Spanish company manufacturing manometers to measure air pressure. A local company making compressors buys your manometers to install on their equipment. They sell their compressors in over a hundred countries. Your products have become part of that export chain because they are now being sold in over a hundred countries.

> ### Example - Starting export when someone else has done the work
> *Sometimes this kind of sale can result in you being required to set up a foreign operation. A European company selling computerized control systems has a client that purchases their equipment to include as part of a complete package of robotics. Over 300 robots were sold to car manufacturers in the US and Canada, who demanded a local service. The European company manufacturing the component had to establish a new operation to satisfy the automotive manufacturer's requirement for service in North America. As an added benefit they could begin start selling computerized systems for other applications in the North American market as they already had a customer base.*

Export Commission Agents

These are individuals or companies who, on a commission basis, arrange orders and perhaps conduct other sales-related activities. Normally, they represent a large number of products or services in a limited number of markets.

Export Merchants

They are similar to Export Commission Agents, but normally buy domestic or foreign products and sell them to foreign purchasers. They are able to compete because they have specialized knowledge about certain types of product or markets and have good expertise with international business, e.g., a company specializing in the aircraft industry or countries in the Caribbean market.

Manufacturer's Export Agents

Export agents could be either an individual or a company. They normally function like a 'rented' export department, receiving payments or commissions or a combination of a retainer and cost reimbursements and commissions. They are similar to export merchants but do not take possession of the products. They find buyers or representatives for you, but as an exporter you retain ownership of the goods and invoice the client directly. The export agent will do most of the marketing. The arrangement could either be for a special project or on a long term basis.

Trading Houses

A Trading House is a company that takes over most of the activities for the exporting company and take on distribution to foreign markets. They buy your product and take all responsibility for selling it in a foreign market. Many small companies begin exporting by using Trading Houses.

In most cases, they assume all export costs and responsibility for any losses resulting from unpaid invoices. Some Trading Houses work on commission. Many specialize either in a geographic area such as Japan or in specific product lines, languages, cultures, etc.

The importance of Trading Houses has declined, in part because of the rapid pace of product development today. They continue to be important for raw material-based products or unique/niche markets where it is not profitable for companies to start their own business or where conditions are too complicated or unstable for an inexperienced exporter.

In Japan, the use of Trading Houses is common practice. They tend to be vertically integrated from raw material suppliers to manufacturers, to banking, financing and shipping. You may be required to work through a Japanese trading house if the only organization permitted to import your product is an accredited Japanese Trading House.

You can obtain more information through an organization called JETRO (Japan External Trade Organization), which has branches in Japan and over 75 offices around the world. They promote both export and import. The web site www.jetro. org includes a wealth of information about JETRO's objectives and regulations and standards, business strategies, import procedures and systems and business procedures. Some examples of a large Japanese trading house (*sogo shosha*) include Mitsui & Co., Ltd., Nichimen Iwai Corp. and Mitsubishi Corp.

Direct Exporting (No Ownership)
Such As Agent and Distributor

Direct export can take place straight to end users, through a company's own office or through local representatives. It is also possible to establish local manufacturing facilities, establish arrangements with licensing partners or set up a joint venture. You will be in charge of exporting.

Before describing the individual channels, let's sort out some definitions and clarify what they mean. Later in this chapter you will find more details.

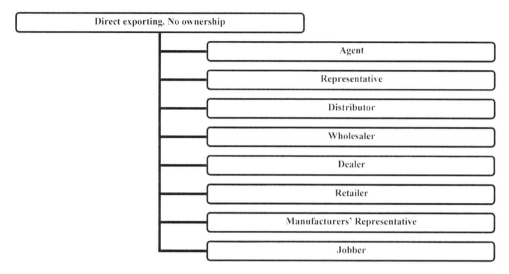

Agent

The word agent is often used incorrectly. Many companies say, "We have agents in 20 countries", when they really mean that they have distributors or representatives.

An agent is someone who negotiates purchases, sales or both but does not "touch" the goods. They are normally paid a commission. An agent is someone who represents you and has the right to use your name and sign agreements on your behalf. The agent can be an alternative to a subsidiary, i.e., the person or the company represents you on site.

If you do not want to delegate this broad range of freedoms to an agent, it would be preferable to retain a representative. In the European Union (EU), there are rules that prevent you from cancelling an agent or representative agreement without compensation.

Using a representative instead of an agent

To limit the other party's powers, sign a representative agreement. First of all, it will indicate to your foreign "client" that they are not authorized to sign contracts on your behalf. The representative is negotiating for you, but you have the final say. The representative solicits orders in exchange for a retainer or commission. They never take possession of the products and generally do not provide after-sales service. They do not take responsibility for delivery of products. Responsibility for the product remains with the manufacturer.

Distributor

This is what many people usually mean when they use the term agent. However, a distributor purchases at a reduced cost and re-sells goods and services at a higher price. A distributor buys from an exporter and in its own name, sells to retailers and dealers or directly to end users such as manufacturers or other industrial customers. The only reason for the distributor to use your name is to take advantage of your promotional material of if they have the right to use your registered name or trade mark. (See more in Legal chapter)

This is the most common type of foreign representative when you need a local partner. The major responsibility is to add as a local presence and bridge linguistic and cultural distances between the importing country and you as an exporter. The more dissimilar and unfamiliar the market is the greater is a need for a local partner. The distributor is established in the market, has an existing customer base and many times already maintains a service organisation.

Wholesaler

A wholesaler is a business entity selling to distributors, dealers, retailers, industrial clients or commercial users. It is similar to a distributor, but normally the wholesaling company does more stocking or warehousing of goods than active selling. It is very common within certain sectors: electrical components, plumbing supplies, small household goods, novelty items. There are many wholesalers with a broader range of products and services than distributors.

Dealer

A dealer distributes and sells directly to commercial end users, usually commercial clients. A dealer and distributor may be the same if there is only one distribution level between you and the client. Perhaps it sounds complicated but with the examples I'll give you later on, you will understand.

Retailer

A retailer is a distributor/dealer who sells a variety of goods to end users and consumers. A retailer is the same as a dealer but with a focus on consumer goods: department stores, hardware stores, grocery stores, etc. Car dealers are actually automobile retailers except when they sell to commercial accounts.

Broker

A broker functions as a liaison or agent but does not have any part in the business or have physical control of the product. They can represent either the buyer or the seller, but do not enter into an exclusive relationship to either. When it comes to prices and other commitments, the broker's responsibility is often limited by the client. Payment is normally in the form of a commission or a lump sum when the business transaction is concluded. Typical broker activity would be negotiating a large order for crude oil between a seller and a buyer. Products could include raw materials like copper or pulp and paper, but sometimes could be a surplus of a large amount of a product such as jeans that a manufacturer wants to get rid of. You can compare their services to a real estate broker who matches a seller and a buyer.

Manufacturer's representative

A manufacturer's representative, sometimes called a manufacturer's agent or manufacturer's rep, is a person or company working on a contract. They may sell within a limited geographical area and have limited flexibility for negotiation of prices and delivery terms.

In North America is it very common to use Manufacturer's Reps as the distances to be covered are large and it is too expensive to maintain a company's own sales force for a limited number of products. The representative is generally a person or company with a suitable customer or client base that allows them to sell directly to a dealer. It is a common method of doing business for hardware products, car accessories and similar industrial products. The Rep deals with many companies with complementary product lines, such as handsaws from one company, pliers from a second and hammers and crowbars from a third. All of them are suited to the same distribution channels. With a broader range of products, this type of sales person can spread the cost of visiting suitable dealers/retailers among several manufacturers.

Most Manufacturers' Reps work on commission. There are exceptions, such as companies that also take responsibility for stocking products. Having a Manufacturers' Rep can be compared to having your own sales force working on commission, but with a broader product range. It is important that your reps have up-to-date product knowledge and good sales support. They tend to sell what is easiest for them and most profitable, so it is up to you to make sure your products fit those criteria.

Jobber

This is synonymous with a wholesaler and distributor. Jobbers are often used for certain products or customer groups. It is a modern type of pedlar and is often a service-oriented dealer. Many jobbers work in the field and maintain a network to deliver products such as oil, grease and grease guns to contractors. Think of a company working in the forest with forestry machines. On a continuous basis, they need replacement parts, tools and lubricants and sometimes spare tires. The Jobber visits the client at the worksite, sells and delivers the items ordered on the spot.

Exporting overseas using your own organisation.

Starting your own organization in a foreign country normally requires a substantial investment. One alternative would be to sell directly from home if the product does not require a lot of service. Direct sales are common in countries where you contract directly with the government or large foreign customers.

Example - Selling directly to end user

You manufacture utility poles. You know that in the foreign country you want to do business in, hydro and telephone authorities are the final customers. In this case, you can approach them directly and export to them from your factory.

Direct Exporting (Ownership) Organisations Like Representative Office and Subsidiary

There are, in principle, three major forms of organization for a company wanting to set up an organisation overseas: a representative office, a branch office or a subsidiary. Note that countries can require slightly different types of company set ups, depending on the legal system. Make sure you check what rules apply.

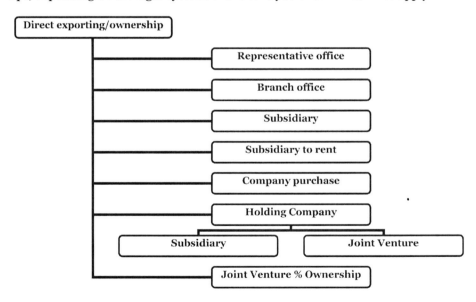

Representative office

A representative office is normally a temporary location established when you want to explore the market. As the representative office is not a legal entity in the host country, (not legally registered) you cannot do business through it. On the other hand, it is normally not taxed either. Setting up a representative office could be a good way for you to investigate the market and identify the right contacts. Later on, the office could be used to support your local representatives. If you bring in staff from outside the country, they could be required to have a work permit or visa because someone who is employed cannot stay as a tourist.

Let's say you are a company in Mexico with potential clients all over Asia. You prefer to work through local distributors who have established relationships with end users and who can buy and sell your product. To start up your business, you place one of your key employees in Bangkok, Thailand. They have a non-immigrant visa but you must also arrange for a work permit or other type of visa that permit their stay as a business person. During this time your representative will not only set up local distributors in the area but will also support and activate them. Beware – the rules are strict. The foreign worker must perform only the work indicated in the work permit. If he/she wants to change employment or the location where they work, the government must approve the change. Anyone who violates the conditions of the work permit could be deported or imprisoned.

By having your own representative, you can arrange to produce sales materials at a lower cost. You are close to your customers from a traveling point of view and time-wise, because there is no 10-14 hour time difference from North America. There will also be an opportunity for you to learn more about the country. You are now local and can more easily search for, select and activate local distributors/ dealers. You also improve your knowledge about each local market. Whenever you relocate staff overseas, it is very important to train them properly. Make sure they learn about the culture, business practices and some of the local language. You eliminate this problem by employing someone local.

Maybe after one year, you might prefer to support the distributors or representatives from farther away or set up a permanent office in another Asian country. If you are not permitted to extend the term of the work visa, foreign authorities could require that you register your company.

Branch office

A branch office is an extension of the parent company in a foreign market. This option allows you to conduct business in the country. Compare it with a sales office in your domestic market. The advantage of a branch office compared with a subsidiary is generally only in the initial stage when branch office operating costs will be greater than income. Your parent company can directly absorb foreign branch office losses. On the other hand, the parent company is also liable if the branch office fails. There will be a direct negative impact on the bottom line.

Many foreign countries impose a 'branch tax'. The branch may not be a legal entity required to pay local taxes, but it produces income from its operations for the parent company. The branch tax is meant to compensate for the taxes that would normally have been paid if the company had been set up as a subsidiary.

Before you choose an export location, you should become familiar with the legal issues, taxation and labour laws. Many countries have tax treaties, so make sure you know what is applicable between your home country and the foreign country.

In the European Union, it will probably not be necessary for you to establish a subsidiary in each member country. In that case, a branch office could be a good solution. You should consult one of the larger auditing firms with international experience to evaluate options for locating your head office and branch offices with respect to tax implications and employment. You will also want to speak with a local lawyer to discuss possible legal implications.

Subsidiary - a buffer if something goes wrong

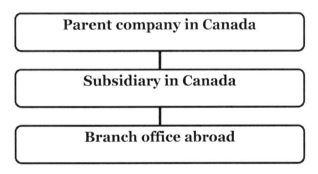

If you want to limit liability for the parent company, it is possible to establish another legal entity such as a subsidiary as a "buffer".

If you have a branch office abroad, your head office is liable for any, losses or lawsuits. Many companies create a subsidiary between them and the branch office. If things go really wrong, you can let the subsidiary go bankrupt and save your parent company.

Subsidiary - sales or manufacturing

The most common form of foreign subsidiary is an incorporated company with share capital. However, there are many different forms of companies and the subsidiary must be guided by domestic laws in the new market.

Starting a subsidiary means making a large investment, whether you have a small company or a large one. The initial costs for staff, office space and equipment, tend to be significant

When starting a subsidiary company, there are many pieces of the puzzle to consider. The company has to be registered, normally with share capital and bookkeeping records kept according to local rules. Some countries do not allow foreign ownership or control and may require you to set up domestic partners as owners. Other countries require that the majority of members of boards of directors have to be local.

There are both advantages and disadvantages to maintaining your own organization. If you plan to manufacture locally, starting a subsidiary is a good option.

However, with a subsidiary you may not be able to apply the same concepts you use at home such as cost analyses from your domestic market and marketing strategies. Many companies are surprised when they examine the real costs and subsequently have to revise plans for their own operations.

Simply sending staff from head office will not work. Someone from Head Office could become President of the new company, but they would have to be accepted as an immigrant, with appropriate visas and work permits. This may take time. It is usually more beneficial to recruit a local executive with the requisite knowledge, contacts and familiarity with economic, political and cultural issues.

To effectively cover the new market, your staff will have to acquire knowledge and establish the right local contacts to achieve the desired results. Understanding the nuances of culture and politics and the rules for doing business is as essential as an established network. You can always bring in specialists, but that is a temporary solution. The learning curve for someone from outside the country can be long and costly.

Do you have long term plans to establish your own operation in the country? If so, start building from day one. Many companies begin with a distributor and when business starts to expand, they decide to set up on their own. However, taking markets from existing distributors can be complex because of legal issues. You risk turning your distributor into a competitor.

One way to start a local company is to buy an existing business or your distributor. You will get an established company with staff, contacts and a service network. You can move selected sales and marketing staff to the new location; however, that is only recommended for some very key people. Staffing with skilled locals can make the difference between success and failure.

> ### Example - Don't forget the formalities
>
> *A foreign company intends to bring out one of their managers as President for their Canadian subsidiary. The new executive requires a work permit or landed immigrant status. The Canadian authorities are willing to approve a work permit for one year at a time. However, they said, "You must prepare a local person to assume this position within a year".*
>
> *The foreign company wants their President to obtain landed immigrant status so that his wife will be allowed to work and their children can have full access to schools without paying high foreign student fees. In this case, the company was a large one. Management put pressure on the government by threatening to move their manufacturing plant to another country if the authorities were not flexible in approving a long term stay.*

Countries use various inducements to attract foreign companies. Sometimes income taxes limit foreign companies' interest in relocating staff to run their operations in another country. Belgium has an arrangement that gives executive ex-patriots (expats) status that will allow them to work there and pay a lower rate of income tax. The difference in taxation can be as much as 40%. However, the foreigner does not enjoy all the rights of a Belgian citizen. They cannot buy property in the country. There may be limitations on whether family members are allowed to work. Expat status is normally only applicable for a limited time period.

Subsidiary 'for rent'

Although a subsidiary may be the best solution for you, start-up and monthly operating costs could be unacceptably high.

A cost containment option is called 'subsidiary for rent'. In this arrangement, you register your company in the new country and use the services of an already-established business there. In other words, you rent or buy part of that company's staff and/or services. One benefit is being seen as a local subsidiary, while retaining your original company's name. The arrangement could vary from renting part of an office and secretarial staff to utilizing all of the foreign company's staff, including their sales people.

Your initial costs and monthly operating expenses will be less. After you have reviewed performance data, you will have better information for assessing long-term growth potential for a stand-alone operation and determining the size of facility and the staff and equipment you want to put in place.

You have the option of choosing the services you buy. At a later stage, you can begin to employ some of your own staff in the new location. When you find that you are ready to 'fly on your own', you can set up a complete organization since you will already have in place an established company with your own staff.

Holmvall International Trading Inc./Export Pro Inc. supplied this service to a number of European companies. We had a separate phone line answered with their company name, separate business cards, etc. We were supplying everything from the receptionist to warehousing, sales, invoicing and bookkeeping. This was a very practical solution for the overseas' companies that wanted their "own" company but not the responsibility and the cost of a full blown foreign operation

Joint Ventures

A joint venture is a cooperative undertaking between two or more parties. It could be a company set up for manufacturing or marketing or a joint interest in research and development. For more details see Joint Venture in the section about local manufacturing.

Local Manufacturing – Licensing, Joint Venture, etc.

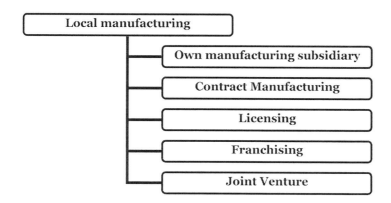

Manufacturing subsidiary

Under this arrangement, sales and production would be handled locally. Such an organizational structure is seen positively, except by your competitors of course. Establishing a bricks and mortar entity sends a message that you are committed to the local market and prepared to stay. In many countries, a manufacturing subsidiary is accepted as a domestic company. In addition to being able to obtain access to government tendering and contracts, your company may be eligible for local employment grants, export assistance and even government export insurance. Arrangement with local universities for R&D as well as research grants can be another possibility.

One of the reasons to select local manufacturing could be that the local market is so large, maybe it is necessary to manufacture locally especially if product customization is extensive and there is a preference for local content.

Manufacturing does not mean you have to produce everything in the country. It could be that you locally assemble the products and ship parts from your domestic manufacturing unit or source some or all parts locally.

If a fast start-up is desirable, it may make sense to purchase an existing company. From a start up and profitability point of view, it can sometimes be an advantage to buy an existing company outright as there would be no need for additional investment in new staff, office or manufacturing facilities, machinery, etc. Depending on profitability, it may be possible to buy the company at book value for only the price of the assets instead of paying for their image or goodwill and outstanding contacts.

Purchasing a local company can be a complex and lengthy process. There are many questions to ask and decisions to make.

1. You have to be clear why you are buying the company and why the seller is willing to dispose of a going concern.

2. Have you taken the 'pulse' of local industry, local politics and the overall economy?

3. What are the transition issues?

4. Will you be able to manage the company by yourself or will you have to hire people to run the business for you? Perhaps you can keep the previous owner on retainer as a manager during a start up period. This could have a downside as well, if neither you nor your trusted advisors are available on site for knowledge transfer or to facilitate a smooth transition.

5. Who are the existing buyers and suppliers? You have to evaluate what the company can deliver in terms of future business growth and profitability, public image and goodwill and market share.

Before buying, you should hire local experts to conduct thorough operational and financial analyses so you won't have unpleasant future surprises. You'll want to know if all of the company's bills have been paid, if there are any outstanding judgments, product liability issues or tax implications. Business ethics, environmental stewardship and human rights practices are also coming under increasing scrutiny. Anticipate problems and prepare for challenges!

Large companies can use local manufacturing for a local market or trading block so as to be closer to customers and prevent paying duty on imported products. Even if you are a foreign company, you will be perceived as a local company. For example, Toyota and Honda have large manufacturing plants in Canada and the US. They are close to the North American market and do not need to pay duties. On the other hand, General Motors has manufacturing facilities in the US and Canada and brings in models from their plants in Korea and Europe they do not make in North America.

So the question is, when is a North American-made car considered North American and when is a foreign-made car, foreign? Or to put it another way, if a Japanese car is made in the US, is it American or Japanese? How about the General Motors car manufactured in Korea and brought into the US? Is it American or Korean? The answers are not black and white.

For every company you are establishing, make sure to learn the local rules. In many countries you are not allowed to own 100% of a company, so analyze the consequences.

Contract manufacturing

With contract manufacturing in different countries, you contract out manufacturing but the product is still yours to sell. No actual investment is made locally in staff and equipment. However, you would have a manufacturing presence and may be able to exert control over production and quality.

This arrangement can be suitable where you do not want to set up your own organisation but manufacturing must be done locally to satisfy the market. Reasons could include high customs duties, quotas or demands for fast product delivery. Freight costs from abroad can make a product too expensive. On the other hand, lower wage levels could make local manufacturing a favourable option.

Warning! You don't want your foreign manufacturer to copy your products and become your competitor. To avoid this, split up the manufacturing so that different parts are made by different companies. Then, have another company that you can trust complete the assembly.

Another advantage to manufacturing locally is that you can qualify for preferential treatment. Some governments will allow you to have a 10-30% higher price for government contracts compared with imported products.

IKEA, the furniture company, designs all products in-house but uses outside manufacturers to produce them. This gives them the flexibility to manufacture in a country with the best quality and best prices, taking into consideration duties, taxes and shipping costs. They can also adapt products to market demand as well as sourcing some local components to add to the product range.

Holding company

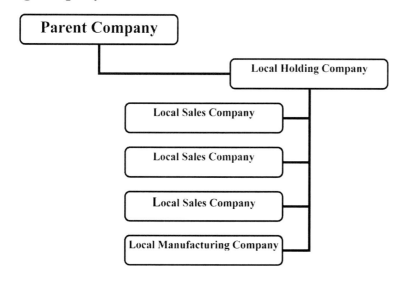

For larger corporations with a presence in many countries, it could be advantageous to create a holding company to "own" foreign companies and take advantage of taxation treaties. This would allow them to consolidate profits in one location where taxes are low.

For example, you can have a number of smaller companies in various Latin American countries, with a holding company placed strategically for them all. This could result in lower taxes on dividends paid out from subsidiaries. Holding companies also provide an opportunity for balancing expenditure and profit results among companies when there is more than one business in the same country, with different rates of return.

Before you establish yourself in a country, research the tax rules. Some countries require that you have a company registered there for any income earned there. Tax rates could differ depending on where your head office is. You may be taxed on a percentage of your worldwide sales and not on your real profit in that country even if you don't make a profit there. So make sure you get expert advice in advance. The same is also applicable for licensing and joint ventures.

Licensing

It is not always possible to sell products directly to another market. Roadblocks could include high price levels, machinery that is too cumbersome or delicate to ship or legislation that prohibits importing certain products. There are occasionally difficulties with local product modifications. Extended manufacturing-to-delivery times in combination with lengthy freight times may make it difficult to export because the market will not accept delay. A company could risk losing an order if manufacturing cannot be done locally. In another situation, an exporting company may not have the personnel and financial resources to quickly establish a presence in a market.

In this case, licensing is a possibility for generating extra income without too much investments and risk.

You might be able to arrange for a qualified local company to manufacture and sell your products. You would have to supply drawings, instructions and marketing material and allow them to fabricate and market your products and/or services for a fee. The licensing fee normally includes a one-time start up payment (down payment) in combination with an annual royalty based on specific conditions or time periods, e.g., annually, sales volumes, number of units sold or a combination of all of these. (See more in Price chapter)

Selling a license means more than transferring a set of drawings. You are also selling the rights to make and sell the product or technique in a specified market during a specified time period. The licensee not only pays for product design but

K.HORNE

also the monetary value placed on transfer of your production and marketing expertise. The licensing arrangement may also include access to a patent or design-protected product, a registered trade mark, a unique technique or complete production systems. In other words, you are transferring more than pieces of paper. If your fee is based on sales volume, your interest will be on high sales volumes. You will want to share your success stories from other markets a well.

Sometimes there are other reasons for entering into a licensing agreement. You find out someone has copied a product for which you hold a patent. The foreign company has been manufacturing this copycat product for a couple of years. Your lawyer sends them a letter threatening a lawsuit for patent infringement if they do not cease and desist. Neither party likely wants a costly legal battle. Frequently, these cases end with negotiations for a licensing arrangement, and include a penalty to compensate for the profits of past unlawful production.

This happened many years ago, when an inventor with a patent for intermittent windshield wipers sued several large automobile manufacturers. The final result of the litigation was a licensing agreement with each of them.

How do you get paid for a licensing agreement?

First of all, both parties have to make money. Otherwise, the licensing arrangement is of no interest. Often, there will be a down payment paid on the day the agreement is signed. There is usually a royalty or agreed-upon amount to be paid based on the number of units sold, the value of sales or a flat fee per year. Sometimes it is difficult to control sales volumes or the patent holding company wants a minimum income each year. With larger systems such as power stations, the manufacturer wants more advanced technical support and is willing to pay a management fee or for technical support in order to install a system or to ensure that the product is manufactured according to their specifications. For more complicated products and systems arrangements are usually made for a continuous transfer of knowledge and technology. (More in the Price chapter).

Many suppliers are concerned that their licensing partner will steal their proprietary knowledge and then cancel the contract. The best way to prevent this is by staying ahead of the game, developing new or improved products and better marketing strategies, so that the licensing partner needs you and your product to remain competitive on the market.

If you do not manufacture and sell the product yourself, the licensing income will provide revenue that increases your profitability and give you wider exposure and increased knowledge of other markets. It also helps you to cover Research and Development costs. Your licensing partner may also have products you want to manufacture for your domestic market.

Franchising

Franchising is a special type of licensing. The parties are the franchisor (the owner) who gives the franchisee (the buyer) the right to distribute its products, techniques, and trademarks by paying a percentage of gross monthly sales and an initial franchising fee. The agreements normally last for 5 to 30 years and are usually for a specific territory.

The franchisor assigns the franchisee the right to use the trademark, the business system and products/services. The franchisor normally promotes or markets sales as well as providing specific training. For this service, the licensee pays a franchise fee at start up, a fixed amount plus a royalty or certain percentage for support, training, etc. Fees differ substantially depending on the business or the market. The Franchisor could maintain a local call center for order taking. This is very common in the fast food industry and is a service you pay extra for. Clients call one, usually easily recognizable number. The call center dispatches the order to the closest location for the customer, for quick delivery.

An initial franchise fee could range from zero to $1 million or more. In the latter case part of the fee is for the down payment and partly for machinery, equipment and furniture. Sometimes, land and construction of a building according to a standard plan are included.

The ongoing royalty could range from zero to 20-25% and would include franchisor services and use of the company name, training and business documentation such as manuals and advertising. When there is no royalty, the franchisor makes money from goods the franchisee is required to purchase like food ingredients or other supplies.

In your country, there are most likely many consumer goods and services franchises - McDonalds in the food business, Best Western hotels, Shell and Esso/Exxon gas stations, Avis and Hertz for car rental. Most of these companies are multi-national. With expanding world markets, many more companies are setting up franchise operations in other countries, giving local entrepreneurs the opportunity to buy into a franchise. In some areas, the majority of restaurants, stores and hotels are franchise arrangements.

A regular licensing arrangement would normally include manufacturing and sales costs. With franchising, it is common to permit or require the use of a trade name as well as the franchising company's marketing strategies. The franchisee is not allowed to depart from the established pattern because uniforms, the facility "look", and packaging are controlled by the franchising company.

What does a franchisee receive for their investment? The opportunity to run an independent business with support from an existing company.

1. An established business with a track record
2. Training for owners, managers and staff
3. Financial management tools
4. Sales and marketing tools
5. Guidelines for operations and consistency in your operation
6. An established image and use of a known trademark
7. Access to the network of other franchisees to compare experiences with
8. Possibility of belonging to a professional association

Depending on the country, there are different types of arrangements and investment costs for a franchisor such as a one-time sign up fee plus an ongoing royalty. Here are some examples:

1. $20,000 plus another $20,000 for a specific territory plus a royalty such as 4-10% on sales.

2. $1 million that includes the franchise location, construction of the building according to franchise standards and all the equipment for a restaurant plus a percentage fee.

3. $200,000 for set-up including equipment plus a percentage fee like 5%. Typically for a printing and copying store that is affiliated with a courier company or supplies postal service, you would sign a lease for the franchise location. Courier companies such as United Parcel Service (UPS) and FedEx offer franchisees the opportunity to dispatch courier packages and mail and can include a long list of services such as post office boxes for rental, retailing packaging, shipping, copying and printing, faxing, passport and identification photography and money transfers. UPS has stores in 45 countries. Some of them operate under the UPS name. Others run under the name of Mail Boxes Etc. and have been established in over 6000 locations. www.mbe.com

4. License the name, with the franchisee required to use the same store name, such as Hallmark Cards. As long as you have the company name on the store and at least 65% of the sales are the franchisor's products, you would pay a small monthly fee. As a franchisor, you would, however, be responsible for start up costs. Setting up of a typical store could cost you $200,000 to $600,000. The benefit of a franchise arrangement is that you will get help with store design, special pricing on inventory, access to other suppliers, advertising and training.

5. A small takeout restaurant for Asian food could have an initial fee of $50,000 plus costs for the building and interior, a supply of ready-to-serve menu items, printed menus and price lists. You have to buy from an approved food supplier but no chef will be needed. The royalty will be 7-9% of which 2% is allotted to marketing.

Depending on the type of product or service and the country, there could be many potential industries and combinations of franchise arrangements. You will find franchising in the teaching profession, consulting services, kitchen supplies, automobile lubrication, building supplies, vehicle repairs, real estate, tax preparation, transportation, accounting and many more.

Joint Ventures

A joint venture is cooperative undertaking between two or more parties. It could be a company set up for manufacturing or marketing or a joint interest in research and development. There is a greater sense of ownership and a stronger commitment among the parties but there is also assumption of greater risk than licensing.

This is not an uncommon arrangement between car manufacturers for development of new products such as engines. It could be a strategic alliance or a short term project-specific initiative where the partners sign a contract for that project. The venture is usually based on common goals and mutual understanding between the partners. A typical example is the bridge between Denmark and

Sweden, where many companies from different countries where involved. When the bridge was completed, the joint venture was dissolved.

When are joint ventures suitable?

An exporting company may have no interest in a fully owned subsidiary in the new country but they want access to local expertise and production capacity. They need a partner with specific attributes but without the technical skills and products they already have. This would be an opportunity for a joint venture. The local company supplies knowledge, facilities and staff and the offshore partner supplies the product and know-how.

Another alternative is a joint venture where shared technology and geographical coverage make each of the partners more competitive in international and domestic markets. On example is Sony Ericsson, a 50:50 joint venture established in 2001 between the Sony Corporation in Japan, an industry leader in electronics, imaging and music and Telefonaktiebolaget LM Ericsson in Sweden, which is a major provider of telecommunications equipment and related services to mobile and fixed network operators. They created an attractive, innovate global brand in mobile handset technology. The joint venture has R&D and manufacturing capacity in more than 175 countries. The management team is comprised of representatives from both partner companies.

Joint venture in a local market

Your local partner likely already has a recognized name and contacts with the clients you are seeking. Instead of using a distribution arrangement where you transfer responsibilities to them, you may want to be an active participant. It is important to understand the market and to have established relationships with clients and with various levels of government. The joint venture provides those benefits.

In some countries where 100% foreign ownership is not allowed, a joint venture is one way to mitigate this restriction. Joint ventures are very common in China.

How much should you own? The ownership split has to be based on how much control you want, how much you are willing to invest, expected profitability, tax implications and special rules applicable in the country. If you hold more than 50%, you will have the controlling share. If you hold less than 25%, you will have very limited control. Despite not having majority ownership, it may be possible for you to exert control by selecting a majority of board members. There may also be a management contract provision requiring the Joint Venture to buy specific products or services from one of the parties.

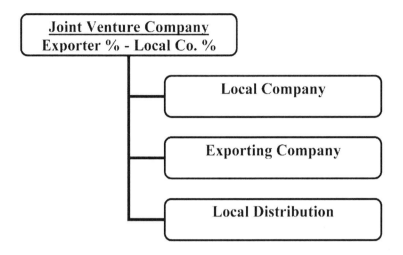

The joint venture may be a freestanding company with its own buildings, production and staff, but this is an expensive solution. It could be a separate legal entity that purchases manufacturing capacity from a local partner, rents space and contracts for staff. Compare this with a Subsidiary to Rent, where start-up costs are limited and there is greater flexibility.

At the outset, you should determine how to divide up the costs. Your partnership agreement might state, for example, that manufacturing expenses should be kept within plus or minus 5% of what they would be if the products were sub-contracted to or purchased from other suppliers. The agreement may include a fixed percentage fee for administration, based on sales or sales costs that are a percentage of sales. You should compare the financial and administrative demands of a joint venture to shared ownership in a subsidiary.

Other reasons why you should consider a joint venture:

You have restrictions on exporting because your production facility cannot handle fluctuations in sales

- Markets are geographically distant, making delivery times too long
- A project is too large for your existing resources or requires staff with special skills
- To extract more value from non-traditional products or services or leverage profits offshore with products that are no longer in demand locally. (extending the life cycle.)

♦ To use the joint venture partner's facilities also outside the territory included in the original agreement

♦ To pool resources and skills between the two organizations (sharing risks and possible rewards)

♦ You plan to "open the doors" in a market but that would not be possible without access to local people, contacts and special expertise

♦ To share your company's marketing and R&D skills and enhance opportunities on the global market

♦ The foreign country does not allow you to have 100% ownership and a joint venture is a compromise.

You have been given an outline of a variety of distribution alternatives. Below is a more comprehensive description of each distribution option. Part Two of the chapter you will also see a description of pros and cons of each alternative.

Distributor

For most exporters, using one or more distributors is the best choice in a foreign market. The organization and number of distributors and sub-distributors is very much dependant on the country you choose, the market and your resources. It is important that you understand the implications of each choice. The closer you are to the end user, the better the communications you can establish to convey information about your products and collect feedback from the market. Long distribution chains mean there will be more people wanting to make money– everyone's profitability will be reduced.

The importer of the goods or the company landing the product is the main distributor. Their main responsibilities are to set pricing, carry out marketing and find sub-distributors or dealers. The importer buys your product and sells directly to end users or via sub-distributors or dealers.

If your organization includes only one distributor for many products in a large country such as Germany, they will be required to establish a network of sub-distributors or dealers in each major geographic area and sometimes for individual consumer products in each major city. Sub-distributors would be responsible for local distribution. In such a scenario, there would be many levels of distribution. At each level or with each added link in the distribution chain, there is increased potential for supply interruptions, communications problems and loss of contact with end-users.

A small company looking for a distributor could be enticed to select a large company with a wide range of products. This could be of interest if your product/service is supplied for large projects. However, you will be one of many suppliers and could "disappear" among many other products and not get the priority you would like. A smaller distributor will have a narrower product range and your product get more attention. It is also easier to work with a small organisation.

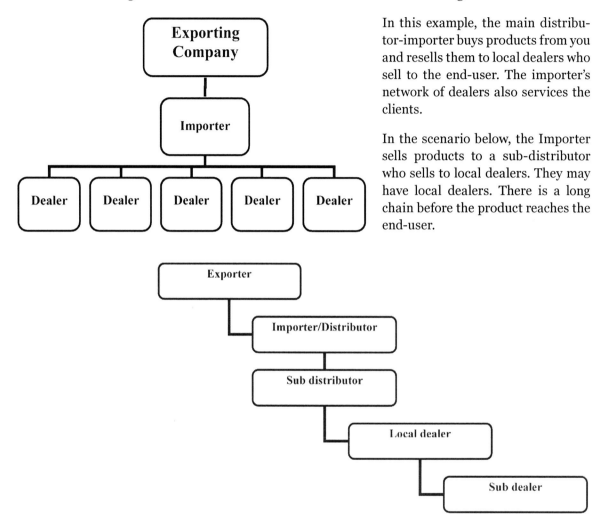

In this example, the main distributor-importer buys products from you and resells them to local dealers who sell to the end-user. The importer's network of dealers also services the clients.

In the scenario below, the Importer sells products to a sub-distributor who sells to local dealers. They may have local dealers. There is a long chain before the product reaches the end-user.

Communication and Distribution

As an exporter, you may feel it is easier to have just one contact who is your main distributor.

When many American companies set up distribution in Europe, it is not uncommon for them to treat Europe as one country and have one main distributor. In the same way, many European companies treat North America as one country, when in fact there are many unique market segments and regional differences in Canada and the US.

With one distributor, business may be easier from your perspective. But beware - you are at greater risk because of lack of regular feedback and fragmented communication networks over as larger geographic area. If that one distributor is incompetent or fails completely, you will have lost the whole market.

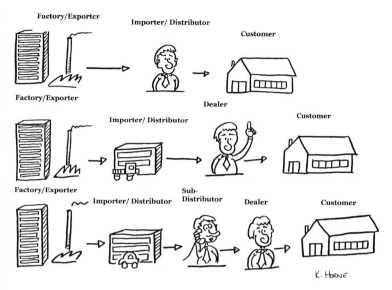

When I was young, we had a game where we whispered something in the next person's ear and that person whispered it to the next person and so on. We might start with the word 'bananas' but by the time we reached the sixth child in line, the word had changed to 'dogs'. The same happens with your communications in long distribution channels. Your message can disappear on the way to the end users and your feedback from the market will be minimum.

To go back to the previous example, if your main distributor in located in northern Germany, there may be a variety of reasons why companies in southern Germany would not want to deal with them. Even worse, if you set up a distributor in the US as the main distributor for all of North America, your buyers in Canada would not like this. Why should they purchase goods via the US? The same would be valid for a product manufactured in Brazil and sold via France to England.

So what is the alternative?

If you take the scenario of a Canadian company exporting to Germany, they can select the best dealers for each geographic area, e.g., two in the north, two in the south and one in the east. With this arrangement, they would have five available local dealers. If one is not working out as expected, they would still have four productive dealers.

With a team of local dealers, lines of communication are shortened. Because there are fewer people involved, business is more profitable for you and the dealers. You may not be able to cover every sales territory, but your overall results will probably

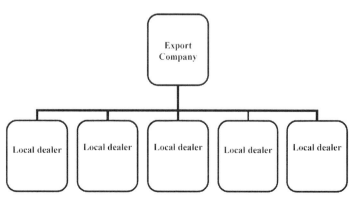

be better than simply using a general importer with sub-distributors. More information about pricing and profit has been included in the Export Pricing Chapter.

One more advantage is that if you have a general importer and they fail, you will lose all sales. If one of the dealers in the example fails, you would only lose small percentage of your distribution.

What are the drawbacks? You will have to find and activate five dealers instead of one. Those may be small and hungrier for your business. They will likely need more sales, financial and technical support. Freight costs may increase because instead of one large shipment you will have five smaller ones.

This approach may fit with your business strategy, but you have to take into consideration the implications of maintaining thirty dealers in the US, six in Italy, eight in France, five in Germany and four in Spain. This solution may seem attractive but you may not have the capacity to manage it effectively. As a small company you can't easily handle all the contacts and business issues and site visits.

An alternative approach

Strong communications and comprehensive market knowledge are essential. The option outlined below would result in the same benefit but at a slightly higher cost. On the plus side, there would be more direct contact with your dealers and the chance to delegate to someone else.

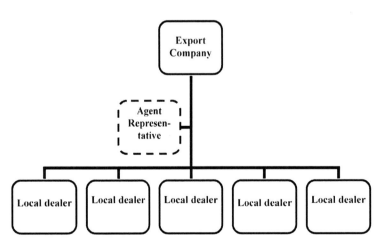

In this option, you work with a foreign representative whose responsibility would be to find and activate local dealers. Shipments and invoicing would go directly between you and the dealer.

You would pay the representative a retainer or commission, but compared with having a general importer, in this scenario you get local dealers who have daily contact with your representative. This representative will be on site, know the market and may even understand the culture of your business. They are your first contact for adding dealers to your network. It's like having your own company's staff person overseas, without the relocation costs. It also reduces the burden on you for market information and daily contact with the market. If there is a problem with payment, your local representative can deal with it.

You will train the representative; he or she will train the dealers. There is an additional benefit to having on on-site representative. A skilled representative who knows that your factory shuts down for vacation during the summer can ensure that dealers place their orders in advance.

The cost of maintaining your rep will vary from a one-time start-up fee with a retainer to a straight commission arrangement. The amount and percentage will depend on how much activity and involvement you demand and their capacity to generate profits. It will certainly cost less than having two level distribution systems with a distributor and dealers.

Resources and the level of control you want over distribution will determine the solution for your organization.

This approach would work well for organizations with limited resources and/or experience and in fact, this has saved many from failing in a foreign country. We have worked as the agent/representative for a number of European, Asian and Canadian companies with good results.

Other Methods of Distribution

Remember that depending on the country, products and services, your distribution solutions can vary. Part Two provides more examples as well as a comparison of the pros and cons of each solution.

Some customer groups and clients require special distribution channels. The illustration that follows is common for hardware products or consumer goods such as building materials.

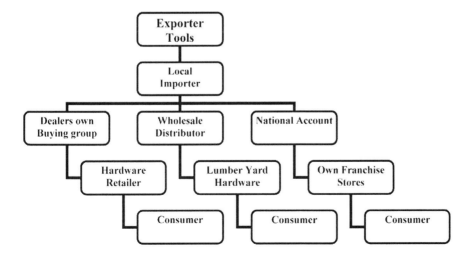

In this case, you have a general importer to cover all of the distributors.

The **dealers' buying group** can be a franchise set-up with a chain of stores using the same name, resulting in a chain of hardware stores spread across the country. There is centralized purchasing and advertising and a designated contact for the local importer. Supplies for the Hardware chain are delivered to the central warehouse that redistributes to the local stores.

A **Wholesale Distributor** can be a company that supplies to local lumber yards as well as to independent hardware stores.

A **National Account** is a company that own its stores. Examples in North America are Sears and The Bay. Tesco which is British but also available throughout Asia is another one as well as the French Carrefour - which is all over Europe and Asia as well.

You can shorten a long distribution chain by eliminating the importer and bypassing one level by going directly to the dealers' buying groups, the wholesale distributor or the National Account. Or you could start with one of them. Understand that if you are selling beauty products or automotive products for new cars and the aftermarket, the set-ups will all be different.

Are there other options?

Each country will have established distribution patterns. For example, in some you can buy groceries at a local gas station. Some have government-owned distribution centres for assistive devices or medical supplies, and they are heavily subsidized or free. Others maintain monopoly stores for sale of pharmaceuticals. You have to examine a variety of approaches before you decide on what is most appropriate for your product in a particular foreign market. Do not try to apply your domestic market distribution approach – it likely will not work.

Each alternative may require that you get closer to the customer. This requires thorough pre-planning, good communications, regular feedback and fewer people who have to make money in the distribution chain. The markets will continue to evolve in terms of complexity and size.

Dell Computers was a typical example of a business with minimal investment in traditional 'bricks and mortar' facilities, with no 'middle man'. If you wanted a Dell computer, you custom-designed the product, then ordered it directly on line or by telephone. The company assembled and shipped the custom computer you ordered. With increased competition, Dell now also sells via dealers, but there is still no distributor and no showrooms. This is an innovative way to keep the distribution channel short and eliminate the need for stocking products. Selling over the internet reduces personal services for the clients and is therefore a negative factor for the customer.

Some More Alternatives

Piggybacking

Find a successful company that has a similar market to yours. If you can join them in the export activities, do so. You both can offer potential clients/distributors a broader range of products/services.

IKEA the Swedish furniture company is familiar for many of you. When you visit their food department you will find Swedish herring and Crisp bread. IKEA is exporting the herring and bread for the Swedish food companies.

Contractors

The 2010 oil spill in the US 2010 highlights what can happen when a company has a broad span of control. When a disaster like this happens, resources are drawn from all over the world to help solve the problem. If you supply products to a domestic contractor with a contract in the US, they may use your products overseas. One more example from the same sector. The drill rigs use lots of drill pipes. If you supply product to a local drill rig operator there is a good chance they will use your products also to their projects overseas.

Multinational Distribution

Perhaps you supply goods to a catalogue house in Belgium. That company also sell to Spain, Italy and Portugal. Because of that you now have distribution in those countries too.

Many household goods suppliers are adopting "just-in-time" principles as a way of reducing overhead and reacting more quickly to consumer demands. If this is the case you have to find a solution to ensure a steady supply of products.

In this chapter, you have learned about many distribution alternatives. There are many more. You have to find the right combination for your business, your product/services and the respective market and customer groups. However, sometimes the market dictates the distribution channel/solution. When that happens you will be "forced" to use a different solution than you wanted to use. So even though you want a solution with few distribution levels the market dictates that you use a longer one with more levels.

Does all this sound complicated? It is and it isn't.

Using common sense, you can select what is most appropriate for your business in each market. As always, it is the customer who decides what and how they want to buy. Follow their advice, do your research, take into account what resources you can commit and you will identify the most appropriate solution for you.

More types of distribution channels

Commission House or Commission Merchant

An agent usually takes physical control and negotiates the sale of the goods they handle. Commission merchants usually have broader powers than a broker.

Consumers' cooperative (CO-OP)

A retail business owned and operated by consumers to sell primarily to its members.

Discount house

A retail business, normally featuring consumer goods and competing on price.

Merchant

A business that buys, takes title to and resells merchandize. Wholesalers and retailers are merchants.

Rack jobber

A wholesaling business unit that markets specialised lines of merchandise to certain type of retail stores, maintains displays and refills inventories. Most common in the food business.

Resident buyer

Either a local purchaser for a client or an agent for an overseas buyer, residing in the country where products are sourced.

Voluntary group

A group of retailers each of whom owns and operates their own store but who are associates who buy and sell jointly with other retailers in the group.

You have covered the basics of distribution in Part One of this chapter. If you would like more detailed information, you can continue reading Part Two. I will give you more examples and distribution alternatives with pros and cons for each one covered in Part One. I will also describe E-commerce. There are exercises at the end of the chapter so that you can practice what you learn.

Summary

This chapter described the most common methods and combinations for distribution as well as some advantages and disadvantages. You have the find the right combination based on the market, your capabilities and business objectives.

When making any business decision, it is important that you analyze what is suitable for your business. The selection of distribution method is dependent on the market's stage of development as well as your company's goals and the resources you have available, the control you want and how much you will delegate to others, what distribution channels there are available and what business practices and organization structures are permitted.

Like any other business strategy, your choice of distribution method should be reviewed regularly. Planning and flexibility will help you adjust to uncontrollable changes such as currency fluctuations, political instability, environmental issues, war and natural disasters. Don't become complacent - keep yourself informed and be prepared to adapt your activities according to conditions.

♦ Remember that you have use the right method of distribution to the end user. Always start with the end-user and work backwards. Your local partner is key to your success.

♦ Decide how much control you want and what you are permitted to do in the market

♦ To maintain effective communications and maximize profitability, you should keep the distribution chain as short as possible

♦ You have to select and adapt an option also based on your company's resources and finances. Unlimited resources allow you to have full control with your own organisation in the market. Limited resources mean that you have to use local companies for your activities

♦ Do your homework first so that you can understand the market you want to enter. If you make an informed selection, you will be in a good position to succeed. If you are wrong, it could be a costly mistake.

♦ Consider a variety of implications for export prices and profitability (political, social, technological, economic, environmental)

♦ Tap into the potential of the internet and e-commerce for your business. (See Part Two of this chapter)

♦ Decide from the beginning if you want your own organization or if you want to use a firm or distributor who is already established. Alternatives to setting up your own company include licensing and joint venture.

♦ The right combination of distribution channel and pricing strategy will help you become more competitive. Your choice will be affected by your resources and what you expect from your international partner.

This is the end of Part One. For more alternatives and details as well as the pros and cons, I suggest you read Part Two. In the Export Pricing chapter you will learn that the selection of a distribution method is also influenced by the price level of your product and how much profit you can make.

Selecting the Right Distribution and Sales Channels – Part Two

E-Commerce

The ease of modern transportation and communications has changed the global business. Let's begin by looking at some other aspects of distribution and international business.

E-Commerce or E-Business is a process of buying and selling on-line, i.e. over electronic systems like Internet or other computer networks.

Growing access to the Internet and the proliferation of web sites have allowed even small companies to advertise their products and services all over the world. It has also created opportunities for them to service and sell to global customers.

There were 1.73 billion Internet users in 2010 or about 25% of the world's population. The major users are: 738 million in Asia (China has 253 million), 418 million in Europe and 253 million in North America and 179 million in Caribbean and Latin American countries.

Almost 247 billion e-mails were sent every day in 2009. Unfortunately for legitimate users, 70% of those messages are spam or virus carriers, so the volume of "real" e-mail is about 47 billion a day. Half of internet users make purchases on-line and another 400 million will join by 2012, resulting in over 1 billion Internet users contributing $1.2 trillion to all global business (B2C or Business to Consumer). Online sales now account for 6% of all retail sales in the United States and are expected to grow to 8% by 2013. Four percent of sales in Great Britain are made online. Many online sales also produce increases in store sales as customers learn more about the products companies offer.

The emerging global interconnectedness will spread ideas and innovations around the world faster than ever before. Online spending rose to $3.2 billion for the week ending on Sunday November 29 2009. This was over 6% more than during the same period previous year, according to comScore, an online market-research firm. (Source: Economist.com, 2009) By 2014, there will be 3 billion Internet subscribers (source: The Economist, 2009). Purchases will also be made by 600 million mobile internet subscribers.

Communication is not only about email and websites. The use of social media in the context of e-commerce has exploded: 350 million subscribers use Facebook every day, 1 billion access You Tube and 27.3 million "Tweet" every day on Twitter. There are hundreds of thousands of blogs. All of these media provide entrepreneurs with free and instant access to customers around the world. Business of the future will have to be part of those social networks if they want to promote themselves, attract new customers and create new ventures using 'online communities'.

E-commerce is an enormous, fast-growing market. Most of us think of e-commerce as a consumer buying books, clothing, tickets or electronics online, but 90% is transactions between businesses, B2B. We are talking of more than 12 trillion dollars a year or 30% of all the business between companies.

Develop a great web site that is easy to find

Before going into too much detail about the different solutions you should know that you can benefit substantially on the global market by using the internet and one or more well-designed web sites. By setting up one or more easy to locate sites, you open the door to advertising and selling your products and delivering customer service.

> ### Example - Better image than you deserve
>
> *About 20 years ago I launched my first web site. The purpose was to explain what I had to offer. One large corporation in Sweden arranging workshops on international business were interested in my services. They told me after we met that they thought my company was too large to do business with, so they did not approach me at that time. I had five people employed and they had 200. The impression created by my website was deceptive.*

With a web site, you create a presence in the global marketplace. You can showcase your products and services in several languages. By using different domain names, you can make them appear local like:..eu, com, ca, sp, etc., creating the image your company is established on many markets.

B2C or Business to Consumer

Amazon.com started by selling books over the internet. Today, the product range includes DVDs, music, games, downloadable books and grocery products. Media comprise only 60% and electronics 35% of sales. Amazon.com keeps track of customer buying patterns and can make personalized recommendations on products of interest. In 2009, the company sold more than $25 billion worth of goods.

When looking at B2C there are two categories: products you can feel, like clothing and products like books, music CDs and computer equipment that you do not. You can download music, books and computer software over the Internet, make stock market trades, complete bank transactions and buy automobile insurance. The market really started to take off in late 2009 with many other companies selling electronics, e-books and mobile phones. In fact by late 2010, Amazon.com sold more e-books that printed books.

Many consumers are making their travel arrangements online. The travel industry is very competitive. Depending on demand and availability, prices can fluctuate considerably. As well, most major airlines have switched to electronic ticketing, online check-in and downloadable boarding passes.

Internet sales cover all products, from food and wine to office supplies, vehicles and luxury goods. With a website a small company located "in the bush" in northern Finland is able to market wild blueberries worldwide, without having a bricks-and-mortar office.

C2B - Customer to Business

At Priceline.com you can buy at a fixed price or submit bids on airline flights, vacation packages, cars, hotels and cruises. You can determine how much you are willing to pay, but according to Priceline terms and conditions, when the seller accepts your bid, you must complete the transaction.

C2C - Customer to Customer

E-Bay is an online auction company. You put in a bid for a product that someone wants to sell or you can list a product that you want to sell. E-Bay takes a small commission ranging from as low as 1.5% for over $1000 to 8.75% on low value goods. Traditional auction firms normally charge around 15 - 25%.

E-Bay is established in 30 international markets and has over 276 million users. They sell about $2000 worth of goods per second. On a daily basis, there are more than 10,000 vehicles offered for auction. More are sold every day on e-Bay than a car dealer can sell in a year – on average, one vehicle every minute. The most expensive item sold on E-Bay was a Gulfstream II Jet valued at $6 million, of which about $75,000 was E-Bay's commission. Unfortunately, you can also find stolen goods sold on-line too.

B2B - Business to Business

This is the largest market, involving many types of companies and products and services. Some companies will only do business this way. Purchasing, order acknowledgement, invoicing as well as payments can be completed online. Here are two examples.

A Singapore Airlines 747 aircraft lands in Buenos Aires and gets a flat tire. The local Singapore Airline flight manager logs onto the Boeing Company Commercial Aviation Services web site to locate the closest replacement tire supplier, places the order and arranges for shipment. Singapore Airlines is invoiced automatically at the agreed-upon price. The tire arrives the next day.

Cisco Systems is one of the largest telecommunications, network and security services and data management systems providers. The company has about $100 million worth of sales a day. Cisco offers certification training, financing options, links to retailers and resellers and tools for customers to manage services ordering, contracts and obtain quotes online. Customers can search for Cisco products on the company web site and make purchases. Since between 80-90% of online orders are initiated by customers, there is a reduced demand for salespeople. This saves Cisco hundreds of millions of dollars every year. Most of the company's subcontracting, after sales service, technical support and trouble shooting is managed online.

There are thousands of B2B marketplaces on the Internet. Many companies maintain joint selling channels. Chrysler purchase manufacturing components from thousands of suppliers electronically.

Examples of B2B marketplaces

♦ **Supplyon** (for Successful Supply Chain Management and Global Supplier Integration) for the manufacturing and automotive industry - www.supplyon.com

♦ **Elemica** (supply chain experts who partner with manufacturers to accelerate revenues through innovative and effective solutions) - www.elemica.com

♦ **Chemconnect** (provides chemical industry customers around the world with on-demand solutions to dramatically improve their supply chain performance) - www.chemconnect.com

- ♦ **Transsora** (community of consumer products manufacturers, retailers and member organizations dedicated to developing technology solutions that lower supply chain costs) - www.transora.com/faqs.html

- ♦ **GHX** (software and services for organizations that buy, sell, track or use medical products - www.ghx.com

The Government Sector

Government procurement is an important aspect of international trade, given the considerable size of the market (often 10-15 percent of GDP) and the benefits for domestic and foreign stakeholders in terms of increased competition. (World Trade Organization, 2010)

Many governments have implemented electronic procurement, some with on-line databases where prospective suppliers can subscribe to receive information. Tenders Electronic Daily (TED) provides free access to business opportunities. It is updated several times a week and lists about 1500 public procurement notices from members of the European Union and in the European Economic Area.

Link the distributor website to your updated information

Say you are a supplier in New Zealand and you have a distributor in England. The two of you can set up a system so that when a client in England logs on to the distributor's web site they get updated information from your web site without having to leave the distributor's site. That way, you can always deliver the most recent information available.

Additional Distribution Solutions

The number of distribution solutions and combinations is almost endless. You have to understand how each market works. Don't just look at how things are done today - look for solutions that haven't been invented yet.

When Dell started selling computers directly to end users, it was a new idea. None of the established vendors like IBM reacted. IBM continued to sell in the same way, through distributors and dealers. Over time the market changed dramatically. Lenovo, the new brand for the former IBM Company, sells directly to customers as does the Hewlett-Packard (HP) Company. Dell has changed the concept of selling directly to customers and now also sell also through dealers.

Many companies think that the more dealers or distributors they have, the more products they will sell. That is completely wrong!

Example - Fewer distributors and more sales

When I took over responsibility for a small European company manufacturing drill presses and exporting to Canada, they were selling to a lot of dealers. In fact, they sold drill presses to any dealer that placed an order. The result was that too many people were competing on price and they had limited interest in promoting the products. There were 15 dealers in Canada alone. I reduced that to four, each of whom had an assigned territory. This allowed them to benefit directly from their sales efforts. Sales increased in the first year by 800%.

Example - Selling under more than one product name

Another company I introduced to the US was competing with large American companies that had hundreds of dealers. We wanted a limited number of distributors either with their own sales force or with a network of dealers. We also wanted to be included in their distribution to a company selling directly to end-users, using a large catalogue.

So how did we do this without creating competition on price?

We selected two different distributors in the United States. One company sold products labelled with the Swedish company name to automotive dealers and quick-lube shops. They also sold the same products labelled with the US Company's name and logo with another product number. The distributors printed up catalogues which were sent to dealers; the dealers sold those products using the catalogues.

We also set up another distributor that was mainly selling to dealers selling to the manufacturing industry. The distributor's product was a private brand and was sold with each company's name and special product number. Both companies knew about each other's existence but they were not competing for the same clients.

Many of the US competitors were selling under their own company name to many dealers in the same geographic area, creating competition on price. There was no guarantee that the salesperson promoting the product would get the order. We were able to take a significant part of the market from our American competitors because our distributors and dealers could promote the Swedish products knowing that nobody else could compete with the same product or pricing.

Private labelling

When you buy a major appliance from Sears's department store, it is not manufactured by Sears. It may carry the Sears Kenmore brand name but it could have been manufactured by Samsung, Whirlpool or LG and private-labelled for Sears. You find similar arrangements for food and health care products which are sold under the name of store or their private brand but manufactured by someone else. Of course, by having more brands you also create competition with yourself. Examples of private brands are Life Brand (Shopper Drug Mart), Kirkland (Costco, Price Club) and President's Choice (Loblaws)

Using Specific Sales Channels

Sometimes you have to follow a certain distributor channel whether you want to or not.

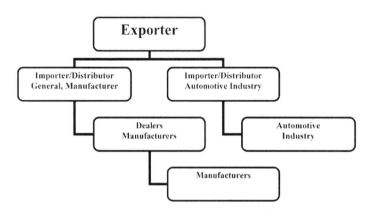

You want to sell your product to the large automobile manufacturers. They do not want to deal with too many companies and in the last couple of years they have reduced the number of approved suppliers. You will have to select one of the approved distributors/dealers to work with. If you sell metalworking machinery and you want to cover the automotive industry and small manufacturers, your distribution arrangement could look like this example.

Selling directly to end users

You are a manager for a Finish company manufacturing snow plow blades. You want to sell them in Sweden, where snow removal on the main highways is done by a transportation authority's maintenance department (Vägverket). For large tenders, the Transport Administration is required by law to advertise their procurements in a publicly available database or on the Transport Authority's website. You can quote and supply direct if you win the contract but you can still sell smaller quantities of your blades directly to the Authority without tender. They will know how many new blades they need each year and can place their order for delivery in time for the winter use.

Why sell directly?

♦   A good option when there is a limited number of potential clients to sell products to

♦   The product can be customized or tailor-made

♦   Products or services are sold through a tendering process

♦   The existence of Complex systems and a strong requirement for ongoing technical support, e.g., power stations

♦   The product is perishable and cannot be stored for long time, such as live lobsters

♦ There is no suitable distribution channel or dealer network for your highly specialized product or service

♦ Government wants to deal directly with the manufacturer under contract or they want to make a counter-trade arrangement

Large companies and major retailers sometimes maintain **resident buyers** in many markets/countries. You can contact them directly to sell your products. Their staff takes care of the logistics and consolidate overseas shipments to their domestic warehouse. One example is BMW having an office for international procurement in India.

Here is another example

A Spanish company sells metal-working equipment. The exporter has set up a representative in Belgium to contact local manufacturers. The machines are shipped and invoiced directly to local clients. The Belgian representative receives his commission when the Spanish exporter's invoice is paid.

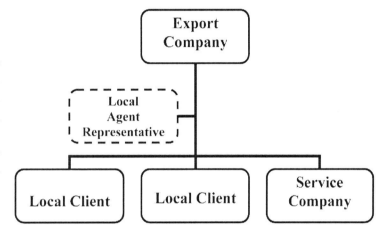

So how is service delivered?

It is very common to have specialized companies that deal with many manufacturers. A company like Volkswagen does not want numerous service companies repairing their metal working-machinery. – If possible, they want one company doing all of the work. That is the one company you should contact to provide spare parts and service for your machines, too.

More distribution channels for the same product

Your company makes steel tracks for skid steer loaders like Bobcat and for forestry machinery. The tracks create a lower ground pressure and allow the machinery to work on soft ground and snow.

So who are the customers?

For the forestry machines:

- Large international forestry companies
- Sawmills and pulp mills
- Small forest management companies
- Farmers who own woodlots
- Contractors in the forestry industry

For the skid steer machines:

- Large and small contractors
- Landscape contractors
- Commercial nurseries and greenhouses
- Airports
- Municipalities
- Equipment rental companies

As you can see from these examples, there are many potential clients and end users. On top of that there will be distribution channels which may be rather complicated. No matter what the arrangements, start with the end user. In this case there will be many different distribution channels based on client requirements and product selected.

Trends in International Sales

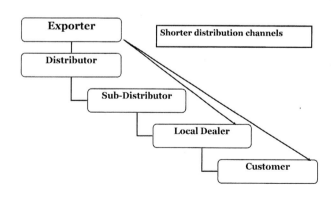

With a rapidly expanding market and increasing competition, more companies try to shorten the distribution chain to improve communications and reduce the number of levels making money. This allows the exporter to become more competitive. Access to the internet makes it easier to advertise products or services at a very low price; take orders and receive payments online. This easy access is not always positive. Your clients can easily compare prices and so can your competitors. More details will be provided in the pricing chapter.

As was common with agents and representatives in the past, now more companies want to shorten the distribution chain to be closer to the clients. They achieve this by eliminating the importer and making direct contact with the manufacturer overseas.

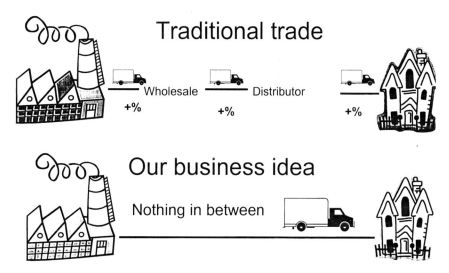

The model above shows a domestic company selling chemicals and cleaning products directly to the end user in neighbouring countries, similar to what Dell computers has been doing. This is direct contact with the end user and eliminates any middleman.

Use your freight forwarder overseas as a distribution center

Increasingly, freight forwarders are offering to manage your shipping services and also to store and distribute your products in foreign markets. You can use these service providers to become more competitive.

For example, you can export full containers to the new country. The local freight forwarder can split up the shipment for delivery to each dealer in several locations. You can also keep the product in a bonded warehouse (see more in the chapter about Freight) to avoid payment of duties and taxes until the goods are shipped to the end user. If you have a registered company overseas, you can have the freight forwarder transport smaller shipments and completing the paperwork for you, including invoicing.

You have to look at local rules and laws to determine what you are allowed to do. If you set up a warehouse in Belgium for product distribution in Europe, the advantage is that you can keep your stock there and supply each market with short turnaround times. You maintain ownership until the goods are sent to your dealers or end users. As long as you have a valid VAT number, the Value Added Tax, you can ship anywhere within the EU using a freight forwarder. However, you cannot modify and assemble product using a third party. So if you use someone to handle the distribution, goods have to be sent as "is". For more information search "fiscal representation EU" on Google.

Export Consortiums

Companies often form partnerships when undertaking joint activities in foreign markets. Instead of each manufacturer of pulp and paper machinery in a domestic market making an individual effort to market their products, they create an association or consortium through which they can work together. Together, the group will have a broader range of products and services to offer. They can even hire local staff and split the costs.

Local Demands on Distribution and Approvals

Each country will have different requirements for approvals and product distribution. Make sure to do advance thorough research so that you can comply. The examples below are from Japan and deal with wine distribution. You can review the source information at www.jetro.org because this is a complicated distribution and approval process. This is common in Japan and you have to use it whether you want or not.

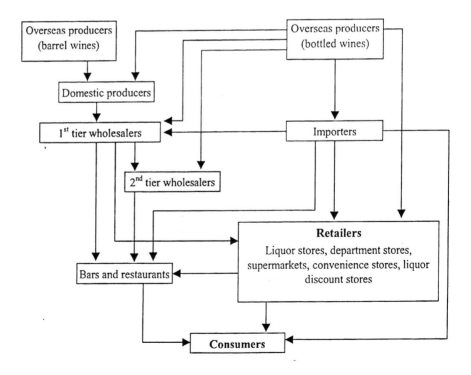

Licensing and tax on licensing fee

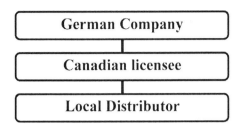

As we have discussed previously, licensing could be a good solution in markets you still want some income from but where you don't have the time or resources to cover on your own. Note that your licensing royalties from the overseas market will be considered as income. The foreign country you work in, will most likely tax you on part of that and require the licensing partner (your Canadian licensee) to retain a withholding tax. In many industrial countries, it will be 15%. If there is a tax treaty between the foreign country and your country, you will most likely be able to deduct the amount withheld on your local tax return.

Licensing examples

The Mine Company was established with a subsidiary and had investigated which products could be manufactured and sold locally. They had previously sold several products manufactured by sub-contractors.

As they did not have their own manufacturing capacity or sufficient resources to market the product, a decision was made to find a licensing partner. At the negotiation stage, they had data on existing sales, established market prices and manufacturing costs from the local sub-contractors. They also had a market survey and a sales forecast. Having already sold products in the market, they knew the profitability and opportunities. In other words, Mine Company was very well prepared.

The contract negotiated with the licensee included:

- ◆ A large down payment - the product was already established
- ◆ A substantial royalty fee (12%) – there was an established high margin on the product. The foreign manufacturer asked for 20% of the gross margin, which was 60%, based on their subcontracted purchases. Those purchases already included a profit for the sub-contractor, so the gross margin for the licensing partner would be higher.
- ◆ The licensee/partner was required to buy a certain number of consulting hours each year to ensure transfer of knowledge and experience

As you can see, the licensing fee is not always a standard percentage. It is based on the anticipated profitability of the product and how much money the licensing partner can make. More detail about this will be provided in the Pricing chapter.

It can be difficult to control sales volume and selling price when a product is included in a licensing package. It may be possible to establish a fixed royalty per year. Also, you could include a provision to convert the licensing agreement to a joint venture at a later date. Once the licensing arrangement is in place, you may find that the market has more potential than you thought. At that point, you may want to be directly involved and take a stronger market position.

In addition to down payments and management fees, there could be imposed taxes. It is important to manage tax liabilities that arise because you conduct business overseas. If you have a profitable domestic company and pay taxes there, it may not matter where you pay them.

There are legal ways to limit taxes such as establishing a subsidiary and arranging an agreement between that subsidiary and your licensing partner. Because, the money earned never leaves the country, you will not have to pay withholding tax.

Joint Venture

Earlier, we described what a joint venture is. However, there is more than one way to utilize it. Let say you are a company in Turkey wanting to establish an operation in Latin America. You understand that you have to manufacture locally but don't want to set up your own manufacturing facility. What do you do? You set up a joint venture with a business in Brazil. You can also utilize that joint venture as a base for expanding your sales to other countries in Latin America.

You establish a subsidiary in Brazil to manufacture and sell refrigerators. That subsidiary is given the rights to the product designs and sales rights. The subsidiary forms a Joint Venture with another Brazilian company. This new company is owned 50/50 by the subsidiary and their local partner. Share capital equals $100,000 or $50,000 each.

The subsidiary (your local company) signs a licensing agreement with the new Joint Venture Company and asks for $50,000 down payment and 6% royalty on sales.

So, the subsidiary pays $50,000 as their share capital and receives $50,000 as a down payment on your license. As you can see the arrangement costs the subsidiary nothing (the share capital amount is netted out by the down payment received). On top of the income earned through the Joint Venture, your subsidiary will also earn income on royalties from licensing. Make sure to investigate the local tax laws so that you can plan for future payments.

What other uses can you make of this type of set up?

A local solution for a joint venture

Another example of what you could do with this company.

It could be a legal entity with headquarters at your lawyer's office address in Brazil. It could be an active company located in facilities your company owns or it could even rent space from your Joint Venture partner. The subsidiary has legal rights to your products. What are the practical implications?

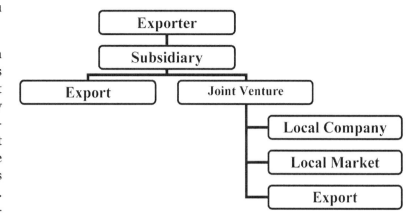

As the licensing fee from the Joint Venture does not leave Brazil, there will be no withholding tax. If the Joint Venture Company makes a profit and pays dividends to its shareholders, it will be to your Brazilian subsidiary and Brazilian partner because they are considered domestic companies.

This solution opens up more opportunities.

- Instead of the Joint Venture Company exporting all the products manufactured, your subsidiary could buy products from the Joint Venture and selling them domestically or export to other markets.

- If your parent company has limited production capacity, you can buy products from your subsidiary for sale at home.

- By being part of the local market you can apply for subsidies and loans that may be available.

- If the government in your domestic market is not prepared to assist your business, the foreign government where your Joint Venture is located can be more supportive. Some countries grant export subsidies and pay for travel and exhibition costs.

- If you are in a free trade zone, you can utilize this to your advantage.

- Some countries do not allow majority foreign ownership. You may be able to negotiate a combination of a Joint Venture with a management contract that gives you a majority of members on the board of directors. You would then have *de facto* (in practice but not by law) control of the foreign company.

Why Some Joint Ventures Don't Work?

The major reason some joint ventures fail is a collision of cultures - two very different cultures trying to work within one company.

You and your partner have to agree from the beginning how you will work together. Perhaps it is natural that with a joint venture in Germany, you will agree to the German culture being predominant in the company. Alternatively, in the United States, American customs and management philosophy would be the prime culture. – Local market decides on business culture and trust. - One approach to eliminating potential culture clashes is to encourage the management-to-be to become involved during the pre-agreement stage of negotiations. Don't forget that circumstances will change during the process of developing the venture. Everyone involved should be prepared to be flexible.

Many large companies have international management team members who have been selected and trained to cope with common pitfalls such as cultural or language barriers that are encountered in international business arrangements. Joint ventures can be more complex than you might expect. They require considerable diplomacy and cooperation to be successful.

Which solution should you select?

We have covered numerous distribution solutions. Because there are so many combinations, it is up to you to find the best solution for each market and customer group. Don't forget that you must **start with the end user** and work backwards. You must also analyze what is appropriate and what is permitted in the country. Find an innovative solution that makes you more competitive! Don't just look at how it is done today; if you discover a better solution, you will have a future advantage.

There are pros and cons with different options. Some of them are listed below. If you don't remember all of the distribution solutions, flip back in the book and review them before reading the pros and cons.

Pros and Cons of Different Distribution Solutions

Indirect Exporting

Indirect Exporting

Advantages	Disadvantages
Requires no or limited investment	You gain limited knowledge about the foreign market
Requires limited knowledge of the export market	As an exporter, you cannot control or influence sales
You will not be faced with local political and finance risks	

Direct Exporting Ownership and No Ownership

Ownership: Where you have own a local company like a subsidiary. No ownership: You use someone else like a distributor.

Export Consortium

Export Consortium

Advantages	Disadvantages
Easier to obtain market contacts and information	Can create problems with partners working together
Allows more active contact with clients	Increased demands on staff
Better service opportunities	Can create delays in receiving payments
Faster market penetration	If disputes are not resolved, it can result in the consortium splitting up
Advantage of a "package" of more products/services	

Representative Office

Representative Office

Advantages	Disadvantages
Can usually be started without any formal registration	Normally a short-term solution
Normally does not require complex bookkeeping or reporting to local authorities as no income is "earned"	Allows only limited activities in the country, otherwise it has to be registered as a branch office.
Low operating costs and easy to close operations	The customer does not see it as a commitment, which can have a negative influence on your business

Branch Office

Branch Office

Advantages	Disadvantages
Easy to register	Can be taxed on sales volumes. Some countries impose a branch tax on all sales to compensate for lost profits
In most cases, the parent company can utilize losses from the foreign branch office start-up and can also transfer profits later on	Your parent company is legally and financially responsible for the foreign company's activities
Better market knowledge	It can be complicated to transform the branch office into a subsidiary, if that is feasible in the future
Seen as a local company by clients	Clients may view the company negatively if you do not do business through a local legal entity. (The clients may not know the legal status). However, more commitment than using local representative.
Better control than using local company	

The Subsidiary as Sales Company

The Subsidiary as Sales Company

Advantages	Disadvantages
You have your own channel into the market	Normally substantial start-up costs, resulting in losses the first few years
You keep control of your company know-how	Larger financial risks
You concentrate on your company products and services	It could be difficult to recruit and train the right local staff
Possibility of consolidating profits. Profitability stays within the company	A risk if you do not succeed it can create negative results even if you later on set up a local representative
Can create increased prestige in the foreign market	It takes more time to shut down if the business does not work
Greater operational freedom and independence	You could lose your good reputation if you have to leave the country
The legal entity is separate from the parent company. If something goes wrong, the parent company has limited legal liability	The subsidiary may have too narrow a product line to make it profitable or be able to compete
You can control and activate the local organization, with an emphasis on your products. You have your own specialists	There could be heavy local taxation. The investments can become locked in because you can't afford to change the structure or shut down
Demonstrates your commitment to the country and may mean lower taxes	Investment is influenced by both economical and political risks
You can quickly implement your own strategies and ideas	You may be required to establish a larger organization than your human resources and finances can practically support
Easier to test the market because you are already there	
Faster, more direct contacts with head office. Better feedback of market information to parent company	
From a business point of view, it is an advantage to have a local legal entity empowered to make agreements	
Easier sales to governments and local authorities	
You can belong to local trade associations	

Subsidiary for Rent

Subsidiary for Rent

Advantages	Disadvantages
Low initial cost	Depends on finding the right partner or landlord to rent from
Low fixed costs	The facility is not yours and you have limited staff of your own, at least in the start-up phase
Access to established office and local staff	Very limited control, unless specified in partnership arrangements
Clear legal and physical establishment on the market	Dependent on partner for level of participation
Allows you to compare what is needed for setting up your own local office	
Flexible expansion	

Local Manufacturing

Local Manufacturing

Advantages	Disadvantages
Seen as a local company; the foreign classification is not applicable. A local product may be given more favourable treatment compared with foreign products. Can also receive local subsidies	The company can lose economies of scale advantages - splitting up production into smaller quantities in many markets
Full control of production	May have to arrange for the factory in one country to obtain a world mandate for a product to compensate for loss of sale
Fewer trade restrictions such as customs duties and quotas; lower transport costs than if sending from your domestic market	Significant financial demands
Can provide more competitive pricing because of lower wages, no customs duties or other charges	Can create internal problems among other units in the company's group, e.g., production, research and design re: who pays for what? The subsidiary does not want to pay for R&D done offshore; Head Office wants to share costs
Greater flexibility for adapting products and production to the host country's standards, culture and economy	Competition locally may affect product development cycles – keeping current could be expensive
Tax benefits, grants for starting up a new activity, including staff training and development subsidies	
Possibility to join local business and professional organizations and associations	
More flexibility with human resource management than at home	
If a large market the local production can translate into a better profitability	
Faster delivery and less shipping cost as well as eliminating customs duties	
Easier to adapt to local cultures as most of the staff are local	
Access to 'competitive intelligence' increases opportunities to influence the market	

Contract Manufacturing

Contract Manufacturing

Advantages	Disadvantages
Does not require significant financial investments	May be difficult to control and administer production and quality
Utilizes lower wage levels for workers	You will transfer production knowledge to someone else you cannot control
Can use the term "made in" on the domestic market	Your manufacturer could be a potential competitor in the future. Can be minimized by using more manufacturers and separate assembly
Political risk is minimized	
Customs and duties eliminated	

Direct Export to End User

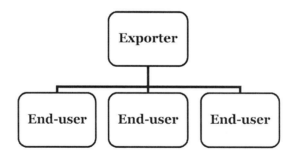

Direct Export to End User

Advantages	Disadvantages
Good direct contact	Heavy workload – you have to do everything yourself
Fewer levels wanting to make money, so you increase your profits and become more competitive	Does not always allow for daily contacts
Small risk. No stock overseas	Increased administration for shipping and payments
Good service to customer	Increased burden for client because of direct import
Gain good knowledge about the market	Could create credit and currency problems

Using Local Distribution (Distributors, Dealers, etc.)

You normally use foreign companies to assist you locally when:

- ♦ You receive frequent orders.

- ♦ There is a requirement for fast deliveries. Goods have to be available locally.

- ♦ You want to reach a specialized market where special representatives are required.

- ♦ You need to distribute a wide range of products and your product line will not be broad enough to cover the marketing costs.

- ♦ There could be a large number of users that continuously need support and possibly local financing.

- ♦ This type of products/service is already established on the market and can use existing distribution channels

- ♦ Local storage is important.

- ♦ The exporter has limited resources to handle local marketing.

Using Local Distribution

Advantages	Disadvantages
Will be well established on the local market with knowledge and customer contacts. The exporting company does not need to build up a local organization or service	Fewer possibilities for the exporting company to control or influence sales
Minimal initial investments costs for the exporting company compared with setting up a subsidiary. Local representative makes substantial commitment by buying your products	Local distributor has less knowledge about your products and will need/require more ongoing support
Local network already has an established customer service organisation with increased goodwill for exporter	Local distributor can sell competing products
Normally lower sales costs	Limited opportunity to direct activities and a risk of losing sales or representatives in the country
Local representative probably has good knowledge about local products and markets that can compensate for lack of knowledge of the distributor's products	A risk that your representative stops selling your product in favour of one of your competitors. Local representative can be future competitor
The local company can adapt their organisation to the products they sell. The exporting company does not need to build a local sales organisation	A poorly-performing representative can cause your product to have a bad image if clients not served properly
No need for you to put local resources in place	If the partner company goes bankrupt it could lead to severe losses for the exporter
Foreign partner takes on most of the risk except perhaps for product liability	Your product could "get lost" or have a low profile if the client has a broad range of products
Less demand on you to develop knowledge of the local market	You gain limited knowledge about the market and fewer customer contacts
Limited market and political risks	Your representative may not be able to fulfill special requests from you or the market

Trading Houses

Trading Houses

Advantages	Disadvantages
You have access to an already established market with local contacts with little or no financial investment and with small risks	Limited possibilities to influence the sales of your products
You will not need your own export department or export personnel. The resource demands for travel, correspondence and shipping can be reduced considerably	Trading Houses demand simple products without a lot of accessories or model selections. Does not work with products that need adaptation to local market or that require service
A quick way to utilize established distribution channels because the Trading House already has a broad customer base	You get one more level between you and the end user. There may be too many distribution levels to be profitable.
The Trading House has special knowledge of the geographical area which makes it possible to export to more distant market than you normally would reach and have the resources to enter those markets	Difficult to know where the product is sold. No customer contact
Trading House staff are knowledgeable about challenging or difficult markets or small markets that would not otherwise be of interest	Less technical service available for clients
Low market and administrative costs; very low business risks. Expenses are incurred by the Trading House as well as the risks	Trading houses usually have a very broad range of products. There is a risk your product will disappear in their product range
Your product will gain a positive image because a reputable Trading House represents your product	Many individuals will have to be educated about your product(s)
You can use your limited resources for other export markets	Many products are too expensive or the export price will be too low for the exporter
Small risk for delayed payment as they are normally fast to pay	
As the Trading Houses normally deals with both import and export, they can take on responsibility for counter trade and arrange low cost financing as well as importing for you	

Licensing

Licensing

Advantages	Disadvantages
Normally you receive a substantial down payment and royalty	Working with a local manufacturer may limit your opportunities to control production and quality
Opportunity to increase income from markets that you would not otherwise reach. You can get a contribution towards paying off your original Research and Development costs and thereby create extra profit.	May be fewer opportunities to influence sales volumes and geographical coverage
Working with a partner can create synergies of ideas for new products and services on other markets	Licensing a product produces less income than if you sold the product itself
Potential to enter political and economically unstable markets or markets with trade barriers	Less exposure of the parent company name if promotion of that name is not part of the agreement
Increased protection against patent infringement because your partner has an interest in protecting your interests	During the licensing period (approximately 5-10 years) you could be locked out of other market opportunities
Increased sales as well as reduced exposure to risk for the exporter	Generally less control than own operation
Low investment cost as the local partner is responsible for manufacturing and marketing costs	Your partner can become a competitor after the contract expires
The local partner has an established knowledge of the market and client base, resulting in a faster start up	Can limit later opportunities in the market
Less freight and duty which makes your product more competitive	May be higher withholding taxes on royalties
Import restrictions and quotas are eliminated as well as non-tariff barriers	Limits rapid local product development
An alternative to test sales or an opportunity to sell older products that are no longer competitive in the home market (see life cycle)	Less income than with direct export
Can be relatively easy to enter markets of interest without a large up-front investment	Local laws and legislations can make it complicated
Good return on investment	

Franchise

Franchise – Franchisor

Advantages	Disadvantages
Gain access to new markets but retains trademark	Gives up responsibility to others; less control
Opportunity to access new markets without losing control	Risk that selection of wrong partner can damage image
Possibility to expand faster than if growing your own operations	Could have legal implications, damage to reputation or inconsistent product quality
Sellers can strongly influence and control activities on local market	
Better income than license	
Good access to local market and knowledge of local market	
Most of the time, you don't have to arrange local approval and permits like liquor licenses, leases, etc.	

Franchise – Franchisee

Advantages	Disadvantages
Quick start with faster expansion and less risk	Less control than owning your operation outright
Access to an established brand and proven business model, so there is no need to re-invent	Have to follow someone else guidelines
Gain access to name, product, operational support and training, assistance in selecting and evaluating location	Risk of selecting a franchisor that does not perform, is not supportive or goes out of business
Benefits of bulk purchasing power	Limited opportunities to buy products and services from other sources
Co-operative advertising	
Continuous access to newly developed products and services	
Reduced risk of failure. Concept already tested. In business for yourself but not by yourself	
Assistance with finding location and design of premises	
Support even before starting operation	
Brand recognition	
Training plus product manuals and access to network of other franchisees	
Established supply chain	
Easier access to financing	

Joint Ventures

It seems that a Joint Venture has many advantages and there are. However, the local market determines the business culture. The partners can have different reasons for entering into the partnership. Make sure they do not collide: you have to establish trust from the beginning. It is important to understand that if you have a joint venture in China; it is the Chinese business culture that will be applicable.

Joint Ventures

Advantages	Disadvantages
You can become established in a market at a lower cost than with your own company and still have good control of the enterprise and shared risk with a partner.	Compared with your own company, there are limits to the controls you can have.
By having an experienced partner, you can contribute your expertise and obtain knowledge about how to do business locally.	Risk of differences of opinions about running the operation
Faster than starting a subsidiary	Can result in protracted decision-making process if there is no strong trust relationship.
You minimize the risk for future competition you could have with licensing.	Cultural differences can lead to difficulties based on management styles and philosophy.
Flexibility for allocation of resources and knowledge. For example, you can contribute a patent and your partner can contribute manufacturing expertise and sales people.	May require extensive resource commitment from management
Opportunity for you to learn about the local market and anticipate future development.	Lower profits and occasional conflicts about how to divide earnings
Potential to adapt products to the new market	Compared to having a subsidiary, you will be required to share your knowledge for a joint venture to work out.
Less risk of being treated as a foreign company	
Smaller investment but still good possibility for profitability	
Access to local products and labour	
Potential to enter markets where 100% ownership is not allowed	

As mentioned earlier, another choice could be to acquire an existing company.

Buying a Company

Buying a Company

Advantages	Disadvantages
You are purchasing an established organisation which is already up and running	It can take a long time negotiating the purchase, could be complicated and take a long time. Local authorities may have rules about company sales to foreign interests.
You buy the company's goodwill and staff including infrastructure, administration systems and distribution network	It may seem like a low cost alternative but can end up being costly because significant financing may be required
You get full control	The company could have financial, legal or product liabilities as well as union contracts or payment arrangements with employees that could be costly.
	May require an extensive resource commitment from management during the negotiation and transition phases.

You have read about many options for distribution methods. It is up to you to find the best alternative based on what the clients want, your resources, knowledge and capacity and how you are allowed to do business in that specific country. Let's practice what you have learned.

Project Work - Exercise

If there are enough people in your class, study group or company, break out into groups of three to five people. The purpose of working in groups is to generate discussions and analysis of the solutions chosen. Each group should write down their answers and be prepared to present them to the other groups and to defend the choices selected. After each group has made their presentation, then you can ask questions or debate that group's solutions.

If this exercise is being completed by groups working in the same company, management should be able to decide on the best solution after hearing the presentations and debates.

In my experience, if there are five groups and each has to present two options few of them will be the same. There may be six to eight different solutions. The beauty of this is that the discussion of alternatives will result in a good exchange of ideas, with many differences of opinion. Highlighting the pros and cons of each solution makes it easier to evaluate the choice that will likely work.

1. Select a product or service and an export market you want to enter.

2. What do you want to achieve? (*For example, a specific sales volume*).

3. What staff resources do you have?

4. Which financial resources do you have?

5. Which control or guidance do you want? (*for example, your own company or another method with less control*)

6. How do you want to split the workload between head office and the foreign market?

7. What risks are there in the export market you selected? What risks are you willing to take?

8. What local rules guide your choice? (*example about ownership*)

9. What is your long term goal for exporting?

Group work – presentation

Take one to two hours to complete the following exercise after answering the 9 questions above.

Using the answer to question 1 (product or service and export market), each group should decide on two alternatives for distribution and then compare them. Some solutions may be eliminated. During the presentation, be sure to include an explanation for why you rejected specific options.

Don't forget to start your analysis with the end user and work backwards so that the distribution chain ends at your company. Make diagrams similar to what you have seen in this chapter for different distribution alternatives.

For each solution/option, list:

1. The advantages and disadvantages for the end user

2. The pros and cons for you, the exporter. Take into consideration workload, how fast you can start up, desired level of control, profitability, etc.

3. The pros and cons for the representatives you select, if this is your choice. If you decide on your own operation, list the potential impacts.

Make a check list of what other activities you might have to do to enter the market you have chosen.

Export Pricing and
How To Influence Profitability – Part One

In This Chapter:

Calculating export prices and profit:

- ◆ Export pricing based on distribution method
- ◆ Export- and end user pricing
- ◆ Negotiating prices
- ◆ Pricing and licensing
- ◆ Intercompany pricing
- ◆ International pricing
- ◆ Pricing for foreign Government contracts
- ◆ Factors influencing pricing
- ◆ Prices and profitability based on external factors.
- ◆ Influence of prices, duties and freight when selecting foreign supplier
- ◆ How discounts or increasing the price, influence sales and profitability

What was the manufacturing cost of the jacket you purchased recently? How much were freight, customs duty and profit margins for each party involved?

Why am I asking these questions, when you don't care? You paid the price you wanted to pay, or what the jacket was worth to you. Good – then we agree.

When you calculate export price, the key factor is how much the end users are willing to pay. Then, you calculate backwards to see how much each individual in the distribution channel needs/wants, the freight costs and customs duties. The remainder is your export price. Now you can calculate the difference between your export price and manufacturing cost and see how much money you will make or lose.

To start these calculations from the manufacturing cost is ridiculous! However, many books and consultants recommend that you should set your export price based on manufacturing cost plus; that is, you use your manufacturing cost and add the profit you want. That is wrong and I'll show you why. Many companies use the domestic price and give a discount for export. The export price has nothing to do with your domestic price.

What Customer Is Willing To Pay

The price of a product or service has to do with what the market is willing to pay plus the number of people on the "journey" that have to make money. This could include the distributors and dealers or the freight company or the local customs authorities.

> ### *"We have to have a higher price than at home,*
> ### *because it costs so much to export."*
> ### *— A statement from many companies. This is not true.*

At home, you have a sales force that travels to customers. You maintain a service department, office workers and other staff, all for whom you have to pay to generate sales for your company. In the overseas market, you will have a local organization that takes care of that for you. This organization will know the market, have built up a customer base and will be able to service the clients. Not only do they manage the selling and service jobs for you, they also increase your sales volumes, lowering your marginal cost. (See earlier chapter "Why International Business, section about marginal costs.)

The customer's price is what they're willing to pay after all discounts. This will change depending on the market. The cost of your jacket you just bought will vary based on where it is being purchased for example in a discount chain or a specialty designer store. When I worked at a Swedish company exporting construction equipment, my department had 36 different export prices for the same product. Price was set for each individual market.

When you go out for dinner, the price changes considerably depending on where you go. A main course in a nice restaurant in the US or France could cost thirty to fifty dollars. The same meal served on a small Greek Island would cost you around eight dollars. At a neighbourhood restaurant in Thailand you'd pay about four dollars. The cost of the meals based on what people are willing to pay, what they can afford to pay and the cost of living in each country.

McDonald's uses a similar pricing system. The Economist magazine, www. economist.com, uses the Big Mac Index compare the cost of a hamburger in the United States and the purchasing power of various world currencies. To see the most recent version, use the Internet and search for "Big Mac index" or go to http://www.oanda.com/currency/big-mac-index for comparisons against current exchange rates.

In July 2009, a Big Mac in the US cost almost twice that in Thailand ($US 3.57 compared to $US 1.98), whereas in Denmark the price was $US 4.90 or 37% higher than in the US.

The news agency Bloomberg made a similar comparison in 2010 using the IKEA Billy book shelf. It showed that the price in Dubai was $47.64 and $103.48 in Israel. The average price was $60.09. An article in the Financial Post (Canada) 2010 stated that a barrel of oil "cost" 10 to 12 Big Macs in 2000-2003 prices, and in 2010 it cost about 22 Big Macs. Not only does the price differ between countries but the price ratio between different products does as well.

When you check online, the cost of airline tickets or vacation packages can change every minute. If you buy far in advance you may be able to negotiate a lower price because the cost for air travel increases as seats are booked and fewer are available for sale. The price of unsold seats will drop the last day before departure because airlines want to fill up the aircraft and make as much money as possible. Demand and availability affect what passengers pay to travel.

When a cruise ship arrives in the port of Puerto Vallarta, Mexico, the prices charged by local shops suddenly go up. They know the clients are willing to pay more.

When we were visiting Thailand in 2009, my wife was looking for a leather handbag. At the first store we went to, the price tag showed 11,000 Baht or about $330US. The salesperson offered a 'special price' of 4,500 Baht because "it was early in the morning and you are the first customers". He also said she could have any designer label she wanted. My wife ended up paying 2,500 Baht or $75 which is a large difference between the tag price and the final price for a bag that in North America would have cost about $500. How did this happen? There were four stores located close to each other, all with similar products. Business was slow so we were able to bargain hard for a better discount.

In this case, the end user price was really dependant on the customer and how tough they were at negotiating. I am sure some people would have paid the full price and felt they got good value; others would be extremely happy to get a 50% discount and feel that they got a great deal.

If you charge too much for a product, you can say goodbye to paying customers. "If you charge too little, say goodbye to your profit." Strike a balance between being competitive and being profitable. If a large part of your business is being in international markets then it is critical that each market is profitable.

How To Calculate Export Prices

You've heard about descriptions like mark-up and profit, margins and profit margins. If you have a product cost of $40 and mark it up 100% you add $40. This means $40 in profit on a selling price of $80 or $40/$80= 50% in profit.

Without going into too much detail about how to set prices, let's look at what happens when you have different distribution channels. If you have a long distribution channel there are more people who have to make money. The result is that you, as an exporter, will get less.

There are now low cost electronic calculators available. In Canada they are called Profit analyzers, (Price $12) and have buttons that perform the calculations for you. My calculator has a Cost/Margin button that calculates what your gross profit will be if your cost is X and the selling price is Y. The Cost/Selling price button calculates what your selling price would be if you want a particular profit. The Sell/Margin button calculates what the price is to achieve a certain margin. This type of inexpensive device makes your calculations much easier. Check your local office supply store to find one.

If you can easily understand the first example below, then you can just skim through the others to follow. But look at the end results. If you have any problems following the calculation and doing them yourself, review each example until you understand.

Care needs to be taken adding or subtracting freight and taxes where applicable.

Calculating Profit

Let me show you how this would work with an example. If you add 25% onto 80 the total will be 100 (80 x .25 = 20; 20 +80 = 100). However, 20% off the top of 100 is 0.2 x 100 or 20. So, in order to get the amount you want off the top, i.e., a 20% profit on the final price, you need to start with: 80÷[(100-20)÷100] = 80÷0.8 = 100.

Let's apply this principle below. In the next example we will use some fixed figures.

Different Cost and Profit Depending on Type of Distribution Selected

Read the following information slowly. It is very important that you understand the concepts so that you can set your export prices.

I've provided some figures for you to use for this calculation. You have two levels of distribution in this example.

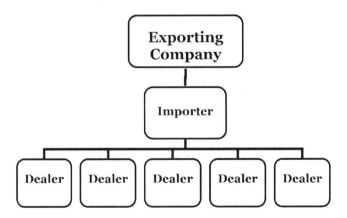

| **Freight is:** | **9%** (You normally have to calculate the cost based on what you are really paying, but after some time you will realize that you can use a percentage figure based on past shipments.) |

| **Duty is:** | **6%.** Of course, this will vary depending on the product and the country of import. |

| **The importer wants:** | **40%** margin or profit margin. (You have to find out what is applicable for your product and the country you are doing business with.) |

The dealer wants: **35%** margin. (You have to find out what is applicable for your product and the country you are doing business with.)

We will use these figures for now to get you to understand what is happening with an export price. We will use the rules from the European Union (EU) to determine how you pay duties. In the EU, you pay duty on the freight and packaging too. We will leave local taxes out of the calculation for now.

1. For easy calculation, let's say you start with an index of **100.** That index represents your export price.

2. Add 9% freight - now you have a total of **109.**

3. Add to this 6% duty - 1.06 x 109 = **115.54**. Note: the product has "landed" in your foreign country with a cost more than 15% higher than when it left your factory.

4. The importer wants 40% profit so you have to divide using (100-40)÷100 or **0.6.** The final figure is 115.54÷06 = **192.57.** This allows for a 40% profit/margin for the importer. – (Forty percent of 192.57 is arrived at this way: 192.57 x .4 = 77.03. Just to see that your figures are correct, you can do this calculation: buying price of 115.54 + profit of 77.03 = **192.57.)**

5. The dealer wants 35% profit after paying the distributor 192.57. This amount will be 192.57÷.65 (100-35) = **296.26**

Activity	Cost or Profit	Total
Export price	100	100
Freight	9% = 9	109
Duty	6% - 6.54	115.54
Importer	40% profit	192.57
Dealer	35% profit	296.26
The customer price is 2.96 times the export price		

In other words, the customer has to pay 2.96 (almost 3) times the export price excluding any local taxes like VAT. Put in another way, your export price is about 1/3 of the end user price.

If you have an even longer distribution chain with two extra levels each wanting 25% (see below) you will now have a price will now be: 296.26/0.75 = **395.01**

For the sub-dealer, the pricing would change like this: 395.01÷ 0.75 = **526.68.** This is more than five times the export price.

Coming back to what the customer is willing to pay, if there is a longer distribution chain, they will not pay more, but you will get less. In this example, that would be about 20% of the end user price.

Note: 100 is the export price and 526.8 is the price the end user will be paying (before any local taxes). The end user pays over 5 times the export price.

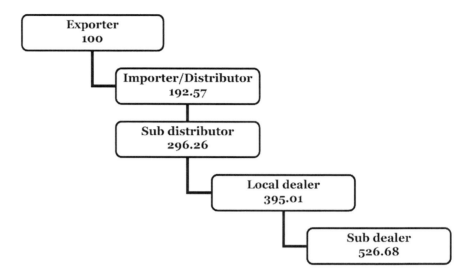

In the next couple of pages, I will show you the actual export price based on what the customer is willing to pay. For now I will just show how different distribution solutions influence the cost, that is, how much you will keep in profit compared to what the customer pays. Later in this chapter you'll see what it means to the actual export price – not only an index.

So what happens if you select another type of distribution?

Selling directly to a local dealer

In the example below, where you sell direct to a local dealer, the duty is the same - 6%.

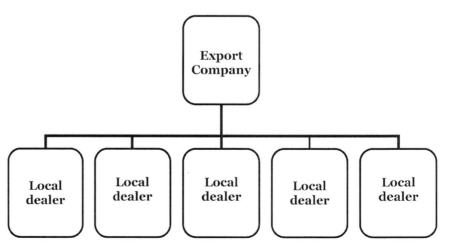

Because you ship a smaller volume of product, shipping costs (freight) increases to 11% (instead of 9%). You are generous and give the local dealer a 45% profit.

The calculation for Example Two looks like this:

> Export price = 100
> Freight 11% = 111. Duty 6% = 111 x 1.06 = 117.66 (landed in the country)

The dealer makes a 45% profit: 117.66 ÷[(100-45)÷100] = 117.66/0.55 = **213.93**

There is a big difference in export price and profit compared to earlier examples. Now the multiplying factor is only about two times the export price, despite higher freight costs and the dealer making a 45% profit. You get almost 50% of the end-user price compared with less than 20% in the example before (526.68). As this example illustrates, the number of levels between you and the end user has a substantial influence on your profitability.

Using a local representative

If you do not remember all the distribution alternatives, refer back to the Distribution chapter.

You plan on using a local representative/agent and give them 15% in commission on the export price. The local dealer wants 40%. In this case, you provide the dealers with local support. Perhaps they will accept a lower profit of 40% instead of the 45% in the earlier example. Normally contact would be between you and the agent. The agent would be responsible finding and activating the dealers. However, you ship to and invoice the dealer directly.

The freight is the same as above: 11%

The duty is: 6%

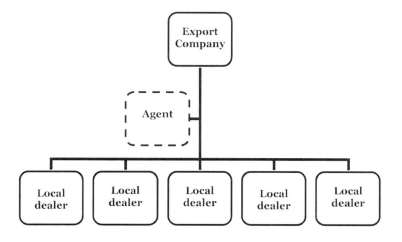

Export Price 100 (note you **get only 85%** of this as you give the representative 15% commission on the export price).

11% freight = 111

6% duty = 111 x 1.06 = **117.66** (landed in the country)

The dealer makes 40% profit: 117.66 ÷ [(100-40) ÷ 100] = 117.66 ÷ 0.60 = **196.10.**

This is less than two times your export price. Note, however, that you only get 85% because a 15% commission is going to the representative.

The factor for you is 196.10 ÷ 0.85 = **230.71** which is the multiplier between what you get and what the end user pays. You pay the agent 15% on the export price so you get 85% of the export price of 100 or 85. You get more than 40% of the selling price. This factor is only slightly higher than when you took care of it yourself in Example two (**213.92**). You can see the importance of shorter distribution chains. What can we do with those figures?

How to use these figures when setting the export price?

Let say you are exporting a hand saw. The local price before taxes is $45 and your manufacturing cost is $12.

Price $45

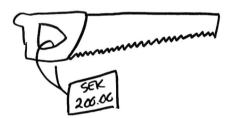

LONG DISTRIBUTION CHAIN

In the first example you have an end price factor of 526.68 for full distribution. That mean the customer price is 5.2668 times the export price. As the customer price is $45 but also 5.2668 times the export price, you get $45 ÷ 5.2668 = $8.54 (export price) which is below your cost of manufacturing ($12).

♦   If you take away one distribution level you will have a factor of 395.01. You get only about 25% of what the customer pays or $45 ÷ 3.9501= **$11.30 as an export price**, which is still less than your manufacturing cost of $12.

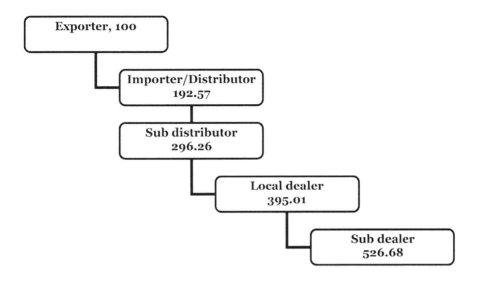

♦   If we take away one more level so you only have Exporter > Importer
> Sub distributor you have a factor of 296.26. Now your export price
is 45 ÷ 2.9626 = **$15.19.**

♦   You make a profit of $15.19 - $12 = **$3.19** or (3.19 ÷ 15.19) x 100 =
21%.

You make some profit but the question is: is it enough for you?

AN ALTERNATIVE – DIRECT TO DEALERS

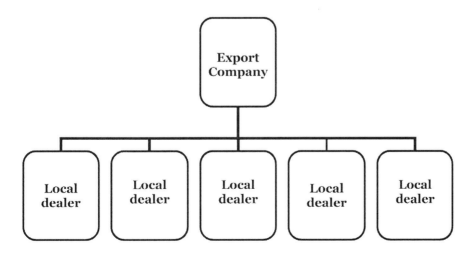

Now the calculation looks like this:

Export price = 100
11% freight = 111
6% duty = 111 x 1.06 = 117.66 (landed in the country)

The dealer makes 45% profit or 117.66÷ [(100-45) ÷100] = 117.66 ÷ 0.55 = **213.93.**

Using Exporter > dealer means you have a factor of **213.93**. Your customer price is 2.1393 times the export price. You know the customer price is $45.

♦ Now your export price is $45 divided by 2.1393 = **$21.03**

♦ Your gross profit margin becomes $21.03 less $12 (the manufacturing cost) = **$9.03**

♦ Hence, the profit (9.03 ÷ 21.03) x100 = **43%.**

As you can see, now you are making some good money. You can keep the profit, give the dealer a better profit or even sell your product at a lower price if you are prepared to a smaller profit.

I hope you can see the advantage of a shorter distribution chain, not only for communications but also to assist you to make more money and be more competitive.

ALTERNATIVE WITH LOCAL REPRESENTATIVE/AGENT

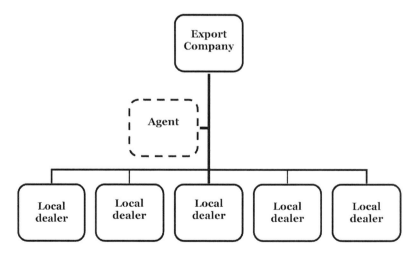

This case is similar to the earlier example. However, now you have an agent assisting you.

Export Price = 100 (You will get only 85% of this as you are giving the representative 15% commission)

Now the calculation looks like this:

Export price = 100
11% freight = 111
6% duty = 111 x 1.06 = **117.66** (landed in the country)

♦   The dealer makes 40% profit: [117.66 ÷ (100-40)] ÷ 100 = 117.66/0.60 = **196.10.** The customer pays 1.961 times the export price.

♦   Now your export price becomes $45 divided by 1.961 = **$22.95**.

However, since you are giving the representative a 15% commission on the export price you will not keep the full $22.95. You keep; $22.95 x 0.85 or $19.51. Your profit will be $19.51 - $12 = **$7.51** or 7.51 ÷ 19.51 x 100 = **38.5%.**

You will make a much better profit than having a distribution chain of Exporter > Importer > Sub Distributor ($3.19 or 21%) but less than the solution with a direct Exporter > Dealer ($9.03 or 43%) arrangement.

Let's put those calculations back in dollar figures step by step:

From Export Price to Customer Price

Export price	**$22.95**
Agent gets 15% on $22.95	**$3.44**
Remaining for exporter	**$19.51**
Manufacturing cost	**$12.00**
Profit for exporter. ($19.51 - $12.00)	**$7.51**
% Profit for exporter ($7.51 :$19.51) x 100	**38.5%**
Freight (11% of $22.95)	**$2.52**
Total cost after freight ($22.95 + $2.52)	**$25.47**
Customs duty (6% on $25.47)	**$1.53**
Total landed cost (export price + freight + duty)	**$27.00**
Dealer wants 40% profit on selling price $45	**$18.00**
Selling price. (landed cost plus dealer profit)	**$45.00**

The calculation adds up correctly. Remember that the landed cost is what it costs the importer after he pays the export price, freight and customs duty. This is the base cost for the importer to use to calculate the final profit.

Make sure you can follow those calculations. **They are important.** If you are unsure, go back and try again. Put in your own numbers and practice again and again, until you are comfortable. Getting this right is your key to making money. There will be more examples in Part Two at the end of the chapter.

We have not taken currency risk into consideration in those examples. That will be covered in detail in the Risk chapter.

As mentioned in the distribution chapter, it is important to select a distribution method based on how customers want to buy, what kind of control you want, and your resources. When you look at what happens to the export price, it makes sense to have a short distribution channel as long as you can handle it. The fewer levels of distribution, the less number of companies that has to make money and more profit for you.

I hope you can understand that selecting the right distribution method is critical to creating the sales and making money. **Don't forget that it is the final user who decides on the price level - it is not decided by your manufacturing cost or your domestic price.**

Freight and Duty Costs As Part of the Cost Calculation

Freight cost could be a small percentage of the total distribution cost, but sometimes it can add up to 15-30% on top of your export price. As you will learn in a later chapter about Freight, you can minimize those costs by negotiating with a freight forwarder for a better price, packing the goods correctly and selecting the right shipping method.

When this book was being written in 2010 the price of oil was around US $80 per barrel. In the middle of 2008 the cost was $133 a barrel. There are some forecasts that oil prices could reach US $200 a barrel in a couple of years. What does that mean for you as an exporter?

Freight costs are driven by fuel costs. A large oil price increase could mean a doubling of freight costs, which would cut into your profits. If the cost rises too high, it could become impossible to export to some markets. Take this into consideration when you plan your distribution and selection of market. Try to keep the number of distribution levels as low as possible. Take one of the examples above and double the freight costs to see what the result would be for export price and profit. Some of the benefits of bringing products from low-cost countries overseas will be reduced by increased freight costs. If you are a manufacturer with high freight costs it will be beneficial for you to focus on markets closer to home.

Take the time to review at the examples you have worked on. Perhaps at first glance it looks complicated, but not if you work through the calculations step by step. Use your own examples so that you really understand. This is the key to whether and how you can compete and make a profit.

In the second section of this chapter there will more examples for you to practice with. There are also calculations specific to the rules in North America, where you do not pay duty on freight and packaging.

Before we go further with pricing, let's sort out a couple of things.

Freight

You must negotiate freight costs. If you can reduce this expense by two percent you will increase your profit by two percent. In the chapter about Freight, I will tell you more about how you can minimize costs.

Duty

You have to minimize duty costs. Although I will describe that in more detail, here is just one example.

If you export to Europe you will pay duty on freight and packaging costs. When shipping to North America, you will only pay duty on the export price. Make sure that you do not include the cost of shipping, packaging and insurance in North American pricing because then the client will have to pay duty on them as well. Show the actual product price and, on the invoice, separately show costs for packaging, shipping and insurance. I suggest you ask your freight forwarder for a freight cost "door-to-door". That makes your calculation much easier.

What Is the End User Price?

When you do the price calculations described above you have to use the ***net*** price the customer pays after deduction of taxes, discounts, etc.

1. Some countries have an value-added tax (VAT) included on the price tag, so if there is 20% tax included in a product priced at $100, price you use for calculation is $100 -20% = $80.

2. Some countries use a manufacturer's suggested retail (MSR) price. Many times this is 20-40% higher than what you really pay. Make sure you use the correct net price in the calculation.

3. In some countries the client will want to negotiate and the final price can end up being much lower. If you have tried to buy at markets in the Caribbean and Asia it is not uncommon to get a 30-50% discount. Remember that they will already have boosted the price before they tell you what it is. What is important is the price **after** all discounts.

4. Industrial clients in some countries get a base discount such as 10%. Make sure to deduct that amount before you complete your pricing calculations.

5. Currency fluctuations will influence export prices and your profit. More information can be found in the chapter on Risks.

6. When you compare prices, remember that "brand names" normally sell at a premium compared with lesser known brands.

Negotiating Prices

When you negotiate with a foreign dealer or distributor:

1. Always find out the local market price. Use that number when you complete your calculations.

2. Remember that in some countries it is mandatory to negotiate pricing. Make sure you have built in allowances for that in your first offer.

3. Some clients have to show their boss they were able to negotiate a better price. Be prepared.

4. Always keep some buffers in your price that will allow you to give a special discount when your distributor has the opportunity to get a large order or wants to run a promotion for a trade show special. You also need to build in some room for currency fluctuations (see later chapter on Risk)

5. Remember the calculation for marginal costs. Today, most likely labour costs will be only a small part of the manufacturing expenses and more money will be spent on research and development, tooling and marketing. Take those factors into consideration before you decide if you can afford to enter a market.

6. As you will see in Part Two of this chapter, the customer benefit is an important part of your pricing. That could be how much the customer can save by using your product.

Example - Not knowing the "starting price"

A group of Nordic suppliers went to Italy to sell their wood products. They returned without an order. I met with the head of delegation. He could not understand what went wrong. "We had the right products and the right prices."

I asked him how much he had allowed for negotiations on price. He said "We gave them our final price at the start."

I told him that approach does not work in Italy. Later, they went back with a price list 20% higher than before, that allowed room for negotiations. That is the way to do business in Italy.

Some importers calculate prices that include the whole import procedure (purchase price + freight + customs + packaging, end-user price, etc.) so they have no problem to get an export price from you and make their own calculations.

Others who are not used to importing will need help and will ask you to make the calculations for them. They want a "package" with the whole price calculation from the exporter to the end user, which you will have done anyhow, using what you have learned in this chapter. They want a price list with the customer price and a full calculation. You have to be prepared for this. Below is such an example.

Export price and local price

Product	Customer price - EURO (via dealer 35% profit)	Distributor price in EURO (35% profit)	Landed cost - EuroUS/Euro 0.8, freight duty 1.15	Export Price US$
A	141.54	92.00	59.8	65
B	119.76	77.85	50.6	55
C	87.11	56.62	36.8	40
D	76.22	49.54	32.20	35

This is a typical chart you can use to show a distributor who wants their price list based on the end-user price, where they can clearly see their discounts.

Wheelchairs in Canada

Many years ago, I helped a Swedish company introduce special wheelchairs to Canada. The chair was light, sporty and easy to move for the person in the wheelchair.

In Sweden, distribution is taken care of by the government department responsible for assistive devices. The price was based on what they were willing to pay.

However, when exporting to Canada from Sweden, there was no competition. One of the large manufacturers of wheel chairs in Canada was hungry to sell and willing to pay a premium for our products. Because of these factors, our export price was higher than what the end-user paid in Sweden. From this example, you can see that the export price is not comparable with your domestic price.

Pricing and Licensing

When you sell a license for your product, you use the same principle as when you set any other prices. You have to look at the market price and make sure everybody along the distribution chain makes money.

♦   The market decides on the price level. Find out what the customer wants to pay for your product.

- How much can your licensing partner make by manufacturing and selling your product?

- Your part, the royalty, is a combination of profitability and what you have to offer.

Example - A product that gives your licensing partner a 60% profit

You want part of the profit, let's say 20%. That makes it 20% of 60% or a 12% royalty. If the partner company only makes a 15% profit and you want 20% of that, you have to make 20% of 15% or a 3% royalty.

You have to figure out how much your partner can make, how much of that profit you want and what is reasonable, based on your product and the service you are prepared to provide. Do not just say that a 4% royalty is common. There is nothing "common" in doing international business. You must perform a calculation that makes sense considering what is of interest to you and your partner.

Example - Mine cars

- *The customer price was based on earlier sales. We had sold products and used subcontractors for local manufacturing, so we knew the manufacturing costs.*

- *Before we signed a licensing agreement, the sub-manufacturer we used had already made some profit producing goods for us, so the net cost for our licensing partner should be lower than what we paid our sub-manufacturer.*

- *We had a 60% profit using a sub-manufacturer, so our licensing partner should make more than that.*

- *We asked for $75,000 down payment to sign the contract. The contract included the design drawings for manufacturing, a list of potential clients, a reference list for clients who had bought units, sales material as well as media articles about the equipment and installations; we wanted 12% Royalty, or 20% of their 60% profit.*

- *We also agreed that they would buy 300 Engineering hours per year at a fixed hourly fee.*

This is just one example. You have to decide:

1. What is the market price?
2. What will be the manufacturing costs?
3. How much profit would the licensee make?
4. How much profit do you want and how much is it worth for the licensee to sell and manufacture your product?
5. How much support can you give and how much do they want?
6. How large is the market and how a big piece can your partner take? Will the licensee and you make money?

7. Don't get hung up on the percentage of the royalty – it is the total amount of money that is the important thing. Note that 20% of nothing is nothing, but 10% royalty on $10 million a year is $1 million a year. It is the combination of percentage and volume that makes profits.

What happens when you have your own company overseas? What export price do you set then?

Intercompany Pricing, Transfer Pricing

- ◆ The market still decides on price
- ◆ Each distribution level has to make money
- ◆ Make the same calculation as if you have a distributor

This is the basis for your calculation. However, there are other parties in the company who may have different opinions and want to have their say.

Management/finance department wants to maximize profit, minimize taxes and risks

They want to make money where they pay the least taxes and where the risks are the lowest; they want to have a high export price to keep more money at home.

Low customs value

The country you are exporting to has high customs duties. By having a low export price, the duty charged will be lower and the local profit higher.

However, your company personnel are not the only ones who influence the price.

Local authorities in the country to which you are exporting will influence what you can do

You have to supply a Customs invoice with your shipment. If that document states that the Supplier and Importer are associated and at arms length, then the Customs department will know that the shipment involves an inter-company transfer. They may ask for more information. You cannot set just any export price. The transfer price should mirror the local price level; if there is a large discrepancy officials may interfere as to the price used for the customs valuation of your shipment.

Customs authority reviews

If you quote an inter-company price that is too low, your local competitor could argue that your competition is not fair. They could request that the Customs department investigate. Even your own authorities can investigate you to make sure that you pay the appropriate taxes on the domestic market.

Selling below fair value prices

If you sell large volumes of product on a foreign market at a lower price than what you sell it for in the domestic market at the same distribution level or for less than your production costs, you could be penalized for predatory pricing or dumping. If a local business can show that it is losing money because of your pricing activity or that you are selling at too low a price, not only will you have to pay a fine, customs authorities may add an extra duty because of your dumping.

There are two distinct criteria considered when deciding if dumping is occurring: if you are selling at too low a price, and/or if a local company is being harmed by your low pricing:

1. Transfer pricing is an income tax concept having to do with determining whether the prices for sale of goods or the amounts charged for services are what they would be if they were supplied to an arms-length customer. If the price is too low, you are considered to be doing it to avoid paying duty on the fair market value. This also restricts a local company's chances to compete.

2. If the transfer price is too high, the income tax authorities in the purchaser's country could disallow the price used for calculation of customs duty and/or taxation. This could result in double taxation because the transfer price for customs purposes would remain the same and the duty would be paid on that same price. Tax authorities would see the high invoice value as a way to avoid paying tax on sales by reducing the profit in that country. You would be penalized you with a "dumping tax".

3. When companies are making intercompany transfers, selling goods or providing services to related parties, it is important that they seek professional advice to ensure that the commercial, tax, customs and other objectives are achieved without unexpected penalties. Governments understand that global business is becoming more competitive. Tax savings can be substantial when an international company uses the right strategies. There can also be substantial penalties when they don't.

Sometimes you may be accused of dumping (selling at a too low price) even if you are not. It is not uncommon in the US for charges to be brought against foreign suppliers of materials such as steel. In most cases, investigation shows there was no dumping but the suppliers incur high legal costs to protect themselves and their companies.

International Companies

International companies conducting business worldwide tend to buy where the price is the best. Many large corporations/suppliers have a specific department to deal with those international clients. They use an international price list which results in consistent pricing no matter which companies or countries they deal with.

Example - International companies

One of your clients is a construction company based in Canada that is working on projects in Tanzania, Brazil and France.

They need equipment in each of these countries. They buy the equipment where it is cheapest, in this case, from Canada. It is manufactured there and shipped to the countries where the projects are. When the job is done, they sell it locally, resulting in exports for the original supplier, as the goods remains in the foreign country. This is a typical company which benefits from international price lists.

Automobile manufacturers

General Motors and Nissan buy components and machinery from all over the world. If you are a supplier of pneumatic blowguns that carry your own product number, these manufacturers will assign their own unique product number to your product. In that way, they can ask for a quotation for that product in any country and order from the lowest bidder. This sometimes creates unfair competition. Your local dealer/distributor that established and serviced an account with the company could be undersold by another distributor in another country who is willing to sell at a lower price, who has not done any work to create the order.

When I dealt with these types of situations I told the dealer that if he was asked for a Ford product number, he should say that we did not have one. This made it easier for local dealers to get the order instead of Ford collecting quotes from all companies selling the product listed with the specific Ford number.

Example - Central purchasing

More oil companies and truck manufacturers use central purchasing with fixed prices for many markets. "We have agreements with Volvo and Scania for their service shops all over the world", states Export Manger Lennart Bergh of Alentec & Orion AB. "It is up to us to make sure in our prices they also get the local service and assistance requested. We have had deliveries of complete installations the last couple of years that include, Ukraine, Kazakhstan, Slovakia, Finland, Poland, Netherlands and Belgium. We not only deliver the products and installation material but also have to make sure the installation is carried out right locally."

Governments and prices

Doing business directly with local governments is different then using a dealer. Sometimes governments will work through a local dealer, but especially in state-controlled countries, they demand a direct business relationship with you. In that case, you will have to follow the rules and, if possible, set aside some commission for your local dealer, to pay for their continued service.

EXAMPLE: Price Calculations for Government Contract

Export Price	100
Financing (For payment over a long time period) Cost you 5%; customer willing to pay 3% during 5 years (difference 10%)	110
Counter trade payment is 3% (described in risk/payment chapter)	113.3
Consulting fee is 3%. Could be fees based on local customs.	116.7
Build in 'room' for customer to negotiate (15%)	134.2
Some governments charge you a "fee" for central processing, e.g., 5%	140.92 Final factor

The factor you have to use in this case is **140.92**. If you plan to pay your local dealer for their services you will have to include that amount in the price factor. As always, the final price is what the client is willing to pay. Use this type of calculation in order to establish customer price, export price and your profit.

Haggling or Bargaining

Many years ago when I visited Greece, I decided to buy a ring for my wife. I went into the jewellery store and the store owner, a 35 year old man, presented me with a ring I liked. He told me a price. I offered him 25% of what he asked. We likely spent around 30 minutes haggling over the price. During that time, he told me that he had three children and a wife to take care of. His grandmother and mother-in-law also lived with his family. We finally agreed that I would pay 50% of the original price.

The owner said, "This was the most enjoyable time I have had for a long time. I close the shop now and take you for lunch."

He probably spent a big part of what I paid for the ring to pay for my lunch. The fact is that negotiating is part of the selling game. Sometimes, it can be fun.

In the first part of this chapter on Pricing you have been given basic information about export pricing. There were a large number of examples. I suggest you work through the calculations once more. Once you read Part Two of this chapter you will get an even deeper understanding of pricing, including examples that you can try on your own. There will also be more aspects to consider including discounts, calculating the real customer price as well the influence of free trade and freight costs on pricing.

Summary

- The local market decides the pricing, not your manufacturing cost. You have to use the local customer price as a base. Your manufacturing cost is only the basis for calculating profit.

- Neither you nor your distributors want to do business without making money.

- Being greedy can lead to a bad investment. Distributors also have to make money. They are your key to success overseas.

- The distribution selection will influence export price, profitability and competitiveness.

- The number of distribution levels influences your export price.

- Distribution margins influence your export price.

- If you can't make distribution profitable with your first option, look at other distribution solutions and calculate again.

- Customs duty and freight influence your export price.

- How you pack the product can decrease freight costs (more in the Freight chapter)

- It is common in many countries for purchasers to negotiate, so make sure you take that into consideration when setting prices.

- Always leave a buffer to allow for special pricing of large orders or promotions.

- If you can reduce distribution and freight costs, you and your distributor can improve your competitiveness.

- Remember what can happen to your marginal costs and take that into account when evaluating your export activities.

- You have to decide on how long your prices are valid for (e.g. one year or can be changed with xx days notice. Some catalogue houses reprint their catalogues every two years and then will require that you keep the prices for that time period.

Export Pricing and How To Influence Profitability – Part Two

There are many ways to set a price. Let's go through some examples to make sure you become familiar with all aspects of setting a price.

Price Based on What the Customer Is Willing To Pay

What are some of the deciding factors for setting a price?

Example - How to decide on customer price

You ask a taxi driver in Singapore to take you to your hotel. What is the price? The cab driver will look at you and try to figure out how much he can charge. He'll ask himself questions like:

- *Is the customer local or a foreigner? If they're a foreigner, perhaps I can charge more.*

- *What is the client willing to pay? Does she or he know the usual rate?*

- *Is there any competition like another taxi nearby? If so, if we do not agree on a price, will the customer leave and negotiate with the other driver?*

- *Are there alternatives such as walking to the hotel, taking the tram, etc?*

- *Is the weather nice or is it pouring rain?*

You could pay more or you could pay less than the going rate. The price depends on the factors listed above and how well prepared you are to negotiate.

Example - Negotiating prices

An American woman visiting Italy walked into a gift shop. She looked around for a while then asked for the price of a vase. The salesperson told her the price. The American woman said "I'll buy it".

The salesperson's response was, "don't you want to negotiate the price?"

Normally you would not pay the full price in Italy for this kind of product. The first price quoted is a starting price for the bargaining process.

Scarcity and new products in high demand

When a large MP3 player manufacturer introduced their new model, demand was higher than the supply. The units were sold at a very high price. The pricing was different in different markets. After one month, when sales slowed down, the company reduced the price by about 30%. In Canada, the price drop happened too soon after the first launch and the company was forced to give refunds to the first customers who bought the higher priced product because of a loud outcry in the daily press. They tried to "skim" the market, that is charge a higher price at the start and then adjust the price downward based on demand for the product.

When the iPhone was introduced, people were sleeping outside the store to be first in line to get one. How do you think Apple priced that product? Some customers even purchased the phone and then resold it at a higher price. - By being greedy and asking too high a price, though this can attract other companies wanting a piece of the market to develop a similar product.

Automobile pricing

How is it that the price of a car can be different depending on which country you buy it in? One factor is what the customer is willing to pay, another is fluctuations in currency. We have seen how currency affects products traded between Canada and the United States. The price could be roughly the same in both countries. When the exchange rate moves up or down regularly, it is tough for car manufacturers to change/adjust the prices.

Another factor influencing price is taxes. Some countries tax motor vehicles heavily, thereby increasing the local price. This difference in pricing sometimes creates a new market. For example, lower car prices in the US and Canada compared with Europe have created a large market for importing used cars to Europe, to sell there.

Taxation, Standard of Living and Controlled Pricing

The price to end user of pharmaceutical products differs substantially among countries. One reason is general pricing levels but also involvement of governments in purchasing when the government is the customer. Another example of government control is alcohol/liquor distribution and pricing. Fuel prices are very high in many markets in Europe because governments have decided to tax auto fuel heavily.

Food in Norway costs three times as much as in Romania. Norway is considered to be rich because of the oil industry. Norwegians have a high standard of living and are willing to spend plenty of money on consumer goods. The people in Romania still have one of the lowest income levels in the European Union. They cannot afford to pay the prices charged in Norway.

If you buy Australian wine instead of beer in Thailand you will pay a premium because the Thai government has placed a high duty on imported wine. A bottle of liquor in Country A could cost two to three times more than in Country B because of heavy taxation. That is one reason why there are so many tax-free stores at airports and on ships. Sometimes the pricing system leads to very odd market situations.

> ### *Example - Buying domestic product cheaper overseas*
>
> *Sweden has high taxes on beer. Denmark does not. Both are members of the European Union. Swedish breweries ship their beer to Denmark. Swedes will take a ferry trip to Denmark, buy Swedish beer at Danish prices then bring it back to Sweden. All of this is allowed according to the EU agreement because the beer they purchased is for personal use.*

Price based on the benefits you think you get

When do we buy cosmetics and fashion? What are we really paying for?

If someone tried to sell you a one litre plastic bottle of perfume for five dollars, you probably would not buy it. How could it be any good?

But if that same type of perfume was packaged in a 15 ml designer glass bottle and priced at $45, you would most likely buy it. Why? We have been 'trained' to expect that good things will cost a certain amount. The same applies to fashion. You can purchase a good quality no-name shirt at a low price, perhaps at a discount store. If you buy a similar shirt with a brand or designer name, from a high-end boutique, you will pay a much higher price for the name and perhaps for the quality.

Why do you think General Motors advertised product lines such as Chevrolet, Pontiac, Buick and Cadillac? All were basically the same cars, but some models included added luxuries like leather seats, sunroofs, climate control, etc. Ford had Mercury and Lincoln model lines, Toyota has Lexus, Honda has Acura and Nissan has the Infiniti luxury model. Consumers have shown they are willing to pay more for a high end name and product. Guess where the car companies make the best profit?

Price based on profit for the client buying your product/service

A company buys a computerized robot to increase manufacturing capacity. They are prepared to pay a price based on the expected return on their investment, how much they can save in labour costs, etc. Using a simple calculation, if the manufacturer can save $100,000 a year and the write-off time is three years, they can pay $300,000 for the robot.

I worked with a company selling a tool that could change accessories on lift trucks. The companies they tried to sell to said the product was too expensive. When we made a Microsoft Excel spreadsheet that the customer could use to estimate their cost savings, they found out their return on investment (ROI) time period would be less than two months. It turned out that because of that quick ROI, our price was too low. The company decided they could lease out the equipment if a client was not willing to make the initial investment.

I introduced air blow-off nozzles into the US. The product was quiet and very safe, with a higher blowing force than the competition. The major selling point was the low air consumption, which produced an energy saving of 60%. It paid for itself in six months.

Pricing based on future profit

You buy an inkjet printer. The price is low, sometimes lower than the cost of the replacement ink cartridges. How can the store sell the printer at such a low price? Because you have to pay for either a refill of your old cartridges or buy new ink cartridges! Usually, no two cartridges from different suppliers will fit another manufacturer's equipment. The printer manufacturers know that by getting you to buy an inexpensive ink jet printer, over time you will spend 20 to 400 times that amount on printer cartridges. That is how they make their money, on consumables. A similar example is razors for men and women. You pay a "good" price for the first package and then you pay handsomely for the refills.

Make that calculation! You will decide to buy a colour laser printer, which does not need to be fed a constant supply of expensive cartridges!

There is a low-priced espresso machine on the market; instead of paying over $1000 for a large machine, you can pay less than $200 for a smaller model. This seems like a huge savings; however, the smaller machine requires a special, single-use container of coffee for each cup you make. Instead of spreading the cost of the coffee machine over hundreds of cups of coffee over time, you will pay the same expensive amount for each cup you brew. This is the same principle as ink jet printer cartridges.

You buy a high efficiency furnace rated at 98% compared with your old one rated at only 65%. This is a saving of 33%. What is it worth to you if you have to pay the cost of the furnace off in three years? That is what the furnace manufacturers calculate. If your furnace is old and not working properly, then you have no choice.

You do the same calculation for replacement windows for your house. If the energy prices are not extremely high and the costs of windows are low, you will see that it is almost impossible to get a payback or that it will take you 25 years to break even, depending on energy prices.

Prices based on urgency or availability

You have to fly out tomorrow to assist a client. What do you think the price of the airline ticket would be today compared to the price of a reservation made two weeks in advance? The airline industry knows you have no choice, so the cost will be higher. The exception of course, if the airline still has many unsold seats.

You book a hotel room in Athens, Greece during the off season. Because most of the tourists have gone home and many rooms are empty, the price charged will be low.

Influence of Prices, Duties, and Freight When Selecting Foreign Supplier

Why is it that a product costing twenty cents to produce in China costs three dollars when you buy it in New York? Just go back to your price calculations and you will understand why.

EXAMPLE: Imports from China or Spain

If you are selling shoes in Holland and want to them to be manufactured overseas, where would you place the order? The cost from China is 10 EURO and from Spain, 11.50 EURO a pair. Would you buy from China or Spain?

The Chinese manufacturer demands a minimum order of 10,000 pairs and payment by Letter of Credit. Delivery time is six weeks. Shipping takes another six weeks.

The Spanish manufacturer has a minimum order quantity of 4,000 pairs. Delivery time is four weeks and shipping time from order placement two days. Payment terms are 30 days after shipment.

The transport cost from Spain is about 3% and from China about 8% based on the export price. There is no duty from Spain to Holland (European Union) but from China the duty is 12.5%. The selling price of the shoes will be 70 Euro in retail stores in Holland.

Where Would You Buy Shoes From?

Cost Comparisons		
Activity	**Origin - China**	**Origin - Spain**
1. Import price	10 EURO	11.5 EURO
2. Freight	8% = 0.8 EURO	3% = 0.345 EURO
3. Total per pair	10.8 EURO	11.845 EURO
4. Duty	12.5% = 1.35 * EURO	0%
5. Total	12.15 EURO	11.845 EURO
6. Customer price	70 EURO	70 EURO
7. Price to store (50% discount)	35 EURO	35 EURO
8. Profit to importer	35-12.15 = 22.85 EURO	35-11.845 = 23.155 EURO
9. % Profit to importer	(22.85/35)x100 = 65.3%	(23.155/35x)100 =66.2%

Note: Duty in EU is based on price plus freight

As you can see, despite the fact that the price for buying shoes from China was lower, in the end, it was still less expensive to buy them from Spain. Furthermore, you did not need to order as large a quantity, you had a longer time to pay, your goods were processed for delivery faster and the shipping time was shorter. Because the distance to Holland was less, you, the buyer, could more easily visit the factory in Spain to check on the quality of goods. There could also be an import quota for shoes from China, making it difficult or even impossible to import from there. There is another possible benefit – your local customers might buy more shoes because "made in Spain" could have a better image for him than "made in China".

Sometimes distribution is more complicated

In the example below, a manufacturer of metal working machinery is setting up distribution for their equipment in Germany. They know that the German car manufacturer only buys from approved suppliers. If they want to sell to the automotive industry, they will have to select one of their approved distributors. On the other hand, they also want to sell to the general manufacturing industry.

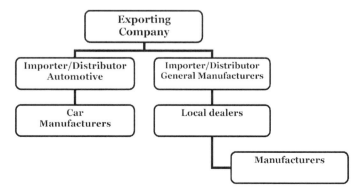

As you can understand, the car manufacturers carry strong buying power. They are not willing to pay the same price as small manufacturers. In this situation, you will need to have two customer price lists, one for the car manufacturers and one for the general manufacturers. I will leave it to you to do the calculations.

Giving Discounts

You will always be asked to give discounts. Make sure your sales people understand the consequences of the discount they agree to. By giving a 10% discount on a product that has 30% profit means they are giving away one third of your profit.

Review the examples in the charts below to see some consequences of giving discounts or increasing the price.

♦   Your salesman gives the client a 5% discount on a product that has 25% profit. You will give away 5/25 = 20% of your profit or you will have to increase sales by 25% to compensate.

♦   How did we get to that figure? Go to the column showing profit 25% then follow that down to the line with 5% decrease in the left column. The result shows you have to increase the sales volume by 25%. If you do the same for a product with 20% profit and 7.5% discount, the result is that you have to increase sales by 60%.

What happens when you decrease the price? Give discount. How much more do you have to sell?									
Profit in percent									
Price Decr. %	10	15	20	25	30	35	40	45	50
Volume increase in % to achieve the same profit									
2	25	15	11	9	7	6	5	5	4
3	43	25	18	14	11	9	8	7	6
4	67	36	25	19	15	13	11	10	9
5	100	50	33	25	20	17	14	13	11
7.5	300	100	60	43	33	27	23	20	18
10		200	100	67	50	40	33	29	25
15			300	150	100	75	60	50	43

♦   You raise the price by 5% for a product that gives 25% profit. You can reduce sales by 17% and still make the same profit.

What happens when you increase the price? How much less do you have to sell?									
Profit in percent									
Price Incr. %	**10**	**15**	**20**	**25**	**30**	**35**	**40**	**45**	**50**
Volume decrease in % to achieve the same profit									
2	17	12	9	7	6	5	5	4	4
3	23	17	13	11	9	8	7	6	6
4	29	21	17	14	12	10	9	8	7
5	33	25	20	17	14	12	11	10	9
7.5	43	33	27	23	20	18	16	14	13
10	50	40	33	29	25	22	20	18	17
15	60	50	43	37	33	30	27	25	23

So how do you deal with being forced to give discounts? You can give away products instead.

If you are asked to reduce your price by 10% for a product that costs $1,000, then you are giving away $100. Instead, why not give your customer another product that is worth $100? If you have a 50% margin on that product, it will really only cost you $50. The client gets his 10% discount but it costs you 5%. If the client likes the product they received as a discount perhaps they will start to buy more.

That is one reason a car dealer is willing to 'give' you some accessories for 'free', instead of reducing the list price. When you buy a TV, the store may 'give' you some fancy cables for 'free'. They most likely have a 65% profit, so those free cables cost them 35%.

When I managed salesmen selling sawmills and sawmilling equipment, they were allowed to give customers a 5% discount to close an order. Eighty percent of the time, they gave the standard price cut. Then, I suggested that they could keep 20% of what they were **not** giving away to customers. That stopped the discounting! After that, they very seldom gave away a discount because they understood that the money was coming out of their own pockets. Remember that it is easy to give away someone else's money, but it hurts to give away your own! The salesmen would earn more money (keeping 20% of what they did not give away) and that was enough for them to stop giving discount.

There are many factors to take into consideration whether you export or import.

Export price calculation

Earlier in this chapter, I gave you some examples for calculating export prices for countries such as Europe, where you have to pay duties on freight, insurance and packaging. When you ship to Canada and the US, you do not have to pay duty on your shipping costs and crating. In these situations, you cannot just use a percentage calculation.

Let us use some figures to show how to calculate for export to the US and Canada. In this example, we will have two levels of distribution, the importer and the dealer.

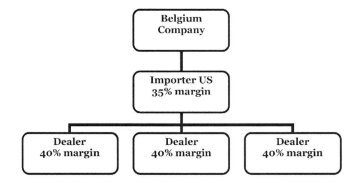

Calculation:export price/import to USA

Customer price	$500
Duty	6% on export price
Freight	8% on export price
Manufacturing cost	$110
Importer wants	35% margin
Dealer wants	40% margin

Calculation: export price/import to USA

Export price	X	We do not know this yet
Customs duty	6% of x (.06 times x)	0.06x
Freight	8% of x (.08 times x)	0.08x
Landed cost.Export price + Duty + Freight	The landed cost in Canada is 1.14 times the export price	1.14x
Distributor selling to dealer 35% margin	1.14x : 0.65	1.754x
Dealer selling to end-user 40% margin	1.754x : 0.60	2.92 x = customer price See calculation below

Profit calculation

Do you remember when we talked about mark-up and profit and profit margin before? If you add 25% of 80 the mark-up is 20. The total will be 100. However, 20% from the top is 0.2 x 100 = 20 is the profit or profit margin. So in order to obtain the profit of 20% price from "80" to arrive at "100", your calculation would be [80:(100-20)]*100] = 80:0.8 = 100.

Distributor wants 35% margin in the example above(profit on their selling price, not add-on) or 1.14x :(100-35)/100) = 1.14x :0.65= **1.754x**. We took the factor 1.14x and divided by 0.65 to get a profit of 35% on the price the distributor sells it for to the dealer. The factor is now 1.754x.

Here is another way to show you that our calculations are right. If we take 35% from 1.754 it will be 1.754 – 35% of 1.754 or 1.754 – 0.614= 1.14, which is the landed cost.

Dealer wants 40% margin or 1.754x : [(100-40)/100)] = 1.754x :0.6 = **2.92x**.

So what is 2.92x? It is the customer price. In other words, the customer pays 2.92 times the export price. We know the customer price, which is $500 (chart above). So 2.92x is equivalent to $500. So x, the export price is 500÷2.92 = **$171.23**

We know that the **manufacturing cost** is **$110.** The difference between our export price and manufacturing cost is profit. There is $171.23 - $110 or **$61.23 in profit**. If you want to know the percentage, it is profit divided by the export price x 100 which would be (61.23÷171.23) x 100 or **35.8%**.

Let's put these figures in chart form so you can see the result.

Calculation: export price/import to Canada

Export price	X	$171.23
Customs duty	6% of x (.06 x 171.23)	+ $10.27
Freight	8% of x (.08 x 171.23)	+ $13.70
Landed cost	(1.14 x 171.23)	= $195.20
Distributor selling to dealer – 35% margin	1.754 x (171.23)	$300.34
Dealer selling to end-user	2.92 x (171.23)	$500 (customer price)

I hope you could follow the calculation.

In this following example we have reduced the number of distribution levels in the foreign country to one: Exporter > Importer > Consumer.

The distributor/importer wants 55% profit margin.

SCENARIO: Distribution: Exporter > Importer > Customer

Customer price $500		
Duty 6% on export price		
Freight 8% on export price		
Manufacturing cost $110		
Importer wants 55% margin		
Export price	x	We do not know this yet
Customs duty	6% of **x (.06 times x)**	**0.06x**
Freight	8% of **x (.08 times x)**	**0.08x**
Landed cost	The landed cost in Canada is 1.14 times the export price	**1.14x**
Distributor selling to end-user	55% margin 1.14x/0.45=2.53x	**2.53x** = customer price

- ♦ Distributor wants 55% margin or 1.14x/[(100-55) ÷ 100)] = 1.14x÷0.45 = **2.53 x**

- ♦ Customer price is 2.53 times the export price.

- ♦ The calculation is $500 ÷ 2.53 = **$197.62** which is the **Export price**.

- ♦ **Profit** is $197.62 - 110 = **$87.62** or 87.62 ÷ 197.62 = **44.3%**

The result is a much better profit. A shorter distribution channel still gives you a better export price and better profit, despite a higher profit margin for the dealer.

There will be some more exercises for you at the end of this chapter.

Other factors to take into consideration

An American company selling products all over the US also has a large catalogue house as their client. Because of large volumes, their purchase prices are low. Catalogue sales allow them to work on smaller margins. The company also send the catalogues to Europe with the same low sales prices, resulting in demand for lower prices by others. This creates a pricing conflict between the local European dealers selling through industrial distribution channels and the US catalogue house working on small margins for mail order. The American Company had to stop selling to the US catalogue house in order to keep the prices in Europe higher, and satisfy their existing distributors.

Price fixing

Price fixing occurs when businesses/competitors agree to sell the same product, commodity or service for the same price or to control supply and demand to maintain a certain market price. Normally, it results in higher prices to customers.

You are driving down the road and suddenly, the gasoline prices posted at all of the stations you passes change, and they change to the same price.

The question is, of course, why did this happen? Is it strong competition, coincidence or fast communication? Price fixing is against the law. When it is prosecuted by governments or trade regulators, the penalty could be hefty fines or even imprisonment.

Price fixing can affect almost any industries, suppliers or clients, including gasoline, beer, microchips, aircraft fuel and sportswear. Other examples of recent incidents of price fixing include:

- the chocolate industry in the US and Germany,
- auction houses in Europe and the US,
- zinc phosphate in Europe,
- plastic additives for food in Europe,
- LCD monitors in Korea,
- Cargo prices on international shipments.

There is also another illegal practice called bid rigging where companies agree on who is going to submit the lowest bid.

- Have you ever wondered how it is that two or more suppliers send in identical bids on one or more of your tenders?

- Are you curious as to why a particular supplier always submits the highest bid on your projects and the lowest one on someone else's projects?

- Have you ever asked why some of the tenders you received are quoted at amounts much higher than the cost you estimated?

- Have you ever questioned why some suppliers bid on some projects and not on others?

- Are you aware of discussions among your suppliers about pricing or whose "turn" it is to win a particular contract?

If you answered "yes" to any of these questions, you may have been the victim of bid-rigging, which is a criminal offence in most countries.

Bid-rigging is an agreement where, in response to a call or request for bids or tenders, one or more bidders agree not to submit a bid, or two or more bidders get together to submit bids that have been prearranged among them.

Bid-rigging eliminates competition among your suppliers, increasing your costs and harming your ability to compete. Whether this occurs on government projects or in the private sector, these increased costs are ultimately passed on to the public. (Competition Bureau Canada, 2010)

This is the end of this chapter. I suggest you complete the exercises below before moving on to the next chapter.

Exercises

It is time for you to practice calculating export prices. In these examples you will complete the more complicated calculations for exporting a product to Canada, so there is no customs duty on freight. Look back to the calculation with X earlier in this chapter.

Answers to the three different examples are provided at the end of this chapter. For each example calculate step by step including the export price, the profit in $ and % profit. Try getting the answer on your own before checking. When you complete the calculation, evaluate the result and look at what you can do increase your profits.

Example 1

a.   Market price is $240 (this is what the customer/end user wants to pay)

b.   Manufacturing cost is $60

c.   Freight is 10%

d.   Customs duty is 5.4%

What is the export price if the distribution chain is:

Exporter > Importer > Local Distributor > Dealer > Customer (Note: there are three levels on the local market <u>before</u> the end user)

The importer wants 25% margin = profit on their selling price to the local distributor.

The local distributor wants 20% margin = profit on their selling price to the local dealer.

The local dealer wants 30% margin = profit when selling to the end user, the customer.

Example 2

a. Market price is $240 (this is what the customer wants to pay)

b. Manufacturing cost is $60

c. Freight is 12% (increased from 10%-12% because of smaller volume to each dealer)

d. Customs duty is 5.4%

What is the export price if the distribution chain is:

> Exporter > Local Distributor/Dealer > Customer (Note: there is one level on the local market between exporter and the end user)

> The local distributor/dealer wants 40% margin = profit on their selling price to the end user/customer.

Example 3

a. Market price is $200 (this is what the customer wants to pay)

b. Manufacturing cost is $50

c. Freight is 10%

d. Customs duty is 6%

What is the export price if the distribution is:

> Exporter > Importer/Distributor > Sub Distributor > Local Dealer > End User (customer). (Note; there are 3 distribution levels)

> Importer wants 35% margin = profit on their selling price

> Sub distributor wants 35% margin = profit

> Dealer wants 45% margin = profit

After making the calculation and seeing the result, how do you deal with this result?

SOLUTIONS

Example 1: Exporter > Importer > Local Distributor > Dealer > Customer

Market price -	$240
Manufacturing cost -	$60
Export price -	X
Freight -	0.1X
Customs duty -	0.054x
Total landed -	1.154x

Importer wants 25% profit 1.154x÷0.75 [(=100-25)/100)] = 1.5387 x. (i.e. the local distributor pays 1.5387 times the export price)

Local distributor wants 20% profit or 1.5387x/0.80= 1.9234 x

The dealer wants 30% profit when they sell to the end user or 1.9234x ÷ 0.7 = 2.7477x

So what is 2.7477x? That is the price the customer pays, 2.7477 times the export price. We know the customer pays $240 which is the same as 2.7476x (2.7477 times the export price). So 2.7477x = 240

X = 240 ÷ 2.7477 = $87.35 The **export price is $87.35**

The profit is the difference between the export price and the manufacturing cost or $87.35 - $60 = $27.35 or 27.35/87.35 x 100 = **31.3%**

Example 2: Exporter > Local Distributor/Dealer > Customer

Market price -	$240
Manufacturing cost -	$60
Export price -	X
Freight -	0.12X
Customs duty -	0.054x
Total landed -	1.174x

In this example the exporter sells directly to an importer who wants 40% profit.

1.174x ÷ 0.60[(100-40/100)] = 1.9567x. The customer price is = $240. In other words, 1.9567 x = $240

X= $240/1.9567 = **$122.66, which is the export price**

Your profit is $122.66 - $60 = **$62.66** or 62.66/122.66 (x 100) = **51.1%**

As you can see, despite higher freight costs and a higher margin paid to your dealer, your profit increases considerably by reducing the number of distribution levels.

Example 3: Exporter > Importer/Distributor > Sub Distributor > Local Dealer > End User (customer).

> Export price is X
> Freight   0.1x
> Duty   0.06x
> **Total**   **1.16x landed cost**

The importer wants 35% or 1.16x ÷ 0.65 [(100-35/100)] = **1.785 x**

The sub distributor wants 35% or 1.85 x÷ 0.65[(100-35/100)] = **2.746x**

The dealer wants 40% or 2.746x÷0.55 [(100-45/100)] = **4.99** x.

The customer pays 4.99 times the export price. 4.99x = $200

X= $200/4.99 = **$40.08 (the export price)**

Your manufacturing cost is $50 so **your "profit"** is $40.08-$50 = **-$9.92**.

You will lose money. Obviously, this solution does not work. What can you do? You can't increase the price. You **have to** "adjust" your distribution. Let's take way the last part in this distribution, the dealer. Now our calculation is:

> Export price is X
> Freight   0.1x
> Duty   0.06x
> **Total**   **1.16x landed cost**

The importer wants 35% or 1.16x ÷ 0.65 (100-35/100) = 1.785 x

The sub-distributor wants 35% or 1.785 x/ 0.65[(100-35/100)] = 2.746x.

Now you the sub distributor selling to the end user, so the customer pays 2.746 times the export price.

2.746x= $200

X= $200/2.7466 = **$72.83 (export price)**

With an **export price of $72.83** and a manufacturing cost of $50, your profit is $72.83 - $50 = **$22.83** or 22.83 ÷ 72.83 x 100 = **31.3%**

In this example, you could still sell to the market and make a profit by reducing the number of levels in the distribution chain.

This is the end of the Pricing chapter. Before moving to the next chapter, I suggest you:

1. Review the content and complete some calculations on your own, using examples from your own business. Make sure you understand how the calculations work. This will ensure that you make money, select the right distribution solution for the market and remain competitive.

2. Go back to the chapter "Why international business" and look at the marginal calculations.

3. After you read the Freight chapter, return to this chapter to see by reducing freight costs can increase your profitability.

Adapting Products/Services and Sales Material

In This Chapter:

- ◆ Adapting products and services
- ◆ Local standards, preferences, approvals and technological level
- ◆ Adapting sales material

John Smith, a manager from Detroit, Michigan, has been asked to fly to Bangkok, Thailand on very short notice. His boss, the Chief of Design, was in hospital and a client in Thailand had complained that the system supplied did not work as specified. The electrical fans in the factory did not perform to specification. John had never been outside North America and looked forward to the trip. However, his daughter has an important birthday in two days and he have to miss that.

His flight from Detroit via Tokyo to Bangkok was, about twenty hours long, of which 14 hours was spent in the air in economy class, on a fully booked flight. He had loaded his computer with all the details about the delivered system and hoped that he had found the answer to the client's problem. In the US, electricity was supplied at a frequency of 60Hz (periods per second) and in Thailand they had 50Hz, which resulted in a 17% slower speed. That could be easily solved with new fan wheels producing a higher air volume than the units supplied. This would produce the air volume per minute output stipulated by the client.

He landed in Bangkok just after midnight the day after he departed. He changed some US dollars to the local currency, Baht. He had been told it would cost about $25 for a taxi to downtown and that he had to pay the driver with exact change for the toll road because drivers tended not to have change.

While he waited for his luggage, he tried to send a text message to his daughter. The local time in Detroit was just before noon. The message service did not work and he would have to try later. In the taxi, he tried again to send, but still could not connect. He asked the driver what could be wrong. The driver said: "No good, American phones, does sometimes not work, we have mainly GSM only some CDMA American phones work here, but you can at a low cost rent a GSM phone here".

After arriving at the hotel 2 a.m. and starting his computer, he decided to use Skype to talk to his daughter; however, his American computer power plug did not work. The voltage in Thailand was 220volt which was no problem because computers operate from 90 volt to 260 volt. He called room service and in two minutes he had an adapter that fit his plug and the wall outlet. Obviously, this was not the first time this had happened to a guest of the hotel. He realized that his phone charger only worked with 120 volt, but he had the USB cable so he could charge it via his computer.

Welcome to the "international standard".

Product & Service Adaption

Every country has legislation, customs, rules and regulations relating to measurements, labelling, electrical standards, etc. If you are an importer, you are the person who has to ensure that you comply with those rules. If you are an exporter, you will have the assistance of your importer.

As foreign companies have to adapt their products to your local market, you have to adapt your products to the export market.

Product adaptation may be necessary because of local regulations or demands from local users based on their preferences or taste. Do your research so that you know if the product or service is sellable in a particular market. For example, you may normally offer a three month warranty on your product in the domestic market, while in the foreign market, customers demand a warranty of 12 months. Sometimes the required adaptation is a minor obstacle; occasionally it will be major, like changing the brand name from the one you use domestically.

As the exporter, you can include a clause in your contract that reads: It is the distributor's responsibility to ensure that the product/service complies with local laws and regulations.

We will cover this in more detail in the Legal chapter.

What do you need to consider?

- The product and services you are providing
- Local taste, fashion, preferences and knowledge
- Sales material and communications presented in the local way
- Measurements (Metric or Imperial)
- Climate and location – extreme heat or cold, high altitude, rural, remote
- Regulations, approvals and standards
- The local language/languages and the methods used to convey information.
- Technological level of the product and end-user knowledge
- Economic strength on the market and potential for future growth

You have to focus on what is important for the customer in each specific country. Product size could be the key criterion in one country, reliability in another and product quality in a third. If the product is good for the environment, this could generate a strong demand. Price could be an important factor in selling your product. It could be a combination of several factors.

What are the market trends? If you don't know this, it could be a costly mistake if your product has gone out of fashion or is too modern or advanced. There are major differences between what high quality means in Pakistan, the US, Europe and Japan. You have to know what local demands are so that you can properly adapt. When you sell a bicycle or other steel-frame product in the US or Europe, it is acceptable to see the weld, although it has been painted over. For a customer in Japan, you have to polish the weld before painting, so that the surface is smooth. For that Japanese client, if the packaging is damaged or poorly made, this reflects on the quality of the product inside.

The education level of the end-user must influence the design of a product. If the customer for your gear-shift mechanism can't read, the product has to be adapted to include visual clues for use instead of written instructions. Most people would know that they have to clean a hydraulic coupling that has been buried in the sand before re-connecting it but some may not. You either have to make a coupling with a filter so that dirt cannot get into the system, or you have to provide clear instructions that all users can understand. In some parts of North America, for example, a paving breaker has to be heavy and sturdy but in northern Europe, the preference is for a slim design with a modern look and low noise.

The user's manual you produce must be in the language of the end user. Where people are illiterate, supplement those instructions with pictures. Remember that the environment of a product in transit could change dramatically – heat, cold, turbulence, moisture, etc. You have to ensure that your shipments are properly protected.

Example - Packing your product

You ship some heavy machinery from Iceland to Hong Kong by boat. The products were painted blue in the factory before shipping but when unpacked at the destination, it has turned red because of rust. You did not apply a rust protection coating and the humidity of seven weeks at sea took its toll on the product finish. There is also mould on the hoses and the operator seats. The instruction manuals have all turned curly and spotted from mildew.

The way you market your products has to be adapted as well. An American client wants information about product appearance and qualities and how much money they can make selling it. A German company wants technical specifications. No matter what the approach, the wording and expressions you use must reflect local customs and customer preferences. Whatever you do, don't have your sister-in-law translate the text, unless she is a professional translator and is very familiar with the industry, the country and how to sell there.

Example - Adapting sales material

When buying a camping trailer in Canada in 1979, I asked for a product brochure. The salesman asked why. I wanted to know the trailer's measurements. He said, you can sleep eight people, there is a shower and you can sit down at the table to eat. What more do you want? I wanted to know how big a car I would need. He looked at my car and said it was large enough. I finally agreed that I did not need the brochure. In Sweden, people buying a product usually want technical details in writing. Then they go home and study the information before making the decision to purchase. So I was still thinking the Swedish way.

We write dates and delivery times in a variety ways. June 12, 2010, is 12/06/2010 in Europe but in the US it is written as 6/12/2010. Many European companies state a delivery time like this - w42. That does not mean in 42 weeks but during week 42 of the calendar or in the middle of October. Some numbers have a negative meaning in some languages and should be avoided wherever possible. The number 4 is considered unlucky in Chinese, Korean, and Japanese cultures because when it is pronounced, it sounds like the word for death.

Most countries have mandatory labelling rules for information that must be provided. In Canada, for instance, text must appear in French and English and packaged or canned food must list the contents and contain a warning when there is a risk of potentially allergic reactions to an ingredient. In Arabic countries, people read from right to left, so if your instructions include only pictures printed in a left-to-right format, they will be reversed and likely misunderstood.

Example - Different taste

A Swedish company was introducing packaged bread to the British market. Before entering the market, they demonstrated the products and offered taste tests outside several food stores and universities. Most people liked the bread but there was one consistent comment – the bread tasted too salty. Changing the bread recipe was something that was easy for the Swedish company to do before officially launching the product.

Countries use one of two systems for measurement: inches, feet and miles are used in the Imperial system. Centimetres, meters and kilometres are used in the metric system. Adapt your measurements to the local system of measurement. You can't expect the user to translate measurements. They may choose not to buy your product! If you are used to the metric system, how do you know if 35 miles per gallon is good gas consumption for a mid-sized vehicle?

Paper sizes vary. The European A4 letter size is narrow and tall, while the 8 ½ by 11" size in Imperial measurement is wide and short. A4 paper will be too large for a North American or British ring binder. Furthermore, the holes in the paper will not be in the same locations. Clothing sizes are not the same, either. The body types of some nationalities are shorter, some are more muscular and some are tall and slim. A dress made for a Norwegian woman will not fit an Asian woman without alteration.

Building standards differ not only between countries but sometimes even within a country. Electrical standards can vary from 120 volt, 240 volt, 360 volt and even more. Electrical plugs and wall sockets have numerous configurations. Electrical motors can be manufactured with a range of shaft sizes and mounting brackets. Computer keyboards have been adapted for many languages.

From the size of file folders to local vehicle emission standards, there are health, safety, public and product safety certification agencies such as CE marking, Underwriters Laboratories (UL), and Canadian Standards Association (CSA). Each covers a range of products and services and has a variety of requirements.

Buying 4" x 4" lumber is not the same size in Europe and North America. In Europe it is 4" x 4" after the wood is dried while in North America it is measured before drying so the end result is more like 3.5" x 3.5". The US gallon and imperial gallon are not the same. The imperial gallon is 4.55 litres and the US gallon is 3.78 litres.

There are three main TV technology production systems: Phase Alternating Line or PAL (used in Western Europe and Australia), Sequential Color with Memory or SECAM (used in Eastern Europe and France) and National Television System Committee or NTSC (used in the United States & Canada). Each standard is different and it is not possible to watch a DVD program recorded in the PAL format on a machine in France without first converting it or using a multisystem system. CDMA or GSM are coding systems used for mobile phones. In some countries the steering wheel in vehicles is on the right side and people drive on the left side of the road. In North American, the steering wheel is on the left side of the car and you drive on the right side of the road. In Australia, England and Singapore it is the opposite. Motor vehicles have to be manufactured according to the driving market.

If you buy a McDonald's hamburger in Poland or Thailand or India, they may look the same but the spice mixture and even the composition of the burger patty will not be the same. In India, your 'hamburger' may be vegetarian. Prepared soups and other convenience foods are spicier in Indonesia than in Italy, even when the same manufacturer's name is on the package.

Your product has to be adapted to the climate of the country where it will be used. Here are some factors you should research in advance. Is the climate cold, hot, dry or humid? Are there a lot of mice or other animals that could get into the packaging and contaminate your product? Is there refrigeration or do you have to reformulate the product so that cold storage is not required. Does your market require that you develop some other type of packaging to preserve the product in hostile conditions? Depending on the location, you may have to supply products that can resist earthquakes, water saturation, mould or termites. At 3000 meters of altitude in Peru, the output of a diesel generator will be reduced by 50%. What is called a road in the bush in Liberia is not the same as the Autobahn in Germany.

You can see that there can be a multitude of product features to adjust, especially if your new market is not at all like your home market in terms of language, culture and technology. Selling to a neighbouring country may be an option for you if you want to limit product adaptation.

Example - Adapting services

Worldwide, consumers want three things: quality products, attractive pricing and excellent service. The key to success is to understand the culture, language and needs of each market.

Religion plays a big role in Islamic culture. Insurance is often prohibited because it is based on risks that people have no control over – only God can decide the outcome of a person's life. We developed a pre-paid health and travel health insurance product for individuals that handled the health concerns of the Muslim market without transgressing their faith. We chose a name, graphics and colours that resonated with their culture, and provided information in Arabic. We even included a special service that would provide an Imam for religious advice if they had a travel medical emergency. By understanding the values and culture of different areas, we could satisfy their needs for product, price and service.

Robin Ingle, Chairman and CEO of Ingle International, which provides insurance products and services worldwide.

Summary

Determine what is appropriate for each market. Investigate what you have to do. Remember:

1. Adapt products and services to the preferences (taste) and knowledge level of the local market.

2. Arrange in advance for required approvals.

3. Label the products according to local rules and legislation.

4. Sales materials and instructions must be produced in the local language and be consistent with local marketing methods.

5. If you are an importer, the burden is on you to ensure that the product/service complies with local regulations, standards, measurements and meets customer demands. As an exporter, you can get assistance with product adaptation from your local importer.

This is a brief chapter with only one section.

Exercise

1. Examine your products/services. What do you need to do to adapt them to the export market you have selected? Consider climate, voltage, local standards, user preferences, etc.

2. Investigate and list some of the rules for approvals, standards and labelling.

3. What features are important for your overseas clients?

4. Outline how you must adapt your sales material and way of selling to fit into the new market's way of thinking and their skill level

Transport, Trade Barriers, Trading Blocs, and International Organizations

In This Chapter:

- ♦ Methods of transportation
- ♦ Freight as part of costs
- ♦ Selecting a forwarder
- ♦ Packaging
- ♦ Responsibility for goods, Incoterms
- ♦ Insurance and documentation
- ♦ Trade barriers
- ♦ Duty free, bonded warehousing, etc.
- ♦ Trading Blocs and Free Trade agreements
- ♦ International organisations

Your company ships cheese from Denmark to Canada. You have a friend in Toronto who will distribute the cheese directly. He has good contacts with Scandinavian restaurants and they are very interested in your product. The price is good and the market is, too.

You send your first shipment and it is delayed at the border by the Canada Revenue Agency. Why? Your partner did not realize that importation of cheese is controlled and a valid cheese import license from the Canadian Food Inspection Agency is required. He did not apply for one. Furthermore, there are Tariff Rate Quotas that limit the amount of foreign cheese allowed into the country. Competitors in the dairy industry are not willing to sell you part of their quota so that your cheese can be imported at their lower customs duty. You've spent and lost a lot of money.

Do your homework next time! Know the rules for the country you are exporting to.

Transport

Transport or shipping is the physical process of moving goods or cargo on the ground, by air or by sea for exporting and importing. Selection of transportation method is dependent on the type of products, final destination, restrictions on transportation of certain types of cargo and how urgently the goods are required. You may have to make compromises based on speed of delivery, transportation safety issues and costs. For example, sending containers of exotic wood flooring from Latin America to Asia requires a different method than shipping live lobsters from Canada to Europe (rail and ship vs. air cargo).

Your product may be moved by a combination of transportation methods. It can leave your factory on a transport truck, travel in the truck container by rail to a port for loading onto a cargo ship, unloaded onto a pickup truck, with final delivery to the end-user by mule.

Ship. This is the most common mode of transporting freight. More than 90% of goods are sent to export markets via ship. Shipping by boat is relatively inexpensive for large volumes of products, for heavy goods and when the schedule for delivery is not time-sensitive.

Cargo vessels are being built with larger capacities than before. Until recently, the maximum size of ships travelling through the Panama Canal (Panamax) has been limited by the width and length of the Canal's three locks, the depth of the locks and the height of the fixed Bridge of the Americas that crosses the Canal.   However, new, larger canals are being constructed. Post-Panamax or super tankers and bulk container ships have the capacity to carry 13,100, twenty foot containers.

When you send goods by sea, the cost is normally calculated on the volume and not the weight if the goods are not heavy. Shipping rates are based on FCL or Full

Container Load or LCL, which is Less than Container Load. One of the drawbacks of sending shipments by sea is that it takes long time.

Air freight. This is a good solution when the goods are not too bulky or too heavy. It is a fast method with less rough handling than for sea freight. Goods are packaged in smaller containers. It can cost more, but you gain in shipping time. In some instances, air freight can cost less than sea freight. Freight cost is normally based on weight, but if the object is bulky, volume is factored into price. There are limits for what can be sent by air: materials like chemicals, hazardous wastes and flammable materials. The classification or value of the product (electronics or fabric), how the goods is packaged (bulky or not or special type of containers) and type of aircraft (courier, air cargo or passenger aircraft) will determine rate and acceptance.

"Why is something sent by ship called cargo, but when it's sent by car/truck it's a shipment?"

Rail. Shipping goods on freight trains can be cost effective over longer distances. It is an environmentally friendly alternative. In large countries such as Russia, Canada, and the United States, where trucking would be unpractical for long distance transportation, bulky products such as lumber, coal, chemicals, machinery and vehicles are sent by rail. In North America and European countries such as Germany, transport truck trailers are placed on rail cars to reduce traffic congestion. Railways networks carry goods throughout Europe and can even have a final destination in Saudi Arabia. In the early 1900s, some companies in Canada and Russia used rail cars for storage as well as transportation of good. Their salesmen used to sell company products as they travelled from town to town. This selling method is still used for some products in some countries.

Trucking. Moving goods along roadways can be profitable for shorter distances, time-sensitive products and smaller loads. You can transport the goods door to door or when you need to reload a number of times. It can be used wherever there is a road. For smaller volumes, it has rather high unit costs. It is not a very environmental friendly alternative and it takes more time than air freight for longer distances.

Parcel Post. This is a good alternative for small shipments and short distances, e.g. spare parts. It is very common for delivery of books, DVDs and small deliveries. Overseas parcels can take weeks to arrive so if the shipment is urgent, a courier would be faster.

Courier. This method promises fast delivery and excellent security. The courier company also facilitates customs clearance. When a customer urgently needs spare parts, or clients/distributors do not want to keep a large inventory in stock, this is a good alternative. Two or three days of transport time is all it takes to the end user. Some freight companies supply the same service but call the service express freight.

Digital transport. We tend to think only of physical transportation of goods. However, you can send products and services digitally. For example, the text and graphics for this book were developed on a computer in Canada then supplied to the printer in the US, UK and Australia electronically. You can send music, photos, software, architectural drawings, etc. You have to determine if the digital transfer is subject to customs duty or taxes at the final destination. Downloading of files may be prohibited in some countries or there could be copyright restrictions or taxes to be paid. It is your responsibility to know what is applicable.

Port of entry

Shipping goods directly to the final destination may not always be the best or lowest cost option. Ask your forwarder about alternative methods and pricing.

Example – Using different route for shipment

We were shipping large quantities of machine parts from Sweden to Chicago, Illinois. The port of entry would be New York, and then the goods would be loaded on a truck for Chicago. All prices were quoted in US dollars (USD). We found that shipping the goods to Halifax, Nova Scotia in Canada then loading them onto rail cars to Chicago would cost less. Generally, freight costs were the same in USD and CDN dollars, but with the value of the US dollar being 25% higher, the cost to ship via Canada would be 25% less. Furthermore, the cost of clearing the shipment in New York was higher than in Chicago.

Freight As Part of Costs

If you remember the calculations for export and import prices, you know that freight costs must be included. It is important to analyze freight costs and whenever possible, to find ways to reduce it. As I stated above, sometimes the cost of shipping by air can be less expensive then by boat.

In the example below, a European company is shipping small oil pumps to California. The client normally sends 40 pumps at a time by sea freight. Remember that freight costs and currency exchange rates change all the time. In the example below, currency values have been converted to USD.

Calculation of Freight Cost - Options

Sea Freight

Number of pumps	20	40	60	80
Total cost *	$470	$470	$470	$470
Freight per pump	$23.50	$11.75	$7.83	$5.88

* You always pay for minimum 1 cubic meter for sea freight. Therefore, the cost is the same for 20, 40, and 80 pumps.

Air Freight

Number of pumps	20	40	60	80
Total cost	$304	$345	$413	$505
Freight per pump	$15.20	$8.63	$6.86	$6.30

It would have cost less to send 40 or even 60 pumps by air. More important, shipping time by air is only 3 days compared with 5 weeks by boat. Because the extra cost is marginal, you could even consider sending 80 pumps by air. Because of gentler handling when the package is sent by air, the exporter could also save by using less costly packaging. Remember that freight companies base their rates on the weight or volume of the shipment as well as on what type of goods are being transported.

> *Example – Cost of freight*
>
> *There will be times when the freight cost is not that important. An international company had to temporarily stop manufacturing their trucks because they did not have the parts to complete production. The container holding the parts was stuck on a ship docked at a port three days away. The daily cost of not being able to get the finished trucks off the assembly line was $100,000 a day. In this case, the cost of shipping was not important because there was an urgent need to get parts delivered fast.*

As I mentioned in the Price chapter, you have to keep an eye on oil price fluctuations. Surcharges to cover increases in the cost of fuel for aircraft, trucks or ships can add considerably to your freight costs.

Transport Pricing

You have to consider a variety of elements:

- ♦ Classification and value of freight to be transported
- ♦ Weight and/or volume of goods
- ♦ Handling costs

- ♦ Loading and unloading expenses
- ♦ Documentation to clients and authorities
- ♦ Customs clearances
- ♦ Port or terminal fees
- ♦ Finance costs
- ♦ Mode of transportation (air, rail, ship, truck, horseback, etc.)
- ♦ Surcharges

When you ask for a price to move your goods, ask your freight forwarder for the door-to-door charge. That way, you don't have to do the calculations for all activities to be taken into account nor currency conversions and you will know the exact cost in one currency. Also, if you have a large shipment, compare the price you are quoted for a partial container (LCL Less than a container load) to the price for a full one. The full container could cost you less if you have large amount of goods and you could save your foreign importer money by filling up the container with even more goods, thus reducing the freight cost per item.

Time for transport

Analyze the time from pick-up to delivery. Shipping by sea is less expensive but a low-cost land carrier could take a longer time as well. Is the cost saving worth it? Perhaps the extra cost for air freight and faster delivery would be a better value.

Security of transport

Analyze how secure the transportation method is. Take into consideration packaging demands, handling, shipping conditions and opportunities for damage or theft. Many companies believe that their insurance coverage is automatic and that they can get reimbursed for lost/stolen goods or damages. In reality, freight companies only cover a small portion of costs. It can also take considerable time and documentation before you receive reimbursement. If you packaged the goods incorrectly, you are likely out of luck. Unfortunately, you may suffer losses due to pilferage and non-delivery or even hijacking, as sometimes happens along the coastline of Somalia. There can also be damage caused by sea water, breakage, contamination by vermin or leakage from other parcels. Your choice of packaging, type of transport and carrier can limit those risks.

Using transport professionals

Most people planning a vacation use the services of a travel agency. They can book an all-inclusive package at a price that includes air and ground transportation, taxes, accommodations and sometimes meals. It is easy to do and costs less than if you bought the individual items by yourself.

When you are shipping goods, you should use a specialist, too. A freight forwarder or agent can negotiate a package deal for you. They will take responsibility for handling the goods from the exporter's door to the importer's loading dock. They can assist with paperwork such as licenses and permits. The forwarder can also analyze the best transportation solution, whether it is boat, air, truck or courier and then suggest the most appropriate packaging.

The seller and buyer have a variety of responsibilities for completing the required documentation and securing the proper permits. Sometimes that responsibility will depend on the Incoterm selected. (See later in this chapter).

The seller has to make sure that product shipping credentials conform to the rules of the exporting authorities and ensure that documents like bills of lading and invoices comply with the rules of the importing countries. The importer has to make sure that any quota, license or permit is applied for in advance and must inform the exporter of any paperwork they must complete to get the goods into the country. A shipment of food could be stopped at the border if the required health inspection certificates and product descriptions are not included. This would mean delayed and extra costs. In a worst-case scenario, entry of the goods would be forbidden and the shipment ordered to be destroyed.

Selecting a Forwarder

When selecting a forwarder you have to make sure they:

♦ have a broad, stable global network positioned to take care of goods from your doorstep to the final destination.

♦ have a contact person who can provide service no matter what the country and method of transportation selected.

♦ are located close to your facility, so they can pick up your goods for dispatch to a partner in the receiving country.

♦ are competent to assist you with documents for export and import statistics, customs invoice requirements, import and export restrictions including licenses and quotas and if required, clearing goods through customs.

♦ can pick up and consolidate shipments from several companies so as to secure competitive prices and supply the most economical solution. If necessary, they can also store the goods before shipping or upon arrival.

♦ can analyze what type of transport is most favourable for you and your client.

♦   arrange for insurance of goods and advise you how to package the goods

♦   monitor goods in transit and inform you and the receiver of the arrival date.

An option for you or for your importer is to store and redistribute the product locally. If required, forwarders may be able to supply a bonded warehouse.

Some forwarders are multi-national companies with offices in hundreds of locations. A large company does not necessarily guarantee that they will deliver the services you need in the way you would prefer.

As a small exporter or importer, it may be easier for you to work with a smaller company that provides more personalized services. The quality of freight forwarders' staff can vary considerably. The profession may be seen as high status and the assistance you receive will be very professional. In other countries, the situation will be different.

There are companies specializing in certain types of transportation such as vehicles, live animals and perishable goods. Check to see if there is a forwarder specializing in your type of product. You may need a specialist in certain countries. A country like Russia may require that a forwarder is pre-approved by them. Companies that transact high volumes of business shipping to one destination tend to be able to react faster. They should also be able to offer you a better price. And because their shipments are loaded and reloaded less often, there is less chance that your goods will be subject to rough treatment, damage or pilferage.

You normally negotiate for better prices in your business. You should do the same for freight. A lower freight cost means that you reduce total costs and that your export price can be higher. Even though the receiver pays for the freight, it is still part of the export price calculation. What you save will increase profit for you or your representative.

The Importance of Packaging

Packaging is important for several reasons.

It must protect the goods from rough handling, theft and a variety of different weather conditions. In some situations, packaging is also part of sales promotion. If this is the case, make sure that the packaging is secure and protects the contents from damage.

Standard measurements are usually stipulated by shipping companies for goods, especially for sea freight. Measurement standards are intended to ensure maximum utilization of container volumes. If you deviate from of those measurements, you will pay a penalty. Ask your forwarder what the standards are. When shipping by boat, freight measurements normally determine the price, so a reduction of 40% in volume means a 40% reduction in costs.

Your freight forwarder will help you comply with requirements such as declaration of origin, bilingual labels, product contents and other standards.

Some countries have rules about packaging materials, including pallets. They may have to be recyclable. Others forbid wooden pallets and require that you use plastic material as the wood can include insects. There are areas in Canada that have been severely affected by disease or destructive insects that entered the country in shipments from overseas. Find out what each receiving country requires.

Package and labelling. If possible label the product in the receiving country's language. Sometimes that is a requirement. There are special rules for labelling hazardous and fragile goods. Specify "this side up", or include cautions about storage at certain temperatures etc. Your forwarder can advise you.

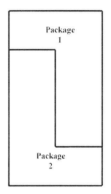

Example – Saving freight costs

> *A European exporter of mobility walkers used standard square boxes when exporting. The result was that a large part what they shipped was "air", and they had to pay for the additional space. By customizing the boxes to tightly fit the folded walkers' shape, they could reduce the shipping volume by 40% and freight costs by 40%.*

Sea freight	Standard packaging	Special packaging
Cost per product	$1000	$1000
Cost for freight	15% or $150	9% or $90
Cost for goods & freight	$1150	$1090

Inform your packing department about what happens when the packaging is done incorrectly. Look at the box on the pallet in the illustration. The box weighs 20 kg and occupies .2 cubic meters. When it was packed on a pallet, the weight increased to 40 kg the volume to 1 cubic meter because of the size and weight of the packaging. This increased freight costs by 500%. The shipping department packed the

goods for international delivery in the same way as for the domestic market, in a small box on a large wooden pallet.

It is one thing to package goods for transportation nearby. However, a shipment going overseas must to be able to withstand a variety of conditions: being picked up and reloaded several times, subjected to movement and moisture at the sea, stacked below or above decks and in changing environments from -15 degrees Celsius to high humidity and temperature. Remember that a ship at sea rolls with the waves five times a minute. During a five week journey, this could add up to 252000 times. If the shipment is loose in a box, there will be a lot of movement and shaking, which means that painted surfaces could be damaged in transit.

Responsibility for Goods

You purchased a shipment of leather boots from Australia, F.O.B. Sydney Harbour. The boat sinks on the way from Sydney to Spain. You are invoiced for payment but refuse to pay because you have not received the goods. Your Australian supplier sends your payment to a collection agency. You are ordered to pay. Why did that happen? The payment terms were F.O.B. Sydney Harbour, which means free on board from the Australian harbour. This means that you are responsible from the time the goods are loaded on the ship.

When you transport goods overseas for export or when goods are shipped to you, the importer, you have to decide who will be arranging for transport, who will negotiate the price and who will pay for it. It is recommended that the seller, who has good contacts in the exporting country, should negotiate freight costs and pay for shipment. Costs for freight and insurance are listed on the invoice as separate items. That way, you will know what has been included. You also eliminate collection charges that otherwise would be added when the receiver pays.

When an exporter sells the goods, the price can be *ex works*. The buyer would be responsible for freight and liability from the factory or when F.O.B. a local harbour. The seller is responsible until the goods are loaded in the ship.

To ensure that both parties are in agreement with the shipping terms, INCOTERM 2000 (see below) is normally stated as the base. This will minimize disagreements between a buyer and seller. I will not be going into too much detail. I suggest that you either ask your forwarder to give you a book that outlines the different terms or that you search on Google for INCOTERMS. Note that the terms were revised January 1, 2011, so update your information.

There are four major groups of Incoterms:

1. **Group E -** The goods are available for the buyer at the seller's site.

2. **Group F -** The seller has to deliver to a carrier appointed by the buyer.

3. **Group C -** The seller arranges for the transport but the buyer is assuming risk.

4. **Group D** - The seller covers all costs and risks to the place of destination.

EXW or Ex works. The buyer is in charge of transport and goods after the goods leave the factory

FOB or Free On Board. The seller is responsible for the goods until loaded into a ship. After that, the buyer is responsible.

CIF or Cost Insurance Freight. CIF Sydney Harbour means the seller has to pay for freight and insurance up to the buyer's port of Sydney. The buyer's responsibility begins when the goods are loaded in the ship.

For information and Incoterms visit the following web sites:

http://www.iccwbo.org/incoterms/id3045/index.html

International Chamber of Commerce. You can find details there, or download their wall chart.

http://www.iccwbo.org/incoterms/wallchart/wallchart.pdf

Some European countries use **Combiterms**. For more details, speak to your freight forwarder.

Local subsidies

Some local governments subsidize inland freight costs for remote locations. A company in the far north of Sweden was shipping goods to Africa. Normally, they would have paid high freight costs to get their goods to port for shipping.

If they sell ex works, however, at the exporter's factory, the seller and buyer do not benefit from those subsidies because the buyer pays the freight cost from the factory. It would be beneficial to use FOB at the exporter's harbour. The exporter could reclaim some of their freight costs for inland shipping by applying for the government subsidy. As an exporter, you can pass on savings from reduced freight costs to your buyer.

To insure or not to insure

Did you know that every second day a ship is damaged, destroyed or hijacked at sea?

You are shipping a machine overseas. The ship encounters rough seas and your machine, which has an exposed steel shaft, shifts inside its container and finally punctures the walls of its wooden container, putting a hole in the next container which contains plastic barrels of olive oil. The olive oil from the broken barrels leaks onto the shipping container packed below. It contains cardboard boxes packed with designer wedding gowns.

Who do you think is responsible? I hope you had insurance, because you could be ruled to be at fault for the damage.

You know from reading the fine print on your ticket that the airline transporting you from one city to another has limited liability if they lose or damage your checked luggage. For that reason, you could buy insurance to cover the difference between your luggage value and what the air carrier may pay. When you ship goods, the same principles apply. The shipping company/transport carrier has very limited liability. Your liability could include damage to third-party goods. Furthermore, you may even be responsible for part of the cost of the vessel if a ship sinks.

The message here is, make sure to arrange adequate insurance coverage for the goods being transported. It is a small expense that could save you a considerable amount of money. Your forwarder can assist with insurance arrangements.

Documentation

When you transport goods domestically, you usually enclose a packing slip or shipping document. You might also send an invoice. When you work internationally, the burden of paperwork will increase. If you are an exporter, your local government will want statistical information about the product or service you are exporting. They are interested in the value, calculated in the local or other currency, the number of units, litres, volume or weight shipped and the customs code (see later this chapter). This data will be used to compile reports on export statistics. If an export license is required, you will have to supply one.

The receiving country will require a packing list describing the contents of the shipment and an invoice that complies with local customs rules. It will contain a product description, the number of units and the price. For those countries that charge duty on freight, insurance and packaging, you will have to include documentation on that as well. Customs authorities and customs brokers at the importer's border will want to know the products country of origin, its place of manufacture or from where the majority of value-added content was sourced, and the declared value for duty and tariff classifications.

If you are an Italian company importing textiles from China for export to South Africa and you simply redirect the textiles to South Africa, they will still be considered to be of Chinese origin. However, if you manufacture clothing from the textiles in Italy, your processing and other costs will be more than the imported value of the textiles, so the clothing will be deemed to be of Italian origin. In reality, the process is not as simple as I have described, so make sure that learn how and comply with the applicable rules.

Some countries require more extensive documentation such as certificates of origin, inspection, quality analysis and product weight, consular invoice, confirmation of insurance or perhaps proof that you are using an approved forwarder. Many of those documents need to be certified by a local authority such as a Chamber of Commerce. Don't worry; your freight forwarder can help. They will know the rules for each country and assist you to fill out the correct forms.

The most frequently-used documents include packing lists, the Bill of Lading (B/L), which is the transport contract prepared by the carrier or freight forwarder. A foreign buyer must have a Bill of Lading to take possession of a shipment. The B/L includes a number which allows you and the receiver to trace the location of the goods. The Air Way Bill (AWB), is used for air shipments. Similar documents are available for trucking, rail courier and other transportation methods. However, the ultimate responsibility for acting in accordance with country requirements is yours.

There may be exceptions to documentation requirements, such as when the seller and buyer already have an established business relationship. Be careful, though, because there are parts of the world where corruption is widespread, and where the rules are not always followed. Don't take chances and try to use shortcuts. See more in the Risk chapter.

Trade Barriers

There are usually legal barriers to importing products. Some countries attempt to protect their domestic industry by limiting access from foreign product competitors. Steps are also taken to safeguard production of military products and protection of the population from illegal drugs, alcohol and dangerous or unsafe products. There are tariff and non-tariff barriers.

Despite the existence of the General Agreement on Tariffs and Trade (GATT) agreement, free trade agreements and a general tendency towards lower tariffs and fewer barriers, trade protectionism is ongoing. Trade tensions are fuelled by numerous economic, political, social, and technological issues.

GATT, now the World Trade Organization (WTO), works is a global international organization regulating the rules of trade between nations, with a focus on reducing trade barriers. There have been significant improvements in the last 30 years with major reductions in customs duties and other trade barriers but there are still restrictions such as licenses, labelling requirements, quotas, packaging rules and local approvals. Many countries also promote purchasing of domestic products.

Tariff barriers

Customs duties are the most common type of trade barrier. This fee, normally a percentage of the product's value, is added to the price of imported goods. Some trading agreements eliminate this duty. For example, if you are a member of the EU or the country you live in has an agreement with the EU, no duties would be applied. The EU also has agreements with developing countries to assist in their industrial development by eliminating duties.

In North America, the customs value is based on the export price FOB port of direct shipment to Canada or the US. In the EU, customs value is based on the CIF value according to Incoterms, which includes the export price, freight costs, insurance and other costs such as packaging and quota licenses.

The **Generalised System of Preferences** or GSP was instituted in 1976 to promote economic growth in developing countries by providing preferential duty-free entry for about 4,800 products from 131 designated countries and territories. Customs duty is calculated at varying rates, depending on the country. http://www.au.af.mil/au/awc/awcgate/crs/rs22183.pdf

Countervailing duty is intended to offset the negative impact of concessions or subsidies paid to foreign exporters of certain products.

Anti-dumping duty. This penalty was covered in the *Price* chapter. When a company sells goods at predatory pricing or for less than their normal value, they may be found guilty of dumping. Commonly dumped products are electronics, textiles, footwear, steel and chemicals from manufacturers in South East Asia and Eastern Europe.

Taxes are imposed to raise money and to control the flow and pricing of goods. There is usually a specific class or special tax on alcohol and tobacco. Cosmetics or luxury items may be taxed more heavily than ordinary consumer goods. Of course, there may also be municipal, provincial/state and/or federal sales or value-added taxes.

Fees can include additional charges for environmental controls on imported products, e.g., recycling electronic equipment components, vehicle tires, aerosol containers.

Non-tariff barriers

An indirect trade barrier restricts trade in certain goods. It can include:

♦ Specific quotas, which limit the amount that can be imported or exported, pricing requirements for imported goods, import licensing for classes of goods such as agricultural products, local content requirements;

♦ Testing and standards requirements for approval of consumer goods and industrial products, technical issues such as voltage, language and packaging rules, building codes, product safety checklists;

♦ Administrative procedures which act as trade roadblocks, such as complex or lengthy customs procedures, product testing certification, corruption, fees for processing documentation;

♦ Government intervention and monopolies such as on the importation and sale of pharmaceuticals or alcohol, buy national policies, subsidizing exports, preventing entry of products such as cultural artefacts, exotic or endangered species or agricultural products.

The list is much longer than what is included above. You will have to become familiar with tariff and non-tariff restrictions so that you understand how they will influence your product/service for each country.

Quotas or limits on quantities of imported goods allowed may be temporary or they can exist for an extended period of time. Sometimes, importers are allocated part of a quota or they may have to compete for a share. When quotas for a product have been distributed or used up before the end of a year, your ability to import goods covered by the quota will be limited.

The status of quotas can, however, change very fast. When a quota for shoes manufactured in China was released in the EU, the application period was for three weeks. However, the quotas sold out in five days! This caused a serious problem for some shoe importers because without a 'piece of the action', they were not allowed to import shoes from China.

Quotas are common for textiles, iron and steel but sometimes also for agricultural products. In the EU a quota applies not just to a single jurisdiction but to the entire European Union. There is a growing tendency to replace quotas with heavy duties. In Canada, all of the previous quantitative limitations were converted to tariff rate quotas (TRQs). So, if a product was formerly subject to 10% duty and the quota was 1,000 units, no more than 1,000 units could be imported. Canadian customs authorities now impose a TRQ of 270% for product volumes over and above the 1,000 units allowed. The end result is the same but is shown on a tariff basis.

An example of special rules can be found in Russia. There, the law stipulates that the majority of locally produced and imported products must be tested and approved by Russian authorities for compliance with national standards. This mandatory review system or Gost certification (http://www.gost.sgs.com) applies to a broad range of consumer, technical, resource, transportation and industrial products and equipment. Multiple certifications and numerous permission documents (permits, licenses, certificates and tests) could be required for a single product or project. Gost documentation must be prepared in the Russian language. As you could expect, this costs a lot of money. If you do not have regular orders/continuous deliveries or if you change your product line, the required re-certifications could be expensive.

Some countries require that goods are inspected at the supplier's or producer's facility before they will approve shipments. For example, I was working with a European company exporting industrial goods to Egypt. The company had to agree to an inspection by an Egyptian government representative. The importer in Egypt had to cover the cost of the inspection visit and arrange for all local permits. Of course, the inspector also expected to be 'treated well' by the European company's managers. Keep these factors in mind when you calculate your export pricing.

An export license may be required for products such as military equipment, certain types of computer software, art and cultural products. Restrictions may be imposed on exports of selected products and services to certain countries. Even electronic currency, documentation or technology transfers may be limited or prohibited to some locations.

Example – Export license

Our company supplies spill control products worldwide. Some of our products use a formula which includes a chemical requiring an export license. Even though this chemical makes up less than 1% of the final product, authorities in the United States insist on an export license which includes a list of all the countries and companies that the end product is exported to. The chemical license has to be renewed every two years, for each and every customer and also for each item/part # it is used in - even if the only difference between the part #s is the size of the package.

Andy Hetzel Jr., President, NPS Corporation, Green Bay, Wisconsin, USA.

Paying customs duty

Whether you are an importer or an exporter, the exporter's invoice detailing the type and value of goods, together with the packing slip, determine what duties will be applied. The international Harmonized Commodity and Coding System or HS code, was developed by the World Customs Organization (WCO) to classify products for trading purposes into categories of increasing complexity (e.g., from crude/natural resources to technology). The HS code is also used by customs departments around the world to determine duties and taxes.

The first hierarchy or level of the HS has 4 digits referred to as headings.

Example:

HS Code 8410 Hydraulic turbines, water wheels & regulators; parts thereof.

A further division into the first 6 digits forms the subheading:

841011 Hydraulic turbines & water wheels, power <= 1000kW

841012 Hydraulic turbines & water wheels, 1000kW < power <= 1000)kW

841013 Hydraulic turbines & water wheels, power > 10000kW

841090 Parts of hydraulic turbines, water wheels, & regulators therefor

The more than 200 nations, trade and economic unions that have adopted the system are not permitted to alter the description of products or sub-categories, so there is standardization of names and numbering. Countries may add subcategories of numbers up to eight or ten digits for export statistics reporting purposes.

More information and clickable examples can be found at: http://www.wcoomd.org/

http://www.foreign-trade.com/reference/hscode.htm (a step-by-step description of each level)

You can find an excellent overview of the American system, with charts detailing units of quantity and rates of duty at http://www.usitc.gov/tata/hts/bychapter/index.htm for each Chapter of the HS

If you have exported before, you will already have the HS code for those goods because the code would have been included on the forms required by local authorities. If you want to find out the customs duty for a new product and specific country, contact your freight forwarder or customs broker, tell them what product you are exporting and ask them for the HS code. They could also find out for you what the customs duty will be for each country you plan to export to. If you want to look up your customs code, and you can't find it on your government website, contact your customs authorities and they could advise you where you could find the information or check the web sites mentioned before.

It is essential that you find and use the appropriate customs code for your product. Using the wrong code can mean that you or your client will pay too much duty. If you use the wrong code and pay too little, customs authorities will eventually find your error and demand that you pay the difference, usually with a penalty. If you are unclear, request a ruling from the customs authorities before making the first shipment. Duties can vary based on country of origin.

Although you can arrange to clear goods through customs yourself, it is not practical. Hire a customs broker to represent your company. Most of the large forwarders have an in-house broker. The smaller forwarders will have an agreement with a larger one. Remember that you will have a short time to unload or get the goods from your forwarder; otherwise, they will charge for storage, which can be very expensive. If you leave clearing the goods in the hands of a forwarder or broker, inform them well in advance when the shipment is to arrive and provide them with a bill of lading, copy of customs invoice and packing slips, so they can prepare all of the paper work in advance and get the goods cleared fast. If you return products for which you have paid duty (i.e., you received the wrong product, it was faulty or damaged), you can request a refund.

Technology is also affecting the customs clearance. There are a number of countries introducing eManifest. The first areas are for trucking companies for border crossings. (Search "eManifest" on Google for update.)

Bonded warehouse

As soon as you import goods to a country, you must pay the appropriate customs duties and taxes. Sometimes, for a number of reasons, you may not want to do that. You can contract for space in your freight forwarder's bonded warehouse. This will allow you to temporarily store the goods and not have to pay any duty or taxes until you take them out. If you frequently use a bonded warehouse, you can set up a one at your facility. The rules are strict and the customs authorities frequently check to secure that you follow procedures.

Duty free manufacturing

Some companies import components that will be included in a manufactured product to be exported. Some countries have 'free trade zones', where no or reduced duties and taxes make them attractive for manufacturers, importers and exporters to set up operations and international distribution centres. The oldest free trade zone was established in Shannon, Ireland in 1947. For smaller manufacturers, if no tax or duty free options are available, they can apply for a drawback to reclaim duties.

Temporary import

You may need to bring in products on a temporary basis. It could be for a trade show, specialized tools for professionals servicing machinery or to transport your horse so that you can participate in a jumping competition.

Major international business organizations such as the US Council for International Business and Chambers of Commerce in India, China, Canada, London, etc.) are permitted to issue an ATA Carnet, which is a customs document allowing the holder to temporarily import goods without paying duties and taxes, as long as the goods are re-exported. Temporary usually means for a period of up to one year. Search online for ATA Carnet for more details.

When you relocate from one country to another, you normally do not pay duty and taxes on furniture and appliances for personal use.

You may also be exempt from duty and taxes if the product you shipped is to be destroyed. Perhaps you are sending a product to be tested for fire resistance and after the test the product will be useless.

We have covered the most important aspects of transport, customs duties, trade barriers and packaging in the first part of this chapter. However, there are other activities and organisations that can influence duties, taxes and quotas. You can read more about those in Part Two. There, we will cover a variety of international organisations, trading blocs and free trade arrangements that will influence your ability to compete on the global arena.

Summary

Remember that:

- The right choice of freight is important to getting the goods to the importer in a safe and fast way. (Sea freight, air freight etc.)

- The pros and cons of different methods of transporting freight such as by sea, air, rail or truck courier have to be analyzed for each shipment.

- Freight costs affect your export or import price. Analyze what is the most cost-effective method for you and your clients.

- Your product packaging has to be adapted to minimize size/volume and weight, keeping in mind the measurements of transportation containers, potential exposure to hazards and damage, depending on the method of shipment.

- Packages must be labelled according to the rules of the receiving location, including language, contents, colours and technical terminology.

- Freight costs should be negotiated and confirmed in advance, in writing. Select a forwarder qualified to assist you at home and at the foreign destination.

- The right delivery terms (INCOTERMS) have to be selected to fit your needs and those of your client.

♦   Do your research and find out if an export or import license is required. Make sure all necessary documents are included for the exporting nation and the importing country.

♦   Double-check to see if the receiving country has quotas or if there is a trade agreement that allows for preferential duty or no duty at all.

♦   If you are an importer, use the correct customs code on all documentation. If you are an exporter, you have to include the Customs code for export statistics.

♦   Insure the goods against a variety of risks.

Shipping
Part Two

Trading Blocks and Free Trade Agreements

In 1995, the approach to world trade changed dramatically. GATT, the General Agreement on Tariffs and Trade (established 1947) evolved into the WTO or World Trade Organisation and the old-style protectionism came to an end. The new global organization was established to assist goods and services producers, exporters and importers to conduct business internationally, using agreed-upon rules of trade. The WTO develops international agreements which reduce custom tariffs between the 155 trading nations who are members. In this multilateral trading system, the WTO also assists developing countries with trade policy issues, acts as a forum for trade negotiations and mediates trade disputes to ensure that trade continues to flow as smoothly, predictably and freely as possible.

Just as workers join labour unions, nations have found that working collaboratively improves profitability and creates stronger trade positions on the global market. Opening up trade, reducing tariffs and imposing consistency have led to improved international communications and larger world markets.

Trade stimulates economic growth and changes in standards of education, health, product quality and day-to-day life. Emerging technologies have increased the speed of movement and the spread of capital and manufacturing around the world, especially to developing nations. WTO negotiations and treaties have been completed for tariff-free trade in telecommunications services, information technology products, financial services, agriculture and a range of services.

Any trade agreement can influence your ability to enter a market and your profitability. It can guide you to select to a specific country or group of countries because of preferential treatment. It will also be an important factor when deciding on local manufacturing.

Examples of Trade Arrangements

Free Trade Area. This type of economic integration is negotiated between several countries. Customs duties, tariffs and quotas are reduced or eliminated for members. However, each country maintains customs tariffs for non-member countries.

Customs Unions. Similar to a free trade area but with a joint or common tariff for non-members. Examples include the Caribbean Community (CARICOM), the Gulf Cooperation Council (GCC) and the Southern Common Market (MERCO-SUR).

Common Market. Like a Customs Union but with common policies on product regulation and also allows free movement of capital, labour, goods, and services and production between and among the member countries. The European Union is an example of a common market.

Economic and Monetary Union. Similar to a Common market but with a shared currency and harmonized economic policies for all member countries. example is part of the European Union and the West African Economic and Monetary Union with eight nations using the West African CFA franc.

Complete Integration. The same as an Economic Union but with full monetary integration and completely harmonized fiscal policy in a single economy. An example would be the United States, which has federal government and quasi-autonomous state governments.

So what does this mean for you?

If you are conducting international business in a nation that operates under any of these arrangements, you will encounter no customs duties when exporting or importing to and from member countries. Note, also, that many trading blocs or individual countries also have agreements with other blocs and countries, which limit or eliminate duties payable. Before you export or import, investigate. Many trading blocs have a common standard and product approval process for all member countries. This makes it easier for companies to comply. Sometimes there are agreements only for specific products. This can determine whether it would be profitable for you to export there.

Below are some of the key trading blocs and economic unions. New ones are being signed all of the time. There are many more being negotiated and listed are web sites where you can find more information and check for updates. Look into arrangements that exist for your specific area. If you belong to a member country of the EU or will be shipping goods there, also look under bilateral agreements on the web site:

Information on all trading blocs

http://www.bilaterals.org – an overview of existing and proposed agreements

http://www.wto.org/english/tratop_e/region_e/region_areagroup_e.htm

http://www.eepcindia.org/trade-blocks.asp - a description of each bloc

Information on individual trading blocs

AANZFTA or Australia and New Zealand for a Free Trade Agreement. Free trade between the Association of Southeast Asian Nations (**ASEAN**) and Australia New Zealand Closer Economic Agreement (**ANZCERTA**).
http://www.dfat.gov.au/trade/fta/asean/index.html

ACP or African, Caribbean and Pacific Group of States, comprised of 79 nations/ states mainly in the Caribbean, Latin America and Africa.
http://www.acpsec.org/index.htm

ACS or **Association of Caribbean States**, has 38 members including Mexico, Venezuela, Caribbean and Central American countries.
http://www.acs-aec.org/index.htm http://www.comunidadandina.org/endex.htm

AFTA or the **Asean Free Trade Area has** members from 10 countries including Brunei Darussalam, Cambodia, Indonesia, Laos and Malaysia
http://www.aseansec.org/index.html

ALADI, the Latin American Integration Association (Associação Latino-Americana de Integração) has 12 Latin American member countries, including Chile, Cuba, Argentina, Ecuador, Mexico and Venezuela.
http://www.aladi.org/nsfweb/sitioIng/

Anzerta (CER) is the Australia New Zealand Closer Economic Agreement. The new name is CER.
http://www.dfat.gov.au/trade/negotiations/afta_cer.html

APEC or **Asia-Pacific Economic Cooperation.** A large organisation of 21 countries from not only Asian economies but also the Americas, including countries like Canada, Chile, Mexico, New Zealand; Papua New Guinea, Russia and Japan.
http://www.apec.org

APTA, the **Asia-Pacific Trade Agreement**, is a preferential trade agreement between Bangladesh, China, India, Republic of Korea, Laos and Sri Lanka
http://www.unescap.org/tid/apta.asp

ASEAN, Association of Southeast Asian Nations, has 10 members including Singapore and Thailand.600 million residents and 1000 languages. It will create a trading block similar to EU with one common currency 2015.
http://www.aseansec.org

AU, the **African Union,** has 53 members in Africa, from Algeria to Zimbabwe.
http://www.africa-union.org

CACM, The **Central American Common Market** includes Guatemala, El Salvador, Honduras and Nicaragua.
http://www.sice.oas.org/SICA/CACM_e.asp

CAN, the Comunidad Andina or **Andean Community** is represented by Bolivia, Columbia, Ecuador and Peru
http://www.comunidadandina.org/endex.htm

Caricom, the Caribbean Community and Common Market, has 15 members and 5 observers or associate members.
http://www.caricom.org/

CEFTA, Central European Free Trade Agreement includes some Eastern European countries that have not joined the EU, such as Albania, Bosnia and Herzegovina, Croatia, and Macedonia.
http://en.wikipedia.org/wiki/Central_European_Free_Trade_Agreement

CEMAC or the **Economic and Monetary Community of Central Africa** is an organization of states of Central Africa with Cameroon, Central African Republic, Chad, Republic of the Congo, Equatorial Guinea, and Gabon as members.
http://www.cemac.cf

CIS, the **Commonwealth of Independent States**, includes Azerbaijan, Armenia, Belarus, Georgia, Kazakhstan, Kyrgyzstan, Moldova, Russia, Tajikistan, Turkmenistan, Uzbekistan and Ukraine.
http://www.cisstat.org/eng/cis.htm

COMESA, the **Common Market for Eastern and Southern Africa**, has 19 members such as Burundi, Egypt, Eritrea, Libya, Rwanda, Sudan and Zambia.
http://about.comesa.int/

DR-CAFTA, **Dominican Republic - Central America Free Trade Agreement**, includes the Dominican Republic, Costa Rica, El Salvador, Guatemala, Honduras and Nicaragua.
http://en.wikipedia.org/wiki/Central_American_Free_Trade_Agreement

EAC is the **East African Community** and includes the Republics of Kenya, Burundi, Rwanda, Uganda and the United Republic of Tanzania.
http://www.eac.int

EAEC Eurasian Economic Community has Kazakhstan, Kyrgyzstan, Russia and Tajikistan as members.
http://www.eurasianhome.org/xml/t/databases.xml?lang=en&nic=databases&
   intorg=3&pid=25

ECO, **Economic Cooperation Organization**. Includes many countries from the former Eastern bloc, such as the Kyrgyz Republic, Tajikistan, Turkey, Iran and Pakistan.
http://www.ecosecretariat.org

ECOWAS is the **Economic Community if West African States** comprised of 15 West African republics like Gambia, Niger, Burkina Faso, Mali and Senegal.
http://www.ecowas.int

EFTA the **European Free Trade Association** is linked to the European Union. Members of the trading bloc include non EU members such as Norway, Iceland, Lichtenstein and Switzerland.
http://www.efta.int

EU, the **European Union**, is made up of 27 members.
http://europa.eu/

FTAA, **Free Trade of the Americas**, includes 33 countries in North America, the Caribbean and Central America, from Canada and the United States in the north to Chile in the south
http://www.ftaa-alca.org/

GAFTA, the **Greater Arab Free Trade Area**, has 17 Arab country members, including Jordan. Amman, Yemen, Lebanon and Libya.
http://www.annd.org/index.php

GCC is the **Gulf Cooperation Council**, with Bahrain, Kuwait, Oman, Qatar, Saudi Arabia and the United Arab Emirates as members.
http://www.globalsecurity.org/military/world/gulf/gcc.htm

GSP, Generalised System of Preferences, is a preferential system as to duties and taxes for less developed countries.
http://www.au.af.mil/au/awc/awcgate/crs/rs22183.pdf

GSTP is the **General System of Trade Preferences among Developing Countries.** Members include a many developing countries in Latin America, Asia and Africa.
http://www.eepcindia.org/trade-block-detail.asp?tbcode=G138

LAIA or ALADI is the **Latin American Integration Association (Asociación Latinoamericana de Integración),** has members from 12 Latin American countries.
http://encarta.msn.com/encyclopedia_761589439/Latin_American_
   Integration_Association_(LAIA).html

MAGREB is an association formed by **Algeria, Morocco and Tunisia**.
http://en.wikipedia.org/wiki/Maghreb

Mashraq, **The Arab countries of eastern Mediterranean**, has Egypt, Jordan, Syria, Lebanon, Palestine, and Iraq as members.

MERCOSUR, (Mercado Común del Sur**) has membership from** Argentina, the Federative Republic of Brazil, Paraguay and the Eastern Republic of Uruguay.
http://www.mercosurtc.com

NAFTA,the **North America Free Trade Agreement**, removed most barriers to trade and investment among the United States, Canada, and Mexico.
http://www.nafta-sec-alena.org

OAS, the **Organization of American States** is comprised of 35 North and South American Countries.
http://www.oas.org

OECS, **Organization of Eastern Caribbean States** includes nine Eastern Caribbean countries such as Antigua and Barbuda, Montserrat, Grenada and St. Lucia.
http://www.oecs.org

SAARC, South Asian Association for Regional Cooperation has members from Bangladesh, Bhutan, India, Nepal, Sri Lanka, Pakistan and Afghanistan.
http://www.saarc-sec.org

SACU, the **Southern African Customs Union** includes Botswana, Lesotho, Namibia, South Africa, and Swaziland as members.
http://www.sacu.int

SADC or **Southern Africa Development Community**, was formed by representatives of 15 southern African countries.
http://www.sadc.int

SAFTA, South Asian Association Free Trade Agreement is affiliated with SAARC is comprised of a mix of members and observers primarily from Asia but also includes other territories.
http://www.saarc-sec.org/main.php

SPARTECA is the **South Pacific Regional Trade and Economic Cooperation Agreement** and includes 16 countries ranging from New Zealand and Australia to Western Samoa.
http://en.wikipedia.org/wiki/South_Pacific_Regional_Trade_and_Economic_
  Cooperation_Agreement

SPC, the **Secretariat of the Pacific Community** has 26 member countries and territories from the Pacific Islands and Australia, France, New Zealand and the US.
http://www.spc.int/corp/

EMOA or **Union Economique et Monetaire Quest Africaine (Economic and Monetary Union of West Africa)** is a sub-regional monetary organization of eight West African countries.
http://www.uemoa.int/index.htm

UMA, Arab Maghreb Union, was formed with members from five Arab countries, Algeria, Libya, Mauritania, Morocco, and Tunisia.
http://www.maghrebarabe.org/en

WAEMU, West African Economic and Monetary Union, is a regional economic and trade group of 15 countries.
http://www.dfa.gov.za/foreign/Multilateral/africa/waemu.htm

Other International Organisations of Interest

ADB. www.adb.org - Asian Development Bank

AFDB. www.afdb.org - African Development Bank

EBRD. www.ebrd.org - European Bank for Reconstruction and Development.

G8. (Group of Eight). France, Germany, Italy, Japan, United Kingdom, USA, Canada and Russia.

IATA. www.iata.org - International Air Transport Association

IBRD. www.worldbank.org - International Bank for Reconstruction and Development. It is part of the World Bank organization.

ICC. www.iccwbo.org - International Chamber of Commerce

IFC. www.ifc.org - International Finance Corporation. A part of the World Bank, intended to stimulate investments in developing countries.

IMF. www.imf.org - International Monetary Fund

ISO. www.iso.ch - International Organization for Standardization

OECD. www.oecd.org - Organization for Economic Co-operation and Development

OPEC. ww.opec.org. Organization for Petroleum Exporting Countries

UN. www.un.org - United Nations

UNCTAD. www.unctad.org - United Nations Conference on Trade and Development. This is the UN's organization for trade and investment.

World Customs Organization. www.wcoomd.org. Considered the voice of the global customs community.

WTCA. www.wtca.org - World Trade Centers Association

WTO. www.wto.org - World Trade Organisation

Exercises

1. Select a country to export your product to. Look up the customs codes for your products. Write down the category number and sub-categories that apply. Find out what the customs duty will be.

2. Select a receiving country and method of transportation. Research the cost for shipping your goods.

3. Compare sea, air and courier transportation to the country you selected in #2. What is the break-even point, i.e., when one method becomes less costly and another. What other benefits will you gain by using one method or the other?

4. Recalculate your export pricing based on the costs for freight and customs duty.

5. Determine if there are quotas for your products and what licenses (if any) are required by the exporting and importing country you chose in question #1.

6. Look up the Incoterms and decide what is most appropriate for you.

7. Contact your local Chamber of Commerce or customs authorities and ask about the process for obtaining an ATA Carnet.

8. Investigate the trade agreements that will influence your import or export.

9. Contact a freight forwarder to ask what instructions or guides they can provide, so you can have more information about freight, Incoterm, etc.

Risks and Payments
in International Business – Part One

In This Chapter:

- ♦ What is risk?
- ♦ Country and political risk
- ♦ Commercial risks
- ♦ Bank risks
- ♦ Currency and liquidity risks
- ♦ Risk for goods and document risks
- ♦ Customs duties, quotas and taxes
- ♦ Technical risks
- ♦ Payment alternatives
- ♦ Transfer payments
- ♦ How to minimize currency risks

On November 2008, you receive an order from Zimbabwe. It looked like there will be a good profit for you, based on that day's exchange rate for the Zimbabwe dollar. The African company will send a money order in advance, calculated in Zimbabwe dollars, and asks that you ship the goods after receiving the money. You confirm acceptance of the order. What do you have to lose?

The money arrives two weeks later, as promised. However, the inflation rate this month in Zimbabwe is 2 million percent. On an annual basis, this works out to 24 million percent. To make this easier to understand, inflation is running at about 462% per minute! The Zimbabwe dollar is virtually worthless, and your bank refuses to cash the money order.

Your first order from Africa did not work out as well as you expected. Aren't you glad you didn't send the shipment?

Risk - Background

Risk is defined as a danger, peril or threat. You will encounter risks in any domestic or international business, but you know more about your domestic market than you do about foreign markets. Risk can range from a domestic upheaval, armed conflict in neighbouring countries, hefty fluctuations in currency, lost markets because of changes to trade regulations or simply because your client does not pay you the money they owe.

So what are the risks and how much risk can you tolerate? First of all, you should complete a risk analysis.

What happens if:

♦ The value of your currency or your buyer's currency drops by 10%?

♦ Product sales go down by 15%?

♦ You don't get paid what is owed?

♦ War erupts in the country you do business with or a country nearby?

♦ Your distributor goes bankrupt?

♦ You encounter production problems?

♦ There are technical problems?

♦ Your sub suppliers can't deliver on time, with good quality?

Competitors try to take over your market?

You want to be prepared if and when any of these risks occur.

There may be many risks for a specific country. You should look into all of them.

Typical Risks in International Business
• Country / Political
• Commercial
• Financial institutions
• Currency
• Interest rates and liquidity
• Goods and document/payment
• Technical

Country and Political Risks

Find out if the government is politically and economically stable. For a variety of reasons, a country could experience significant currency fluctuations, high inflation, recession and even deflation. There may be preferential policies for domestic or local products/services or embargoes against buying from some other nations. There may be money shortages in the market or limited convertible currency available, which would make it difficult for locals to pay with foreign funds.

The country may be bureaucratic or corrupt, so doing business there will be a challenge. Investigate economic growth forecasts for the country. If you plan to invest there, know the specific investment risks and opportunities you might face. Just as you would if you were planning to work with another company, look at the country's balance sheet, i.e., the current accounts and debt outlook.

There may be political risks associated with the product and services being exported, for example, medical or military equipment or computer software. Is the country at war or are there strained relations with other countries? Laws can be surprisingly different. (See more in the Legal chapter). In Venezuela, the President may decide to confiscate foreign assets by nationalizing an industry. Some governments impose special taxes and other barriers.

Political risks in other countries can influence the global economy. For example, in the 1980s there were conflicts and crises in Iran, Afghanistan and some Latin American countries, the Tiananmen Square protests of 1989 in the People's Republic of China, the Asian Financial Crisis of 1997-98, the Gulf War from 1990 to 1991 and the September 11, 2001 terrorist attacks in the US. The dot.com crash and the economic meltdown of 2007-2010 are examples of crises with international impacts.

According to a report by The Economist in 2009, 77 out of 166 countries are at high risk of social unrest, with 22 considered very high risk. Areas represented in the high risk are Sub Saharan Africa, large parts of Eastern Europe. There are also risk areas in Latin America and Asia. Be wary of countries where there are considerably risk when doing business, like Iraq, Guinea, Zimbabwe, Venezuela.

Search on Google for "country risk" or "international country risk guide" and add the country.

There are many web sites that provide some information - www.countryrisk.com and http://external.worldbankimflib.org/external.htm. Look at the JOLIS library catalogue. The Economist and Dun & Bradstreet also make country reports. (See more about insurance below and the chapter about Market Research.)

Commercial Risks

What if your client delays payment, is a credit risk, or has decided not to pay? Before you establish a business relationship with a client, check their credit rating and take steps to secure your payment.

You may think that you have an agreement but somehow, you have misunderstood your foreign partner about the products being ordered. The country in question does not permit the sale of your type of product or else the standards are different. What if you, the seller want one type of payment term but the buyer wants a different one? Clarify well in advance of when payment will be due. If the terms are 60 days net, you have to explain to the purchaser exactly what that means in terms of your timetable for payment.

In some countries, a purchaser will pay on the day they receive an invoice. In others, payment is customarily made after 120 days. In some locations, you may have to threaten legal action to get the money owed to you. Companies I've worked with have had to call in a lawyer or the local police because of criminal behaviour on the part of non-payers. Trying to collect past-due monies, especially from a debtor in a foreign country, can be expensive.

Get to know the tax system and transportation available in each country you are shipping to. Determine the creditworthiness of the client in advance. Say you've received a large order from a company overseas and the payment is delayed. You may not want to complain, but you must! If you don't communicate your requirements for punctuality from the beginning, you are setting yourself up for future payment problems.

Depending on the country's laws and culture, the security of payment could be good or poor. Conditions can change quickly for a company and a country, for many reasons. You will find that Finland is a reliable country for payments, that financial transactions from Portugal may be slightly less reliable and the reliability of payments from institutions in Venezuela and Nigeria could be difficult unless you set up special arrangements in advance. Always keep yourself updated on local events.

Bank Risks

No matter what country you are in or where you are doing business, you will eventually encounter a problem with foreign exchange and the banking system. There will always be cultural differences that affect the way business is carried out. Some of these differences will benefit you but others will put you at a disadvantage.

A foreign bank may be unable or uninterested in processing payments to pay an exporter. What is considered a safe method of payment in your country perhaps will not be as safe or reliable in a foreign country. For example, if the overseas bank does not honour the payment terms, your "secure" Letter of Credit or Cash against Document will not receive the appropriate treatment.

Governments set restrictions on the amount of money that can be transferred out or deposited into a bank account without documentation or some type of detailed explanation. Some financial institutions have such complicated systems that it may take a long time before you receive payment.

Currency, interest, and liquidity risks

There are 203 sovereign states in the world and about 174 currencies. The total number has reduced over time as more countries harmonize their currencies. When you do business internationally, you will likely be dealing with different currencies. As was mentioned in the Price chapter, currency fluctuations will influence your ability to compete and make money.

Currency risk arises when a payment is made in other currency than the seller's. The exchange rate between your currency (e.g., the local currency you convert to) and the foreign currency (value they will pay) can change the next day. If the value of the foreign country's currency declines, you will get paid less in your currency. The difference will eat into your profitability. Keep in mind that when you are purchasing foreign-made components to use in manufacturing another product, foreign exchange risks still must be factored in.

I have provided more detail in Part Two of this chapter about how to minimize currency risks.

Which currency should you use? If you require payment in your own currency then you know what payment you will get. However, your distributor likely wants a fixed price in their currency, so they know their exact cost. Let's look at some other examples.

- ♦ You receive a request from the World Bank to submit a quote for consulting services. They want the project pricing in a specific currency such as the US dollar or Euro.

- ♦ You are importing from a country where the currency is non-convertible, so you must use a common currency like the US dollar or Euro.

- ♦ You are exporting to a country with non-convertible currency. They just received payment from another purchaser in Japanese Yen and they want to pay you in that currency.

- ♦ Just after you've shipped a large order of chemicals and agricultural equipment, the country receiving the shipment goes to war with its neighbour.

The borders are closed. They have no money to pay for your products. The next shipment is ready to go, but now there are international sanctions or restrictions on what you are allowed to export. In the past, the United Nations, the US and various other nations have imposed arms, trade and economic embargoes on countries such as Cuba and Iraq.

Whether you select the currency of the exporting or importing country, your ability to compete successfully will be influenced by the value of the respective currency. If you are competing against a supplier in a third country, you have to factor in their currency values as well.

> ***Example – Currency change***
>
> *You are exporting wooden flooring from Canada to Germany. If the Canadian dollar drops in value compared to the Euro, your "cost" will go down in relation to the Euro. This will allow you to charge a lower Euro export price or obtain a higher profit keeping the same price. On the other hand, if one of your competitors is a Taiwanese company and their currency drops in comparison with the Canadian dollar, they will have an advantage in the German market because they will be able to reduce their prices lower than yours.*

Your company borrows money to cover some of your manufacturing costs and to finance export activities. You offer credit terms to your foreign distributor. If you allow them 60 days credit and you pay 5% interest on your outstanding loan, it is easy to calculate what it will cost you to extend credit for those 60 days. However, if interest rates increase to 10% and you get paid in 120 days, you interest charges go up by 200%. You can see the obvious influence on your financing cost and how your profit will be substantially reduced.

With extended payment periods and larger investments to fund expansion to new markets, you will need access to more money. Liquidity will be affected and you have to plan proactively by making arrangements with your local banker for increased credit.

Risks for Goods, Document Risks, Customs Duty, and Taxes

As you learned in the Freight chapter, goods being transported can be subjected to delay, leakage, loss or misdirection, shrinkage in weight or volume, damage or loss caused by insufficient or unsuitable packaging, fraud, wear and tear, hijacking and theft.

Loss or delay causes inconvenience to you and your customers and, if you have not purchased enough of the right kind of insurance, you will lose money. Make sure you know the limitations or exclusions on any insurance you buy for shipments.

The claims process can be long and complicated. Depending on the reasons for loss, some companies will only refund part of the value of the goods.

The various trade barriers, import restrictions and customs rules can make exporting difficult. Check for quotas that control entry of your product to certain markets.

If you fill out the export forms incorrectly, there is a risk that foreign authorities may not allow clearance of the goods or that your foreign buyer could pay too much in duties and taxes.

Technical Risks

If there is a design fault if the product doesn't work or you haven't adapted the product to the country, you could be sued for the harm caused to your importer or customers. You could have a quality problem. The term "high quality" means something different in Pakistan than it does in Europe. The demand for "high quality" by Japanese consumers is higher than that in Europe and North America. Overseas production is more difficult to control than domestic manufacturing.

After you have spent a considerable amount of money developing new products or adapting old ones to a particular market, you may find out that the market is small. You will have a hard time recovering your investment. Alternatively, someone could buy a sample of your product, copy it then sell it at a cheaper price. If you are in the technology field, products can become obsolete quickly or fail under certain conditions. If your business relies on electronic transactions, you could be 'hacked' and proprietary information stolen without your knowledge.

Production disruptions that occur at home or with an overseas producer could mean that you won't be able to meet your on-time delivery schedule. A sub-supplier of essential components could experience production delays or not be able to obtain raw materials. An example is the earthquake and tsunami 2011 in Japan resulting in lack of supply of parts in Japan, the US and other countries. This led to temporary closing of some auto manufacturers.

Payment Alternatives

How do you get paid by a buyer in a foreign market? The first question you have to answer is, how are payments usually transacted there?

If you ask domestic purchasers for payment within 30 days, that gives your local distributor 30 days to sell the goods before having to pay your invoice. However, what happens when you have to ship your products from Australia to the east coast of the US? Shipping time by boat is 6-7 weeks. Do you think the American distributor will want to pay you before the shipment arrives? No! They want to receive and inspect the goods first, then have some time to pay. As a result, they will ask for 60 or even 90 days credit.

What type of payments can you select from?

Payment Risks and Security

1.   Consignment

2.   Open credit

3.   Document against acceptance. D/A

4.   Export Factoring

5.   Cash again document. (CAD) also called (D/P) Document against payment

6.   Letter of credit

7.   Bank guarantee

8.   Payment in advance

The higher the number is on the list, the lower the risk.

Consignment. You deliver the goods to the client. They pay you when they have sold the goods, based on agreed-upon payment terms, such as 30 days after sales. You have virtually no payment security. You will have interest or carrying costs until you receive payment.

Open credit can extend to 30, 60, 90 days or even longer. You deliver the goods and assign the client a time frame within which to pay. You still have no security for payment and you lose interest on the money during the period before payment.

Document Against Acceptance (D/A), is similar to Document Against Payment (see below). However, the buyer signs a *promissory note* or accepts a *usance draft* from the bank. This requires payment at a certain time in the future, in order for the buyer to obtain access to the document that allows release of the shipment. A promissory note is a written undertaking to pay a specified amount of money at a stated time. This is relatively safe in most countries, as the buyer's credit rating will be damaged if the note is not paid on time.

In Germany, if you sign a D/A and then don't pay, the banks will enforce payment; however, in Canada, the banks do not take the same approach. To strengthen the security of payments, an exporter may request that their banker's collecting institution add their *aval* or endorsement to the draft. If the collecting bank chooses to do this, the exporter will have the collecting bank's undertaking to honour the draft at maturity.

Export Factoring. Although factoring is common domestically, in many countries it is not common in exporting. In principle, the exporter sells their receivables or invoices to a factoring company. This allows the exporter to obtain a portion of the amount owing up front. It is a somewhat costly solution and only commonly used by companies in need of cash flow.

Cash Against Document (CAD) or Document Against Payment (D/P). An exporter sends their invoice along with the shipping documentation to a bank in the receiving country. For the importer to gain access to the goods, they have to pay the bank the full amount before the necessary documents are released to the shipping company. The bank then forwards the payment to the exporter. The cost of the service varies and can range from $50 to several hundred dollars. Of course, the exporter will lose interest earnings until payment is received.

Letter of credit (L/C) This transaction is more complicated. If you are interested in using this or other payment methods which involve a financial institution, I suggest you consult with your bank and ask for a handbook that will provide more details.

In principle, the importer would instruct his bank to issue a letter of credit to secure payment to the exporter. The L/C stipulates the value, product weight/volume, time of payment and rules for payment. The exporter has to fulfill all of the stipulated conditions, otherwise the **L/C** will not be considered valid. The Rules on credit transactions, including L/Cs, are governed by the Uniform Customs and Practice for Documentary Credits, *UCP 600,* issued by the ICC (International Chamber of Commerce). You can get more information by searching the web for Letter of Credit or specifically Letter of Credit, UCP 600.

In order to have any significance, however, it should be an **Irrevocable L/C,** so the buyer can't renege on the agreement. The status should be confirmed by the foreign bank, (a **Confirmed L/C)** which means that the bank guarantees the payment. As you know, some foreign banks are not considered to be secure, so to be safe the L/C should be confirmed by another bank outside the issuing bank's country. For example, you could have your bank do this for you, and they will guarantee the payment.

For those who continuously use Letters of Credit, there is also a **Revolving L/C.** As long it remains open and there are funds left in the account, the client can continue to buy against the L/C.

An L/C is a good instrument for a manufacturer of custom-make products or equipment with a long production time, and when the seller wants a guarantee for payment even before the goods are ready to be shipped or even manufactured.

The L/C is an expensive financial instrument as both the buyer and the seller pay, so banks are, of course, happy to offer this service. If you want a payment confirmed by the foreign bank or by your bank, it will cost you several hundred dollars plus a percentage of the shipment value as well as a confirmation fee. The description of the goods, the stated shipment methods and all of the documentation must match exactly and conform to the L/C.

When you use an L/C, the business banker deals only with documents – they will not be inspecting the shipment. Their objective is to confirm that the exporter's shipping documentation complies with the terms and conditions contained in the Letter of Credit. If the L/C states that the shipment contains 300 pair of shoes and you ship 320 pairs, the Letter of Credit is invalid. The L/C will state how long the instrument is open for or valid. The valid date is the last date by which the documents must be presented at the bank. If your goods are delayed in transit and you can't convince the buyer to alter the original L/C to extend the date, it becomes invalid. Sounds complicated? Make sure you sort out all the rules with your bank before accepting any Letter of Credit.

Bank guarantee. Instead of using an L/C you can use a bank guarantee. Your importer contacts their bank to have them set up or "open" a guarantee. The bank promises to pay the outstanding financial liability if the importer does not fulfill their responsibility to pay. The importer/buyer will pay a fee for this service. Normally, it is a percentage like 2%. You can also arrange for a bank-to-bank guarantee, which means the foreign bank undertakes to pay your bank if your buyer fails. Of course, it is a more secure arrangement when your bank promises payment. With this type of collateral, your bank may be willing to lend you money against the guarantee.

Payment in advance. The best payment for an exporter is a company that sends the money they owe, in advance. You have the money in your bank account. Your cash flow is positive.

I have outlined for you the most common types of payments. Your bank will be more than happy to give you information booklets on each topic. However, the easiest way for you to become more informed is to search on each key word on the Internet. To give you an example, if you search on Google for *letter of credit* you will get more than 64 million hits, which should give you more than enough resources to start with.

Example – Different payment, better for both parties

What payment method is best for you and your distributor? Sometimes, we only look at one side of the equation. I had a Swedish supplier using Cash Against Document as a payment term to a Canadian distributor. The Canadian distributor was not happy because he could get better payment terms from Spain with open credit for 60 days. He wanted the same arrangements with the Swedish company.

I asked the supplier how long it usually took for them to get paid from the day of shipment. They said it was about 60 days. With that information, I was able to offer the Canadian distributor terms of 60 days credit against a bank guarantee, which they accepted. Both parties won - the Canadian distributor got the 60 days credit that they wanted and the Swedish company got even better payment terms than before. They received their money at the same time but payment was guaranteed by the bank, with less paperwork and no risk for return of the goods.

We will cover payment plus terms in more detail later in this chapter.

How to Transmit Money

Electronic business transactions have increased at an explosive pace. Not only do we order books, music and food over the Internet, we can also do E-invoicing, and save a great deal of money in the process. Payment methods are also changing. There are numerous formal and informal methods of transferring funds from one jurisdiction to another. Remember that the security of payments is important, especially if you are selling large volumes of products or high-value goods.

Sending a payment for goods using a regular bank cheque (**buyer's cheque**) from one country to another does not work that well. The bank in the receiving country must put a hold on the cheque until they receive confirmation from the bank where the cheque was issued, that there are sufficient funds in the account to cover the cheque. A better way is to send a **cashier's cheque** or **bank draft**. This type of financial instrument is issued against the funds held by a financial institution (the bank) rather than an individual's personal or business account. The funds behind a banker's draft are set aside when the draft is drawn up, and then held until the draft is cashed. Payment by the issuing bank is guaranteed. Because the banks have already processed or cleared the payment, the money is immediately accessible. The drawback is that sending the draft through the mail system takes time. There is always a risk that the letter becomes lost or is stolen. You would then have to ask the foreign bank to cancel the original draft and issue a replacement.

You can transfer funds electronically or "wire" money across a network of banks around the world. One way is to use **SWIFT**, a data carrier or clearing service. SWIFT stands for the Society for Worldwide Interbank Financial Telecommunication, a cooperative of 9000 banks, security companies and financial institutions. Another 250 non-banking organizations such as Microsoft and General Electric belong too. With SWIFT, the foreign bank wires information about an approved funds transfer to your bank and the money is usually available to you within two days. No money actually changes hands and there is nothing for you to "see".

The way it works is that banks clear their liabilities between themselves using SWIFT. In processing a transaction to transfer money from Australia to Germany, the Australian bank notifies the German bank to pay you; they are "owed" the same amount by the Australian bank. On the other hand, the German bank most likely owes the Australian bank money – all of the transactions are cleared between the banks via SWIFT. Look for more information at http://www.swift.com/.

You should know that some banks are not members of the SWIFT system, so they still have to use a local bank that is a member. In the United States, I have a run into this situation a number of times. My client's bank had to get their transactions cleared through Citibank, a bank with SWIFT arrangement. If you work internationally, make sure that your financial institution has an arrangement to access the SWIFT system. In some countries, staff in any bank branch will know about it; in other countries, you may have to call several people in your bank before you can find someone who is familiar with SWIFT.

When I opened my office in Canada in 1982, I decided to open US and Canadian currency business bank accounts at the international head office of the bank in downtown Toronto, even though I more frequently used a local branch close to my office to make deposits. The reason I did this was to ensure that I had access to a bank office with staff who knew about international transactions.

Because I did so much business in Sweden, I had bank accounts in three different currencies in Sweden, for my consulting fees and commissions from various companies. The difference was that I could use a local branch, knowing that almost all of the staff were familiar with international business transactions.

Example – Different ways to transfer money

Many of you are familiar with eBay's PayPal but there are many other solutions, many of which have been invented locally. The Government of India allows financial transactions over the internet. That means that rural residents can have their wages deposited into their bank account. They can also set up transactions with local retailers to pay for goods they purchase. One more example is the M-PESA, a money transfer service operated by Safaricom, Kenya's largest mobile operator. The service allows 9.5 million people or over 20% of the nation's population to transfer money over their mobile phones, even if they do not have a bank account.

This is a brief introduction to risks in international business. In Part Two of this chapter you will get more detailed information about how minimize potential risks.

Summary - Risks and Payments

- ♦ You will encounter more risks when conducting international business and they will be more difficult to handle than domestic risks.

- ♦ Make sure you understand what risks you can take and what their impact might be.

- ♦ Complete a risk analysis for each country. Given what you know about each country, what could happen and how can you prepare to deal with events? That will give you a good base if and when you are doing business there.

- ♦ Beware of political risks and know how to prevent losses.

- ♦ You have to decide when it is too risky to do business in a country or whether it is possible for you to insure your goods and as payments.

- ♦ Analyze the technical risks for each country. Look at the skill level, working environment and other aspects and make sure you use them appropriately.

- ♦ Assess bank risks. Is your foreign bank safe to deal with?

- ♦ Analyze currency risks and take steps to minimize them:

  a. Select a currency and how you can prevent losses, taking into consideration the market and client. (See Part Two of this chapter).

  b. Remember there may be a lack of currency in developing countries

- ♦ Open a foreign currency account if appropriate. (See Part Two of this chapter).

- ♦ Minimize document risks by ensuring that for each country and each product, the paperwork complies with local laws.

- ♦ Analyze the payment risks and select the right method for you and your client.

  a. Select payment terms based on the stability and sophistication of the market.

  b. Evaluate the client's ability to pay and pay on time.

  c. Positive payment terms for you may be negative for your client.

    d.   Payment terms have different security in different countries.

    e.   Payment terms are a combination of safety and way of competing.

    f.   Contact the bank and local companies to identify suitable methods of payment in that specific country.

    g.   Insure the payment when possible, especially for large payments and if you are not sure of the credit-worthiness of the client. (See more in Part Two)

    h.   When insuring payment, allow for processing time for the insuring company.

♦   Analyze what can happen if interest rates rise and plan for how you can deal with the impact on cash flow. Arrange for financing to allow a positive cash flow.

Risks and Payments
in International Business – Part Two

Political Risks and How To Protect Yourself

Political instability in a country where you do business can certainly affect you. How can you protect yourself? First of all, talk with someone at the foreign embassy about the political situation and risks in the country. Organizations such as The Economist and Dun & Bradstreet (D&B) produce and sell reports on business and political risks in each country.

You can buy insurance against non-payment of invoices and for political risks and natural disasters. (See more below.) If an insurance company is not willing to insure against risks in that country, then you should consider not taking the risks either.

Technical risks

Test market your product in the foreign country. Adapt the product to local requirements or preferences. Make sure the product complies with local standards, laws and regulations. If more components are needed than in the domestic market, test those too, to ensure they work and comply with local standards. Remember, labour force and end-user skill levels and perceptions of quality differ between countries. What may be considered high quality in one country may be seen as low quality in another country.

Document risks

Check with your freight forwarder and find out what kind of documents you will need.

Commercial risks

As mentioned in Part One, you should select a method that makes your payments more secure. However, you can also use a Government sponsored insurance company to insure payments. In Canada, the Export Development Corporation or EDC (http://edc.ca.) can insure your export invoices, including against political risks. A similar organization in Sweden is called Exportkreditnämnden (EKN) - http://www.ekn.se. Most countries have export financing or insurance organizations. Insurance can be taken out on continuous business as well as for single orders.

The web site for the International Trade Centre contains a list of Export Credit Insurance Agencies and guides on a variety of credit and financial topics. They also provide advisory services on trade financing and credit insurance and regional and country reports. www.intracen.org/tfs/welcome2.htm?http&&&www.intracen.org/tfs/mciagencies/welcome.htm.

Premiums for this type of insurance are based on the anticipated level of risk. Is the country safe? Is the client credit worthy? How much deductible do you want, i.e., how much of the dollar loss are you willing to share?

If an insurance company will not issue coverage, you know that the risk is high. If the premium is high, you will have to decide if you want to risk doing business in that country and with that client. Normally, the client will not know that you've taken out insurance.

The website http://www.intrum.com/en/european-payment-index.html contains an index of payment risks in Europe. I suggest you search Google for "payment risk rankings" to find out more about country and business sector risks and business climate or look at http://en.wikipedia.org/wiki/Country_risk

Risks for goods (see more in the Freight chapter)

Export Financing

As I have mentioned before, you will probably require additional financing when you begin exporting. If you have a good relationship with a local bank, they likely will be interested in assisting you with overseas expansion. Find a bank with experience in international business; otherwise, staff may not understand what you are doing, or being able to obtain payment overseas. The "international" office can also supply you with contacts on the foreign market.

In many countries, there are consortia of financial institutions to assist with financing overseas expansion. There may also be government-sponsored export financing. Many organizations promote business in developing countries and provide funding or financial aid. In these cases, there may exist pre-approved export financing and insurance to those countries. Investigate with your local government what domestic and international aid organisations there are supporting the country you target. You can find some of them at http://en.wikipedia.org/wiki/Category:International_development_agencies

Currency and Currency Risks

Which currency should I use and how can I protect myself?

Invoice in your own currency. You will always get the same amount of money, but your distributor may not be happy because they will have to arrange for currency conversion. Furthermore, the importer will have to assume the risk of the cost of buying your currency. They would likely prefer a fixed price in their currency.

Borrow funds in the same currency you are selling in. If you are an Asian exporter selling to a country using the Euro and invoicing in Euros, you can borrow the same amount in Euros as you have sold your goods for. That way, if the Euro increases in value, you will receive more in your local currency but you will also owe more on the loan. However, it will all even out and you minimize the currency risk. Remember - you still have to pay interest on your loan.

Foreign exchange contract (FX contract or FEC). This is a contract between parties to buy or sell a specific amount of a certain foreign currency in exchange for another one, at a fixed price at a certain date. When you make an FX arrangement with a bank to convert funds on a certain date, at a certain exchange rate, you are required to carry through with the transaction, because it is a joint commitment.

Let's say you are Brazilian company shipping footwear to Europe. You prepare an invoice valued at 200,000 Euros with a payment date of January 31. You arrange a foreign exchange contract with the bank to exchange 200,000 Euros into Brazil reals (BRL) on February 7. Why the later date? Schedule the transaction to occur one week after the expected payment date to make sure that you have received the payment from Europe. When you signed the contract with the bank, you received a confirmed exchange rate for February 7.

Go to www.oanda.com to find today's exchange rate. You can also check historical exchange rates on www.oanda.com/currency/historical-rates. Your bank can give you exchange rates for various periods of time, e.g., 3 months, 6 months, 12 months, so you can see what the anticipated currency trend will be. Many daily newspapers and business magazines publish a forecast rate on key currencies. By using a foreign exchange contract, you can minimize currency risks and ensure you get to keep the profit you calculated.

Foreign exchange option or FX option. This is a contract that gives the right, but not the obligation, for you to buy or sell a specific amount of a foreign currency for another currency, at a fixed price. It is similar to the exchange contract but in this case, you buy an option to convert a certain amount at a later date, but you are not obligated to complete the transaction. You have the benefit of a guaranteed rate but if the exchange value is not in your favour you would not exercise the FX option.

Of course, this option costs more than the foreign exchange contract. You can compare it with buying a stock option. There are different types of FX options: A call option is a right to buy a currency. A sell option is a right to sell.

What are the advantages with an option? When you send a company a quote for a selling them goods, get a promised rate. When you receive the order priced in a foreign currency, the margins will be small, so you don't want to lose if the currency drops in value. You would buy an option to be guaranteed a specific exchange rate.

Example – Foreign exchange option

You are an American company supplying a European buyer with propane barbecue units. They will pay you 300,000 Euro within 3 months. The current exchange rate is 1.4512 Euro to the US dollar.

You buy an option to sell 300,000 Euro at a rate of 1.44 (for a total of $432,000). You pay a premium of 2% for the option contract. The exchange rate after 3 months is 1.47. In other words, the value of the Euro has gone up and you do not use the option because you will now receive more US dollars in payment.

You made (1.47 -1.44) x 300,000 or $9000, minus the insurance premium you paid on 2% of 300,000 Euro x 1.44 = $8640, leaving you with a net profit of $260 on the option for the exchange rate.

If the rate had gone down to 1.33 Euro, you would use the option and get your exchange rate of 300,000 x 1.44 = $432,000. You still paid the 2% premium, but have limited your currency loss.

There is also something called a currency swap. As the name states you can make arrangements to exchange funds at a certain date and later trade it back.

You can add a buffer (5-10%) in your export price calculation, so if there are small fluctuations in the exchange rate, you can absorb them.

Foreign exchange accounts. If you continuously get paid in a foreign currency, open an account in that currency at your bank or another financial institution if your bank does not offer this service. Foreign currency accounts allow you to exchange payments for receivables and payables in the same currency. That means money is deposited in the foreign currency and you can build up savings in that currency, which allows you to "hedge" the impact of fluctuations. You can follow currency trends and make the exchange when you can get the best rate. You can usually earn interest on your foreign account.

Another benefit of using this type of account is that your invoices and commissions to foreign representatives can easily be paid in the appropriate currency. When you have many distributors in the EU, open a bank account there to make it easy for the clients to pay directly into your account.

By keeping money in a foreign currency, you can better negotiate with banks for a more favourable exchange rate. If you are not happy with the rate your present bank offers, you can negotiate with an alternative bank. There are banks/financial institutions that only process exchange trades, so they will normally be able to offer you a better rate.

If you simply transfer the foreign currency directly into your domestic account, the bank will dictate the exchange rate. You will probably also be charged an administration fee for each transaction.

Remember that there are many ways to protect against currency fluctuations. In this chapter, you have read that you can:

- Invoice in your own currency. Not good for the buyer
- Borrow in the same currency as your invoices will be paid
- Arrange foreign exchange contract
- Use foreign exchange accounts

Changes in interest rates

You borrow money to keep your cash flow positive. With extended payment periods, you will have to pay more in interest charges. A sudden increase in interest rates will affect your profits.

Letters of Credit (L/C)

This is issued by a bank and authorizes the bearer to withdraw a stated amount of money from the issuing bank. There are several other types of L/C such as Transferable or Back-to-Back L/C, which we will not cover here. They are not that commonly used.

Many companies use L/Cs. The documents will be accepted, as long as they conform to the content of the shipments. What are the most common reasons an L/C would be refused?

♦ The time frame for the L/C has expired, which means the L/C is no longer valid.

♦ The shipment has been delayed and the delivery time is past the date on the documentation

♦ Lack of consistency between the documents presented

♦ Documentation is presented too late to the advising/presenting bank, so by the time they are processed, the L/C has expired

♦ The insurance policy is issued in another currency than the L/C

♦ Both parties have not completed the agreement to endorse the L/C or the endorsement document is missing from the Bill of Lading or insurance policy

♦ Invoice

  ○ Discrepancies in the description of the goods. The L/C has one description and the invoice has another

  ○ Discrepancies in delivery terms or no delivery terms are given

  ○ The referral in the L/C to the stated pro forma invoice or the order is missing

  ○ The exporter has included costs which have not been agreed on in the L/C

  ○ The invoice does not show the same prices as agreed to in the L/C

♦ Insurance policy

  ○ All of the prescribed risks stated in the L/C are not covered

  ○ Does not contain the correct shipment departure date

  ○ Does not cover the whole value of CIF, (Cost/Insurance/Freight) or DDP (Delivered Duty Paid) value

  ○ Has a different place/location for payment than the L/C

♦ Bill of lading

  ○ Does not correspond to the requirements in the L/C

  ○ Presented too late, (after the expiry date of the L/C)

  ○ All of the specified documents associated with the Bill of Lading have not been presented

As you can see, it is essential that the documents presented by the exporter comply with the terms and conditions stipulated in the L/C. Letters of Credit are not the easiest payment method to use. I always recommend that you get professional help. Ask your bank to assist you.

Advantages and Disadvantages of Letters of Credit

For Seller	For Buyer
Advantages	**Advantages**
◆ Guarantees payment as long as documents comply with terms and conditions in the L/C	◆ Ensures that the seller complies with what is ordered as to products and delivering in time
◆ Especially useful for long delivery times and/or custom-made products	◆ As the L/C is a rather complicated transaction, it is profitable for banks. They tend to be more actively involved with the buyer's business and more eager to assist with other transactions
◆ Not dependent on buyer's creditworthiness, solvency or willingness to pay. Make sure that you have the right type of L/C for that	
◆ Possible to get money earlier by borrowing against the L/C	
Disadvantages	**Disadvantages**
◆ Documents have to comply with the term in the L/C	◆ Requires the buyer to have credit available. The bank will "lock in" money from their account/credit
◆ Expensive	◆ Offers limited safety as to quality or quantity of goods
	◆ Expensive

Different Payment Methods and Their Implications.
Top More Risk. Bottom Less Risk.

Method	Normal-Payment	Goods available to buyer	Risk for seller	Risk for buyer	Comments
Payment in advance	Before shipping	After payment	None	Totally dependent on the seller shipping the goods	Useful for custom-made goods or when you have doubts about the buyer
Open credit	According to agreement	Before payment	Depending on buyer	None	Suitable for firms with ongoing business
Cash against document. CAD, D/P	When goods arrive at buyer's harbour	When payment has been made at the bank	Limited risk. Mainly if buyer does not accept goods or the bank is not reliable	None	Normally when you do not give open credit or you cannot get bank guarantee
Document against acceptance. D/A	After bill of exchange	After the buyer has signed bill of exchange	Depends on the banking system in the country	Limited, depending on the bank system	Safe in some countries, but not in others
Bank to bank guarantee	According to invoice	When goods arrive	Limited. More risk if you only have bank guarantee (depending on country)	Limited	Safe but dependent on the country
Irrevocable Letter of credit	After shipment and documents delivered to the bank	Normally after payment or on presentation at the bank	Risk is dependent on the bank	Risk is dependent on the bank	Risk if the foreign bank is not reliable
Confirmed L/C (e.g., by exporter's bank)	After shipment and documents delivered to the bank	Normally after payment or on presentation at the bank	Risk low, is dependent on the bank	Risk low, is dependent on the bank	Minimum because of guarantees

Other Forms of Payment

Countertrade

There are many ways to get paid. In the past, countries in Eastern Europe did not have convertible currencies, so when they sold something to a neighbouring country, they bought something for the corresponding amount. When the Soviet Union sold farm machinery to Poland for 200,000 roubles, they could receive payment in tomatoes and oats valued at the same amount as the machinery.

When trading with western nations, the old Eastern Bloc countries would usually arrange for part payment in a western currency like dollars, but part of the deal was that the seller would buy products worth a certain dollar amount of the value of the total sale, e.g., 20% from the Eastern Bloc country. In those days, many business organizations accepted these trade conditions. However, there were companies specializing in countertrade and a company could sell their outstanding liabilities for a fee.

There were also occasions where an Eastern European company would sell a factory and the payment would be made in the form of goods from the new manufacturing company/buyer.

Types of Countertrade

- **Barter.** When you swap or exchange goods or services of equal value, e.g., you buy an amount of goods equal to those you sold.

- **Counter purchase.** Where two parties undertake to provide business to one another, e.g., they buy goods from each other or contract to purchase a certain percentage of the value of sales.

- **Advance purchase.** When you want to ensure you will get paid and obtain compensation before you ship your goods.

- **Offsets.** This is very common in large capital projects or where there is a substantial level of government procurement. As an approved supplier, you are supposed to deliver some economic benefit to the country you are selling to. It could be that you promise to produce some of the products in the country, that you license production, sub-contract some production, transfer technology or even invest in the country. You are selling military marine vessels to a country. In return you commit to buy certain percentage of the order in local goods and do part of the manufacturing locally.

- **Buyback.** An offer to buy back some of the production that is created by the machinery you are selling. You are selling a steel production plant. You offer to buy x number of tons of steel during a five year period.

As this is not a very common activity today, I suggest if you are pressured into this type of trade arrangement that you ask for help. The first time this happens you can often buy yourself out of a countertrade commitment by giving a special discount. If the order if very large and when there is a commitment to continuous purchases of your products, you may have to agree to the countertrade.

The volume of countertrade is increasing for other reasons. Countries/companies make special offers to obtain large contracts. When a Swedish company attempted to sell military aircraft to Thailand, they offered to buy chicken from Thailand. This was not a very popular solution for chicken producers in Sweden. At other times, companies offer to produce a certain amount of goods in the country they are exporting to.

There could be an offer from a specific country to purchase goods from your country, based on a countertrade. An American company negotiated a large contract to sell jet aircraft to a government in Europe. The American company agreed to purchase industrial machinery valued at 20% of the value of the sale.

If the American company only buys 10% worth of machinery from the European country, they still have a legal obligation. If you are a supplier of machinery from that specific country, you could utilize this countertrade requirement to your advantage. Your local Trade Commissioner should know about these types of countertrade agreements and be able to advise you.

Before you go on to the next chapter, I suggest you complete some exercises.

Exercise

1. Select a country to export to. Select a product or service to export to that country. Make a list of risks that can occur and identify how to prevent them.

2. What steps can you take to find out about political risks?

3. Ask your freight forwarder for a checklist of the documents to include when exporting to the country you selected in question 1.

4. What payment period and method would you use for the product or service you selected in question 1?

5. What foreign currency will you use for the invoicing? Ask your bank for the 3 month, 6 month and 24 month future exchange rates for the country you are exporting to and also the cost of an FX option. You can also try to find future exchange rates in the financial section of your local newspaper.

6. Check if your bank provides SWIFT transfer and receiving. If not, find an alternate bank to work with.

7. Can you open bank accounts in foreign currencies at your bank? Which currencies are available? Are there any specific rules or limitations?

8. Discuss with your bank how they can assist you with export financing. Are there any associations of bankers for export financing? What government programs are there? Do they have special arrangements or aid programs for developing countries to assist them to buy from you?

9. Investigate which organizations provide export insurance and to which countries.

10. Ask your bank for handbooks on international payments. Ask them too what organisations offer export insurance.

11. Ask your freight forwarder the same questions.

Importing

In This Chapter:

♦ **Importing methods**

♦ **Difference between exporting and importing**

♦ **Activities included in importing**

♦ **Finding suppliers**

♦ **Test marketing a product**

You have been marketing farmers' work clothes like pants, jackets, overalls, gloves and other work wear on the domestic market for a long time. You have been selling to them directly, using your own telemarketers. The problem, however, is that you sell the same product as everybody else and have to compete on price. When you ask the supplier for product improvements you are always neglected. To make things worse, you are paying a middle-man who also makes money.

Why not put all of that money into your own pocket? You have good sales volumes and decide that you want to market under your own trade mark. You buy directly from the manufacturers and have the clothing designed to your own specifications. You have decided to import.

How To Import?

When you look at distribution and pricing, instead of considering the exporter's point of view, you are now the importer. With respect to payments and currencies, you will be dealing with the same questions.

Where do I find the suppliers? What will it cost? How do I make sure the products are the right quality? What price should I pay? How much would it cost me to get the products to my country? How do I comply with local legislation and import rules?

If you have read the earlier chapters on international business you already have answers to many of those questions. Most of what is applicable to exporting also applies to importing. The main difference is that instead of finding a foreign distributor, you have to find foreign suppliers.

By now, you will have developed a basic understanding of culture and business practices in your domestic market, but you still have to understand the culture in the country you are buying from.

Markets are global, not local. Not only do we sell products and services internationally, we buy internationally as well. Why? Sometimes products that are in demand are not available locally and we have to source them overseas. We may find alternatives to domestic products that have more advanced technology and lower prices.

Many companies try to develop their components in-house rather than source from outside. When you buy a car, however, it contains manufactured parts from many suppliers located in several countries. If you carry a wide range of products and services, you can source complementary products from other markets. In fact, you can use those suppliers as distributors for your products. You can also source components for domestic manufactured products, which may make you even more competitive.

In the next few pages, we will look at importing step by step.

Distribution

What is the distribution process for importing? Of course, you could import directly and eliminate all the middlemen.

You could import via a distributor or agent who sources the products and also assists you with the whole process. Especially if a manufacturer requires

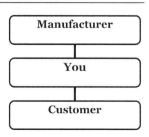

large quantity purchasing, this would allow the distributor/agent to split orders and shipments between several importers and distribute them at the same time. Freight costs would be reduced because of the large quantities being shipped. You may pay a bit more to buy rather than produce the goods but you will save on wages and freight costs and still be able to use your work force to produce other products at home. If you prefer to manufacture locally, instead of having your manufacturing done overseas, you could sign a licensing agreement with a foreign manufacturer allowing you to make the product.

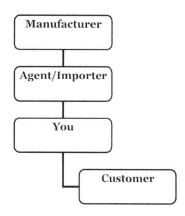

Differences Between Exporting and Importing

When you buy from a domestic manufacturer, it may be easier to control quality. You both speak the same language and there are likely few cultural differences. When you work with people in other countries, their standards for product quality and scheduling deliveries could be completely different. As in exporting, you must build up a relationship. To do that, you must visit your partner where your products are going to be made. You might be surprised to discover that what they described as a modern factory is, in fact, a large open building with packed dirt floors and large numbers of workers using antiquated machinery in unsafe conditions. On the other hand, you might find a more modern facility than what you have.

At home, you may shut down for public holidays and summer vacation. Your foreign supplier probably does the same, but may also close for a variety of religious holidays. A large segment of their labour force may be from the same family. If there are family disagreements or other events leading to work stoppages, they could experience problems with keeping production and deliveries on a consistent schedule.

If you are not familiar with importing, you should join a specialist professional organization such as the Food & Beverage Importers Association, the Importers Association of Australia, the Chilean Avocado Importers Association or Japan Machine Tools Importers' Association. Some of the larger international Chambers of Commerce such as the Singapore Chinese Chamber of Commerce & Industry, the Huizhou Merchants Chamber of Commerce or the Associated Chambers of Commerce and Industry of India also function in a similar way. They all offer expertise and information. Invest in a membership. You will gain access to industry contacts, experienced business people and a large international network.

Finding a Supplier

Use the same principles as you did to find new markets for exporting. (*Also see the chapter on Market Research*) You have to investigate where in the world the products and services you seek are.

Limit your search for suppliers to those locations it is practical to buy from, for example, countries with a stable economy, secure delivery channels and sufficient supply of goods in the quality and quantity you need. Find out if shipping distances will result in you paying high freight costs. For manufacturing countries such as China, it is common to require minimum order sizes that are quite large. This can make it less practical for you to buy from them, if your orders are for less quantity.

As you now are importing, the foreign representatives in your country such as embassies and trade commissioners are really interested in dealing with you. Before you contact them prepare a clear description of what you are looking for so they can source the suppliers and provide them with adequate information. Some countries are really aggressive. When I sourced products in Korea 15 years ago, the news spread like a "wild fire" and hundreds of companies contacted me. Some still do despite the fact I do not work in that field any more. Utilize contacts from trade associations, trade shows, trade show organisations and trade press.

You can, of course make a search on Google for a product like "safety shoes". The problem is that you will get so many hits. When I did a search I got 36 million safety shoe manufacturers of which 18.4 million where in China. A better search is commercial data bases. (*See Part Two of the Market Research chapter, and then you can make a more specific search.*) If your product covers a specific industry, contact the local trade magazine for that industry and they can help you with contacts. They often have buyers' guides that list manufacturers and distributors.

Before you sign up a supplier, find out what your rights are. Will they deliver to you and can you get exclusivity? You don't want to build up a distribution network and sales to find out later on the supplier will sell to any company in your country. Perhaps you should sell the product under your own trade name. That way, you can swap suppliers if you are not happy or the price level is not satisfactory. If possible, arrange for alternative suppliers so if you have problem with one you can order from the other. When you have more than one supplier, you can also compare quality, security of deliveries, etc. As with exporting don't miss the opportunity to use your supplier as a distributor in their country. Two-way trade is always better.

Investigate Customs Duties, Quotas, Freight Costs, and Other Restrictions

Ask your freight forwarder what duties and taxes apply in your country for the goods you are importing and for each country you are importing from. Check if there are any specific restrictions such as import quotas. You can, of course, also contact your local customs authority. See if any of the countries you plan to buy from have free trade agreements or preferential duties. Some countries have special agreements to lower or eliminate customs duties for goods from some developing countries, e.g., the EU's Generalised System of Preferences (GSP). What that means is that if you are a European company, you can import certain products duty free. This includes products such as textiles from Africa.

Find out what regulatory approvals must be met or what product testing requirements, labelling rules or other standards have to be complied with. Examples are electrical standards, building codes, label appearance and language requirements. Look into environmental rules (e.g., no lead in toys) as well as special sizing. Footwear and clothing sizes are measured differently in Europe and North America. Southern European and North American women tend to have rounder hips than northern European women. Product liability issues vary from country to country. In North America, it is the country selling the product that is considered liable; in the EU, it is the manufacturer. This will be discussed at greater length in the Legal chapter. Remember from the Pricing chapter that freight costs can have a significant influence on your total cost and if you are going to be profitable.

When you sell consumer goods and your manufacturer supplies the packaging, make sure to have them apply the appropriate barcodes. This will help your warehouse to track inventory and for stores to easily find the selling price.

Is There a Market for the Product? Can You Sell It?

Whenever possible, bring home some samples of the product you want to import. Be aware that some suppliers provide free samples, but there cannot be sold. I was working with a company in China, to import children's clothing to Sweden. They provided me with samples of sweaters, but only the left half of the garment. If you want complete products, be prepared to pay for them.

You have to test the product on potential clients. Depending on the product – a pair of shoes or a large piece of equipment the test period may be short or lengthy. Find out the market price, what the customers are willing to pay. When you have the products on hand, you will be able to find out what customers think, what they like about them and what they want changed. Is the quality as you expected or will modifications or improvements need to be made? What is the warranty and how is that handled?

Decide on your type of distribution and, as you did in the Pricing chapter, complete a calculation to see if that alternative will be profitable. The Export Pricing chapter includes a cost comparison of importing from Spain or China. Review that material. With your end-user price, distribution channels, freight costs and duties and taxes, you should be able to calculate if you can make money. Look at the Distribution chapter again to review the list of alternatives.

You must have clear information about delivery terms, payment rules/terms, currency, etc. When calculating your real costs, is the price you have been given from your supplier and freight forwarder the right price? What happens if the currency changes? Is the country from which you are importing safe or could political instability create problems? If you buy goods such as machinery or electronics, does the manufacturer supply product instructions or manuals? If so, do they have to be adapted to your market or accepted as is?

Find products	Search for suppliers of your product
Buy samples	Buy/obtain samples from one or more suppliers. Negotiate contracts to secure future prices and delivery.
Bring home the goods	Check for delivery terms. Negotiate and analyze transport options. Insure goods. Investigate customs duties. Pay for goods.
Test sales	Contact potential end-users and/or distributors to evaluate product, packaging and prices.
Revise design and packaging	Adapt product and packaging after feedback from customer and/or dealers.
Order	Place order for sales.
Launch and sell products	Prepare sales material, advertising, etc., and launch the product.

If the first test sales are successful and no modifications are necessary, you will be ready to order larger quantities. Before doing that, however, you have to confirm that:

♦ the manufacturer/seller has the capacity to consistently supply the product now and in the foreseeable future;

♦ the product and quality will be the same as originally ordered;

♦ product packaging is sturdy enough for transport;

♦ the language and design of the labels are correct and according to your requirements for size, barcodes, etc.;

♦ freight arrangements for your shipments meet your specifications

It would be wise for you to visit the factory again, before the first shipment is sent out. If you cannot do this, then recruit someone locally to physically examine the shipment before it leaves the manufacturer/supplier's premises. You would be in a difficult situation if you found out after delivery to your destination that the goods you ordered do not meet your requirements, especially if you have paid in advance.

Summary

♦ Be very specific about what are you looking for in a product and what is important when you source a supplier.

♦ When you source products, follow a selection process similar to that you would use when selecting a market. Look for complementary products.

♦ Look for alternate suppliers to your domestic suppliers.

♦ Look for suppliers who can also act as distributors in that market. Two-way trade is always better than one way.

♦ Investigate whether you can sell the product/service in your market before you begin to import. Who is your competition?

♦ You can source product components and become even more competitive.

♦ Evaluate the pros and cons of different suppliers with respect to price, quality, flexibility in delivery and production and ease/difficulty to do business with. Find out warranty coverage and warranty costs, total costs and the time for shipment and delivery.

♦ Evaluate freight costs, customs duties, distribution, etc. Don't forget packaging costs. Make sure to investigate issues relating to quotas, licenses, testing, standards and approved labelling, etc.

♦ Does the foreign country have export financing that you can utilize?

♦ Ensure that you have the proper documentation for both exporting and importing, so that your goods can easily be cleared at the border.

♦ Compare duties, taxes and freight costs as well as quotas for each country/manufacturer you are importing from.

♦ What currency are you buying in? Have you checked projected currency rates?

♦ Complete cost calculations for importing as well as selling price and selling costs. Will you make money? Show the whole chain of distribution. List all activities.

♦ Who is supplying sales materials and service handbooks?

♦ Get expert advice. It is better to ask beforehand than when it is too late.

♦ Remember that quality levels and security of delivery will vary in different countries.

♦ There are many activities to think about when importing. Make sure you look at all of the aspects.

♦ Review the Distribution, Pricing, Risks and Shipping chapters.

Exercise

1. List the products and services you are considering importing.

2. What countries may be of interest to import from? Select one or two to use in the questions below.

3. Identify the appropriate contacts to source products/services. Contact them for further analysis.

4. Make a chart outlining the distribution chain from manufacturer to end user.

5. Write out a list of freight costs, customs duties, and any quotas you found.

6. What is the maximum price you can pay to the foreign manufacturer so that you can be profitable? Calculate backwards.

7. List the activities that are necessary for importing and selling the product/service you selected.

Legalities in International Business
Part One

In This Chapter:

- ♦ Company and product names
- ♦ Trade names and trade marks
- ♦ Patents and design protection
- ♦ Copyright
- ♦ Contracts and what should be included
- ♦ What laws apply?
- ♦ What happens if you do not have a contract?
- ♦ Should you use a lawyer?
- ♦ Sample contract with explanations
- ♦ Product liability

Example – Cancelling contract

You have had a distributor in Italy for 15 years. He hasn't sold much but you haven't shown an interest in that market. You have found a more suitable distributor and write a letter to the existing distributor cancelling your working relationship.

Shortly afterwards, you receive a letter from his lawyer demanding a large amount of money as compensation for the 15 years he has been working for you. You reply that you didn't have a written agreement with him and you're not willing to pay. You get a second letter with a scheduled court date in Milan. You're upset because you think you're being intimidated, so you contact your lawyer.

What you didn't know is that the legal system in Europe protects the distributor. Even though you didn't have a written contract specifying the process for cancellation, he can now demand compensation. If you had been smart enough to have set up a written contract, you could have cancelled according to the clause in the contract.

Example - Trademark

You are a manufacturer of wheelchairs, with a factory in China. The model name is Champ. You have just begun exporting them to Canada. A month after the first shipment arrives in Canada, you get a letter from a trademark attorney stating that you have committed a trademark infringement. The trademark Champ is registered to the War Amps in Canada. The lawyer issues several cease and desist demands: you cannot use the name Champ on any product sales materials and you must stop selling your wheelchairs in Canada until you have complied. If you do not act immediately, he will sue you for damages on behalf of his clients. You could be liable to pay a hefty fine for the infringement.

How did you get into this situation? Did you not research whether your product name was in use before you started to export?

Legal issues in international business

Hopefully, you are familiar with the legal issues that affect your domestic market. In international business, you have to adapt to the legalities of each market you enter as well as complying with international laws and regulations.

Product Names

The product name and company name you use can have a positive meaning or association in your domestic market. However, that same name can mean something completely different, and perhaps negative, in a foreign language. There is a cultural element to naming as well. For example, in China, certain numbers are lucky or auspicious (two, three, five, eight) and other numbers are unlucky or inauspicious (four, six) because of how they sound and what other words they sound like when translated. The word for the number eight also sounds like the word for "wealth" or "prosperity", while the word for the number four sounds like the word for "death".

Have the names, you are considering translated into various languages and investigate their literal and slang meanings before you invest in marketing and advertising materials. Even if you don't find a name in the dictionary, it could be used informally to mean something that is rude or inappropriate.

♦ The Crayola crayon company in the US changed the name of a colour from Prussian Blue to midnight blue in 1953 because of teacher requests. ("Prussian" was associated with the war-time Germany)

♦ An Italian mineral water company entering the Spanish market was puzzled that their product was not selling well. The product was called *Traficante*, which translates into "drug dealer" in Spanish.

♦ A multi-national food company started selling baby food in Africa. The jars of food had a picture of a smiling blue-eyed baby on the label. This was the same packaging used in the US. The problem was, because so many consumers in Africa cannot read, most companies put pictures of what is inside a container on the label.

I could fill this book with examples of marketing mistakes! You'll find many others by searching the Internet.

When you're setting up a contract with a distributor, you have to decide if you want them to use your company name and product names. If so, make sure to register the names in that country and license the distributor with the right to use the name as your representative. If you let them register the name, they will own it. If you change distributors, you wouldn't be able to use your own name.

You have to register you licensing arrangement with the local authorities for it to be valid. You will also be able to cancel the arrangement if you change distributors. In any case, make sure all sales material includes the ™ and/or ® symbol.

The rules about who can register a trade name and when, vary from country to country. In Jordan, for example, it is the date when you apply to register and not whether a name has been previously used that decides who can register. Recognized trade names such as Safeway, Microsoft and McDonalds have been registered and owned by Jordanians.

In most countries, to register a name, you have to show that you have used it or that you are planning to so.

Trademark

What is a trademark?

According to the US Patent and Trademark Office, a trademark is defined as: "any word, name, symbol, or device, or any combination used, or intended to be used in commerce to identify and distinguish the goods of one manufacturer or seller from goods manufactured or sold by others, and to indicate the source of the goods. In short, a trademark is a brand name."

Generally a trademark is a sign, word, logotype or some combination of these that is specific to your product, service or company. There is no doubt that products with trademarks can carry higher prices, support more rapid sales development, lower than average marketing costs and for your website, more visitors.

The most people are familiar with trademarks like Coca Cola, Ford, IBM, IKEA, Lenovo, Absolut Vodka, Apple iPhone and more. So how do you protect your trademark? You can use the symbol ™, which signifies an unregistered trademark but indicates that you want to protect the product or you can use the symbol ®, if it is a registered trademark.

Most recognized trademarks are:

1. **Coca Cola**
2. **IBM**
3. **Microsoft**
4. **Google**
5. **GE, General Electric**

Source www.interbrand.com

Registering your trademark

To keep your company or product name from being misappropriated, you have to:

1. Register your trademark in each country where you will be doing business or in several countries, including the major international markets. You can only register the name and trademark for special goods or services, not for general use. What I have done is register the name Export Master® for the consulting and education services I deliver for international business. That means someone else could register the same name for another product or service like crating systems for export. Normally, you have to continuously use the trademark to keep the protection active. You can't just register a trademark to protect it. Someone who intends to use the name could challenge the protection.

2. The McDonald's corporation has spent fifty years developing their trademarks and logos. The "Golden Arches" and stylized letter "M" have been trademarked, so no one else can use them without permission.

3. There is always a risk that someone will try to use your name or a look-alike name to benefit from your established image. This is illegal. In legal terms that is called trademark infringement or passing off, which is misrepresenting goods or services from one person by using the same name or a name similar to a recognized brand.

> ### *Example – Trademark dispute*
>
> *In 2006, Mattel, the company that manufactures and licenses the Barbie doll line of products, sued a restaurant chain in Montreal, Canada, for trademark infringement. The restaurants were called Barbie's and had been in business for a number of years. The Supreme Court of Canada found that while the trademark name Barbie clearly covered dolls and similar products, a trademark could not be used to absolutely restrict other legitimate uses of the name. The target market for the chain of Barbie's restaurants was adults and not children. The Court found there was no attempt to misrepresent the restaurant and that there would be no confusion on the part of consumers between a food service establishment and toys.*

Before you enter a market, check that your company and/or product name is available and appropriate and that no one else has registered to use that name for a similar product or service (i.e., in the same classification).

What do you do if the name you want to use is already registered or in use?

*   Look at the classification of the product or service. Is it the same as yours? Does the classification cover your area?

*   If the product or service is in your classification, you can ask the registered owner for permission to use it.

*   Change the name of your product or service.

You can normally not register a trade name that is a person's name, for example, "Grant" but you can register "Graant's", which is a line of work wear products.

Patent and Design Protection

Many companies arrange patent and design protection for their products and services. You need to learn how patent laws work. By filing for a patent, you state your intention to protect the product and service from others copying it. It is very common to first apply for a patent in the domestic markets and then apply for patent protection in other markets. Many markets allow you a period of one year in which to apply in secondary markets. However, there are exceptions such as in Taiwan, where you have to apply for all patents at the same time or at least in your domestic market plus Taiwan.

In many jurisdictions, you will be protected during the patent application period, as long as you are granted approval for the patent. Therefore, once the patent has been granted, you can take legal action on any infringement that occurred before you received final approval. This may not be the case elsewhere, because someone could produce and sell a "infringing" product up to the date when you get the patent approved. Investigate the procedures in each country you do business in.

You can apply for a patent in individual countries, within trading blocs like the European Union or for what is called a world patent. The latter does not mean you get a patent for all over the world, but it will cover key global markets.

The rules for patent applications differ between countries. In the United States, patents are granted to the 'first to invent" while in Japan it is the "first to register". In the US, patents are valid for 17 years and in Japan for 20 years from the application date. The patent application process in the US is confidential and in Japan it is public. These are only some of the differences. I find that American patents are frequently challenged, because they were granted when they should perhaps not have been. The result of the challenge is that the patent is overturned.

It is very common to see the words, "patent pending" on products. This signals that someone has applied for a patent; however, it does not necessarily mean the patent will be approved. You want to protect your product patent during the application period. I suggest you do some research when you start and then speak with a patent lawyer about how to proceed.

Example – Patents large corporations

There are ongoing patent disputes. When I began writing this book in early 2010, Nokia had taken Apple Corporation to court, accusing them of infringing on Nokia patents on all Apple products such as computers, iPod and iPhone. Apple countersued Nokia for infringing on a number of their patents.

In another case in 2009, an American court awarded a small Canadian company over $200 million after finding Microsoft Corporation guilty of patent infringement. There is, however, always the risk that companies found guilty of patent infringement will challenge the ruling in a higher court.

There are about 2 million patents awarded every year, so it can be difficult to find out if you are committing an infringement. Multi-national companies such as Nokia, which has about 15,000 people working in research and development, owns thousands of patents. In fact, Nokia applies for about 1000 patents every year. As with a trademark, make sure to register your patent, and then put a contract in place, if you want to allow someone else to use your patent, such as in licensing agreement. The same rules are also applicable for design protection.

The symbol ©, which stands for copyright, applies to this book but also for music, articles, art and other creations characterized as intellectual property. It also applies to photographs and some statistical information. If you want to use a Toyota car in an advertisement then you have to get approval. Consider, however, that if you hire a professional photographer to take promotional shots of your product or wedding photos, the photographer can retain control of those photos as the formal or recognized owner of a copyright. If it is not stated in your contract for service who will own the rights to the photographs, you may not be able to copy them.

Which Law Is Applicable?

When you conduct business in another country, you will be faced with laws and regulations that you have to adapt to. When you sign a legal contract, you must specify what country's law is applicable.

Common Law is used in England, Australia and New Zealand and North America, except in Quebec, Canada and Louisiana, US. The law is based on common sense. However, very little has been written about trade law, so business contracts tend to be lengthy because so many items have to be specified.

You should use common sense when there is no contract. If a distributor has not been performing well, there would normally be no problem for you to cancel the working arrangement. If they have met your performance expectations and you want to cancel the arrangement because you will be starting your own company, then you have an obligation to give them adequate notice and/or to compensate them. All of this applies if there is no contract, so I always recommend some kind of written agreement to protect your interests and the distributors.

In most European countries except for the United Kingdom, the laws are based on the **Napoleonic Code**, which is also called the **French Civil Code or Civil Law.** There is considerable detail in the law on the subject of trade. Whether you have a contract or not, there are normally clear guidelines in terms of what is applicable.

In Europe, there are laws about agent agreements that outline the minimum rules for cancelling a contract. If you have an agent and cancel your working arrangement with them, the law states how much you have to pay in compensation and the required notice period for cancellation. You can't include anything in a contract that is in conflict with the law. Local laws will apply, no matter what is in the contract. You can, of course, include more favourable conditions for the agent or distributor than the law stipulates. In the European Union, there are laws pertaining specifically to the EU. They take precedence over the local laws of each member country. You should be aware that EU laws restrict you from inserting non-competing clauses in contracts. The Napoleonic Code is also the basis for laws in Latin America, the French Colonies, South Korea and Thailand.

Scotland, South Africa and Sri Lanka use a combination of Common Law and Civil Law, while in North Africa and the Middle East, the French Civilian Code applies, except for matters relating to family and property issues, where Islamic tradition seems to be the prevalent approach.

Islamic Law is an interpretation of the Koran and is used in Saudi Arabia, Iran, Pakistan and other Islamic countries. In countries such as Russia, Eastern Europe and China, social, government policies and political considerations guide how the law is applied (e.g., communism, socialism, etc.).

Does this seem really complicated? It isn't, but I suggest that you always obtain legal advice before entering a new market.

Do I need to sign a contract?

♦ Yes, if you want to ensure that the parties agree on what has been discussed. Due to cultural and language differences, your distributor could translate the terms discussed in a way that benefits him and not you. You thought you had a clear agreement but in reality, you did not.

♦ Someone you negotiated an agreement with leaves the company. No one else remembers the terms and conditions the two of you agreed on. A contract would have alleviated this risk.

♦ Even if you don't draw up an official contract, keep a written record of the terms you agree to, such as a protocol or the minutes of a meeting. Send this documentation to the other party and ask them to sign it, to signify that they agree. Include as many details as possible.

♦ Your company and a foreign company want to set up an arrangement for your product to be manufactured there. You prepare a Letter of Intent. A letter of intent is a legally binding contract that enables you both to exchange commercial and technical information before the final agreement is completed. This protects you when exchanging confidential business or trade information.

♦ Your counterpart is not used to making a detailed agreement, so you both sign a **Gentlemen's Agreement**, stating that you will only sell your products and services through the other company on their market. They agree not to sell competing products. This works in some Asian countries where relationships are the foundation for conducting business.

What can happen when you don't have a contract?

♦ In the European Union, trade law specifies what is appropriate. If you don't know the law or try to circumvent it, you will likely get into trouble.

♦ In a country using common law, common sense very much dictates what is applicable

♦ In Japan, the existence of a contract is not as important as the relationship you have established. If there are issues with non-performance, there will be difficulties because of the personal/working relationship. "You can not cancel a relationship."

♦ In China, even when you have a signed contract, in reality, it means that you have agreed to continue to negotiate.

How do you cancel when there is no signed contract?

Example – Cancelling a non existent contract

When I joined a company in Europe, they had partners in more than 20 countries. Some of them were good partners and some were not performing. Of course, I wanted to get rid of the ones who weren't productive.

As the new Vice President of Marketing, I developed a contract for all of the partners. I informed them that I was the new manager and that I wanted to establish clear lines of communication and accountability with every partner.

I mailed out the contract and included a positive message about what we were going to do to support them. I also included a cancellation clause that allowed me to cancel the working arrangement with three months notice, after a one year period,

All the partners signed the contract. After the twelve months was up, I gave notice and cancelled 80% of them. I could do that because they had signed a legally binding agreement that gave me the authority to cancel.

Should You Use a Lawyer?

♦ Always obtain legal advice from someone familiar with business law. Laws change regularly, so you can't expect to keep up to date. There are so many things that can go wrong and then it can be expensive. To buy some hours from a lawyer is a low cost insurance.

- ◆ Even if you have a domestic lawyer, it is wise to consult with one who has knowledge of the law in the foreign country where you plan you sign the contract. It can make a big difference. In some countries you can arrange for a non-compete clause, while in some others, that is not allowed. How would you know? In the US and the EU, non-compete clauses are not permitted but in Canada, they generally are. What this means is that, in principle, you cannot legally contract with someone in Belgium for the exclusive right to sell your product there. You can't stop a distributor in France from also selling your product in Belgium. There are exceptions, so check first.

- ◆ The laws for using agents in Europe are very specific. You must know these before signing a contract. Even if you don't, you will be required to comply.

- ◆ In Muslim countries, it is illegal to charge interest on loans or overdue payments. Know what is allowed and what alternatives may be available.

Examples of marketing rules

- ◆ All countries have controls for marketing activities such as promotion, labelling, pricing and distribution channels.

- ◆ In Austria, premiums or offers like coupons and free gifts are considered to be the same as cash discounts and are prohibited.

- ◆ In Canada, labels must be in both English and French, the two official languages.

- ◆ In some countries, food and chemical product labels have to list the product contents.

- ◆ Marketing claims in some countries have to be provable and in others you are not permitted to make claims you can't prove, like 25% fuel savings.

- ◆ If you go to the opera in Barcelona, you can either buy the program in Spanish or in Catalonian.

The first part of this chapter has given you some basics in terms of laws and regulations influencing your foreign activities.

In Part Two, I will provide more detail about legal issues as well as some sample text for a contract.

Summary

♦ Familiarize yourself with the legalities for conducting international business in your own country.

♦ Make sure you are allowed to use your name and trade name in a foreign country. If you are allowed find out if someone else has registered the name and for what classification.

♦ Make sure you know what your name or trade name means in a foreign language, so you can avoid mistakes or embarrassments.

♦ Register the name with the appropriate authorities. Use ™ and ® with the names and logotypes you want to protect. Don't forget to sign a licensing agreement with your partner. This will allow them to use the name or logotype and allow you to withdraw the use arrangement when the distributor contract is cancelled. Make sure you own the registration.

♦ Protect your design and technology with design protection and patents.

♦ Be aware of the rules relating to registering and using © copyright for products, services or images.

♦ Know what laws and regulations apply in each country where you do business and what you have to do to adjust to their requirements. What are the implications for your business practices, your products, distributors, staff, etc.?

♦ Always put in writing what you and your foreign business partner agree to. This is good practice and prevents future disagreements.

♦ It is preferable to have a signed legal contract. You'll find that a contract is necessary, especially when there is a dispute or if you want to cancel an arrangement. (More details are provided in Part Two of this chapter).

♦ You can use the contract text in Part Two of this chapter as a check list.

♦ Seek advice from lawyers in your country and in the foreign country you want to do business in.

Legalities in International Business
Part Two

Contract

What should a distributor contract include? Even if you use a lawyer, here is a checklist of what to include and why. A contract should be forward thinking. You have to think about what might happen. What issues might arise in the future?

The contract should mirror what you and your partner have agreed upon. The importance of the contract becomes evident the day you disagree. You can't just write what you want in a contract. Local laws and regulations will dictate what can be included. For example, if you include a cancellation clause stating that after 10 years, you can dismiss your European agent without final compensation by giving them three months notice; this will likely not be legal. European law specifies the timeframe for notice and the level and type of compensation required. You cannot give someone exclusivity if that is against the law.

Exporters tend to write a one-sided contract demanding an extensive list of activities from a distributor but offering very little themselves. Don't do that. You should consider this as an equal partnership where you, the exporter, offer your partner something and you ask for something in return.

A contract includes two major parts:

1. The main body of the contract will include headings or sections that you are not going to change: applicable law, parties involved, responsibilities of the parties, termination options, etc.

2. An Appendix, which could include sections that can be revised more often, such as lists of prices and products.

By developing a contract in this way, you will not need to amend the main contract but you would be able to make changes to the appendix.

Main Contract

The legal text and paragraphs below are **only** to be used as <u>**examples.**</u> They are included to help you to understand contract content and provide a checklist to prepare you to discuss and draft your agreement based on the terms you and your partner negotiate. The text in bold is the legal wording and the other text is explanation. **I urge you to consult with a lawyer for the final text.** – You can make a suggested contract based on the below text, but have a local lawyer do the final fine tuning.

DISTRIBUTOR AGREEMENT

1. **The Parties signing the contract** (e.g., you and the distributor)

   THIS AGREEMENT dated the xxth day of xx 201x

   >   **B E T W E E N:**

   (Name of exporting company).................

   Address: Street
   >   **City/Postal code**
   >   **Country** (Japan in this example)

   (Hereinafter called "the exporter". Use a short name for the company, e.g. ABC Steel Inc is called "ABC")

   - and -

   (Name of distributor) xxxxxxxxxxx

   Address: Street
   >   **City/Postal code**
   >   **Country**

   (Hereinafter called "the distributor". Use a short name for the company, as above)

   WITNESSETH as follows:

2. **Description of territory, area**

   For example, Germany is the primary territory (but the Appendix will contain more details). Protection of territory - if the law allows, you can state that you will not establish another distributor in their territory and that the distributor will not be permitted to sell outside of the territory.

SCOPE AND TERRITORY

Subject to the terms and conditions hereinafter set forth, the EXPORTER hereby grants to the DISTRIBUTOR the exclusive right throughout (*write in country name*) **specified in Appendix A, to sell and distribute the Products, hereinafter specified in Appendix C and to appoint other distributors and dealers for the sale and distribution of the Products in** (country name).

Without the prior consent of the DISTRIBUTOR, the EXPORTER shall avoid, to the best of their knowledge and ability, selling any Products to other persons or companies within (country name) **or outside the country for delivery to or resale in** (country name).

This means that the exporter shall not sell directly to clients of the distributor or to other companies that would sell in the distributor's country

Exception: as the EXPORTER has global customers who export (name of product) that contains (SEE PART 3 BELOW), the EXPORTER shall be permitted to sell to those customers even though that may result in sales to (country name).

As was mentioned in the Distribution and Pricing chapters, this could be a large construction company that brings equipment for a large international contract or an Original Equipment Manufacturer or OEM into the territory

Without the prior consent of the EXPORTER, the DISTRIBUTOR shall avoid, to the best of their ability, selling any Products to other persons or companies within (country name) **or outside** (country name) **for delivery to or resale outside of** (country name).

This clause may be illegal in the EU because of laws against non-competition

For more details relating to Territory, see Appendix A.

3. **General description of Products**

You are currently selling drill-presses for the manufacturing industry. You buy a company making cosmetics. If you do not specify the particular product line, the cosmetics would automatically be included too.

Specify if your distributor will have the right or will be required to use your company name and trademark (as a licensee).

♦ The Products covered by this Agreement and herein referred to as "the Product" or "the Products" as the context requires, are specified in Appendix B. They are to be sold or manufactured by the EXPORTER, as well as related accessories, tools and spare parts pertaining thereto and including any changes, modifications, enhancements or improvement thereof.

The products shall be sold under the name of the EXPORTER.

The DISTRIBUTOR shall, as part of this agreement, sign a licensing agreement to allow the use of the Trademarks by the EXPORTER.

This is a critical clause and should include both your company name and product name. Make sure that you as an exporter register those trade names in the country.

Note: In the case where any product is specifically designed or developed by the EXPORTER for the DISTRIBUTOR, those product designs remain the property of the EXPORTER.

You must include this clause, as you, the exporter may develop a new or revised product for the distributor. Even if the suggestions for design changes come from the distributor, ownership of the redesigned product is still the exporter's.

In the event of any warranty claim, the rules applicable are as contained in Appendix E.

4. *What is the EXPORTER to deliver?* This includes not only products but also supports and services, sales material, participating in trade shows, etc.

♦ Exporter SERVICES

The EXPORTER will transfer information to the DISTRIBUTOR in order to facilitate marketing, sales and technical support activities.

The EXPORTER will supply to the DISTRIBUTOR, free of charge, 500 sets of sales material in English, per year.

If the DISTRIBUTOR so requires, the EXPORTER will, at cost, supply the DISTRIBUTOR with additional materials, artwork, film or digital formats, in order for the DISTRIBUTOR to produce the sales material locally.

The reason for this clause is to clarify how much and in what form sales materials and support will be provided by the exporter.

The EXPORTER will provide technical support from Japan by mail, email, fax and telephone.

The EXPORTER will supply support staff at large exhibitions and when negotiating larger contracts, if so agreed upon.

The EXPORTER will deliver training to the DISTRIBUTOR's personnel on the Exporter products free of charge. Duration of the training will be for one week within the first 12-month period, at the EXPORTER's premises in (location), **Japan. The DISTRIBUTOR will be required to pay for their travel to and from Japan as well as any accommodation costs**.

5. **What is the responsibility of the distributor, agent, etc?**

   ♦ **DISTRIBUTOR SERVICES**

   The DISTRIBUTOR shall search for, select and service suitable clients. DISTRIBUTOR shall, on their own behalf, import, sell and distribute the Products in *(name of country)*.

   The DISTRIBUTOR shall recruit, educate and retain qualified staff to **(***insert a description of the work to be done*).

   The *(job title)* **shall have the following qualifications:**

(This clause is only applicable if specialist skills or knowledge is required, such as information technology specialists, computer programmers, certified welders, etc.)

   The DISTRIBUTOR shall maintain an adequate stock/inventory of Exporter products to meet customer demands.

   The DISTRIBUTOR will have on hand the required demo kits and training systems for sales people to learn from and use when demonstrating the functions and features of the Products.

Do you want to include an orientation or test period during which time the distributor has to prove that they can perform in accordance with Appendix C before the distributorship is validated?

To comply with this contract, the Distributor is required to buy Products from the Exporter in accordance with the volumes and values contained in Appendix C.

This is a way, during the start-up period, to make it possible for the exporter to cancel the contract for non-performance. It also gives the Distributor time to show that they can meet performance targets without being at risk of losing the distributorship.

To ensure that all Products sold and delivered in *(name of country)* **comply with local standards and legislation, the DISTRIBUTOR will inform the Exporter of any applicable rules and regulations, so that the Exporter's products can be brought into compliance with same.**

Remember that your product/services must meet the terms of local laws, regulations and standards. Because you can't keep up to date on these requirements, you have to trust that your distributor will keep informed and also inform you in a timely way, so that no problems arise with product or service compliance locally. You also must agree who would pay for local approvals and any required registrations. If the product has to be tested and certified/approved by local safety authorities, will you the exporter, pay those costs or should the distributor?

6. Competing activities

♦ **COMPETITIVE ACTIVITIES**

In compliance with this contract, the DISTRIBUTOR shall not, during the term of this contract, sell any competing products. The Exporter agrees not to sell to any direct competitors.

In some countries, it is allowable to include non-compete clauses, so that the distributor is not allowed to sell competing products during the term of the contract with you. There may also be a provision that a distributor is not permitted to sell competing products for a specific period after your contract expires or is cancelled, e.g., 2 years after. In other jurisdictions it may be against the law to include non-compete clauses, so even if you put it in the contract, it is not enforceable. Adapt your text accordingly.

7. Exchange of information

What are the rules for exchange of information? Is it the distributor's responsibility to provide reports? In what format (verbal or written), how frequently (weekly, monthly, quarterly) and using what methods (telephone, email, fax)?

- **REPORTS AND RECORDS**

  The DISTRIBUTOR shall keep the Exporter continuously informed with (*the type of reporting, e.g.,* quarterly written) reports regarding marketing conditions in (*name of country*) *inter alia*, competitors, prices, sales, service issues, stock/inventory, publicity, major customers, prospective customers and other market activities not specified.

Most of the time, it is better to discuss these topics over the phone. This provides you with more details and the option to ask questions and get clarifications.

  According to how the Products are to be sold, whether as individual products or as part of a system, the parties (i.e. the DISTRIBUTOR and Exporter) shall jointly agree on a suitable customer price level.

There are two reasons for including a similar clause adapted to your company. If the distributor sets prices that are too high, their profit per product and the total profit may be high, but as an exporter, you will lose on volume. If the distributor does not comply with this clause, you could increase your export price, which would make their profit margin lower.

8. **Secrecy/confidentiality agreement**

This is very important. You do not want any trade secrets being shared with a third party.

  During the term of this Agreement or any time thereafter, the DISTRIBUTOR shall not use or communicate to third parties any technical, process, industrial or other trade secrets which it has come to know through the business relationship with the Exporter and which are not otherwise in the public domain.

  The DISTRIBUTOR shall also, therefore, caused to be signed by its employees a similar secrecy/confidentiality agreement to ensure that no employee of the Distributor will share or otherwise transfer this type of information.

It is essential for you to confirm that the distributor has a confidentiality agreement with their staff. If not, the staff could leave the distributor's company and use your confidential information in a competing business. I know it can sometimes be difficult to get the distributor to sign this type of agreement with their staff. If you cannot get that confirmation, at least include the first part of this clause to bind the distributor to secrecy. Of course, all of this depends on the product and service you will supply. If the product is complex software, I think the employer would have a standard contract with their staff. If they sell used farming machinery, they most likely would not have a secrecy agreement.

9. **The right to terminate the contract**

This section sets out the timeframe for giving notice and the process for terminating a contract.

♦   **TERMS AND TERMINATION PROCESS**

This Agreement shall come into force on the date set forth on page one (the "Effective Date") and shall continue until termination, as provided for below.

This Agreement may be terminated by written notice which shall be given at least 90 days prior to the date on which the Agreement is to be terminated (the "Termination Date").

The Exporter shall not give notice of termination earlier than xxxx, 201x, provided that this contract has been fulfilled and the purchase volumes comply with Appendix C.

If the Distributor does not meet these volume targets (dollars or number of units) you will have the option to cancel the contract based on non- performance.

If no notice of termination is delivered by either party, this Agreement will automatically be extended for one year at a time.

The term could be for any period of time that has been agreed upon in the contract.

Notwithstanding the foregoing termination provisions, this Agreement may be terminated by either party at any time with 60 days prior written notice if the other party should commit a material breach of any of the provisions of this Agreement unless such breach is remedied within the 60-day period.

This agreement may be terminated immediately, by either party, with written notice, if:

•   **the other party should become insolvent, or;**

- **if a petition for bankruptcy should be made against the other party, or:**

- **if one of the parties files for bankruptcy, and said petition is not discharged within 60 days, or;**

- **an assignment or lien is made for the benefit of its creditors or a receiver of its property or a substantial part thereof are to be appointed elsewhere.**

If you or the distributor goes bankrupt, the contract can be immediately cancelled)

By either party with 60 days prior written notice, if the ownership of one of the parties changes.

If the ownership of the distributor changes, the contract should be cancelled immediately. It could be that your strongest competitor has bought out your distributor.

At the Termination Date, irrespective of the cause of termination, the DISTRIBUTOR shall return to the Exporter all drawings, models, designs and pertinent technical material which the DISTRIBUTOR has received from the Exporter or otherwise obtained as part of the rights which enjoyed under this Agreement.

If there is a breach of the contract terms, what remedies are available to you? What are your options for cancelling the contract?

As an example, if the distributor has not paid the exporter's invoices within 60 days, the contract will automatically be cancelled if you have included this type of clause in your contract. If there is a non-compete clause and your distributor is selling similar products from another company, the contract will automatically be deemed to be cancelled.

10. **Terms of notice**

If you want to provide notice of cancellation or renewal of a contract, how should that be done?

- **NOTICES**

  Any notice, demand, request, consent or approval required or contemplated, to be given or made hereunder shall be in

writing and either delivered personally or sent by courier, fax
or other means of verifiable communication or by registered or
certified mail, postage prepaid, addressed as follows:

(a)   If to the DISTRIBUTOR:

> DISTRIBUTOR xxxxxxx.
> Address: xxxxx
> xxxxx
> Country
>
> Attention: President

(b) If to the Exporter

> Address: xxxxxxxxxxxxx
> xxxxxxxxx
> Country
>
> Attention: President

♦   **GOVERNING LAW**

This is the law that will apply when interpreting the contract terms. For example, in the case of an American company exporting to France, most likely French or Napoleonic law will be the governing legislation. You will have difficult suing the French company for non-payment in an American court, as they most likely have no assets in the US. This will, of course, depend on what the parties have agreed upon and what is practical.

> **This Agreement shall be governed by the laws of** (the country you
> select and/or the parties agree to).

You have to select laws of one country, otherwise the contract will not be considered legal. You should also have the jurisdiction specified in the event there is a dispute of lawsuit.

♦   **DISPUTE RESOLUTION**

How will disputes be resolved? What kinds of dispute will be subject to formal resolution? You have to specify the methods for alternate dispute resolution, e.g., arbitration, mediation or litigation. I always believe you, as a party, have the most protection if you have the option of taking a dispute to court. Note that it can be very complicated and expensive to arbitrate a dispute in a foreign country.

♦ **ASSIGNMENT**

You should include a clause stating that the contract is not transferable or assignable to any other parties. The contract could also include a requirement that you have the right to approve any sub-distributors.

Neither party shall assign any of its rights or obligations hereunder without the prior written consent of the other party.

IN WITNESS WHEREOF the parties hereto have executed this Agreement on the day and year first above written.

Exporter name

By: _____

(Name of person signing)

(Position title, e.g., President)

DISTRIBUTOR name

By: _____

(Name of person signing)

(Position title, e.g., President)

Make sure that you know who has the authority to sign the contract. If there are amendments required later, it must be clear who can approve them.

Appendix

This is the part that can be changed or amended without affecting the main provisions of the contract.

♦ **APPENDIX A**

Geographical area described in detail. Customer groups described in detail.

For example, the Appendix could state Germany, if the distributor's territory is to be all of Germany or it could refer to a certain part of the country and specify the boundaries or name of the geographic area (county, province, state.). Be as descriptive as possible.

You can also describe the customer groups to be included and excluded. If, for instance, you want to exclude certain companies within the territory from the contract, you should stipulate that. You can also restrict certain customers or customer groups from being included.

You can specify that you retain the right to sell directly to some large companies such as General Motors, or that the contract covers the primary manufacturing industry and you will sell to satellite industries. The contract may also state that because you will be selling to large OEMs, your products can be sold via their networks into the distributor's territory and will not constitute a conflict. As was stated in the chapters "Selecting the Right Distribution… and Export Pricing…", you will deal with large international buyers under separate agreements

♦ **APPENDIX B**

Products/Services (in detail)

A part of the contract, list the individual items along with identifying details, so that there is no confusion. This list protects you from misunderstandings and also ensures that any new products or new product lines will not automatically be included unless you amend the list in the Appendix. If you are not specific, your distributor would have access to any product or service you launch in the future, regardless of whether it is in the same industry or not.

♦ **APPENDIX C**

SALES

Include here a description of the expected target to be reached or minimum sales volumes. Once you and your distributor agree on an expected sales volume, there could be various stages or increments for reaching the goal, e.g., month-over-month increases, and the performance target totals could be increased every year.

You could also include targets during an 18 month start-up or test period. If the sales volume is met, then the contract would be automatically renewed.

♦ **To comply with this contract, DISTRIBUTOR shall buy from and get delivered from the Exporter Product valued in the following amounts.**

   - **First 6 months** $ xxxx
   - **Month 6-12** $ xxxxx
   - **Month 13 – 18** $ xxxxxx
   - **Month 19 – 24** $ xxxxxxx

Instead of a purchase dollar amount, you could use either the number of units or sales/purchase volume.

> **If the above-noted targets are not achieved and the DISTRIBU-TOR does not accept delivery of purchases in accordance with performance levels agreed hereto, the Exporter has the right to cancel the contract with 3 months prior notice.**
>
> **Following the initial 24 month period, the** *(number of units or sales/purchase volume)* **shall be as agreed upon by both parties for a further 12 month period. This** *(number of units or sales/purchase volume)* **shall be set not later than 90 days before the annual renewal date. If no new agreement is established, the above-noted performance target shall be increased by x% per year.**

♦   **APPENDIX D**

Price list

Prices and currency

What currency will be used in costing the contracted amounts? What happens if the currency fluctuates significantly?

To be on the safe side, include a price list and indicate what steps will be taken if, for example, the selected currency fluctuates more than + or -5%. State whether the prices are calculated ex works, f.o.b., etc. There is more information on this in the Shipping chapter.

What are the procedures and the schedule for reviewing and changing prices? You could include a clause stating that prices are to be reviewed annually and will remain unchanged for a period of one year after the review. However, if the currency changes by more than 5%, prices can be adjusted with three months notice.

Some distributors sell to large catalogue houses and they have to guarantee prices during the life of the catalogue. You could be forced into a similar arrangement if you sell to them. It could mean you have to agree to a price freeze for up to two years, if that is how long a time the catalogue is valid for.

Who will pay for freight and insurance? You can state that this is the responsibility of the distributor. However, if you have a practical reason such as strong buying power in your market and the ability to negotiate lower freight costs and insurance, then you can offer to cover these expenses and add them to the invoice for the goods.

♦ **Enclosed as Appendix D** is a price list that includes an effective date. Note that these prices are in Japanese Yen and can be changed with 3 months notice. The prices are ex works xxxxx, excluding packaging. Any freight and insurance charges will be covered by the DISTRIBUTOR.

Payment term is 60 days after date of invoice. A late payment penalty of 1.5% per month or 18% a year will be charged on the outstanding balance.

Late payment charges

Will you impose a charge for late payment and if so, how much? Some countries have rules that automatically apply. In others, you have to include the charge in the contract. It is forbidden to charge interest in most nations using Islamic law. You may also find yourself in a situation where a foreign government interferes with the transfer of money, e.g., through embargoes, currency restrictions, nationalizing an industry or other methods that can delay payment.

Payment and export packaging

How and when is the payment to be made, and who is paying for the export packaging?

Terms of payment

Is it 30 days, 60 days or 90 days, document against acceptance or with a bank guarantee? (Also see Payment chapter)

Who decides on market prices?

You want to be involved in this decision. If your distributor sells your product at very high prices, their profits will be good but the sales volume will be lower. You want to make sure that this doesn't happen. You can, of course, choose to increase your prices, but this won't help you to increase sales volume.

Who pays for what?

You could indicate in the contract that you will provide the first 100 promotional leaflets free of charge to the distributor. Any requirements over and above that will be priced at x amount per leaflet. Alternatively, you could agree to supply an original electronic or hard copy file so that the distributor can print their own.

Trade shows are important marketing venues. You might agree to send your own staff to one show a year. Whenever possible, specify which trade show and the location, the number of staff providing support, the kinds of demonstration or marketing materials to be provided and the dollar value of any advertising and related expenses.

Training

What training will be provided? Whenever possible itemize the types of training, the frequency and the duration. Are there certain technical standards, certifications or proficiency testing that must be completed? Will training be delivered in your distributor's premises, at another location in that market or will they be required to send their staff to your location? Who will be responsible for the cost of training (facilitator/trainer, facilities, travel, accommodations and meal.)?

* **APPENDIX E**

  ◆ **WARRANTIES**

What are the conditions under which a warranty can be exercised? You may usually provide for three months of warranty but the local market demands a six month warranty. You need to know this in advance, because it will impact your costs. What is the timeframe for processing and approving a warranty claim?

Do consumers have to register with you to get warranty coverage or is their sales receipt sufficient? How will you deal with warranty claims – locally, through the distributor or through head office? Will the distributor have the authority to make decisions on warranty claims, have repairs made and obtain compensation from you? Do you want the goods returned and an exchange made instead of a repair?

When you begin your relationship with the distributor, set up guidelines for how the process will work and how frequently they will report on warranty claims.

> **The Exporter warrants that the Products at delivery are free of defects.**
>
> **The warranty period is limited to a period of 12 months from the delivery/invoice date. The Exporter's liability is limited to manufacturing defects. The Exporter has the choice of repairing or replacing the product. The same warranty conditions will apply to any exchanged product.**
>
> **The DISTRIBUTOR shall inform the Exporter, in writing,** (specify how often and in what detail) **of any warranty claims within the stated product warranty period.**
>
> **The Exporter will not honour a warranty for products which have been altered or put to uses not in accordance with the Product Instruction Manual.**

The DISTRIBUTOR shall, at their cost, ship the product for which a warranty claim has been approved, to the Exporter. The Exporter shall accept the cost of return shipping the repaired or replaced product to the DISTRIBUTOR.

This may not always be practical, depending on the value of the original product and associated shipping costs, so you will have to find a cost effective solution. You could send the distributor spare product/parts free of charge, so that you can clear warranty claims every three months. Decide if you will pay for all or a portion of the labour costs warranty repairs.

If there are any major problems, you will want the distributor to return the product to you so that you can verify the seriousness of the problem. Note also that there may be additional paperwork, costs and requests for reimbursements of customs duties when products under warranty are shipped between countries.

♦ **It is up to the DISTRIBUTOR to claim any duties or taxes paid to xxxx authorities as a result of the transfer out of and into the country.**

♦ **The Exporter is not liable for any claims over and above the product value.**

♦ **The Exporter carries product liability insurance. If a claim is made by a client of the DISTRIBUTOR, the liability of the Exporter for personal or property damage shall be limited to what is covered by said insurance. It is the responsibility of the DISTRIBUTOR to carry sufficient liability insurance to cover any amount over the limits of the Exporter's policy**.

Other items you perhaps want to include:

1. **If the contract is cancelled:**

   a. **Return of stock**

Most likely you'll want the stock returned and not sold at a discount. There are pros and cons to this. You don't want your former distributor to dump your products at a low price but on the other hand, there will be a cost you to get them back.

   b. **Return of documentation**

You want the distributor to promptly return all of the promotional materials, training documents, binders, drawings, electronic files and pricelists to prevent re-use or mis-use.

Other issues

Don't forget to make provision for the commercial or trade secrets you or your partners may exchange. How will they be affected by your working relationship?

There is variation in how different cultures perceive contracts and similar legal agreements. If you sign a contract with a company in Finland, you can trust that they will keep to the agreement. If you sign a contract with a Japanese company, the personal relationship you have with them is more important than the contents of the contract. If you sign with a Chinese company, it means you have agreed to ongoing negotiations of the terms.

You have to become familiar with what is applicable in the country you are dealing with. In China, for example, a joint venture agreement is often a good alternative to trying to establish your own arrangements. The local representative will have established local relationships that you can benefit from. Furthermore, there are restrictions on foreign ownership in China.

Product Liability

I'm sure you have read about product liability lawsuits in the US. Often, people engage in what is called a "nuisance" lawsuit, to gain financial advantage or notoriety. Whether there is merit to a claim or not, defending yourself will cost time and money.

Do you know how product liability will influence you as an exporter? Laws vary around the world. Yes, you may be sued in the US, but with the right preparation and expert advice before the fact, you can protect yourself and reduce the chance of a law suit. I suggest that you arrange for product liability insurance coverage in the country where your office is located. The distributor can link their local insurance to that. Be sure to specify in the contract with the distributor their responsibility ensuring that the product/service complies with local laws and regulations. (refer back to Section 5)

Canadian law does not support lawsuits to the same extent as in the US, although they are becoming more frequent. In the European Union, responsibility for product liability rests with the original manufacturer. The results are that the rules are tougher than in the US. The risks for lawsuits are also much lower. Frequently, it is not the product that is the problem but rather inadequate or improper documentation.

How Can You Minimize Risk?

◆ Clarify that the responsibility for compliance with local regulatory requirements belongs to your local partner.

◆ Consult with a business or product insurance specialist and arrange for adequate liability insurance coverage.

◆ Develop product instructions that dictate how the product is to be used properly, so as to minimize the potential for accidents and misuse.

> **Example – Product liability**
>
> *I asked a representative of a company selling chainsaws in the US if the parent company had ever had any lawsuits. He said no. When I asked him why not, he said that their product documentation clearly stated that the purchaser was required to read and initial that they had read the complete instructions before using the chainsaw. Sometimes that written confirmation was required even before the customer was allowed to take the chainsaw from the retail store. With this kind of added protection, no consumer could claim that they were not told how to use the equipment properly.*

You must become familiar with the legal aspects of international business so that you can instruct legal counsel, negotiate contract terms from a position of knowledge and strength and protect yourself and your company from being taken advantage of. There are many elements of the law and a variety of country interpretations that must be taken into consideration.

I have given you a great deal of information in this chapter, but it simply is not possible to cover every eventuality. Nor can I give you legal advice – you have to obtain this for yourself. It is up to you to do your advance research and ensure that you are aware of what other legal aspects might be applicable in your business situation.

Use the sample contract you've read as a check list when you negotiate with a foreign partner. Once you've completed it, you can also share the contents with your lawyer. Being prepared with all the details will make it easier for the lawyer and likely reduce the cost to you for legal advice.

Competent legal advice is great insurance – consider it an investment to protect yourself against future problems.

Exercise

1. Make a search on Google for "Orion trademark Europe". Look at the trademarks and different classifications on the results page. Do the same for some of your products.

2. List your company name and your product/service names. Decide which of these you want to use and protect. Are any of them already in use in the foreign country where you want to do business? Which will you protect with a registered trade mark and what uses or applications will the protection cover? Which do you want to protect with ™?

3. Check to see if your company name and product names have the right meaning in the foreign country (you may have to change the name). If you go to "Google translate" and instead of using the name "Amra", translate the name of your product to mean "high tech fast train" in Danish (e.g., *højteknologiske iltog*). Do the same for Chinese and Spanish translations.

4. Determine if you want your foreign partner to use your company name and product name?

5. What patents and design protections do you have? Are they registered in the foreign country? If not, can you meet the required time limit? Do you want to register the name or product?

6. For the country you are going to, check to see what trade laws are applicable and how they will affect your company and ability to do business there. For example you can run a Google search on "French Trade Law". That will give you a number of sites to study. Do the same for "Japanese Trade Law".

7. Using the contract example I provided, fill in the appropriate information and design your own contract.

International Business in the Future

In This Chapter:

- ♦ **Your input for future books**
- ♦ **Future markets and customers**
- ♦ **Future production and services**
- ♦ **The future in marketing and education**
- ♦ **The customer of the future**

This is the final chapter. I hope you enjoyed the book and now feel more prepared to start or accelerate the growth of your business on the global market. Because the market will continue to change, your activities have to do so as well. You will never become an expert on international business and you must commit to continuous learning.

Whether you are working in a company expanding into new markets or if you are a student with plans to join a company doing international business, you will have the benefit of experiencing new cultures and new markets. One day, you will be able to say proudly on your company's website, "Our products are available in over 30 countries."

No book can ever be perfect or suit the needs of every reader. My hope is that since you've reached this point, you will have gained fresh insights into the global marketplace.

I would appreciate receiving your feedback:

♦ What did you like in the book?

♦ What can be improved?

♦ What was missing that you wanted to know more about?

♦ Any other suggestions?

Send your comments to me at: book@exportpro.com

If you have any examples from your experience that I can use, please share them with me. I will try to include them when I update this text or in new books. Of course, before I use any of your material, I'll let you know.

My website at www.exportpro.com will be regularly updated with new links, additional questions and answers and of course, new books as they are published. I'll also include information about teacher's handbooks. I would certainly appreciate any suggestions you have for the website too.

Future Markets and Customers

If you think you are safe in your domestic market because you've sold locally for a long time, you are probably wrong. Most likely there are similar products to yours available from other markets. When they enter your "safe" market and you are not competing internationally, your previously secure position will be at risk.

Map out your future, but do it in pencil. The road ahead is as long as you make it. Make it worth the trip."
— Jon Bon Jovi

We must learn to "read" global markets and adjust our planning constantly, so that we can be prepared for change. If we knew what was going to happen in the future, life would certainly be easy, wouldn't it? There will always be shifts that are almost impossible to predict – caused by natural disasters, business uncertainty, energy supply issues, political and economic upheavals. The only thing we can do is make qualified guesses. You have to maintain a forward-looking approach and keep on collecting and analyzing information. You want to have the best possible knowledge about what might happen two, five or ten years in the future, so that you can plan, adapt yourself and your organization.

Population and Work Force

♦ We know that the world population will reach about 9.3 billion people by 2050, which is a 50% increase from 2009. The majority of the increase is taking place in developing countries.

♦ Nearly 500 million people will move from rural to urban centres.

- About 2.8 billion live on less than $2 a day.

- 195 million people are living and working outside their home country.

- The industrial age is not about money, it is about knowledge. Political decisions can't stop the spread of knowledge because it belongs to individuals, who decide where they want to live.

- In the past, it took 14 years before knowledge became obsolete. Today, 50% what we learned three to five years ago is outdated or no longer valid.

- Aging populations in traditional industrial nations will have a major impact on country economies because of increased costs for pensions and health care. Also, an increasingly larger segment of the population will be out of the labour force.

If you have products and services for this customer group, however, you would have an ever-increasing market.

Developing nations will have a large labour force of young workers, the majority of whom will be under 25 years of age. This means a larger segment of productive working population and less of an economic burden of older people. By 2020, India's labour force is expected to increase by 110 million, while China and the US may only increase by 15 million and 11 million respectively. In contrast, Japan will experience a population reduction of three million people (Goldman Sachs, July 2010).

Industrial nations will adopt more flexible and innovative working arrangements such as telecommuting and job-sharing. Many employees are now working from home, more jobs are being contracted out and there has been a growth in part time work. The traditional 9-5 office or factory jobs will eventually disappear.

An increasing number of people will retire to locations overseas. The reasons are better climates, lower cost of living, taxes and medical costs.

Unfortunately, there is also increasing environmental migration. Between 25 million and one billion people around the world will be forced to move by 2050 because rising water levels and flooding will make their current locations uninhabitable (islands in the South Pacific) or drought and extreme heat will create unliveable conditions (Africa, Central Asia, South and Latin America).

Trade and Consumption

As international trade grows, the world is becoming increasingly borderless. Growing populations lead to greater consumption of a wider variety of products – agricultural, manufactured, technology, housing, etc. Consumers in emerging economies will become more demanding for better quality, quantity and prices and local markets will have to update their infrastructure to remain competitive.

An example of this is India, which has experienced serious capacity constraints caused by reliance on outdated housing, production, communications and transportation infrastructure and an outdated energy grid. On the other hand, China has invested heavily in expanding railways, airports, roads and power plants.

Competition is not just about labour costs. A drastic future increase in crude oil prices from about $80 (2009-2010) to $200 per barrel would result in freight costs increasing by 200 to 300% which would seriously disrupt global trade development. The advantage of low wage levels would be offset by the high cost of transporting goods, which for some products would cause them to become less price-competitive and more difficult to sell on far distant markets.

If you are an automobile manufacturer, your future markets will be in emerging economies. In China, more than 1 million cars a month were sold in 2009, more than in the US. This volume represented 25% of world consumption. The forecast for automobile sales in China for 2010 are 17 million units. General Motors expects to sell over 3 million cars there by 2015. Currently only 60 to 80 people per thousand in China own a car, while in the United States, 800 people per thousand own a vehicle. Asia will account for 70% of the Ford Motor Company's global growth in the next 10 years. Most of this market expansion will be in China and India, with India becoming the third largest global auto market by the end of this decade, behind China and the US. Significant production increases will occur in India, Thailand and China. Thailand is called "the Detroit of Asia" for good reason, because all of the major manufacturers have located production of components and assembly of complete vehicles there. They export to Asia, Saudi Arabia and other parts of the world. There are over 1,800 automotive parts manufacturers, in Thailand, of which 700 are OEM.

Market demands are shifting from products to services and complete systems. As an exporter, you are selling solutions and profitability. Developing markets require more raw materials and energy. This benefits countries like Canada, Brazil and Chile, large parts of Africa, Australia and Russia, all of which have abundant supplies of resources. Today (2010) China accounts for 50% of the world's steel production, creating an enormous demand for raw materials. As well, Chinese steel exports exert considerable pressure on other steel producing nations.

Energy

The availability and costs of producing and distributing energy will influence not only the economy but also product development. The developing world will soon surpass the OECD countries in oil consumption. This growth trend will continue as the developing countries grow, increase production and increase usage of vehicles.

Even though the share of fossil fuels will decrease because of alternative energy sources, the absolute quantities of those fossil fuels will increase because of total energy demand. 80% of energy consumption will still be from coal, oil and natural gas for the foreseeable future.

Coal consumption in China and India will double between 2005 and 2030, which will represent 70% of the global increase. China will bring over 500 coal-fired generating plants online between 2008 and 2012. India, Taiwan, Vietnam, Indonesia and Malaysia will double their coal- fired power plant capacity during the same time period. Today, an individual in China uses only 1/10th of the energy consumed by the average person in North America. This is a frightening indication on what will likely happen to future energy consumption when the ordinary consumer in China begins to use more resources. There is also a direct relationship between demand, supply and a correspondingly increase in energy prices.

There is a clear link between rising energy prices and negative implications for an economy. For example, China is both a high consumer of imported energy and a major contributor to the production of environmental emissions. According to the New York Times of August 9, 2010, the situation in China has become so severe that a list was recently published of 2,087 old, low technology non-energy efficient steel mills, cement works and other energy-intensive factories that were required to close by Sept. 30 2010.

The listed factories were barred from obtaining bank loans, export credits, business licenses and land and the electricity to those factories could be shut down if they failed to close on the date ordered. The current Chinese plan calls for 20% less energy consumption in 2010, compared to 2005. This closing of factories can be achieved because of labour shortages in many cities, which make it easier for those laid off from closed plants to get another job. This emphasizes the trend in the developing countries to invest in better technology and taking energy compensative measures.

Alternative and renewal energy sources such as wind power and solar power will play an important role for all nations. Any technology and service that can reduce energy consumption without negatively affecting the environment will have a market advantage in the future. Geothermal or ground heating, synthetic and biofuels, tidal or wave power and other alternatives are being tested and will increase in importance as costs fall. Electrical and hybrid vehicles will form an even larger part of the market because of consumer interest and new legislation forcing manufacturers to produce cars which consume less fuel. Years ago, there were plans to reduce dependence of nuclear power; however, that has been reversed in the face of increased energy demands. With today's focus on environmental controls and "clean" energy with limited "dirty" emissions, nuclear power is once again seen as a viable alternative. According to Nuclear Energy Institute, 16 countries rely on nuclear power for at least 25%, (30% in Japan and Europe, in France over 75%). The number of nuclear power plants will double by 2030 and demand will double or triple.

Productivity, Currencies, and Payments

A fluctuation in global currencies, particularly in emerging economies, has a strong influence on the cost of manufacturing and the cost of goods sold. When a currency appreciates or rises in value against the US dollar or the Euro, the country's exported goods become more expensive and can have the effect of reducing demand. However, companies selling to these fast-developing consumer markets can benefit.

A variety of political, economic and industrial factors have led to significant global currency fluctuations. The strength of a currency is very dependent on the country's economic situation, e.g., stability, value of investments, diversification of industry, expected results, level of debt and resource base. Some countries such as China do not allow a market adapted valuation rate for their currency, so they can control their exchange rate, no matter what happens in the rest of the world (fixed vs. floating rate). Because of pressure from industrialized nations, China will slowly release some controls on their currency and let it increase in value.

Instability in the value of the US Dollar, the Euro, the British pound and Japanese Yen, will continue, making it more challenging for exporters and importers to calculate pricing and control costs. How dramatic the valuation shifts are, will depend on global market confidence. Many of the larger countries now have such significant government debt and growing structural deficits that a fiscal tightening in those economies is inevitable. Management of risk will continue to be an important focus. The question is, who is going to be first to return their economy to financial stability?

Electronic money transfer has become very common. However, even more customer-friendly solutions are on the way with the expansion of mobile commerce for purchases of products and services and introduction of money transfers via cell phone. This technology is growing rapidly in Africa, the Middle East and Asia. According to the World Bank, the current value of formal remittances is about $318 billion worldwide, with another $315 billion in informal transactions. Financial transactions can even be completed using applications on Facebook.

High Tech, Information Technology, and Commerce

By 2013, about 2.2 billion people will be using the internet, 17% of them in China, 47% in Asia and 13% in Africa and the Middle East (Forrester Research). E-commerce will be a significant part of future markets, including electronic tools such as online bidding, quoting, invoicing and payments.

Technological innovations and new gadgets will continue to influence global business, especially in developing countries where mobile communications devices allow for more rapid market penetration than land lines. An added benefit is that users can quickly obtain market information and access to financial institutions. Cell phone features are becoming more advanced every day. It will soon be common to watch television, videos and music on smart phones, mini computers and tablet PCs.

There are almost five times as many cell phones today as landlines, with a steady increase in the number of new users, especially in areas where land line installation has stalled. Cellular telephone networks are not only a dominant communication route between individuals and between companies. Wireless technology has changed methods of communication within hospitals. Radiologist's reports and diagnostic images such as electrocardiograms can now be sent over the Internet between hospitals, family physicians and medical specialists. Medical facilities now track patient information such as test results, medical records, treatments and insurance information wirelessly. Patients can be monitored in the hospital and remotely, at home, with an alarm sent to a central system monitor if the individual's condition changes or when medication is required. Allowing patients to remain at home, while still remaining under medical observation, frees up hospital beds for more urgently ill patients.

Within the medical field, technological advances will revolutionize the design of hospitals in the future. More complexity will demand innovative approaches to educating medical staff and keeping them current with new developments. Hospital staff will have to become comfortable using expensive, high tech equipment, including robotics in operating rooms. In fact, there are several studies showing that simulations and playing computer games may enhance the skill level of physicians manipulating laparoscopic and robotic surgery equipment in the operating room. This is a recent development that has required a re-thinking of medical training techniques and one more reason that the market for computer games will increase.

Medical imaging has progressed to 3-D displays on sophisticated, less expensive computers, allowing for more complex but less intrusive surgeries. The focus on development of vaccines and other pharmaceutical products will shift to a balance of preventing ailments as well as combating a broader spectrum of severe sicknesses, to allow people to live longer and enjoy a more pleasant quality of life. Today, one of every 10 people is over the age of 60. By 2050, the number will rise to more than one in five. Even though the percent of old people per capita is highest in the industrial nations, more than 64% of older people live in developing nations. In Asia, Africa, the Caribbean and Latin America, the numbers of people between the ages of 60 to 79 years are growing the fastest. Medical advancements could create a huge market for products for people over 60.

Global expansion of medical tourism has provided patients who can afford to travel with the choice to select and pay for private medical treatment in locations such as South Africa, India, Thailand, Europe, the Middle East, the Philippines, Singapore and Malaysia. Continued fiscal pressure and increasing service demands on health care systems in industrialized countries will lead to approval of additional procedures being paid for. Insurance companies and even governments wanting to contain costs will shift towards allowing more of those offshore medical services to be covered.

In what is called "the services revolution", technology has contributed to an increasingly competitive international marketplace. Traditional employment is becoming a thing of the past. Information-based professions in fields such as accounting, telemarketing, engineering, banking, publishing, financial and legal services are becoming increasingly marketable, to the lowest bidder. Off-shoring or outsourcing of special projects and day-to-day functions will continue to increase as long as labour costs in emerging economies remain price-competitive.

The online gambling industry has developed into an international, borderless, around-the-clock activity. You can logon to play poker from your home in Manila in the Philippines and your opponents could be located in Singapore, Lima, Peru and Helsinki, Finland. Even if on-line gambling only counts for 8% of the total market today, market penetration will continue to grow beyond the current level of $30 billion a year.

The nature of work will continue to change dramatically. While some traditional jobs have disappeared, more job opportunities have been created. One of the fastest growing development areas is video gaming, which has created employment for specialized designers, writers and program developers and for those developing equipment to run the programs. Video games were worth $52 billion in 2010. The value is expected to rise to $91 billion by 2015. Many of the games or apps (applications) are played on smart phones. According to TechCrunch (July 2010), that specific market will shortly be valued at about $11.4 billion.

Who could have predicted that the majority of movies in the 21st century would be produced with the help of sophisticated cinematic software? Or that special effects and Computer Generated Images (CGI) would populate the world we watch on television programs and in film? Investment costs are huge but so are the rewards when consumers are served with the right product. The film Avatar, in which the director used advanced stereoscopic filmmaking techniques, was one of the highest-grossing films of all time in North America, earning hundreds of millions of dollars.

In the future, your 3-D television and peripherals will become the hub of your home. Through connections to your personal computers, the system will monitor internal and external security, control lighting, air conditioning and heating, appliances and entertainment devices, answer the telephone, allow you to see who is ringing the door bell or walking around your house or apartment and order groceries, movies or other media. You will be able to program functions and activities either via the computer or remotely via your mobile phone.

You'll know where your children are when they borrow your car, because the built-in Global Positioning System (GPS) connected to the central monitoring panel at home will show you their location and the speed they are driving. Anyone, including younger children, will be traceable with personal monitoring devices such as GPS on mobile phones.

Outsourcing

Outsourcing is defined as contracting out a business process or function to an external provider. Similar contracting out arrangements is also called off-shoring or multi-sourcing.

Industrial nations wanting a better competitive position against emerging economies with lower employment costs have usually sub-contracted manufacturing of labour-intensive products to countries with lower wage levels. Domestically, they have increased productivity by investing in technology such as robotics, computer-assisted design and automation, all of which reduce dependence on human labour and expenditures on salaries and benefits.

Until recently, outsourcing was associated with call centres and the technology sector, with almost 30% of the jobs sent offshore. However, manufacturing and customer service tasks in sectors such as finance, sales and marketing are also being outsourced. Today, diagnostic images can be sent securely over the internet. Laboratory test samples can be delivered by overnight courier. Instead of paying technicians and radiologists a rate of $30-100 per hour in western countries, the same functions can be performed at a much lower cost by individuals overseas who have the same education and skill levels.

It is estimated that about 4-5 million jobs have been transferred to India, China and the Philippines, with a value in the trillions of dollars. An average monthly salary for a call center employee in Philippines is about $350 or about 50% above the country's minimum wage level. The turnover of labour is, however high at 60-80% a year. The reason why Philippines is so popular is that Filipinos generally speak better American English than Indian workers. Emerging economies are experiencing some of the same labour force disruptions that industrialized countries have. Recently, labour strife and worker demands for wage increases and benefits have challenged tradition and caused concerns about the future rapid pace of economic expansion in China.

When you call a toll-free number for support for your broken computer or for questions about billing problems with your credit card, you will probably speak with an agent in a call centre somewhere in India or the Philippines. Establishing call centres in India has become the norm for numerous global companies. However, many clients complained when they didn't receive service from someone "local". Although the call takers may be fluent in English and have English names, cultural barriers created problems, especially when the call-takers could not make decisions quickly but stuck to their scripted messages. In competitive economic conditions, customer service becomes even more important, no matter what the original price of the product. Many companies fail to take this into account, especially when cost becomes the determining factor in profitability. If you have a good product but unsatisfactory customer service, word will get around and customers won't buy from you.

The nature of outsourcing is, changing. Preparing for a court case in North America requires many hours of high-priced legal labour - reading similar cases and court judgments, researching, sifting through evidence to find what is relevant, reading police reports and witness statements, etc. With knowledge of the applicable laws and access to all the case materials, a trained, competent lawyer located in a country with lower labour costs could easily complete the same work.

In the financial sector, specialist functions in labour intensive operations such as accounting, bookkeeping, credit checking, financial auditing, financial analysis and research, investment analysis, payroll preparation and credit management are being outsourced to third parties in locations like India, which has a highly educated English-speaking population. Cash-strapped financial institutions and those wishing to diversify their labour force and save money can pay under $30,000 a year for the same skills that would cost them more than $80,000 in North America.

Another approach is called near-sourcing, in which primarily American countries establish production and manufacturing facilities outside the US territorial boundaries but nearby, in Latin American countries or Mexico. Chrysler and General Motors have large assembly plants in Mexico, which is the 10th largest vehicle producer in the world. Workers produce about 2 million cars a year and of that number, about three quarters are for export. Offshore auto parts and component production will continue to grow in importance. General Electric and Cessna Aircraft, both American companies, as well as Spanish and French aircraft manufacturers and Bombardier, a Canadian company, have also established aerospace related assembly and manufacturing plants in Mexico, to take advantage of less expensive labour costs.

Education

While the level of education has become an increasingly important criterion when staff are hired, the methods of delivery have changed dramatically over the years.

Students no longer learn in traditional ways, especially in developed countries. Information technology, communications and electronic-supported teaching is becoming commonplace. The use of e-books and e-learning applications is expanding. New solutions are being developed in which individual students sit in a classroom and receive instructions on a computer screen, from a teacher in a remote location. Because the students would also be equipped with cell phones and headsets, the teacher are able to interact with each individual over the network.

Employees have to study new skills on an ongoing basis and become more international in their outlook. Sales and marketing require international skills, as do R&D, production and finance and the legal department.

Increasing number of students from industrialized countries will enrol in programs overseas. They will want access to specialized education or to the same curriculum as at home, but delivered at a lower price, from a location where the cost of living is less.

Developing countries graduate significant numbers of trained professionals. India has 380 universities and 11,200 institutions of higher learning which produce 6000 PhDs, 200,000 engineers and 300,000 science graduates and postgraduates annually. Despite these impressive numbers, there continues to be a shortage of post secondary institutions. According to India's National Knowledge Commission, the country needs a total of 1,500 universities. That would also open the door for foreign companies and training institutions who want to participate in a rapidly-expanding education market. Foreign countries will have to recruit instructors from overseas to educate local staff to produce enough qualified labour.

China produces about 5 million university graduates every year, which seems like a significant number. However, economic growth has put serious pressure on the availability of skilled workers. An even larger pool of highly-educated people will be required if business and industry are to keep pace.

Another factor affecting industrial growth is the mix and level of skills and knowledge available. Even though China has a large labour force, there will be a shortage of trained workers in the high growth sectors. There is an ongoing need for at least 2,200 civil aviation pilots every year or 40,000 by 2025. To help reduce the acute shortages, the Chinese government has given approval for companies to recruit trained pilots from overseas, but there simply are not enough trained pilots in the world to fill their enormous need. As well, language, political and cultural differences may pose some interesting challenges for foreign pilots. Salaries and benefits are escalating quickly. "Job-hopping" between air-cargo companies and commercial airlines has become such a problem that private airlines now charge "compensation for the cost of training" fees when a pilot resigns to go to another airline. Government labour relations regulators are trying to deal with a growing number of disputes over breaches of contracts. On the plus side, China's need to train many new pilots locally has opened up a huge market for flight simulators.

China has 122,000 lawyers. In the state of California, there are close to 200,000 lawyers. When you consider that China has a population 30 times larger than the United States, you can get a sense of how significant the shortage of trained legal personnel is. This will become more problematic as China expands its business globally, because without enough lawyers to serve local clients, they will be hard-pressed to meet an increasing demand from international clients for legal services.

China requires an additional 120,000 medical doctors, particularly in rural areas where there are fewer facilities, service delivery costs tend to be higher and annual incomes lower. There is a shortage of 500,000 information technology technicians.

As you can see, a large population is not a predictor of business success. Sufficient numbers of trained and skilled labour are essential to maintaining consistent development; without them, industrial growth will stall. With predications of growth of 8-11% per year, the pressure for skilled labour and services will continue.

Although China and India will require these graduates for their own markets, they face strong international competition. Indian and Chinese students will also be attracted to and recruited by industrial nations seeking to fill their needs for educated staff. Because so many of these new workers will be young, the average age in those industrial countries will drop as the imported graduates enter the workforce. Canada needs about 250,000 to 350,000 immigrants every year to maintain a skilled labour force. One reason is an aging population coupled with the low number of children born each year.

Even if many Chinese citizens are to be trained overseas, it is a fact that 70% may not return. There is also strong resistance from foreign professionals about relocating to China. Attracting qualified candidates to senior positions in fields such as economics, engineering, human resource management, project management, etc. has been difficult, competition is fierce and salary levels are very high. Foreign companies in China are also dependant on local resources in a country that has up to 30% workforce turnover annually and is experiencing more frequent labour unrest.

The New York Times reported that, although the wages of Chinese factory workers are still very low compared to traditional industrialized countries in Europe and North America, the impact of rising production costs will affect the global economy by driving up the price of a wide range of manufactured goods.

The Bureau of Labour Statistics in the US has compiled data on hourly compensation costs for production workers (fabricating, assembly, and related activities) in the manufacturing industry. Between 2005 and 2008, wages in China rose from 5.95 Yuan an hour to 9.48 Yuan, or from approximately $.73 US to $1.36 US. According to *Credit Suisse*, there have been significant increases in wage levels for general labourers and factory workers from $1,000 US a year in 2000 to $3,900 a year in 2010.

A new trend has been developing at a time (2009) when the world's GDP experienced negative development of 0.8% and European Union's GDP was 4.00%. The manufacture of labour-intensive products is being relocated to countries like Bangladesh (+5.6% GDP in 2009), Vietnam (+5.30% GDP in 2009) and Indonesia (+ 4.5% GDP in 2009), all of which have low wage costs. The impact is that there are greater numbers of developing countries to invest in.

Closer links between education and industry

There is a growing interdependence of industry with business schools, community colleges, universities and schools of technology.

In the health field, universities have been working in close cooperation with the medical products and pharmaceutical industries for some time. Initiatives such as the Academic Innovation Alliance, a funding arrangement between the Microsoft Corporation and the University of Waterloo in Ontario, Canada and grants from the Intel Corporation to the University of California, are examples of how large companies are collaborating with educational institutions on research and attracting new employees from those universities. Because graduates of the University of Waterloo's Electrical and Computer Engineering programs are already familiar with Microsoft's programming language, their learning curve on the job will be much shorter. Another benefit of the focus on innovation, patent development and company-building is that new high tech companies have originated in the university environment.

Design, Production, and Distribution

You could design a product in Italy, contract for completion of Research & Development in India and then have the product manufactured in Thailand for sale in Chile.

Product cycles are getting shorter and there is high pressure for faster R&D. To date, less than five percent of all basic and applied research and experimental development in science and technology engineering has been carried out in rapidly developing countries. That situation is changing.

In a 1997 research paper presented to the Research Policy Institute, at Lund University, Sweden, it was noted that "transnational corporations (TNCs) have started performing some of their strategic research and development (R&D) in some developing countries. The primary driving forces behind such a move by TNCs are technology-related i.e. to gain access to science and technology (S&T)

resources and cost-related i.e. to exploit the cost differentials. R&D activities related to product development for regional/global markets and generic technologies by TNCs are diffusing skills and knowledge to the host countries."

The *2009 EU Industrial R&D Investment Scoreboard* noted that: "For the second straight year, the R&D growth rate of EU companies (8.1%) has been higher than that of the US (5.7%). It also outpaced Japanese companies (4.4%) for the fourth straight year. Companies from emerging economies, which account for a small share of the total R&D, continued the trend of high R&D growth e.g. China (40%), India (27.3%) and Taiwan (25.1%). Companies based in Switzerland and South Korea also increased their R&D investments well above the Scoreboard average."

R&D expenditures in sectors such as energy, pharmaceuticals & biotechnology, aerospace, electronics, health care and automotive equipment and services, communications and information technology hardware, software and data services will continue to grow. Emerging economies need to further develop their own technology. Industrialized countries are outsourcing/contracting out more R&D activities because of lower costs. Having product development completed offshore also facilitates adaptation of products and services to those markets.

The top ten global R&D investors are: Toyota Motor Company, Microsoft, General Motors, Pfizer, Johnson & Johnson, Ford Motor Company, Volkswagen, Nokia, Roche and Novartis.

The average cost of bringing a new drug to the market is US$800 million or more (National Post, Canada, July 2010). This expensive, time consuming process is subject to extensive government regulations and testing requirements before clinical trials can begin on humans.

A significant component of expenditures can be reduced by having the pharmaceutical R&D done in India where the cost of skilled staff, many of whom were trained in American or European universities, is about 80% less expensive than in Europe and North America. The financial advantage to companies is enormous, because of the multiplier factor of their investments.

Unfortunately, authorities in China and India have not been strict in enforcing compliance with patent and copyright rules. Infringements on foreign technologies continue, especially counterfeiting of popular brands and copying intellectual property such as movies and music. More overseas companies are taking the patent infringers to court, and succeeding in winning financial damages, payment of legal fees and cease-and-desist orders. Infringement will hopefully be reduced as new technologies are developed in those countries.

The US and Japan continue to lead in the field of patent applications, but in 2009, the Republic of Korea moved into 4th place and China into 5th place. In fact, according to the World Intellectual Property Organization (WIPO), Huawai a telecommunications solutions provider, was the first Chinese company to top patent applications in 2009 with 6,770 patent filings; cumulative filings have been 42,543 patents. Another Chinese company is a competitor called ZTE (also in the telecom sector) with 5,719 patent applications. The company invests 10% of its revenue in research and development. Source - http://tmt.interfaxchina.com 2010.

Advertising and Information

Just as the market is changing, so is technology. Traditional advertising in newspapers, magazines and on TV is losing ground to online media and new methods of ad placement, including pop-up and banner ads, electronic billboards, telemarketing, chat groups and web pages. Credit card suppliers and online merchandisers track your purchasing patterns and can deliver targeted marketing campaigns and website ads based on your preferences. A sudden switch from purchasing sports equipment to diapers would likely indicate that there is a new baby in the family. This buying pattern signals that it's time for the marketer to tell you about promotions on children's products as well as on fire alarms and registered educational savings programs as parents look for home security and plan for their child's financial future.

Google earns considerable revenues from AdWords by allowing advertisers to place ads on web search and result pages. Advertisers pay according to how many times the site visitor clicks through and is forwarded to their client's web site. They benefit from a lot of Internet exposure. Increased web site traffic benefits both advertisers and the clients. Google monitors activity carefully, so they always know how many searches have been made, the subject of the searches and the number of web pages viewed.

Publicis' Zenith Optimedia Group predicts that online advertising spending will account for 13.8% of worldwide advertising in 2010, at a value of $63 billion. Users of mobile and smart phones and portable computers such as iPads, which all have wireless capability, are new targets. The total mobile device ad market is expected to grow to $13.5 billion by 2013 from less than $1 billion in 2009. (Source - Gartner Inc, USA)

Several major North American and European advertising companies have relocated resources to India and China to cover those markets as well as western countries.

Accessing information

Using a software application, you can now point your cell phone camera at the barcode on the time table screen at the railway station, scan it and download the entire time table to your device. Scan the barcode in a retail store or supermarket and you will have full product data and the user's manual, as well as a comparison with similar products.

Servers at restaurants and retail stores use devices like the iPhone to place food and drink orders in the kitchen and complete your billing. In fact, for some restaurants and fast-food outlets, you can now download the menu from their website to their phone and order online, for home delivery or pickup.

By February 2012 Singaporeans will not need to carry cash or credit cards. According to Asia News Network, they can just tap their cell phones on sensors that automatically complete the payment. The NFC Near Field Communication short-range wireless interaction system will be used.

Languages

Cross-border, multi-country work will require more knowledge and complex skills from each person involved. English will still be the primary language of commerce and technology, but over time, facility in other languages will become necessary. If you want to pursue business opportunities in China, you will need to learn the basics of one of the local languages (Mandarin or Cantonese). With appropriate language skills, you will be able to speak directly to the right person in the factory, e.g., production manager, service coordinator.

Alternatively, you could employ someone with the language skills and knowledge of the culture to ensure that there are no misunderstandings and that you receive the proper feedback. If you hire a local translator, you cannot be sure that they understand your business. They likely will not be familiar with the technical terms and details of your product. Perhaps they'll be reluctant to translate accurately because they don't want to share bad news or negative comments. If this happens, you'll miss out and you risk offending a potential business partner.

Overseas Investments

In the past, it was common for industrial countries to invest in low-cost developing countries to reduce costs and to get closer to a new growth market. That practice has, changed. China and India, for example, are heavily dependent on foreign raw materials. That has created a buying spree of oilfields and oil companies, coal, copper and iron ore mines and of producers of steel. China is scheduled to construct more than 60 new nuclear power reactors by 2020 to reduce their dependence on coal-fired energy. How can they meet that goal? By buying one or more uranium mines to ensure continuous supply of raw materials.

Not only is the resource industry attracting foreign investors. Nine of the twenty soccer clubs in the English Premier League are owned by foreigners.

"Rowing harder doesn't help if the boat is headed in the wrong direction."
— Kenichi Ohmae

Future Consumer

In the next decade, the way in which you buy products, get deliveries and pay for your purchases will change. Here is an example.

Your wife is celebrating her birthday. You want to do something special for tonight, but there's a problem, because you have meetings all day and won't be able to do any shopping. You use your cell phone to order some groceries and a bottle of champagne. You order a dozen of her favourite flowers and the store sends you a photo of the bouquet for approval. You order a download of a movie to watch with your wife and another one for your son and daughter. You check with your home monitoring system to confirm that the children are at home. You send a message to the appliance control panel to start the convection oven so that the roast beef and vegetables will be cooked by the time you get home. You go online and check the birthday wish list your wife posted last year and make sure that no one else has ordered the gift you have in mind. You place the order for delivery at 8 p.m., during dinner. All of the products have been paid for using your cell phone. Your phone provider subsidises your telephone bill because they earn money from the retailers on the payment transfer through your phone account instead of a traditional credit card. Next, you use your phone as an intercom and ask the children to program the robot to start setting the table.

Your wife is using the electrical moped today so you have to use the car driven by hybrid electrical/green diesel with fuel from algae. You press the home button on the auto pilot in the car and relax, watching the news on TV and using the picture in picture to talk to and watch your children play as you sip your coffee latte. The computer indicates a traffic jam ahead and reroutes the car. You arrive at home in 34 minutes and 6 seconds.

This will be a fact of life – the future is just around the corner.

"You think you know what the situation is today without realizing it has already changed."

This book was prepared to supply you with the information and knowledge you need to conduct international business and importing/exporting. I wish you much success in your endeavours working in tomorrow's global markets.

You reached the finish line of your journey of learning international business the practical way. However, the finish line for international business does not exist.

— Leif Holmvall

Glossary

AANZFTA or Australia and New Zealand for a Free Trade Agreement. Free trade between the Association of Southeast Asian Nations (**ASEAN**) and Australia New Zealand Closer Economic Agreement (**ANZCERTA**). http://www.dfat.gov.au/trade/fta/asean/index.html

ACP or African, Caribbean and Pacific Group of States, comprised of 79 nations/states mainly in the Caribbean, Latin America and Africa. http://www.acpsec.org/index.htm

ACS or **Association of Caribbean States**, has 38 members including Mexico, Venezuela, Caribbean and Central American countries. http://www.acs-aec.org/index.htm http://www.comunidadandina.org/endex.htm

ADB, Asian Development Bank. Total 67 members of which 48 are from the region. http://www.adb.org

AFTA or the **Asean Free Trade Area** has members from 10 countries including Brunei, Darussalam, Cambodia, Indonesia, Laos and Malaysia. http://www.aseansec.org/index.html

AFDB, African Development Bank, includes 53 independent African countries and 24 non-African countries. http://www.afdb.org

Agent, someone who negotiates purchases or sales or both between buyer and seller, but who does not "touch" the goods. Normally paid a commission or lump sum for the service either by seller or buyer depending who they represent.

ALADI, the Latin American Integration Association (Associação Latino-Americana de Integração) has 12 Latin American member countries including Chile, Cuba, Argentina, Ecuador, Mexico and Venezuela. http://www.aladi.org/nsfweb/sitioIng/

Anti-dumping Duty. This is special duty assessed when a company is found selling goods at a too low a cost.

Anzerta (CER) is the Australia New Zealand Closer Economic Agreement. The new name is CER. http://www.dfat.gov.au/trade/negotiations/afta_cer.html

APEC or **Asia-Pacific Economic Cooperation.** A large organisation of 21 countries from Asian economies and the Americas, including countries like Canada, Chile, Mexico, New Zealand, Papua New Guinea, Russia and Japan. http://www.apec.org

APTA, the **Asia-Pacific Trade Agreement**, is a preferential trade agreement between Bangladesh, China, India, Republic of Korea, Laos and Sri Lanka. http://www.unescap.org/tid/apta.asp

ASEAN, Association of Southeast Asian Nations, has 10 members including Singapore and Thailand, with 600 million residents and 1000 languages. It will create a trading block similar to EU with one common currency 2015. http://www.aseansec.org

AU, the **African Union**, has 53 members in Africa, from Algeria to Zimbabwe. http://www.africa-union.org

Aval, a guarantee added to a debt obligation by a third party who ensures payment should the issuing person default.

AWB, Air Way Bill is the freight "contract" for air shipments.

B2B, Business to Business in E-commerce.

B2B marketplaces, E-commerce sources with more than one supplier. Normally for a specific industry or product type like chemicals, automotive parts etc.

B2C, Business to Consumer in E-commerce.

Bank draft or banker's draft is a "cheque" payable to a corresponding bank, such as in your country. It is a type of cheque where the payment is guaranteed to be available by the issuing bank.

Bank guarantee. The buyer's bank "promises" to pay the amount if the importer does not fulfill their payment obligations.

Bank to Bank guarantee, similar to Bank guarantee but the seller's bank guarantees the payment.

Bid rigging, where a group of companies agree on who is going to submit the lowest bid.

Bilateral agreements are trade agreements between a number of countries or trade unions.

B/L, Bill of Lading is the contract for shipment for sea shipments.

Bonded warehousing, is an area where you can store goods without paying taxes and customs duty until goods is taken out.

Branch office, is an extension of the parent company in a foreign or domestic market. Compare it with a local sales office in your domestic market.

Bribe, is a "gift" to influence the buyers or authority's' decision.

Broker functions as a liaison or agent but does not have any part in the business or have physical control of the product. Compare to a real estate broker.

Buyers Cheque,   a regular cheque from one country as a payment. It does not normally work in international business as the receiving bank does not know if funds are available in the foreign bank.

CACM, The **Central American Common Market** includes Guatemala, El Salvador, Honduras and Nicaragua. http://www.sice.oas.org/SICA/CACM_e.asp

C2B, Customer to Business in E-commerce.

C2C, Customer to Customer in E-commerce.

CAD, Cash Against Document. A payment method where the buyer has to pay before obtaining the documents to get access to goods.

CAN, the Comunidad Andina or **Andean Community** is represented by Bolivia, Columbia, Ecuador and Peru. http://www.comunidadandina.org/endex.htm

Caricom, the Caribbean Community and Common Market, has 15 members and 5 observers or associate members. http://www.caricom.org/

CEFTA, Central European Free Trade Agreement includes some Eastern European countries that have not joined the EU, such as Albania, Bosnia and Herzegovina, Croatia and Macedonia.
 http://en.wikipedia.org/wiki/Central_European_Free_Trade_Agreement

CEMAC or the **Economic and Monetary Community of Central Africa** is an organization of states of Central Africa with Cameroon, Central African Republic, Chad, Republic of the Congo, Equatorial Guinea, and Gabon as members.
 http://www.cemac.cf

CEO, Chief Executive Officer.

CIF, Cost Insurance Freight. Incoterms rule clarifying the responsibility (ownership) of goods during transport.

CIS the **Commonwealth of Independent States**, includes Azerbaijan, Armenia, Belarus, Georgia, Kazakhstan, Kyrgyzstan, Moldova, Russia, Tajikistan, Turkmenistan, Uzbekistan and Ukraine.
http://www.cisstat.org/eng/cis.htm

Civil Law, also called Napoleonic Code and French Civilian Code. A law very common in Europe.

COMESA, the **Common Market for Eastern and Southern Africa**, has 19 members such as Burundi, Egypt, Eritrea, Libya, Rwanda, Sudan and Zambia.
http://about.comesa.int/

Commission, a payment, normally a percentage paid to brokers and agents for their performance.

Combiterms, terms clarifying the responsibility for shipments, mainly used by European companies (see also Incoterms).

Commission House or Commission Merchant, an agent that usually takes physical control and negotiates the sale of goods they handle.

Common Law as trade law is used in North America. (Except for Quebec, Canada and Louisiana, USA), England, Australia and New Zeeland. The law is generally based on common sense.

Common Market, like a Customs Union but allows free movement and production between the member countries.

Complete Integration, is the same as Economic Union but with complete integration.

Consignment, a payment term where the buyer keeps the goods in stock and pays the seller when they are sold.

CO-OP, Consumers' cooperative is a retail business owned and operated by consumers to sell primarily to members.

Contract, a legal document stating terms e.g. between a buyer and a seller.

Contract manufacturing, when the owner of the product sub contracts manufacturing to another company.

Copyright is the exclusive right granted to the author or creator of an original work like music, books, etc including the right to copy, distribute and adapt the work.

Countervailing duty is a special fee to offset a subsidy paid to a foreign exporter.

Customer price, the price including taxes the customer is willing to pay or has to pay after all discounts.

Customs duty, the most common trade barrier or fee, is normally a percentage of the value, which is added to the price of goods imported.

Customs Unions, the same as free trade area but with a common tariff for non members.

Customs value is the value that customs authorities use to apply any customs duties and taxes.

D/A or Document against acceptance, when the buyer signs a promissory note or accepts a usance draft at the bank to pay at a certain time in the future to get access to the document to release the shipment.

Dealer distributes and sells directly to commercial end users.

Design protection is a protection by the owner of the design of a product, prohibiting others from copying it.

Developing countries is a term used for less developed countries.

Direct Exporting is exporting directly to the market through your company/ organization or using other companies' assistance.

Discount is a reduction of cost based on the list price.

Discount house is a retail business, normally featuring consumer goods and competing on price.

Distributor, a company that buys products and services and resells them in their own name.

Door to door, a complete shipping cost from "door" of seller to "door" of buyer.

Down payment, an up-front payment used in connection with licensing agreements.

D/P, Document against payment, a method to secure payments.

DR-CAFTA, Dominican Republic - Central America Free Trade Agreement, includes the Dominican Republic, Costa Rica, El Salvador, Guatemala, Honduras and Nicaragua.
http://en.wikipedia.org/wiki/Central_American_Free_Trade_Agreement

Dumping, a term used when a company sells at a much lower price to a foreign market than on the domestic market.

Duty, see customs duty

EAC is the **East African Community** and includes the Republics of Kenya, Burundi, Rwanda, Uganda and the United Republic of Tanzania.
http://www.eac.int

EAEC Eurasian Economic Community has Kazakhstan, Kyrgyzstan, Russia and Tajikistan as members.
http://www.eurasianhome.org/xml/t/databases.xml?lang=en&nic=databases&in torg=3&pid=25

EBRD, European Bank for reconstruction and Development.
http://www.ebrd.org

ECO, Economic Cooperation Organization. Includes many countries from the former Eastern bloc, such as the Kyrgyz Republic, Tajikistan, Turkey, Iran and Pakistan.
http://www.ecosecretariat.org

E-Commerce or E-Business, is a process of buying and selling on-line using electronic systems like Internet or other computer networks.

ECOWAS is the **Economic Community of West African States** comprised of 15 West African republics like Gambia, Niger, Burkina Faso, Mali and Senegal.
http://www.ecowas.int

EFTA, the **European Free Trade Association** is linked to the European Union. Members of the trading bloc include non EU members such as Norway, Iceland, Lichtenstein and Switzerland.
http://www.efta.int

E-invoicing, a system to invoice electronically.

End user price. See customer price.

EU, the **European Union**, is made up of 27 members.
http://europa.eu/

EURO, the common currency of most of the European Union members.

Export agents or **Manufacturers' Export Agents** could be either an individual or a company. They normally function like a 'rented' export department.

Export Commission Agents are individuals or companies who, on a commission basis, arrange orders and perhaps conduct other sales-related activities.

Export Consortiums is a partnership for undertaking joint activities foreign markets.

Export Factoring is an exporter selling receivables/invoices to a factoring company, allowing the exporter to get part of or the major part of the payment up front.

Export Financing, a special method of financing exporting either via bank or special export financing organisations.

Export Merchants, are similar to Export Commission Agents, but normally buy domestic or foreign products and sell them to foreign purchasers.

Export Price is the price the exporter charges the foreign buyer or importer.

EXW, Ex Works means that the buyer is in charge of transport and goods after the goods leave the factory. Incoterms specify who is responsible for goods.

Fair value prices are when deciding if an export price is consistent with the rules as to valuation of goods imported.

FCL, Full Container Load.

Fees, normally used by foreign authorities to add on import value. It could be a special fee for environmental control on products imported.

FOB, Free On Board, Incoterms stating that the buyer has the responsibility from when then goods are loaded in. e.g. a ship.

Foreign exchange accounts, an account in foreign currency.

Franchising is a special type of licensing. The parties are the franchisor (the owner) who gives the franchisee (the buyer) the right to distribute its products, techniques, and trademarks by paying a percentage of gross monthly sales and an initial franchising fee.

Free Trade Area. This is free trade between the member countries, with no customs duties between them.

Freight cost is the cost to transfer the goods from location "a" to location "b".

French Civilian Code, also called Civil Law or Napoleonic Code. (See Civil Law).

Freight forwarder, is a company supplying services to transfer goods from point A to point B.

FTAA, **Free Trade of the Americas**, includes 33 countries in North America, the Caribbean and Central America, from Canada and the United States in the north to Chile in the south.
http://www.ftaa-alca.org/

FX contract, **FEC,** Foreign exchange contract. A contract between parties to buy or sell a specific amount of a certain foreign currency in exchange for another currency at a fixed price.

FX option, Foreign exchange option. This is a contract giving the right, but not the obligation to buy or sell a specific amount of a foreign currency for another one at a fixed price.

G8, (Group of Eight). France, Germany, Italy, Japan, United Kingdom, USA, Canada and Russia.

GAFTA, the **Greater Arab Free Trade Area**, has 17 Arab country members, including Jordan. Amman, Yemen , Lebanon and Libya.
http://www.annd.org/index.php

GATT, General Agreement on Tariffs and Trade, now WTO.

GCC is the **Gulf Cooperation Council**, with Bahrain, Kuwait, Oman, Qatar, Saudi Arabia and the United Arab Emirates as members.
http://www.globalsecurity.org/military/world/gulf/gcc.htm

Gost certificate. A special certificate required for export to Russia.

GDP, Gross Domestic Product, similar to a company's annual sales, but for a country.

GSP, Generalised System of Preferences, is a preferential system for duties and taxes for less developed countries.
http://www.au.af.mil/au/awc/awcgate/crs/rs22183.pdf

GSTP is the **General System of Trade Preferences among Developing Countries.** Members include many developing countries in Latin America, Asia and Africa.
http://www.eepcindia.org/trade-block-detail.asp?tbcode=G138

Guanxi, in China, the personal relationship is very important.

Holding company, a "central" company that owns other companies like subsidiaries (whether sales companies or manufacturing companies) in different countries. By doing so, they can consolidate profits and losses and pay taxes where it is most favourable.

HS code, (Harmonized Commodity and Coding System), developed by the World Customs Organization (WCO) to classify products for trading purposes, like statistics and customs duty.

IATA, International Air Transport Association.
http://www.iata.org

IBRD, International Bank for Reconstruction and Development.
http://www.worldbank.org

ICC, International Chamber of commerce.
http://www.iccwbo.org

IFC, International Finance Corporation is part of the World Bank, intended to stimulate investments in developing countries.
http://www.ifc.org

IMF, International Monetary Fund.
http://www.imf.org

Importer, the company bringing the product into a country.

Incoterm, an international standard, outlining the responsibility between exporter and importer as to responsibility (ownership) when shipping goods.

International, involving more than one country

Indirect Exporting, using someone else to do the exporting. You are not actively involved

International Firm or International Company. This is a company conducting international business in many markets, such as large engineering or construction companies

Islamic Law, interpretation of the Koran as used in Saudi Arabia. Iran, Pakistan, and other Islamic countries.

ISO, International Organization for Standardization.
http://www.iso.ch

Jobber is synonymous with a wholesaler and distributor. Jobbers are often used for certain products or customer groups.

Joint venture is a cooperative undertaking between two or more parties. It could be a company set up for construction, manufacturing or marketing or a joint interest in research and development.

LAIA or ALADI is the **Latin American Integration Association (Asociación Latinoamericana de Integración),** are members from 12 Latin American countries.
http://encarta.msn.com/encyclopedia_761589439/Latin_American_ Integration_Association_(LAIA).html

Landed cost. The total cost for the goods received or landed in the foreign country. Includes export price, freight, duties, taxes and any clearing costs.

L/C, Letter of credit.

LCL, Less than Container Load.

Licence is an agreement, "selling" the rights to make and sell the product or technique in a specified market during a specified time period.

MAGREB is an association formed by **Algeria, Morocco and Tunisia**.
http://en.wikipedia.org/wiki/Maghreb

Manufacturing cost. The total cost of all production costs including tooling costs, research and development, material, labour and administration.

Manufacturers' Export Agents or Export Agents could be either an individual or a company. They normally function like a 'rented' export department.

Manufacturer's Representative, sometimes called a **Manufacturer's Agent** or Manufacturer's Rep, is a person or company working on a contract to sell/market a range of products from one or more companies. They are normally paid a commission.

Mashraq, **The Arab countries of eastern Mediterranean**, has Egypt, Jordan, Syria, Lebanon, Palestine, and Iraq as members.

Merchant. A business that buys, takes title to and resells merchandize. Wholesalers and retailers are merchants.

Margin, the difference between what you get paid to what it cost you.

Marginal cost. The cost of increased production volume. That means the marginal cost to manufacture certain products is added to the production volume the manufacturing cost was based on. That is normally only cost of labour and material as tools and R&D is already included in the "normal" manufacturing cost.

Mark-up, the add on to achieve a profit. For example, a. 100% mark-up on $100 is $100 and total price= $200.

MERCOSUR, (Mercado Común del Sur) has membership from Argentina, the Federative Republic of Brazil, Paraguay and the Eastern Republic of Uruguay. http://www.mercosurtc.com

MSR, Manufacturers' suggested retail price.

NAFTA, the **North America Free Trade Agreement**, removed most barriers to trade and investment among the United States, Canada, and Mexico. http://www.nafta-sec-alena.org

Napoleonic Code also called French Civilian Code or Civil Law. (See Civil Law.)

Non-Tariff barriers. These are indirect trade barriers. It can be quota limiting the amount of import or export; it can be requirements for an import license that limit import of categories of products.

OAS, the **Organization of American States** is comprised of 35 North and South American Countries. http://www.oas.org

OECS, **Organization of Eastern Caribbean States** includes nine Eastern Caribbean countries such as Antigua and Barbuda, Montserrat, Grenada and St. Lucia. http://www.oecs.org

OECD, Organization for Economic Co-operation and Development. http://www.oecd.org

OEM (Original Equipment Manufacturer). This is a company that builds machinery to be exported, either using your products as components of the final product or as an integral part of a complete system.

On-line databases. Commercial databases that can be accessed via internet or data-lines.

OPEC, Organization for Petroleum Exporting Countries. http://www.opec.org

Open credit, where you give a client a payment term without security being required.

Patent is an exclusive right during a limited time for the inventor to make, sell and modify a product or service.

Payment in advance. The buyer sends the money in advance before goods are shipped.

Port of entry, the port where the goods arrive.

Price fixing occurs when several companies agree to offer a certain price.

Product liability, when manufacturers, distributors, suppliers, retailers, and others who make products available are held responsible for the injuries or damage those products cause.

Profit is the difference between the total cost and selling price.

Quota is a restriction that only a limited amount of products will be allowed into the country.

Rack jobber. A wholesaling business unit that markets specialised lines of merchandise to certain types of retail stores and maintains and restocks goods.

Representative office is a temporary office established where a company wants to explore a new market.

Resident buyer is either a local purchaser for a client or an agent for an overseas buyer, residing in the country where products are sourced.

Retailer is a distributor/dealer who sells a variety of goods to end users and consumers.

SAARC, South Asian Association for Regional Cooperation includes members from Bangladesh, Bhutan, India, Nepal, Sri Lanka, Pakistan and Afghanistan. http://www.saarc-sec.org

SACU, the **Southern African Customs Union** includes Botswana, Lesotho, Namibia, South Africa, and Swaziland as members. http://www.sacu.int

SADC, South African Development Community, Community has members from Angola, Botswana, Lesotho, Malawi, Mauritius, Mozambique, Namibia, South Africa, Swaziland, Tanzania, Zambia and Zimbabwe. http://www.sadc.int/

SAFTA, South Asian Association Free Trade Agreement is affiliated with SAARC and is comprised of a mix of members and observers primarily from Asia but also including other territories. http://www.saarc-sec.org/main.php

SIM card, Subscriber Identification Module. A electronic card used in mobile phones.

Skimming. A way to charge a higher price to make more profit, when introducing a new attractive product and later reduce the price when demand is reduced.

SPARTECA is the **South Pacific Regional Trade and Economic Cooperation Agreement** and includes 16 countries ranging from New Zealand and Australia to Western Samoa. http://en.wikipedia.org/wiki/South_Pacific_Regional_Trade_and_Economic_Cooperation_Agreement

SPC, the **Secretariat of the Pacific Community** has 26 member countries and territories from the Pacific Islands and Australia, France, New Zealand and the US. http://www.spc.int/corp/

Sub dealer, is a dealer that buys from another dealer and sells it to the end user.

Sub distributor, a distributor that buys from another distributor and resells to either dealers or to end users.

Subsidiary is an incorporated company with share capital owned by a parent company.

Subsidiary for rent. In this arrangement, you register your company in the new country and use and pay for the services of an already-established business there.

Swift, Society for Worldwide Interbank Financial Telecommunication, which means the foreign bank wires the money to your bank and releases the money to you in about two days. http://www.swift.com/

Taric (Tariff Code) a system to obtain customs tariffs in Europe.

Taxes and special taxes are "fees" charged by authorities in the importing countries. It is one more income source like special tax for goods such as alcohol and tobacco but also sometimes on cosmetics or "luxury items."

Trademark, ™ is a distinctive symbol, logotype and/or name normally for a special classification.

Trade name is a name used for sales of products and services. It can be a company name.

Trading House is a company that buys and resells products and services under its own name. It takes over most of the activities for the exporting company and assumes distribution and risks to foreign markets.

Transfer pricing is the price charged/invoiced by the parent company to its own subsidiaries.

Transnational company, a company that supplies products/services or maintains production in multiple countries.

Transparency International. An organisation evaluating corruption around the world.
http://www.transparency.org/

UEMOA or **Union Economique et Monetaire Quest Africaine (Economic and Monetary Union of West Africa)** is a sub-regional monetary organization of eight West African countries
http://www.uemoa.int/index.htm

UMA, Arab Maghreb Union, was formed with members from five Arab countries - Algeria, Libya, Mauritania, Morocco, and Tunisia.
http://www.maghrebarabe.org/en

UN, United Nation.
http://www.un.org

UNCTAD. United Nation's Conference on Trade and Development is UN's organization for trade and investment.
http://www.unctad.org

Usance, a period allowed for payment of a bill of exchange, especially in international trade.

VAT, Value Added Tax.

Voluntary group is a group of retailers each of whom owns and operates their own store but who are associates to buy and sell jointly with other retailers in the group.

WAEMU, West African Economic and Monetary Union, is a regional economic and trade group of 15 countries.
http://www.dfa.gov.za/foreign/Multilateral/africa/waemu.htm

World Customs Organization. An international organisation focused on customs questions. Considered the voice of the global customs community.
http://www.wcoomd.org

WTCA, World Trade Centers Association.
http://www.wtca.org

WTO, World Trade Organization.
http://www.wto.org

Links on the Web

Many of the links below have already been mentioned in the previous chapters. Where no description is provided, the websites contain general information.

Web site addresses change, so visit our web site at: http://www.exportpro.com for updated information.

General Information

http://www.qwiki.com/
Put in a key word and the site will give you answer to most of your questions. E.g. type in letter of credit. The site will show you what it is but also read you an explanation in English.

Another similar website is http://www.wolframalpha.com/
Type in Africa and it will list the countries and links to each of them. Type in "currency future US dollar Euro" and it will give you today's rate and a future forecast

Country Information: General

Global Edge – International business portal providing country guides, links to global information resources and a discussion forum.
http://globaledge.msu.edu/resourceDesk/

Global Finance - Good statistics including general information.
http://www.gfmag.com/tools/global-database/economic-data.html?utm_
    source=gfmag&utm_medium=email&utm_content=link15&utm_
    campaign=globaldatabase

http://www.gfmag.com/tools/global-database/ne-data.html?utm_
source=gfmag&utm_medium=email&utm_content=link16&utm_
campaign=globaldatabase

Wikipedia geography portal.
http://en.wikipedia.org/wiki/Portal:Geography

List information on many countries. http://www.worldinfozone.com/

Covers Russia and Eastern Europe. http://www.ucis.pitt.edu/reesweb.

Library of Congress. Have different studies of countries. Arranged by country, common categories include Business, Commerce & Economy; Government, politics & law.
http://lcweb2.loc.gov/frd/cs/cshome.html

Country Briefings, free online 60 countries – News, country profiles, forecasts, statistics etc.
http://www.loc.gov/rr/international/portals.html
http://www.economist.com/countries

Country Profile, Country Reports (Top Products). You have to purchase these reports. http://store.eiu.com

Good source for **market profiles**.
http://www.visitbritain.org/insightsandstatistics/publications/marketprofiles.aspx

CIA World Factbook. CIA information about countries. If the link does not work, start with the main page and look for World Fact Book. World facts and figures.
https://www.cia.gov/library/publications/index.html
https://www.cia.gov/library/publications/the-world-factbook/index.html

World Fact and Figures. Has plenty of information, however many of the statistics are taken from other sources, so the data could be out of date.
http://www.worldfactsandfigures.com

US Commercial Service. Contains information on a numerous countries.
http://www.state.gov/www/about_state/business/com_guides/2001/index.html

US government site with country information.
http://www.state.gov/r/pa/ei/subject/index.htm

Also see:
http://www.state.gov/www/background_notes/
http://www.state.gov/www/about_state/business/com_guides/2001/index.html

Country Commercial Guides

IMD business School, evaluations of different countries' competitiveness.
http://www.imd.ch

US department of commerce, information on countries and general information on exporting.
http://www.ita.doc.gov/

Country Information: By Country

International Business Information on the Web – Online Directory.

Information Today. Links to the web sites described in the book titled: "International Business Information on the Web".
http://www.infotoday.com/ibidirectory.htm

The World Bank, links for different countries and trade.
http://data.worldbank.org

Aneki.com. Country Information, Regional and World Rankings. Facts, statistics, and rankings for over 190 countries. Current listings are divided into four categories – economic, social, technological, and environmental – and are retrieved from sources such as the CIA World Factbook and Forbes.com.
http://www.aneki.com/index.html

Maps and geographic information.
http://geography.about.com/library/maps/blrasia.htm

Australian website, has information on individual countries and industries.
http://www.austrade.gov.au/Country/default.aspx

Europe, EU, European Union

General sites

General Information about EU.
http://europa.eu.int/

Information EU as to trade.
http://ec.europa.eu/trade/index_en.htm

Information on the expansion of EU.
http://europa.eu/pol/enlarg/index_en.htm

By law, in the **EU**, governments including local municipalities have to hold open **tenders** and award the contract to the company with the best bid, despite which country they reside in within the EU.
http://ted.europa.eu/

For trade barriers, http://mkaccdb.eu.int/

Europages Information on companies. Search engine in 26 languages.
http://www.europages.com/

US based has a large number of links and information
http://www.eurunion.org/

Statistics http://epp.eurostat.ec.europa.eu

Information by Country

Belgium. Belgium Government. http://www.belgium.be/en/

Czech Republic. Main web site: http://www.czech.cz

Denmark. Main Government web site: http://www.um.dk/en

Germany. German Government Website:
http://www.auswaertiges-amt.de/1_fremsp/english/Index2.htm

Greece. Website of Federal Government:
http://www.ypex.gov.gr/www.mfa.gr/en-US

Hungary. Hungarian Investment and Trade Agency
http://www.itdh.com/Engine.aspx

Iceland. Iceland export Directory:
http://www.icelandexport.is/english/

Ireland. Enterprise Ireland
http://www.enterprise-ireland.com/english.asp

Netherland. Netherland International Home Page
http://www.minbuza.nl/en/home

Sweden
http://en.wikipedia.org/wiki/Sweden
http://www.sweden.se/
http://www.state.gov/r/pa/ei/bgn/2880.htm
http://www.sweden.gov.se/

http://www.sweden.se/eng/Home/
http://www.worldinfozone.com/facts.php?country=Sweden

You can also find information on the pages:
http://www.riksdagen.se
http://www.un.int/sweden/pages/links.htm
http://www.tillvaxtverket.se/english
http://www.riksbank.se
http://www.regeringen.se/euro

Import license Sweden. You can see in taric if license required.
http://www.kommers.se.

Trade statistics Sweden see: http://www.kommers.se

Quota. To see how much is available for Sweden go to:
http://ec.europa.eu/taxation_customs/dds/en/home.htm

Swedish customs, quota etc.
http://www.tullverket.se

Customer association **Svensk Handel.** Has an import office .
http://www.svenskhandel.se/Default.asp

Link to trade information
http://www.swedishtrade.se/exportinformation/

Updated info on **trade statistics** you can obtain on:
http://www.scb.se/default_____2154.aspx or

Look for **trade statistics** at:
http://www.intrastat.scb.se/defaulteng.asp

Swedish Trade Council.
http://www.swedishtrade.se/english/

Bizbook. List Swedish Industry executives
http://www.bizbook.se

North America

Canada

Department of foreign affairs, start for a lot of information on Canada.
http://www.strategis.ic.gc.ca

Canadian Government website.
http://www.canada.gc.ca/main_e.html

Canadian business information.
http://www.canadianbusiness.com/

Doing business with Canada.
http://investincanada.gc.ca/eng/default.aspx

Canadian Statistics
http://strategis.ic.gc.ca/engdoc/main.html

Mexico

United States Mexico Chamber of Commerce
http://www.usmcoc.org

Mexican Trade
http://www.mextrade.com

USA

US Census bureau statistics on population and many other things.
http://www.census.gov/

Latin America

Latin American Network Information Center (LANIC)
http://lanic.utexas.edu

Internet Resources for Latin America. Links to internet guides, directories, databases.
http://lib.nmsu.edu/subject/bord/laguia

Chile. Source for exporters.
http://www.prochile.cl

Africa

http://en.wikipedia.org/wiki/Africa
http://www.pbs.org/wnet/africa/
http://www.africaguide.com/afmap.htm
http://www.worldbank.org/africa
http://www.hmnet.com/africa/1africa.html
http://en.wikipedia.org/wiki/South_Africa

Asia

Asia General

http://en.wikipedia.org/wiki/Asia

Gives information on each country.
http://www.nationsonline.org/oneworld/asia.htm

China

Wikipedia, http://en.wikipedia.org/wiki/China

Information on products and producers.
http://english.china.com/

www.chinachemnet.com
www.chinashare.com

India

http://en.wikipedia.org/wiki/India
http://www.tourindia.com/htm/homepage.htm
http://india.gov.in/
http://goidirectory.nic.in/
http://lcweb2.loc.gov/frd/cs/intoc.html
http://www.india.org/
http://www.geographia.com/india/
http://www.state.gov/r/pa/ei/bgn/3454.htm
http://www.india-today.com/
http://www.worldbank.org/india
http://meaindia.nic.in/

Japan

http://www.jetro.org

Malaysia

http://en.wikipedia.org/wiki/Malaysia
http://www.economist.com/countries/Malaysia/
http://travel.state.gov/travel/cis_pa_tw/cis/cis_960.html

International Organizations

Federation of International Trade Associations
http://fita.org

Directory of 450 international trade associations in the USA, Canada, and Mexico at: http://fita.org/members.html

Also Web Resources for International Trade, a directory of 4000 sites covering finance, logistics, standards, legal, business travel, etc. See "short cuts" list for trade shows, business directories, international market research, country profiles etc. http://fita.org/webindex/index.html

ArabDataNet
National US-Arab Chamber of Commerce. News, country profiles, industries, government contacts, US trade statistics, legal information, trade shows, organizations, US embassies in Arab countries.
http://www.arabdatanet.com

Association of American Chambers of Commerce in Latin America
http://www.aaccla.org

Association of Balkan Chambers. Includes country profiles and a market research section.
http://www.abcinfos.com

Canadian Government. Has links for travelers.
http://www.dfait-maeci.gc.ca

World Bank. Gives specific profile and information as to countries.
http://www.worldbank.org

WTO. Has trade statistics and country information worldwide. Also try:
http://stat.wto.org www.wto.org

UNCTAD. International Trade Centre.
http://www.intracen.org

Products & Services: Aggregated trade stats by commodity and country (from UN's COMTRADE database). Look also at these links:
http://www.intracen.org/menus/products.htm
http://www.intracen.org/menus/countries.htm

OECD. Frequently Requested Statistics – Includes GDP, standardized unemployment rates, population, purchasing power parities, and short-term economic statistics.

By country:
http://www.oecd.org/home/0,2987,en_2649_201185_1_1_1_1_1,00.html

By topic:
http://www.oecd.org/maintopic/0,3348,en_2649_201185_1_1_1_1_1,00.html

OAS Foreign Trade Information System. SICE – Trade-Related Links – Good set of links for each country in the Americas, incl. local banks, stats offices, etc.
http://www.sice.oas.org/ http://www.sice.oas.org/countries_e.asp

Eldis. Funded by Danish development agency, Danida. Asia, Africa & Latin America. Statistics, agriculture, government, industry. Links to docs, other sites, & citations for printed materials.
http://www.eldis.org/country/

OECD. http://www.oecd.org

OPEC. http://www.opec.org

NAFTA, North American Free Trade Agreement
http://www.sice.oas.org

NAFTA. http://www.dfait-maeci.gc.ca/nafta-alena/menu-en.asp

Development Banks

World Bank Group. Click on Countries & Regions to find background information on 100 developing countries, click on Data & Statistics for country data. Also have statistics on the OECD countries.
http://www.worldbank.org

International Monetary Fund. Good information on different publications. Gives information on the countries' policies too.
http://www.imf.org/external/pubind.htm
http://www.imf.org/external/country/index.htm.

Asian Development Bank Economics & Statistics. Economic Resource Center – Statistics, key indicators, reports and review related to Asian development.
http://www.adb.org/Economics/

Also Country Economic Review. Economic situation & prospects, & social indicators, for Asian countries (PDF)
http://www.adb.org/Documents/CERs

Central American Bank for Economic Integration. Links to regional information sources and newspapers.
http://www.bcie.org/english/index.php

Inter American Development Bank
http://www.iadb.org

Universities

GlobalEDGE Resource Desk. Center for International Business & Research, Michigan State U. Info such as trade, stats, companies, government sources, and currency is arranged under Regional & Country-Specific Information, for Africa, Asia & Oceana, Europe, Central & South America, and North America. Also under Statistical Data & Info Resources for links to UN and other international statistical sources.
http://globaledge.msu.edu/ibrd/ibrd.asp

How To Do Business in a Country, Including Culture and Language

Economist. Go to this page and type in the country (search audio and video) e.g., Spain or the city Tokyo and you will have an array of videos and audios describing the places and how to do business there. Or click on Audio on the left side and click on "doing business in".
http://audiovideo.economist.com/

Lex Mundi – Guides to Doing Business
http://www.lexmundi.com/lexmundi/Guides_to_Doing_Business1.
     asp?SnID=2045787476

Aspects of doing business in different countries. Information on doing business in different countries.
http://www.businessculture.com/
http://www.worldbusinessculture.com/

Gift giving
http://www.cyborlink.com/besite/international_gift_giving.htm
http://www.4hb.com/0113intergift.html
Search Google "gift giving in business"

Bribing
http://en.wikipedia.org/wiki/
http://www.tranparency.org
http://www.allbusiness.com/human-resources/employee-development-
     employee-ethics/686469-1.html

Women in International Business

A travel magazine for women, the website is a good source of information, what to wear in different countries and travel tips.
http://www.journeywoman.com/

A non-profit service with information about cultures.
http://canada.servas.org/english.htm

An international friendship and travel network for women
http://www.womenwelcomewomen.org.uk/

Her Own Way: A Woman's Guide to Safe and Successful Travel, Foreign Affairs and International Trade Canada.
http://www.voyage.gc.ca/publications/pdf/her_own_way-en.pdf

Global_Competitiveness_ Reports/Reports/gender_gap.pdf. This report from the World Economic Forum reports on the global gender gap. Sweden and Norway are at the top of the list with respect to women's empowerment. China ranks 33, India ranks 53 and Turkey and Egypt are at 57 and 58 of the fifty-eight countries listed. http://www.weforum.org/pdf/

Articles on women and international business.
http://www.we-inc.org/resources/

Travel

Seating diagrams on aircraft. http://www.seatguru.com/

Good information as to visa and medical information.
http://www.oneworld.com/ow/airports-and-destinations/visa-and-health-
   information

The Centers for Disease Control and Prevention list global destinations and travel health information. http://www.cdc.gov/

Statistics

Various Countries

WTO. http://stat.wto.org

Strategis. The Canadian Government website gives trade information for Canada and US (Trade Data Online) and links to other countries.
http://strategis.ic.gc.ca/engdoc/main.html

Food and resource industry
http://faostat.fao.org/
http://unstats.un.org/unsd/default.htm

Europe

http://epp.eurostat.ec.europa.eu/portal/page/portal/eurostat/home/
http://epp.eurostat.ec.europa.eu/

Swedish Federal Bank in Swedish. Trade statistics.
http://www.riksbank.se

North America

For USA and Canada
http://strategis.ic.gc.ca/epic/site/eas-aes.nsf/en/h_ra01888e.html
http://strategis.ic.gc.ca/sc_mrkti/tdst/engdoc/tr_homep.html

Trade resources by geographical region
http://strategis.ic.gc.ca/sc_mrkti/ibin/engdoc/1a2.html

Canada

Strategis. The Canadian Government website gives trade information for Canada and USA (Trade Data Online) but also links to other countries.
http://strategis.ic.gc.ca/sc_mrkti/tdst/engdoc/tr_homep.html

USA

US Census Bureau
http://www.census.gov/foreign-trade/www/ http://tse.export.gov/

UN

United Nations Statistics Division. Millennium Profiles – Statistics on development indicators including computer use, Internet use, phone use, urban population. Social Statistics has data on housing, water treatment, education, income (per capita GDP), unemployment, aging population etc.
http://www.un.org/depts/unsd/
http://unstats.un.org/unsd/default.htm

BUBL World Area Studies. http://bubl.ac.uk

Customs, Customs Duties, and Shipping

Harmonized Description and Coding System (HS) World Customs Organization
http://www.wcoomd.org

Customs codes for import and export.
http://www.foreign-trade.com/reference/hscode.htm

See how much is left of **quota remains.**
http://europa.eu.int/comm/taxation_customs/dds/sv/home.htm

Freight and Deliveries

ICC, International Chamber of Commerce home page, with a lot of information including Incoterms.
http://www.iccwbo.org/incoterms/id3040/index.html

Incoterms
http://en.wikipedia.org/wiki/Incoterms
http://www.pbb.com/en/tools/incoterms/incoterms2000.pdf

ATA carnet. Updated info at:
http://www.chamber.ca/carnet

Links to **trade barrier and market access**. Good info about importing.
http://mkaccdb.eu.int/

Online Databases

Data Star databases.
http://www.dialog.com/products/datastar/

For online search, you need an account.
http://www.datastarweb.com

Online training Datastar
http://training.dialog.com/sem_info/dstar_ontap.html

Dialog. Information on all Dialog products including **Datastar.**
http://www.dialog.com/info/products/

Takes you on a tour on dialogweb. Note the different selection at the bottom of the page.
http://www.dialog.com/

Online training and seminars.
http://training.dialog.com/

Dialog reference material.
http://library.dialog.com/

Online search, you need an account.
http://www.dialogselect.com

Example of searches on **Dialog**
http://www.exportpro.com

Kompass. http://www.kompass.com

Info USA. http://www.infousa.com

Database, to purchase information
You can buy prepared reports on a specific product and market. For example when searching on energy drinks France, a large number of companies show on the search. Below are some examples:
http://www.marketresearch.com/
ttp://www.researchandmarkets.com/reports/256811
http://www.reportlinker.com
http://www.euromonitor.com/
http://www.frost.com/prod/servlet/frost-home.pag
http://www.datamonitor.com/
http://research.thomsonib.com/
http://www.ibisworld.com/
http://www.marketresearch.com/
http://www.researchandmarkets.com/

Tenders. European Tenders Electronic Daily
http://ted.europa.eu/

Miscellaneous Sources

Currencies and Transfer of Money

Oanda - currencies and historic info in most currencies.
http://www.oanda.com
http://www.oanda.com/currency/historical-rates

XE net - a currency converter
http://www.xe.net/currency

The Economist magazine. http://www.economist.com
Uses a **Big Mac Index** as a comparison between the cost of a hamburger in the
United States and purchasing power of various world currencies. To see the most
recent version, use the Internet and search for "Big Mac index" or go to:
http://www.oanda.com/currency/big-mac-index

Information to transfer of money.
http://www.swift.com/

Directories:
Aid organisations. You can find some of them at:
http://en.wikipedia.org/wiki/Category:International_development_agencies

World Federation of Trading House Associations (WFTA)
http://www.wfta.org

World Pages, US and Canadian white and yellow pages as well as e-mail and URLs.
http:// www.worldpages.com

Risks and Export Insurance

http://www.countryrisk.com/
http://external.worldbankimflib.org/external.htm (look at the JOLIS library
catalog)
http://www.intrum.com/en/european-payment-index.
http://en.wikipedia.org/wiki/Country_risk

Export Development Corporation. EDC insures your export invoices,
including political risks.
http://edc.ca
A similar organization exists in Sweden.

EKN, Exportkreditnämnden. Most countries have similar organizations. The
insurance can be taken on continuous business as well as single orders.
http://www.ekn.se

For organizations in other countries see:
http://www.intracen.org/tfs/welcome2.htm?http&&&www.intracen.org/tfs/
    mciagencies/welcome.htm

Trade Shows

http://eventseeker.com
www.tsnn.com
www.cyberexpo.com
www.tscentral.com

Trading Blocs, International Organisations, and Bilateral Agreements

Bilateral Agreements

http://www.bilaterals.org

Trading Blocs

http://www.wto.org/english/tratop_e/region_e/region_areagroup_e.htm
http://www.eepcindia.org/trade-blocks.asp

ACP, African, Caribbean, and Pacific States
http://www.acpsec.org/index.htm

ACS.Association of Caribbean States
http://www.comunidadandina.org/endex.htm

AFTA Asean Free Trade Area. 10 countries.
http://www.aseansec.org/4920.htm

(ALADI) Latin American Integration Association.
http://www.aladi.org/nsfweb/sitioIng/

Anzerta (CER) Australian New Zeeland Closer Economic Agreement.
The new name is CER.
http://www.dfat.gov.au/trade/negotiations/afta_cer.html

APEC, Asia-Pacific Economic Cooperation.
http://www.apec.org/

APTA Asia-Pacific Trade Agreement.
http://www.unescap.org/tid/apta.asp_

ARF, Asean Regional Forum.
http://www.aseanregionalforum.org/

ASEAN, Association of Southeast Asian Nations.
http://www.aseansec.org/

AU. African Union.
http://www.africa-union.org/

CACM. Central American Common Market.
http://www.sice.oas.org/SICA/CACM_e.asp

CAN Andean community.
http://www.comunidadandina.org/endex.htm

Caricom, Caribbean Community.
http://www.caricom.org/

CEFTA, Central European Free Trade Agreement.
http://en.wikipedia.org/wiki/Central_European_Free_Trade_Agreement

CEMAC Economic and Monetary Community of Central.
http://www.cemac.cf/

CIS Commonwealth of Independent states.
http://www.cisstat.org/eng/cis.htm

COMESA, Common market for eastern and southern Africa.
http://about.comesa.int/

DR-CAFTA , Dominican Republic - Central America Free Trade Agreement.
http://en.wikipedia.org/wiki/Central_American_Free_Trade_Agreement

EAC, East African Community.
http://www.eac.int/

EAEC Eurasian Economic Community.
http://www.eurasianhome.org/xml/t/databases.xml?lang=en&nic=databases&in
    torg=3&pid=25

ECO, Economic Cooperation Organization.
http://www.ecosecretariat.org/

ECOWASN, Economic Community if West African States.
http://www.ecowas.int/

EFTA the **European Free Trade Association.**
http://www.efta.int/

EU, **European Union.**
http://europa.eu/

FTAA, Free Trade of the Americas.
http://www.ftaa-alca.org/

GCC Gulf Cooperation Council.
http://www.globalsecurity.org/military/world/gulf/gcc.htm

GAFTA, Greater Arab Free Trade Area. http://www.annd.org/index.php

GSP, Generalised System of Preferences.
http://www.au.af.mil/au/awc/awcgate/crs/rs22183.pdf

GSTP General System of Trade Preferences among Developing countries.
http://www.eepcindia.org/trade-block-detail.asp?tbcode=G138

LAIA, Latin American Integration Association.
http://encarta.msn.com/encyclopedia_761589439/Latin_American_
    Integration_Association_(LAIA).html

Magreb, Algeria, Morocco and Tunisia.
http://en.wikipedia.org/wiki/Maghreb

MERCOSUR. http://www.mercosurtc.com/

NAFTA North America Free Trade Agreement.
http://www.nafta-sec-alena.org/

OAS, Organization of American States.
http://www.oas.org/

OECS, Organization of Eastern Caribbean States.
http://www.oecs.org/

Pacific Community. http://www.spc.int/corp/

SAAC, South Asian Association for regional cooperation.
http://www.saarc-sec.org/

(SACU) Southern African Customs Union.
http://en.wikipedia.org/wiki/Southern_African_Customs_Union

SADC. Southern Africa Development Community.
http://www.sadc.int/

SAFTA, South Asian Association Free Trade Agreement.
http://www.saarc-sec.org/main.php .

SPARTECA South Pacific Regional Trade and Economic Cooperation Agreement.
http://en.wikipedia.org/wiki/South_Pacific_Regional_Trade_and_Economic_
    Cooperation_Agreement

WAEMU, West African Economic and Monetary Union.
http://www.dfa.gov.za/foreign/Multilateral/africa/waemu.htm

UEMOA Union Econmique et Monetaire Quest Africaine.
http://www.uemoa.int/index.htm

UMA, Arab Maghreb Union.
http://www.maghrebarabe.org/en/

Other International Organisations of Interest

ADB. Asian Development Bank
http://www.adb.org

AFDB. African Development Bank
http://www.afdb.org

EBRD. European Bank for reconstruction and Development.
http://www.ebrd.org

G8. (Group Eight).
http://www.g8.utoronto.ca/

IATA. International Air Transport Association
http://www.iata.org

IBRD. International Bank for Reconstruction and Development. It is part of the World Bank.
http:// www.worldbank.org

ICC. International Chamber of commerce
http://www.iccwbo.org

IFC. International Finance Corporation. Part of World Bank to stimulate investments in developing countries.
http://www.ifc.org.

IMF. International Monetary Fund
http://www.imf.org

ISO. International Organization for Standardization
http://www.iso.ch

OECD. Organization for Economic Co-operation and Development.
http://www.oecd.org.

OPEC. Organization for Petroleum Exporting Countries
http://www.opec.org..

UN. United Nation
http://www.un.org

UNCTAD. United Nation's Conference on Trade and Development is UN's organization for trade and investment.
http://www.unctad.org.

World Customs Organization.
http://www.wcoomd.org

WTCA. World Trade Centers Association
http://www.wtca.org.

WTO. World Trade Organisation (Former GATT)
http://www.wto.org

Index

CPSIA information can be obtained at www.ICGtesting.com
Printed in the USA
BVOW061905220513

321397BV00005B/108/P